PITY AND POWER IN ANCIENT ATHENS

One way Ancient Athenians resembled modern Americans was their moral discomfort with empire. Athenians had power and used it ruthlessly, but the infliction of suffering did not mesh well with their civic self-image. Embracing the concepts of democracy and freedom, they proudly pitted themselves against tyranny and oppression, but in practice they often acted tyrannically. *Pity and Power in Ancient Athens* argues that the exercise of power in democratic Athens, especially during its brief fifth-century empire, raised troubling questions about the alleviation and infliction of suffering, and pity emerged as a topic in Athenian culture at this time. The ten chapters collectively examine the role of pity in the literature, art, and society of Classical Athens by analyzing evidence from tragedy, philosophy, historiography, epic, oratory, vase painting, sculpture, and medical writings.

Rachel Hall Sternberg is assistant professor of Classics at Case Western Reserve University.

PITY AND POWER
IN ANCIENT ATHENS

EDITED BY RACHEL HALL STERNBERG

Case Western Reserve University

CAMBRIDGE
UNIVERSITY PRESS

CAMBRIDGE UNIVERSITY PRESS
Cambridge, New York, Melbourne, Madrid, Cape Town, Singapore, São Paulo

Cambridge University Press
40 West 20th Street, New York, NY 10011-4211, USA

www.cambridge.org
Information on this title: www.cambridge.org/9780521845526

First published 2005

Printed in Hong Kong by Golden Cup

A catalog record for this publication is available from the British Library.

Library of Congress Cataloging in Publication Data

Pity and power in ancient Athens / edited by Rachel Hall Sternberg.
p.   cm.
Includes bibliographical references and index.
ISBN 0-521-84552-1 (hardback)
1. Sympathy – Greece – Athens – History – To 1500.   2. Athens (Greece) – Civilization.
I. Sternberg, Rachel Hall.   II. Title.
DF289.P56   2005
177′.7 – dc22   2005006324

ISBN-13   978-0-521-84552-6 hardback
ISBN-10   0-521-84552-1 hardback

CONTENTS

ILLUSTRATIONS

LIST OF CONTRIBUTORS

AILEEN AJOOTIAN is an associate professor of Classics and Art at the University of Mississippi and has published extensively on topics in sculpture, mythical iconography, and Mediterranean archaeology.

DOUGLAS C. CLAPP is an assistant professor of Classics at Samford University in Birmingham, Alabama, and investigates pity in the plays of Sophocles.

THOMAS M. FALKNER, who taught Classics at The College of Wooster for twenty-seven years, is now provost and dean of the faculty at McDaniel College. He is the author of *The Poetics of Old Age in Greek Epic, Lyric, and Tragedy* (1995).

JAMES F. JOHNSON is a professor of Classics at Austin College in Sherman, Texas. He is working on a comprehensive study of compassion in Greek tragedy.

DAVID KONSTAN is the John Rowe Workman Distinguished Professor of Classics and the Humanistic Tradition at Brown University. His many books include *Pity Transformed* (2001).

JENNIFER CLARKE KOSAK is an assistant professor of Classics at Bowdoin College. She is the author of *Heroic Measures: Hippocratic Medicine in the Making of Euripidean Tragedy* (2004).

DONALD LATEINER is the John R. Wright Professor of Greek and Humanities at Ohio Wesleyan University. His publications include *The Historical Method of Herodotus* (1989).

JOHN H. OAKLEY is the Forrest D. Murden, Jr., Professor of Classical Studies at the College of William & Mary. His latest book, *Picturing Death in Classical Athens: The Evidence of the White Lekythoi*, was published by Cambridge University Press.

CHRISTOPHER PELLING is Regius Professor of Greek at Oxford University. His numerous publications include *Plutarch and History* (2002).

RACHEL HALL STERNBERG is an assistant professor of Classics at Case Western Reserve University. She is completing a book entitled *Tragedy Offstage: Responses to Suffering in Everyday Ancient Athens.*

ANGELIKI TZANETOU is an assistant professor of Classics at the University of Illinois at Urbana-Champaign. She is working on a book about exile, democracy, and empire in Athenian tragedy.

ACKNOWLEDGMENTS

HAVING BEEN FOREWARNED BY A WISE ADVISOR, IN THE BEST Herodotean fashion, that an edited volume was a fool's errand and would prove a tremendous headache, I was all the more pleased to discover the deep and genuine rewards of collaborating with the colleagues whose work is represented here.

The central concerns of this volume crystallized at Bryn Mawr College during my graduate studies and began to take shape as I wrote my dissertation under the direction of T. Corey Brennan and Richard Hamilton. Thanks are owed them both. In particular, I can never thank Corey enough for the unflagging support, logistical genius, and sheer conviviality that set the present work in motion. Next, I wish to acknowledge gratefully the Gladys Krieble Delmas Foundation in New York, as well as The College of Wooster and Rutgers University, for the generous funding that allowed us to hold in March 2002 the conference Pity in Ancient Athenian Life & Letters, upon which this volume is based. David Konstan graciously promised to serve as keynote speaker, and then kept that promise at considerable inconvenience to himself. Angeliki Tzanetou furnished the linchpin of the argument. John Oakley was extraordinarily helpful with the illustrations. I am grateful, as well, to the other distinguished scholars who signed on to *Pity and Power in Ancient Athens* and whose hard work and intellectual camaraderie made the project flourish. I learned more from all of them than I could possibly have imagined. Over the past months, I have keenly appreciated the encouragement, dry wit, and perspicacity of Beatrice Rehl, our editor at Cambridge. I shall be indebted to those readers who imperturbably accept certain inconsistencies in the transliteration of Greek proper nouns. And finally, I would like to thank my family for all their patience and support.

   – Rachel Hall Sternberg, *Case Western Reserve University*

INTRODUCTION

RACHEL HALL STERNBERG

◎▣◎

ONE WAY ANCIENT ATHENIANS RESEMBLED MODERN AMERICANS WAS their moral discomfort with empire. The Athenians had power and used it ruthlessly; they celebrated martial prowess and glory; but in certain contexts, violence worried them. The infliction of suffering, it seems, did not fit well with their civic self-image. Athenians, like us, embraced democracy and freedom – indeed, they invented those concepts. They proudly pitted themselves against tyranny and oppression. As it happens, their very concept of the tyrant entailed, to a considerable extent, his abuse of power, his violence against innocent victims whose sufferings merited pity. Athenians therefore were deeply troubled when they saw themselves behaving in tyrannical and oppressive ways. And they discovered what we Americans are continually rediscovering: that the use of power often entails violence and the infliction of suffering even when one's aim is ostensibly lofty – even when, for example, one seeks to prevent unjust bloodshed, to intervene on behalf of the oppressed.

The aim of this volume is to explore the moral discomfort of Athenians through the theme of pity or compassion. The chapters, taken as a whole, examine the place of pity in the culture of an idealistic city-state faced with the recurrent question, "How do we maintain our hegemony?" Some authors question whether there was a role for pity in political decision making; others study the refraction of pity through tragedy, philosophy, the visual arts, and medicine. As an interdisciplinary collection embracing at a minimum history, art history, and literary criticism, this book raises diverse theoretical and interpretive issues. The authors' common purpose, however, is to describe Athenian pity in the light of historical circumstances – during the city-state's

1

brief age of empire in the fifth century BCE and also during the century that followed, when Athens lost its hegemony yet retained and perpetuated its civic self-image and cultural prestige. Such an inquiry is relevant to contemporary society on both sides of the Atlantic because it can help us think about thorny questions of American and European pity, American and European power, and the ever-present issue of what to do in the face of suffering both at home and around the globe.

Nowadays, of course, the preferred term is "compassion" rather than "pity," since the latter can convey scorn, a sense of superiority greatly at odds with an egalitarian ethos. Pity, it is feared, can be a bad thing, while compassion, a word derived from church Latin for "suffering with," is conceived of as a good thing. Modern views of compassion are set firmly within a double framework of Christianity and secular humanism. Within Christianity, compassion is a virtue illustrated by Christ's parable of the Good Samaritan (Luke 10:29–37). Within secular humanism, philosophers since Hume and Rousseau have suspected that fellow-feeling among human beings, whether it is called pity or compassion or sympathy, forms the basis for a moral society.[1] Yet a hundred years before Nietzsche rejected pity as "the greatest danger," Kant complained that sympathy is a "good-natured passion [that] is nevertheless weak and always blind."[2] He and his followers argued that reason rather than emotion must provide the foundation for morality. The last few years have witnessed attempts to bridge the supposed gap between the two. Psychologists have sought the pathways in the brain involved in generating the physiological symptoms of emotion.[3] In the field of classical philosophy, Richard Sorabji and others have revived the ancient idea, developed most of all by the Stoics, that emotion is cognitive. Martha Nussbaum, in *Upheavals of Thought* (2001), argues that affect and cognition work together and that compassion has an evaluative component. It is not a raw instinct, like fear, but something more intellectual: a feeling that rests upon judgment.[4]

The political implications of pity or compassion have been strongly felt in the United States throughout much of its history, not least in abolitionism, and especially since the nineteenth century when realist literature exposed the hardships and horrors imposed upon the poor by free-wheeling industrialization. Ironically, wealthy capitalists of that era helped shape American philanthropy.[5] Domestic political debate today focuses on public welfare and private charity. The political right and left have long squared off against one another over the efficacy of compassion. The right claims that compassion tends to weaken its recipients and in any case should be practiced by private individuals rather than by governmental agencies; the left has traditionally urged compassion as a corrective to social injustice, although lately it is seeking more hard-headed approaches.[6] In foreign policy, right and left alike are divided over the wisdom of aid and interventions, as potent images of suffering in far-flung parts of the world reach our living rooms on a nightly basis.[7] Such images convey information, but also, more overtly, they stir feelings of pity. Susan Sontag, in *Regarding the Pain of Others* (2003), explores the ambivalent shock value of film footage and still photographs depicting violence. She warns that compassion is inherently unstable, that the globalization of suffering can induce despair and apathy. Yet images of pain, she insists, are an invitation to reflect on who caused the pain, and whether it is morally excusable.

THE PROBLEM OF PITY IN ATHENS

As competing groups, then, lay claim to unjust suffering, some of it inflicted by the United States or by its allies, modern observers are left wondering how to respond – and whether pity can reliably guide the world's sole remaining superpower. But what of ancient Athens? To start with, pity there was not a virtue. It never ranked among traditional forms of moral achievement such as justness (*dikaiosunê*), self-control (*sôphrosunê*), or general excellence (*aretê*). This fact emerges clearly in

the moralizing writings of Xenophon and Isocrates, whose occasional
catalogues of virtues reveal the centrality of justness and self-control.[8]
Piety ranks next in importance, with wisdom not far after. In such
contexts, Isocrates sometimes praises mildness and love of humanity
but he never mentions *eleos* or *oiktos*, the two classical Greek words for
pity. Still, in the courts of law, one way to convince jurors of a man's
good character was to praise him for his pity; one way to vilify him was
to decry his pitilessness.[9] Isocrates approvingly calls his fellow citizens
the most pitying, *eleêmonestatous* (15.20).[10] We are faced, then, with a
seeming paradox: pity was not a virtue, yet it somehow merited praise.

That paradox deepens in Book Three of Thucydides, when the
Athenians reopen debate on the fate of Mytilene, a city whose rebellion
against the hegemony of Athens has just been crushed. Should all male
Mytileneans be put to death, or just the ringleaders? Kleon, whom
Thucydides portrays as ruthless, urges extreme measures and dispar-
ages pity as a weakness that places Athens in danger (Thuc. 3.37.2): "You
don't realize how dangerous it is for you whether you go awry because you are persuaded by self-interested arguments, or whether you
yield to pity . . . " Later in the speech (Thuc. 3.40.2–3), Kleon warns the
Athenians of the three things most prejudicial to rule: "pity, delight
in argument, or fairness. For pity is right when given reciprocally to
one's peers[11] but not to those who will not pity in return and who are,
by necessity, permanent enemies." Yet when Diodotos urges limiting
the executions, he not only retains Kleon's focus on expediency but also
mimics his warning against pity and fairness (3.48.1). The Mytilenean
episode epitomizes the tension within Athenian culture with regard to
pity, for Thucydides frames the explicit rejection of pity in the debate
itself with a tacit acceptance of pity in the passages immediately preceding and following.[12] First, he implies that humanitarian pangs were
what caused the issue to be reopened on a second day, and he uses the
adjective *ômon*, or savage, to describe that initial vote of the Athenian

assembly that condemned the Mytileneans to wholesale destruction (Thuc. 3.36.4).[13] Second, Thucydides implies that similar pangs slowed the progress of the first trireme sent to Mytilene with the terrible order (Thuc. 3.49.4). Both Kleon and Diodotos, then, reject pity as a motive for decision and political action in ancient Athens, yet their admonitions presuppose that the citizen body can be moved by *oiktos*.

Fifth-century Athenian voters, in running an empire, must often have dealt with issues of pity and the infliction of suffering. Yet most scholarly discussions of Greek pity have focused instead on Aristotle's concept of *katharsis*, the "purification" of pity and terror experienced by spectators of tragedy in the ancient theater. His treatment of pity in rhetoric stirred little interest, and until recently, pity outside the court-room and theater was overlooked even by philosophers who studied ancient ethics. One reason for this is simple: Plato and Aristotle set the ethical agenda, and pity was not on it. In nineteenth- and twentieth-century scholarship prior to World War Two, the issue was seldom raised and, when it was, it received curt dismissal.[14] Grace Macurdy, in 1940, looked at mercy in Greek literature from a Christian vantage point. Walter Burkert, in 1955, completed his dissertation on *oiktos* and *eleos* in the Homeric poems, but then turned his attention to other themes.

The moral turbulence of the 1960s sparked a broader interest in Greek popular morality, but again, pity received short shrift. Lionel Pearson, in *Popular Ethics in Ancient Greece* (1962), analyzed the place of justice in the moral outlook of the Greeks but never considered pity. Sir Kenneth Dover, writing a dozen years later in *Greek Popular Morality*, devoted just six pages to compassion (1974: 195–201). Arthur R. Hands spent twelve pages on pity for the destitute in his *Charities and Social Aid in Greece and Rome* (1968). Willem Den Boer, in *Private Morality in Greece and Rome* (1979), examined the treatment of widows and orphans. Jacqueline de Romilly, in her 1979 volume *La douceur dans la pensée grecque*, delineated the history of humanity and gentleness in Greek literature, approaching her subject through the Greek words *praos*, *philanthrôpos*, *epieikês*, and *sungnômê* – but never *eleos* or *oiktos*.

It is generally acknowledged that Hellenists of each successive generation live in a climate of thought that leads them, within the limits of the evidence, to find their own Athens. Today's climate of thought will be more easily summarized tomorrow, but it appears that some scholars, tired of intellectual cynicism and distressed by global events, want either to build anew the moral grounds for altruism and compassion – or understand why they cannot.[15] Julia Annas, in *The Morality of Happiness* (1993), analyzed Aristotelian concepts of friendship, self-love, and justice in a section on "other-concern," and David Konstan several years ago published *Pity Transformed* (2001), the first full-length book on pity in the ancient world. In it, he traces the history of ideas about pity in Greece and Rome over a period of more than a thousand years. He acknowledges the sociological underpinnings of such ideas: "If emotions depend at least in part on beliefs," he writes, "then they have a history analogous to that of the cultures or societies that have generated them" (Konstan 2001: 9). Yet the place of pity in classical Athens accounted for only part of *Pity Transformed*, and a number of complex questions about Athenian society and culture remain to be explored in depth: In what ways did the exercise of power in the Athenian democracy affect ancient views of pity and vice versa? How did citizens develop and express their emotional responses – and ethical attitudes – toward the suffering of others? What is the relationship between pity in Athenian life and Athenian arts and letters? Why is much of Greek tragedy imbued with pity? Why do writers like Thucydides and Plato give the impression of rejecting it?

This set of questions is so daunting and so complex as to require multiple answers from scholars in different subfields of Classics. The present volume is based on a conference on Pity in Ancient Athenian Life &

Letters held at Rutgers University in March 2002. All the contributors have attempted to understand the moral universe of ancient Athens by thinking across genres and trying to understand Athenian society as a whole. They analyze pity in historiography, oratory, tragedy, vase painting, sculpture, and medical writings – with reference to philosophy and epic along the way. Certain key texts turn up in more than one chapter: the Mytilenean debate, for example, and the suppliant plays. Most modern readers find the latter quite dull, but their dynamic of pity and suppliancy clearly commanded the interest of their original audiences and they furnish valuable evidence for fifth-century Athenian attitudes. Several of our contributors turn to these plays to elucidate ways in which pity was embedded within the discourse of power (Konstan, Tzanetou) or, alternatively, was distanced from it (Johnson and Clapp).[16] The genre of tragedy as a whole receives considerable attention in this volume because of its salience in Athenian culture and because the themes of tragedy can be looked at from many points of view – through the lens of oratory, for example, or vase painting.

Yet the historical context remains paramount. One premise shared by the present authors is that evidence from different literary genres, and from the visual arts as well, can be used to cross-check readings of passages and images in the rest and can, we hope, lead toward more secure interpretations of Athenian pity. The contributors do not agree on every point, but the chapters coalesce around the central theme of pity and power because, it will be argued, the development of pity as a *topos* in literature and art was linked to the emergence of Athens as a hegemonic city-state. Ultimately, we aim to contribute to the social and cultural history of Athens in ways suggested more than half a century ago by the *Annales* school. The interest in private lives, pursued by Paul Veyne, Peter Brown, and numerous other classicists, is also flourishing, and ancient emotions are nowadays under scrutiny: Douglas Cairns has written on shame or *aidôs* in ancient Greece, William V.

Harris on classical anger. Like Cairns and Harris, we do not aspire to
a cross-cultural analysis, although Greek pity could fruitfully be compared to the sympathetic emotions of Brazilian highlanders, studied
by Nancy Scheper-Hughes, or those of Micronesian islanders, studied
by Catherine Lutz, or especially those of contemporary Americans,
studied by Candace Clark. Ancient Rome is deliberately overlooked,
except in the final chapter, although some fascinating work on Roman
emotion has been done by Carlin Barton and others. Nevertheless, we
hope that our narrow focus on a single historical era will bring with it
a concomitant depth.

SUMMARY OF PAPERS

The starting point for this investigation is the editor's chapter on the
fundamental meaning and nature of Greek pity. Conceptions of *oiktos*
and *eleos* are examined through their occurrence in two prose genres –
oratory and historiography – that are arguably closer to ordinary experience than epic or tragedy or philosophy. Since the private controver-
sies, public speeches, and storytelling found in the Attic orators and the
writings of Herodotus, Thucydides, and Xenophon responded, in their
own age, to actual events as well as to the practical needs and interests
of a wide audience, they yield abundant evidence for everyday pity and
allow its definition. The exploration of pity as an emotion, complete
with its physiological dimensions, permits conjecture about why pity,
in ancient Athens, was not a virtue. The privileging of oratorical and
historiographical texts, meanwhile, confers an interpretive advantage:
it allows us to look at Greek pity without the aid of Aristotle. The explanations he offers are not the only ones possible, and it will be argued
that Aristotle, perceptive as he is, should not necessarily be considered
the last word on the subject.

In his chapter, David Konstan poses a key question: "What place
does pity have in the cold and calculating arena of political debate?"

His answer starts with historical scenes of supplication represented in Thucydides and Isocrates and then turns to scenes of supplication in tragedy – Euripides' *Suppliant Women* and *Heraclidae*, and Aeschylus' *Suppliant Women* – that allow him to study private motives as well as public considerations. He counts on Aristotle to elucidate concepts of deserved and undeserved pity that would have shaped the outcome of actual instances of supplication. Konstan ultimately concludes that, in public debate, pity could raise political questions but not dictate political answers because the self-interest or advantage of the city mattered more.

Donald Lateiner's findings, by and large, corroborate those of Konstan. His starting point is pity in the *Iliad* – most conspicuously, the pity of Achilles – because Homeric epic enjoyed unrivaled prestige and influence within Greek culture. He then argues, from the texts of two fifth-century historians who observed the Athenian empire at work, that pity played a scant role in contemporary politics. The pity of quasi-legendary despots in Herodotus' *History* merely displayed the unlimited power at their disposal. The political expediency that Thucydides emphasized, on the other hand, was real and compelling. And pity was a luxury the weak could not afford. Rather, the strong had the power to act and "an appeal for pity [was] a sign of weakness in the world of *Machtpolitik*."

Angeliki Tzanetou supplies a pivotal explanation for the emergence of pity as a *topos* in classical Athens. Analyzing oratory and the suppliant plays, she argues that pity became a feature of civic ideology at the moment when Athens, having fended off Persia, assumed the leadership of the Delian League and acquired an empire. For concrete historical reasons, Athens claimed to be not only powerful but also compassionate, able to rise above mere self-interest. Yet "power emerges as the other face of pity," Tzanetou writes, and in reality "Athens helped those who recognized its political and military superiority and punished those who did not." The principle of expediency, which Thucydides revealed so incisively, could be hidden by the public self-image of Athens as a generous city.

Was pity, then, a mirage in ancient Athens, a shimmering illusion on the sands of bad faith? The most cynical observers might agree. But in that case, why did Athenians place so much emphasis on the artistic spectacle of suffering, the anguish of Hecuba or Oedipus? Pathetic images, whether brought to life on stage, or on the surface of a vase, or in stone, dramatized human plights that called for an emotional and evaluative response. They captured the inherent inequality between the pitier and the pitied. They also reminded viewers of their own precarious good fortune and kept them from becoming smug. If pity was not a mirage in ancient Athens, it was because Athenians, in keeping with their Homeric and Archaic Greek heritage, seem often to have reminded themselves that no one, no matter how powerful, was invulnerable to the blows of fate. They seem, moreover, to have believed that the spectacle of suffering in art and tragedy might play a role in the cultivation of pity. This is especially the case for tragedy, the only genre of art or literature that is thoroughly imbued with pity.

James Johnson and Douglas Clapp study the idealization of pity in Greek tragedy – its positive value and the "horror and pain of life and relationships which lack compassion and understanding." They identify, for example, a stark contrast between the human pity that permeates the action of Sophocles' *Ajax* and the lack thereof in Euripides' *Hippolytus*. Most importantly, they differ from Konstan and Tzanetou in urging that the compassion shown on the tragic stage was a genuine and uncynical element in the civic education of Athenian citizens, that it was depicted as a powerful response to human suffering based on a deep awareness of human insecurity and of the corresponding need for human interdependence. Plato's attack on tragedy, they further argue, was based on a distrust of emotion and was unwarranted.

Thomas Falkner, in a detailed reading of Sophocles' *Trachiniae*, suggests how scenes of pity embedded within this and other plays modeled for Athenian spectators the response they should have to the suffering of others. He foregrounds the power and status of Athenian spectators presented with pitiable tragic scenes. Identifying gender as "one of the primary metaphors through which the audience is encouraged to regard the objects of its pity," Falkner argues that the exercise of tragic pity required a "sympathetic and nonhierarchical perspective" – which was considered feminine by nature and was therefore problematic for an Athenian audience bounded by masculine ideals.

Evidence from the visual arts proves harder to find, and also harder to interpret. John Oakley proposes a series of parameters for reading emotion in the images on fifth-century Athenian vases. In the absence of any specific iconography for pity, the gestures and facial expressions of painted figures are frequently ambiguous. It is also difficult to know who in ancient Athens viewed the painted scenes and what they thought of them, especially since many pots were exported. Oakley finds, however, that pity was one of the emotions first explored in the Early Classical period, when Athens was acquiring its hegemony.

Aileen Ajootian, working from the inherent vulnerability of babies and children, is more willing than Oakley to speculate on pity in the visual arts. She considers representations, in sculpture and vase paintings, of disturbing myths about mothers who kill their children, especially the story of Prokne and her young son Itys. Ajootian raises significant questions about how Athenians may have responded to sculptures displayed in civic settings, especially when the stories they evoked ran parallel to those recounted in the courtroom or dramatized in the theater. She also links the iconography of the *kourotrophos*, the male caretaker mostly famously exemplified by the Hermes of Praxiteles, with formal supplication.

Jennifer Kosak's chapter raises interesting questions about the exercise of pity in the private sphere. Working from Hippocratic treatises and selected scenes from tragedy, she argues that the sense of touch – the fact of physical contact – altered the dynamic between doctor and healer. It shortened the distance that power created and transformed the sufferer from a painful spectacle into a human being whose suffering would be remedied through empathy more so than pity. To understand an illness, doctors needed to observe their patients, and also to interact with them either verbally or nonverbally; but most importantly, doctors often needed to act, and pity could get in the way.

The final chapter in the collection furnishes a retrospective, as Christopher Pelling uses the writings of Plutarch to explore what happened to Greek conceptions of pity after the political pre-eminence of Classical Athens had long since vanished and all power lay with Rome. Plutarch, a Greek biographer and philosopher writing in the late first and early second centuries CE, was less concerned with whether a sufferer deserved pity for his specific situation, as Aristotle held, than with the merits of that individual's entire life. Plutarch often expressed the even broader view that all human beings have flaws that lead to pitiable suffering. An heir to classical Athenian culture, Plutarch nevertheless moved beyond the Aristotelian view toward a more compassionate stance.

These chapters, taken together, suggest that the power of Athens raised issues of pity that became part of the culture – a *topos* in art and literature and public discourse that helped to educate Athenians.[17] A theme that was problematized in the fifth century remained, in the fourth century, the object of controversy. Plato rejected the tragic experiment on the grounds that it weakened men in real life; and Aristotle, predictably, urged moderation. But the popular moralizers Isocrates, Xenophon, and Demosthenes touted a vision of Athens that was firmly rooted in the capacity for pity. In the same century that witnessed the diminution of Athenian power, the challenge of rival states, and the rise of Macedon, the idea of Athens as a once-benign power became firmly enshrined. Isocrates went so far as to claim, in his *Panegyricus*, that the Athenian empire was won through kindness. Throughout the fourth century, and long after the city-state's political prime, Athenians continued to explore pity in their private lives – and later Greeks, including Plutarch's contemporaries, believed that their ancestors had erected an altar to pity in the middle of the city.[18]

ENDNOTES

1. Hume 1998: 8–12; Rousseau 1972: 175, 181–96.
2. Nietzsche 1964: 226; Kant 1960: 58.
3. See Damasio 1994. Research on the emotions is a rapidly developing multidisciplinary field. Oatley and Jenkins 1996 furnish an excellent introduction. Principal trends, from the neurophysical to the psychological and cultural, are reflected in Lewis and Haviland-Jones 2000. A cultural historian's summative analysis of recent work in cognitive psychology and anthropology is found in Reddy 2001.
4. Nussbaum emphasizes Stoic ideas. Cooper 1999 offers detailed essays on Plato and Aristotle.
5. Bremer writes (1988: 102): "According to the gospel of wealth, philanthropy was less the handmaid of social reform than a substitute for it. Wise administration of wealth was an antidote for radical proposals for redistributing property and a method of reconciling the poor and the rich."
6. For a history of the debate viewed from the right, see Olasky 1992 and Sykes 1992. For the troubled left, see Wagner 2000. Willis, writing in *The New Yorker* (30 Sept. 1996: 5), rejects liberal and right-wing moralizing alike in favor of "deeper, harder questions, like how people can wrest from the corporations power over economic and political decision-making."
7. See Hancock 1989. In the wake of the September 11 terrorist attacks, Oriana Fallaci (2002) delivered a polemic against blindly and compassionately allowing Muslim immigrants – "poor-little-things" – to threaten Europe.
8. Three come from Xenophon (*Ages.* 11.1–12, *Cyr.* 8.1.23–33, *Mem.* 4.8.11) and five from Isocrates (2.15–54, 3.29–64, 8.63, 9.22–46, and 12.30–32). For corroborating epigraphic evidence, see Whitehead 1993.

9. Dem. 21.185 and Xen. *Cyr.* 6.1.47 offer praise, while excoriation of the pitiless is found at Ant. 1.26–27; Dem. 19.309, 21.182, 24.197, 24.201, 25.84, 27.65; Aeschin. 1.188; Din. 1.24.
10. Compare Lys. 24.7, Isoc. 15.20, and Dem. 22.57, 24.171, 27.65.
11. Kleon's suggestion of reciprocity is somewhat sophistic: the political issue of pity in Thucydides gets raised only in the context of a radical power gap, where the pitier enjoys a superior position and the power to determine the fate of the pitied.
12. Hornblower (1991: 1.421) notes the disparity, as do Pelling (2000: 11) and MacMullen (2003: 3). In the Melian dialogue, also, Thucydides implicitly condemns the Athenians' lack of compassion in utterly destroying the island community of Melos, which had sought only to maintain its neutrality in the conflict between Athens and Sparta. MacMullen comments (2–3): "Thucydides' readers are chilled to the bone by both tone and outcome of the story, as he intended. Inexorable rationality, the Athenian way of mind, is held up to them for detestation. . . . Pure reason in the service of force *was* inhuman, and [Thucydides] evidently felt it to be so, himself."
13. Thucydides uses the word only two other times, to characterize the civil war in Corcyra (3.82.1 and 3.84.1). For the moral condemnation of savagery, see Dem. 9.26, 18.231, 18.275, 20.109, 21.88, 21.97, 21.109, 24.171, 25.83–84, 27.26–28, 29.2; Isoc. 12.90, 15.300, 15.315. Isocrates (4.112) depicts Spartan domination at the end of the Peloponnesian War as a moral low point in Athenian history, when citizens were so deeply embroiled in troubles of their own that they had no time to pity or help one another and were reduced to savagery.
14. The Reverend J. P. Mahaffy, writing in the late nineteenth century, called Athenians "deeply selfish" (1883: 146) and commented that "with all their intellect, and all their subtlety, the Greeks were wanting in heart" (243).
15. See for example Wuthnow 1991; Menlowe and Smith 1993; Clark 1997; Sober and Wilson 1998.
16. David Konstan finds that the political decision to grant or refuse suppliant requests in scenes from tragedy rested on considerations of advantage more so than pity; James Johnson and Douglas Clapp contend, to the contrary, that compassion was operative in those decisions; and Angeliki Tzanetou explores the ideological underpinnings of suppliant dramas, especially Athenian attitudes toward non-Athenian exiles.
17. Indeed, the propensity for pity was recognized as a sign of education. In the *Electra* of Euripides, Orestes says, "There is pity not among the ignorant, but among learned men" (294–95).
18. Thompson 1952; Zuntz 1953; Vanderpool 1974.

The Nature of Pity

Rachel Hall Sternberg

◎▣◎

HERODOTUS TELLS HOW THE PERSIAN KING XERXES, UPON VIEWING his troops arrayed at the Hellespont, suddenly weeps. As the king explains to his uncle Artabanos, it has just occurred to him that not one of the men he is looking at will be alive a hundred years hence, and so he pities (*katoikteirai*) the brevity of life. Artabanos responds (7.46.2–3): "In the course of life we suffer other things more pitiable (*oiktrotera*) than this. For in so short a lifetime, no human being is born so blessed . . . that it shall not happen, often and not just once, that he will wish to die rather than to live. For there are calamities that meet him and diseases that confound him, so that they make life, short as it is, seem long."

This anecdote, which dramatizes the ominous massing of Persian forces prior to their descent on Europe, reveals an unexpected facet of the tyrant and allows Herodotus, through the figure of the wise advisor, to comment on the tragic ebb and flow of life, whose calamities and diseases are more pitiable than the mere fact of death. It also allows us to examine the pity attributed to Xerxes. Though inspired by a thought, it is an emotion, sudden in onset and sharp enough to draw tears. Xerxes speaks of it as entering into him while he thinks and calculates. Yet as an example of pity, it is curiously pure. Its object is abstract rather than personal. No suppliant demands it; no decision rests upon it; it changes nothing. Despite his ironic premonition of doom, Xerxes takes no action and indeed none is possible. He could halt the invasion, but he cannot extend man's natural life span. And so the tyrant's moment of pity stands alone, unbidden and without consequence.

The image of Xerxes at the Hellespont invites us to explore the Greek concept of pity: the words that expressed it – *oiktos* and *eleos* – and the nature of the emotion. We ought to be wary of the invitation, for such an exploration will inevitably be fraught with difficulty. Can we proceed without wrongly mapping our own conceptual universe onto an alien culture? Anthropologists who study living people often struggle with this problem; for classicists, it is compounded by time. The ancient Greeks left behind mere fragments of evidence for pity, which was in any case a "fuzzy" concept. Across the abyss of millennia, they cannot explain themselves to us nor can they correct our misreadings. How can we hope to discern what they thought or felt? Can we even translate the Greek terms *oiktos* and *eleos* into English without stumbling?

These difficulties are daunting but not lethal.[1] Let us walk for a moment on the sunny side of the hermeneutic street. First, we know that the Greeks, like us, drew a distinction in common parlance between thought and feeling. Indeed, Anna Wierzbicka has identified "think" and "feel" as two of more than sixty lexical universals – concepts expressed as separate words or morphemes in all languages. Her success at using semantic primitives to explicate emotions found in various languages and cultures is encouraging.[2] It suggests that we can hope to understand what the Greeks meant when they talked about emotion. Second, we know that the Greeks did classify *oiktos* or *eleos* as an emotion, a point to be discussed in greater detail later. Third, we possess hundreds of references to pity in Greek texts, including plays, treatises, and some intriguing anecdotes in which pity plays a part. In sum, we can attempt a cross-cultural analysis by using the evidence we have to describe the "folk psychology" of the ancient Greeks – their everyday understanding of *oiktos* and *eleos*.[3]

Herodotus and subsequent Greek historians offer tantalizing insights into the folk psychology of pity because in recounting events they interpret human motives. So do orators like Demosthenes, whether in forensic or deliberative contexts; and even their deployment of pity as an oratorical *tekhnê* is revealing. These two genres – historiography and oratory – offer a solid starting point for the study of pity in ancient Athens because they are in some ways closer to real life than the heroic scenes of epic and tragedy. Granted, all literary genres reflect ancient thought in different ways, and none holds up an unblemished mirror of society. But what distinguishes the historians and orators is that they at least purport to describe reality or to offer a convincing fiction. The present chapter concentrates on the usage of *oiktos*, *eleos*, and their cognates in Herodotus, Thucydides, Xenophon, and works attributed to the ten Attic orators, a sample consisting of 257 separate occurrences. Aside from rhetorical arguments for and against pity, and various gnomic observations, the sample yields twenty-nine reported cases of pity that are either historically authentic, such as Athenian pity for women taken captive at Olynthos,[4] or quasi-legendary, like those found in the *History* of Herodotus and Xenophon's *Cyropaedia*.[5]

Although lexically complete, the sample fails to capture every scene of pity or compassion because Greek writers had other ways to denote feelings of sympathetic sorrow. They could, for example, use various *sun-* compounds, such as *sunakhthomai* or *sullupeô*.[6] They could also suggest pity through an accumulation of pathetic images, the recounting of atrocities, or the mention of pleading and tears. Nevertheless, a lexical approach lays a practical foundation on which further discussions of pity can be built.[7] One benefit of this foundation is that it does not rest upon Aristotle and therefore can be used to check his views. It will be interesting to watch the interplay between folk psychology and philosophical analysis within the ancient sources.

DEFINITIONS

But definitions first. I start by following standard procedures for lexical analysis. My first goal is to establish the denotation or core meaning of the Greek terms. My second goal is to distinguish, if possible, between them. I offer "pity" as a makeshift translation for both but beg the reader to set aside, as far as possible, the distracting and largely negative connotations of the English word within our own culture.[8] Rather, we should become alert to the connotations of *oiktos* and *eleos* within Greek culture insofar as these can be deduced from the stories and examples presented here and elsewhere in this volume.

Like most words, *oiktos* and *eleos* are polysemic: that is to say, they possess multiple meanings and can denote more than one thing. Typically, both denote Person A's feeling of sorrow or distress aroused by the misfortunes of Person B, who is in pain or jeopardy. Their reference to a feeling of sorrow rather than a dispassionate calculation seems obvious and indisputable when an ancient author classifies either *eleos* or *oiktos* with other emotions. Aristotle does this,[9] and so does Demosthenes. The latter lists *eleos* among a myriad of emotions, including envy, anger, and a desire to please, that can lead Athenians astray (Dem. 19.228). Elsewhere he names *eleos* in opposition to hatred, envy, and anger (Dem. 21.196).[10] Very occasionally, however, *eleos* and *oiktos* seem as much a moral or emotional propensity as an immediate feeling: Demosthenes (25.81) describes *eleos* as something that one brings from home.[11] It is almost an attitude.

What about other meanings? Sometimes *eleos*, *oiktos*, and their cognates do not denote "pity" at all but rather an "audible and pitiful expression of misery." When Andocides describes his first night in prison after the mutilation of the Hermes, for example, *oiktos* must refer to something that can be heard (1.48):[12] "There was the clamor (*boê*) and lamentation (*oiktos*) of those weeping and grieving over their present evils."

Another possible meaning, "to show pity," poses greater problems in interpretation because the context is sometimes ambiguous. Dover in particular (1974: 195–96) observes that *eleos* and *oiktos* can denote an action rather than a feeling. Perhaps so, yet there are grounds for caution. Of the twenty-nine cases of reported pity in oratory and historiography, eighteen entail action of some kind. Croesus, for instance, pities Adrestos and spares his life; Kambyses pities Psammenitos and tries to halt the execution of his son. In a real-life example, the Areopagus Council pities and acquits Theogenes, who was duped into marrying an impure daughter of Neaira and narrowly escapes blame for letting her perform religious rites on behalf of Athens. Pity and action are often closely related. From a lexical point of view, however, there is a world of difference between cases in which the feeling of pity and the resultant action are clearly separated in the narrative and those in which they are virtually simultaneous, with the *eleos* or *oiktos* word seeming to denote both.

It turns out that sixteen of the eighteen passages make a clear lexical separation between pity and action. Herodotus, for example, writes, "And at that point this man Aryandes, pitying Pheretime, gives her the entire army of Egypt."[13] Such a separation is lacking in only two cases, and it would be difficult to prove in either of them that the pity word denotes an action wholly divorced from feeling. In the *Cyropaedia* (6.1.47) it almost certainly does not: Panthea, in praising Cyrus for pity (*katoiktisin*), must be referring to his protection of her, but Cyrus is later said to *feel* pity for her as well (7.3.14). A passage from *Against Theomnestus* (Lys. 10.22) presents a more complicated situation: the speaker says his opponent, in an earlier case, was pitied (*êleêthê*), that is, acquitted, by the Areopagus Council. Certainly it could be argued that stock expressions of "pity and pardon" were used so often in forensic speeches as to be leeched of meaning, with the result that *êleêthê* was simply an alternative way for the speaker to express the fact of acquittal. Yet the speaker's own goal is to win the pity of the jury. He seeks it partly on the grounds that he himself was orphaned at age thirteen when his father was put to death by the Thirty (10.4) and partly because he is now the victim of wrongdoing (10.13). The issue of pity, it seems, is very much alive in this speech, and the word *êleêthê* at 10.22 may well have been uttered in a tone of meaningful indignation.[14] This example points to yet another semantic difficulty: we are unable to account for the range of meanings that can be imparted in the performance of any speech act. A speaker may use irony or sarcasm. He or she may, through body language or vocal inflection, subtly shift the meaning of a word away from its standard denotation. It is impossible to capture the living qualities of classical Greek, but we should assume that pity words denote the emotion unless a given text clearly indicates otherwise.

As a feeling of sorrow, *oiktos* and *eleos* require an object to complete their meaning: a Person B who suffers or is expected to suffer terrible things, like the calamities and diseases of which Artabanos spoke.[15] When classed according to the object of pity, twelve of the twenty-nine cases involve people captured or defeated in war; four involve the sick, the old, or the emasculated; four involve wrongdoers; two involve the financially strapped; and three involve babies, children, or adult offspring.[16] These categories match some of the situations that Aristotle designates as pitiable: death, bodily injury, sickness, and old age.[17] But they point to others that the philosopher does not mention: warfare, wrongdoing, financial difficulty, and incidents involving babies or older children.

The single largest category comprises people captured or defeated in warfare. Six such cases can be deemed historically authentic,[18] and a passage in Demosthenes conveys the pathos of defeat (19.65): "For when recently we were traveling to Delphi, by necessity we had to see all these things: houses demolished, city walls taken away, the place stripped of men in their prime, only women and a few little children, and miserable old people." The special pitiability of old people is clear: in forensic speeches, the orators routinely mention a litigant's old age or his elderly parents in order to stir pity.[19] The sick are not a *topos* in oratory, but Thucydides and Xenophon provide authentic examples of pity for them. Wrongdoers form a category that dovetails with a major preoccupation of forensic oratory, namely, whether a person accused of a given crime can in some way merit or deserve pity. His right to be pitied may be argued on the grounds that he is innocent. Then again, if he admits guilt, pity may be urged in view of extenuating circumstances or prospective suffering on the part of his innocent dependents. The category of the financially strapped is underrepresented, given that Lysias and Demosthenes, in numerous other passages, lambaste the rich and drum up sympathy for the poor without necessarily using *oiktos* and *eleos* or their cognates.[20] Other people's small children or one's own offspring at any age are fitting objects of pity, a point underscored by constant oratorical references to children. Wives are rarely mentioned in the courtroom context, but historiography gives us a number of pitiable women: the wife of Intaphrenes, Pheretime, Panthea, and captive Olynthians. Of all these, only the war prisoner Panthea is pitied, in part because she is a woman and embodies feminine beauty. The others are pitied for rather different reasons.

How does this material compare with Aristotle's definition of pity in the *Rhetoric*? David Konstan translates: "Let pity, then, be a kind of pain in the case of an apparent destructive or painful harm of one not deserving to encounter it, which one might expect oneself, or one of one's own, to suffer, and this when it seems near."[21] The first component of the definition, that pity is a kind of pain or distress (*lupê tis*), fits closely with the evidence from oratory and historiography. But the second component of the philosopher's definition, attributing the arousal of pity to "an apparent destructive or painful harm *of one not deserving to encounter it*," seems unduly narrow. Aristotle is saying that *oiktos* and *eleos* are not merely Person A's feeling of sorrow or distress aroused by the misfortunes of Person B, who is in pain or jeopardy. Rather, Person A, in order to feel *oiktos* or *eleos*, must first judge the suffering of Person B to be undeserved. This certainly holds true in the courtroom: dozens of passages in oratory raise the issue of whether, from the standpoint of justice, a given person deserves to be pitied, and we must not forget that Aristotle offers this definition in the context of rhetoric and persuasion (Fortenbaugh 2002: 114). Among the twenty-nine cases of pity analyzed in this chapter, considerations of merit or desert sometimes play a determining role, as when Croesus judges that Adrestos, his son's unwitting killer, does not deserve to die (Hdt. 1.45.2).[22] But this is not invariably the case. In Xenophon's *Anabasis* (1.4.7), some Greek soldiers pity defectors whom others condemn as cowards. In the *History*, Phokaians pity their abandoned city (Hdt. 1.165.3) and break their oath never to return there. More importantly, it appears that certain misfortunes were considered pitiable in and of themselves. Hence, survivors of the plague pity the stricken (Thuc. 2.51.6) and Xerxes indiscriminately pities all mankind (Hdt. 7.46.2).

A bit later in the *Rhetoric*, Aristotle imposes yet another limitation on *oiktos* and *eleos*: he says that the pitier and the pitied cannot be too close, *an mê sphodra engus ôsin oikeiotêti* (2.8, 1386a18–19). The feeling of pity depends on a certain detachment, exemplified by the story of Amasis, a reprise of the story that Herodotus attaches to Psammenitos (see p. 78). Nevertheless, Herodotus tells us (3.52.3) that Periander pitied his son Lykophron, an incident discussed later. Timokrates is criticized for failing to pity his own father, who has suffered *atimia* (Dem. 24.201).[23] Cases of self-pity, where detachment is impossible, also occur among the twenty-nine historiographical and oratorical cases of *oiktos* and *eleos*: Athenians under siege pity themselves (Xen. *Apol.* 18); Xenophon as one of the Ten Thousand pities them (*An.* 3.1.19); and Isocrates pities his own old age (Isoc. 12.232).[24] It would seem, then, that Aristotle identifies genuine themes in Greek pity – merit and detachment – but perhaps overstates them.

Finally, it remains to consider the difference between the words *oiktos* and *eleos*. They are synonyms in the broad sense. In their range of application, however, they are not completely identical and interchangeable, and scholars have often suspected them of having different shades of meaning.[25] The Liddell and Scott lexicon defines both *oiktos* and *eleos* as "pity" or "compassion" while adding for *eleos* a third meaning, "mercy," and some have wanted to bring Greek into conformance with English by translating *eleos* as "pity" and *oiktos* as "compassion." But the two words are sometimes used in close association with no apparent difference in semantic content, most conspicuously in the Mytilenean debate. Kleon urges the Athenians not to be led astray by *oiktos*. The reason he offers is that *eleos* is right only in a context of reciprocal relations (Thuc. 3.40.2–3).[26] *Oiktos* and *eleos* are used interchangeably here and also in phrases such as "worthy of pity," "pity and pardon," and so forth.[27]

Now it is true that *eleos* is found much more frequently in these stock phrases,[28] so one may be tempted to imagine that *eleos* is milder than *oiktos*: more detached, more reasoned, less emotional. The problem is that this preponderance of *eleos* words can also be understood as a function of literary genre. From one genre to the next, Greek authors show clear-cut preferences for either *oiktos* or *eleos*. In Homer, *eleos* words constitute 76 percent of the total. The philosophers also prefer *eleos* at a rate of 84 percent and employ *eleos* even when discussing tragic pity – although tragic poets Aeschylus, Sophocles, and Euripides overwhelmingly prefer *oiktos* words, which they use 95 percent of the time, possibly for reasons of scansion. The historians, like the tragedians, prefer *oiktos* words, which they use 93 percent of the time, while the orators prefer *eleos* words, which they use 89 percent of the time. Since most of the stock phrases are found in oratory, the very genre that prefers *eleos* and, at the same time, has occasion to discuss merited pity or pity and pardon,[29] we are left wandering in circles, unable to tell whether the orators chose *eleos* because it was more detached and more reasoned, or whether *eleos* seems more detached and more reasoned because the orators chose it. A similar conundrum obtains in historiography, where we cannot know whether the historians used *oiktos* in dramatic portions of their narratives because it connoted deep emotion, or whether *oiktos* seems to connote deep emotion because the historians used it so dramatically.

Stock phrases aside, oratory offers several instances where *eleos* and *oiktos* are juxtaposed in such a way as to suggest that they do connote different things. So, for example, the *Funeral Oration* attributed to Lysias says that the Greeks fighting at Salamis felt *eleos* for their children, *pothos* (longing) for their wives, and *oiktos* for their fathers and mothers (Lys. 2.39). Is there something about aging parents that makes them suitable objects of *oiktos* as opposed to *eleos*? Does their old age make them pathetic in a distinctive way? Other *oiktos* words are used of old people at Dem. 19.65 and Isoc. 12.232. Inconveniently, however, *eleos* too is used of old people, at Lys. 20.35 and Dem. 49.17, 19.283, and 24.201. Let us consider another possibility. Could one of the two words imply that the pitier has the power to help the pitied and is inclined to do so? But the eighteen cases of pity where the pitier intervenes are almost evenly divided between *oiktos* and *eleos*.[30] Once again, any effort to tease out a difference in meaning leads precisely nowhere. There must have been some semantic distinction between the two, but for us it remains highly elusive. Cyrus pities the war captive Panthea with *oiktos* much as Athenians pity the captive Olynthian women with *eleos*. Assassins pity the infant Kypselos with *oiktos*, while the Spartan conquerors pity the young nephews of Nicias with *eleos*. Perhaps a close study of other fifth- and fourth-century genres would yield greater insights.

The two word groups of *oiktos* and *eleos* definitely offered Greek writers the possibility of literary *variatio*. When the speaker in Antiphon's *Against the Stepmother* (1.25) alleges that the defendant murdered her husband *aneleêmonôs* and *anoiktistôs*, we would very much like to understand the shades of meaning in those two rare adverbs. Yet the weight of evidence suggests that there was little difference, and that Antiphon was pitilessly indulging in pleonasm.

SIGHT, HEARING, AND TEARS

Having considered the meaning of *oiktos* and *eleos*, we may now examine in greater detail the Greek folk psychology of pity: the sense perceptions that trigger the feeling, its relation to weeping and tears, and the locus of pity within the human body. Greek historians and orators are remarkably consistent in how they describe or allude to the emotional response of pity and surely draw on conventional concepts within Greek culture. Sources that provide full psychological detail, however, are limited in number. Thucydides, despite an underlying humanity,[31] writes in a minimalist style and is not apt to describe emotions. Xenophon is more expansive, especially in the *Cyropaedia*, because the fictional Cyrus needs to understand the mentality of the people around him in order to control them (Tatum 1989: 65–66) and is shown pitying Gadatas, Panthea, and Croesus. But by far the richest descriptions of pity are found in the *History* of Herodotus, especially when he elaborates on traditional tales or develops the character portrait of a nearly contemporary historical figure like Xerxes. His are not real-life anecdotes, though they purport to be, but the attitudes they reveal are genuine, and they are arguably as Greek as their author even when the setting and characters are foreign. Unfortunately, Herodotus is unique in the depth of insight he offers into Greek conceptions of pity. The Attic orators offer piecemeal clues, but rarely dwell on the moment of pity long enough to reveal its proximate causes or effects on the pitier. Demosthenes is the most profuse and informative, but most of the genre's purportedly true-life anecdotes are frustratingly concise. Still, oratorical allusions to pity dovetail neatly with the fuller descriptions offered by Herodotus and Xenophon. All these authors appear to conceptualize the emotion in much the same way, and all concede the power of sight, hearing, and tears, each of which will be considered in turn.

In Book Five of the *History*, Herodotus tells how ten men forewarned by an oracle come to kill the newborn Kypselos of Corinth. The first man to take the baby from the arms of its mother is supposed to dash it to the ground (Hdt. 5.92c3–4). Pity restrains him, though, because he sees the child's smile. Herodotus implies that had the man not seen it, he would have carried out the killing. Sight, then, is pivotal. A number of scholars have noticed that ancient Greeks considered sight a privileged sense, as Aristotle does in the *Metaphysics*.[32] Jenny Strauss Clay (1983: 12) writes that they "thought hearing immeasurably inferior to seeing, since the latter sense yielded incomparably more certain knowledge. The equation between seeing and knowing . . . can be summed up in the Greek verb *oida*, which means 'I have seen,' hence, 'I know.'" Ruth Padel (1992: 62) observes that eyes "have a key role in fifth-century language describing relations between a human being and the outside world, physical, social, or daemonic."[33] The ancient sources suggest that the ability of human beings to see one another creates the possibility of mutual sympathy and understanding, the very bonds that hold society together. Xenophon captures this sense of psychological proximity in the *Cyropaedia* (2.1.25), when his fictional Cyrus the Great orders that each army company of 100 men share a tent so that the soldiers will get to know each other, developing consideration and respect, since "those who are unacquainted seem somehow more indifferent – like people in the dark."

It is often sight that triggers pity, as with Xerxes at the Hellespont, or earlier in the *History*, when Periander drives his son Lykophron from the royal house of Corinth but later relents (Hdt. 3.52.3): "On the fourth day Periander, seeing him in an unwashed and hungry state, pitied him." One common ploy of contestants in a lawsuit demonstrates the importance of seeing for oneself. In the epilogue, when the water in the clock was nearly spent, a litigant might bring his small children or other pitiable dependents into court so that the jurors could witness with their own eyes the human beings who would suffer from an unfavorable verdict. This practice was apparently so routine that Aristophanes has the litigious Philokleon ask at the mock trial (*Wasps* 976), "Where are the children?" Plato's Socrates, in the *Apology* (34c), says that bringing in children and other relatives and friends is something that he, at least, will not do. In extant oratory, the ploy is more often alluded to than expressly carried out.[34] *On the Embassy* is the only speech that refers to children and other relatives actually present in court (Aeschin. 2.152). Aeschines exploits their presence in the epilogue (2.179) in very much the manner Plato and Aristophanes deride.

Seeing becomes a dramatic act of the imagination in *Against Ctesiphon*, where Aeschines describes the condition of Thebes after the defeat at Chaeronea in 338 BCE, some eight years prior to the speech (Aeschin. 3.157):

> But since you were not present in person, yet in your minds at least look steadfastly at their misfortunes and imagine that you see their city conquered, the razing of their walls, the burning of their homes; their women and children led into slavery; their old men, their old women, late in life unlearning freedom; weeping, supplicating you, angry not with those taking vengeance upon them, but with those responsible for these things.

Aeschines employs no *eleos* or *oiktos* words in this passage, but people captured or defeated in war are typical objects of pity; so are children and old people. The orator piles one pathetic image upon another so that each juror will feel pity and indignation as he sees conquered Thebes in his mind's eye.[35]

The power of sight, then, was commonly linked to fellow-feeling and the capacity for pity – what modern psychologists would describe as sympathy or empathy. This is not to say that pity was the only possible response to the spectacle of another's misfortune. Isocrates comments that people cry over the fabrications of poets[36] but view real sufferings with something like pleasure (Isoc. 4.168): "Looking upon many

and terrible actual experiences brought about by war, they are so far
from pitying that they rejoice more in the evils of others than in their
own private advantages." Indifference was another possible response,
for one could look upon a pathetic sight and yet remain unmoved. The
unknown author of *Against Alcibiades* observes (And. 4.23): "When you
are shown things of this kind on the tragic stage, you think them terrible, but when you see them happening in the city, you think nothing
of it."

Seeing and hearing are often paired, as in the *Third Tetralogy*
(Antiph. 4.4.2), where "seeing with the eyes and hearing with the ears"
is held up as a standard of naturalness.[37] In the context of pity, one may
simultaneously see and hear a suffering person, but hearing gains its
full importance only at the recounting of an event remote in time or
space, where one must grasp the truth through hearing and imagining.
Xenophon's Cyrus, for example, pities Gadatas when the latter tells of
having been unjustly emasculated by the Assyrian king (*Cyr.* 5.4.32).
An effective story or *logos* brings the event close to the hearer, produc-
ing the effect of psychological proximity. The quasi-magical power of
words is a familiar *topos* in Greek thought, and the *Defense of Helen* by
Gorgias describes the impact of a story well told (9): "Fearful shuddering and tearful pity [*eleos poludakrus*] and sad yearning enter into the
hearers; and the soul, affected by the words, experiences as its own the
emotion aroused by the good and ill fortunes of other people's doings
and lives."[38]

Hearing triggers pity in the tale of Kambyses and Psammenitos in
Book Three of the *History*. Kambyses makes a cruel test of the defeated
Egyptian king: he parades past him his condemned son and enslaved
daughter. Psammenitos remains impassive until he catches sight of an
old companion reduced to beggary, at which point he cries out, calls
upon his friend by name, and strikes his own head in grief. Everything
Psammenitos does is reported to Kambyses, who is confounded and

sends a messenger to question him. Psammenitos explains that the woes of his household are too great to bewail, but the misfortune of his friend is worthy of tears.[39] When this speech is reported to Kambyses, his courtiers and the deposed Croesus, who was also present, listen and weep (Hdt. 3.14.10–11):

> When this reply was carried back, it seemed to [Kambyses and his courtiers] well said. And the Egyptians say that Croesus cried . . . and the Persians present cried too, and a certain pity entered Kambyses himself (eselthein oikton tina) and he ordered them at once to save the boy from among those to be destroyed and to bring Psammenitos himself from the city's outskirts to his side.

Here it is not sight that inspires pity, but rather a messenger's speech, a device reminiscent of tragedy. Herodotus does not say that Croesus and the Persians pitied Psammenitos; he only says they cried, but from this observation we are given to understand that they, along with Kambyses and perhaps in advance of him, did feel pity.

Sometimes the *logos* that is heard can mitigate the image that is seen, as the hearer's understanding of a situation deepens. This happens in Book One of the *History*, where Croesus must deal with the death of his son, brought about inadvertently by Adrestos, the very man whom he had mercifully accepted as a suppliant. When the Lydians bring home the corpse, Adrestos is following behind and begs Croesus to kill him then and there (Hdt. 1.45.1–2). Herodotus places great emphasis on Adrestos' self-incriminating speech and the king's reaction to it. Croesus sees his young son's corpse, he sees the killer ready to die; yet hearing the confession stirs his pity and so he spares Adrestos. Interestingly, he disregards the literal entreaties of the suppliant, who asks to be killed and demonstrates his sincere desire to die by taking his own life afterward.

As might be expected, tales of suffering can achieve superlative results in the courtroom. Hermogenes remarks in the *Apology* of Xenophon that jurors often acquit the guilty "either pitying them because of their speech or because they spoke winningly" (Xen. *Apol.* 4). The actual hearing of a story is twice linked to *eleos*. First, in *Against Polycles*, the plaintiff claims that "my domestic affairs were in such a sorry state at that critical point that you would pity me if you heard them" (Dem. 50.59). Second, the same plaintiff, in *Against Nicostratus*, tells how he once pitied Nicostratus and gave him money. This anecdote, one of our few historically authentic cases of pity, is worth reviewing in some detail.

Nicostratus had been a neighbor and close friend of Apollodoros. One day, however, he was taken captive in a trireme and sold into slavery on the island of Aegina. Apollodoros, who was absent from the country at the time, later heard the news and gave Nicostratus' brother travel money to Aegina. Nicostratus was successfully ransomed and came home (Dem. 53.7–8):

> And [Nicostratus], arriving home and coming to my house first, embraced me and praised me because I had provided travel money for his brother, and he bewailed his own misfortune, and while complaining of his own relatives begged me to help him, just as in time past I had been a true friend to him. At the same time he was crying, and saying that he had been ransomed for twenty-six minae, and he beseeched me to contribute something toward his ransom. Hearing these things and taking pity on him (tauta d'egô akouôn kai eleêsas touton), and at the same time seeing how badly off he was, displaying the wounds on his calves that were made by fetters . . . I answered him that . . . I would come to his aid.

Apollodoros therefore gave Nicostratus a thousand drachmas; nor is this the whole story of his misplaced generosity, which allegedly led to an assault and ended in a lawsuit. But at this juncture, we are told, he was deeply affected by the sight of his friend's wounds, and he also heard what Nicostratus said: his thanking, bewailing, complaining, begging, crying, telling, and urging. Hearing these things, he pitied him.

The art of persuasion, as it developed throughout the fifth and fourth centuries, carried the power of words to new heights.[40] Aristotle, recognizing the cognitive element in emotion, explores how rhetoric could be used to induce anger, fear, shame, benevolence, pity, indignation, envy, and emulation.[41] But tears and lamentation, as well as language, were also effective instruments, a fact that Plato recognizes in his complaints about courtroom weeping.[42] Historiography and oratory both demonstrate that tears can trigger pity. The unknown author of *Against Alcibiades* refers to pitiful supplication and weeping (And. 4.39), while two Greek words for tears and crying, the noun *to dakruon* and the verb *dakruô*, are often found in close association with *eleos* or *oiktos*.[43] All in all, references to pathetic tears far outnumber references to pathetic sights or pathetic stories.

Herodotus once again provides useful psychological details, this time in his story of Darius and the wife of Intaphrenes. The Persian king has just imprisoned Intaphrenes and all the males in his household on the grounds of suspected treason (Hdt. 3.119.2–3):

> *He seized them and put them in prison to await their death. The wife of Intaphrenes, coming constantly to the doors of the king, wailed and lamented. And doing always this same thing she persuaded Darius to pity her* (epeise oiktirai min). *And sending his messenger to her he said, "Woman, King Darius grants you the release of one of your imprisoned relatives, whomever you choose out of all of them."*

For Herodotus, the chief interest in this tale lies in the woman's oddly calculated choice of whom to save from death; she names her brother, and explains why in a speech echoed in Sophocles' *Antigone* (908–12).

Nonetheless, we should look closely at the pity of Darius. Herodotus says it is the woman's constant clamor, her wailing and lamenting,[44] that commands the king's attention: always doing this same thing, she persuades him to pity her. The use of the verb *peithô* here is striking: her tears achieve the same result as a verbal argument.

We have seen that Nicostratus was weeping when he pleaded with Apollodoros and won his pity (Dem. 53.7). Gadatas, too, was crying as he told Cyrus his story (Xen. *Cyr.* 5.4.32), and Aeschines' pathetic vision of defeated Thebes included weeping war victims whom the jury was expected to find pitiable (Aeschin. 3.157). In Athenian courtrooms, weeping was standard practice because litigants believed that tears would trigger pity in the jurors. The speaker in *Against Epicrates* assumes a causal connection between tears and pity (Lys. 27.12): "Most absurd of all, while in private suits it is the wronged who weep and are pitiable, in public suits it is the wrongdoers who are pitiable and you, the wronged, who pity them." Demosthenes, in *Against Onetor*, describes Onetor's behavior at an earlier trial in which his brother-in-law Aphobos had been found guilty (Dem. 30.32):

> *After the case had been decided, he got up before the court and begged, supplicating on behalf of Aphobos and entreating them and weeping with tears to fix the damages at a talent, and he offered himself as surety for this amount.*

Weeping children are equated with pardon and pity in *On the Embassy* (Dem. 19.281): "Will you be content that all these men . . . should derive benefit from neither pardon, nor pity, nor weeping children bearing names of public benefactors, nor anything else?"

So tears can trigger pity. But pity can, in turn, trigger tears. Gorgias, as noted earlier (see p. 28), speaks of "tearful pity," and Demosthenes equates the feeling of pity with a tearful response when he says that Aeschines lacked feeling for the Olynthian war captives (Dem. 19.309): "Yet Aeschines did not pity [the women] nor did he weep for Greece."[45]

The notion is so commonplace that we can infer pity in passages where *oiktos* and *eleos* are lacking but a character is said to witness pathetic things and weep. Pity is certainly implied in the miraculous birth story of Cyrus the Great as recounted in the *History*. Astyages, king of the Medes, marries his daughter to a lowly Persian and then orders her newborn baby killed. A herdsman is enjoined to expose the infant, but his wife, who has just given birth to a stillborn child, persuades him to switch the two so that Cyrus might live (1.112): "At the same time he said these things, the herdsman uncovered [the infant Cyrus] and showed it to her. And when his wife saw the child so big and beautiful, she burst into tears, and taking her man by the knees she begged him by no means to expose it." As with the would-be assassins of the infant Kypselos (Hdt. 5.92c3–4), sight triggers her reaction. Since the emotion that gives rise to her tears goes unnamed, one might object that grief and longing are intended here rather than pity. But the woman does not immediately ask to keep the baby for herself; rather, she begs her husband not to expose it. She next suggests a plan that will allow their dead son to receive a princely burial and the other child to live. Herodotus, then, focuses twice on her desire to preserve the baby's life. This scene also draws upon pathos established earlier in the story. When the newborn Cyrus was first handed over to Harpagos, the kinsman of Astyages, all decked out for death, Harpagos wept (Hdt. 1.109) and so did members of his household. The seemingly doomed baby is a pathetic sight, and neither Harpagos nor the herdsman wants to kill him. Pity for the child is implied at every juncture.[46] As in the story of Psammenitos, then, Herodotus uses tears as a literary shorthand for pity. They could also be considered metonymic: tears, which are one part of the emotional response, stand for the whole.[47]

The same shorthand or metonymy occurs in the *Against Diogeiton* of Lysias, a lawsuit brought against a guardian who allegedly deprived three wards, two boys and a girl, of their inheritance.[48] The speaker, who married the girl, recounts how the two boys were cast out by Diogeiton and came with their mother to ask his help, "pitifully affected by the blow and wretchedly laid low, weeping and calling upon me not to look the other way while they were deprived of their patrimony and reduced to beggary" (Lys. 32.10). The speaker convokes a family meeting at which the mother accuses Diogeiton, her own father, of mistreating the children. She cites every financial and practical detail: they are cast out of their house in worn-out clothes, without shoes, attendants, bedding, cloaks, or the furniture and money that was their due. She says Diogeiton values money over everything else. Then the speaker continues (Lys. 32.18):

> At that point, gentlemen of the jury, after many terrible things had been said by the woman, all of us present were so affected by this man's conduct and by her statements, seeing the children, the sorts of things they were suffering; remembering the dead man and how he had left his estate to an unworthy guardian; reflecting how difficult it is to find a person who can be trusted with one's affairs; so that, gentlemen of the jury, no one of us present was able to say a thing, but weeping no less than the sufferers we left to go our ways in silence.

Here we have the terrible things, the sufferings, the mother's affecting *logos*, and the sight of the children. Finally, when the assembled relatives all begin to cry, we know they feel pity for the disinherited orphans along with indignation over the treachery of Diogeiton.

Tears can draw sympathetic tears, as in Xenophon's *Cyropaedia* when Cyrus confronts his uncle Kyaxares, who is jealous of him (5.5.6ff). Cyrus begs an explanation; Kyaxares describes at length his sense of political impotence and humiliation (5.5.8–10): "And as he said this he was still more overpowered by tears so that he drew Cyrus along too, and *his* eyes filled with tears." The emotional bond between the two men is obvious. Cyrus, as the story goes, quickly recovers and launches into a defense of his own motives and acts that leads to a complete reconciliation in which the uncle accepts his nephew's kiss.

Xenophon also supplies us with a quasi-historical anecdote in the *Hellenica*, dated to 378 BCE, showing that tears are contagious and suggesting a moment of pity although neither *eleos* nor *oiktos* is named. The Thebans had induced Sphodrias, the Spartan governor at the Boeotian city of Thespiae, to invade Attica without official sanction. The ephors impeached Sphodrias on a capital charge but he was acquitted, and Xenophon purports to tell us why. Sphodrias had a son, Kleonymos, who was friendly with Archidamos, the son of King Agesilaus. Kleonymos asked Archidamos for help. He did so tearfully (5.4.27): "And when Archidamos saw Kleonymos weeping, he wept with him standing by his side, and when he heard what he was asking he replied, 'Kleonymos, be assured that I am not even able to look my father in the face.... Nevertheless, since you urge me, believe that I shall make every effort to get this done for you.'" The acts of seeing and hearing, in that order, are key features of the psychological analysis embedded in the narrative. Archidamos sees his friend crying and starts crying, too. He then hears the request and grants it by approaching his father and securing a pardon for Sphodrias.

One last scene of pity from Xenophon's *Cyropaedia* features Panthea, the devoted wife of an Assyrian. Captured in war, she has been chosen as a prize for Cyrus. A friend tells Cyrus how he found Panthea inside her tent, seated among her servants, bowed down with grief and dread. Xenophon's chief interest lies in creating a heroine of great nobility and beauty, but she is also a spectacular weeper (*Cyr.* 5.1.5–6):

> But when we ordered her to rise, all her attendants stood up with her,
> and then she was conspicuous both for her stature and for her nobility
> and grace, even though she stood there in humble clothing. And her
> tears were obvious as they fell in drops, some down her dress, some even
> to her feet. Then the oldest of us said, "Take heart, lady; for though we
> hear that your husband also is a good and noble man, yet we are
> choosing you out for a man who, be assured, is not his inferior.... We

think that if any man deserves admiration, that man is Cyrus; and you
shall belong to him from now on." Now when the lady heard that, she
tore her outer garment from top to bottom and started wailing; and her
servants also cried aloud with her.

Her tears, which spill more profusely than real tears ever could, fail to secure her release, but they do elicit kindly words from one of her Persian captors; as the eldest, he seems to speak for the entire group of men, and so Xenophon creates the unlikely picture of a lovely war captive surrounded by victorious soldiers who respond to her weeping with sympathy and respect.[49] Their behavior is consistent with that of their leader, Cyrus, who is so kind to Panthea that she praises his compassion (6.1.47). Later, when Panthea is grieving over her dead husband's mutilated body, Cyrus pities them both (7.3.14). He offers to help her – in vain, since Panthea then takes her own life. From her first appearance to her last, Panthea is presented as a woman both lovely and deserving of pity.

In summary, oratory and historiography supply an abundance of psychological detail not found in Aristotle. The philosopher does emphasize the role of sight, but briefly: he says that those whose appearance, voice, and dress are pitiable "make the evil appear nearby, putting it before our eyes [*pro ommatôn poiountes*]."[50] His interest in the spoken word underlies the entire *Rhetoric*, but he elaborates the role of hearing only once: the words of the sufferer may arouse pity (2.8, 1386b2). And he never talks about the power of tears.

The Physiology of Pity

A great deal of recent scientific research on emotion has explored its biological underpinnings: autonomic responses, hormonal and electrocortical changes, muscle tension and tremor, facial expression, and so forth.[51] Nico Frijda, for example, regards emotional experience as an "output" from various phases of a complex process that begins with the appraisal of a stimulus event (1986: 463). Greek pity, whether or not we choose to view it as an output, begins in the same way: Person A must perceive the pain or jeopardy of Person B in order to feel sorrow. Passages from oratory and historiography, as explained in the preceding section, account abundantly for appraisal: when a person is confronted with a stimulus event, the senses of sight and hearing, and especially the perception of tears, are often said to trigger *eleos* or *oiktos*.

Greek writers describe the feeling of pity as something that "enters into" the pitier. This notion is very much in keeping with the Greek tendency, starting with Homer, to attribute strong feelings or powerful thoughts to an external source. Herodotus says that pity entered into Kambyses (3.14.11), and Plato uses the same expression, in the negative, when he says that pity did not enter into Phaedo (58e–59a). Once it is within a person, pity can displace other emotions, as with Periander (Hdt. 3.52.3), who pities his son and then lets go of his anger; or it can check the pitier from injuring the object of pity, as with the infant Kypselos' would-be assassin, whom pity restrains (Hdt. 5.92c3). Thucydides and Lysias both locate pity in the mind, or *gnômê*. The Plataians appealing to the Spartans for mercy in the *Peloponnesian War* say (Thuc. 3.59.1): "[You should] spare us and be bent in the mind, taking us with prudent pity." Lysias, in *Against Eratosthenes* (12.79), tells the jurors that this is the critical moment in which "there should be no pardon or pity in your minds." Speaking in another vein, Lycurgus warns his listeners that Leokrates, the defendant, might lead the "moist" part of their characters into a state of pity by means of tears (1.33).

These figurative turns of phrase raise the question of precisely where within the person pity was imagined to go. Modern psychologists argue about whether emotions arise as bodily sensations or in the brain (Oatley and Jenkins 1996: 111). Which bodily organs, which aspects of a human being, did the Greeks associate with the experience of pity? In the *Rhetoric*, Aristotle locates aversion, pity, anger, and similar emotions in the *psukhê*, or consciousness. Elsewhere, in *On the Soul* (408b), he further refines this idea, claiming that the *psukhê* probably does not generate pity or other emotions but is the instrument for them.[52] A rather obscure Hippocratic treatise, *Regimen II*, explains precisely how sight and hearing act upon the *psukhê*, which here seems more like a tangible organ than some intangible consciousness or life force. After all, it can be moved, warmed, dried, and shaken, and can in turn have a slimming effect on a person (*Regimen* 2.61):

> *The faculty of sight is like this: the* psukhê, *attending to the visible object, is moved and warmed. Since it is warmed, it dries, the moisture having been emptied out. And through the sense of hearing, when a sound intrudes, the* psukhê *is shaken and it works hard, and as it works it is warmed and dried. The* psukhê *is moved by as many things as a person thinks about, and it is warmed and dried, and spending its moisture it works hard, and it empties the flesh and makes a man thin.*

This account is reminiscent of the theory, described by Plato in the *Phaedo*, that the *psukhê* is the *harmonia* of hot, cold, moisture, and dryness in the body.[53] Our Hippocratic writer does not separate thought from feeling, but the effects produced by visual or aural stimulation do suggest emotion, in that the *psukhê* is literally moved.[54]

Still, which part of the human body accommodated the *psukhê*? The two leading possibilities were the brain and the chest. John Beare, in an old but still useful work, traces the view that the *enkephalos* or brain was the seat of consciousness to the physician Alkmaeon of Kroton (1906: 251–52). Most likely a younger contemporary of Pythagoras in the late sixth century BCE, Alkmaeon postulated that the brain received stimuli from eyes, ears, and nose. Through dissection, he reportedly found the optic nerves that connect the eyes to the brain (Beare 1906: 11–12; cf. the Hippocratic treatise *Fleshes*, 17), although he could not know precisely how they worked. Another physician, the unknown author of the Hippocratic treatise *The Sacred Disease* (17), assigned to the brain many facets of consciousness:

> *People ought to know that from no other place than there [the brain] arise our pleasures and high spirits and jokes and witticisms, as well as pains and griefs and anxieties and weeping. And most especially we think by means of it, and see and hear, and distinguish the ugly from the beautiful, the bad from the good, the pleasant from the unpleasant.... And these things that we experience all come from the brain [apo tou enkephalou].*

People ought to know, perhaps, but they easily might not. Although Plato subscribed to Alkmaeon's theory, Aristotle rejected it (Beare 1906: 329–31). He thought the cardiac muscle was responsible for consciousness. And the tragic poets often situated thoughts and feelings in the *phrên* (pl. *phrenes*), a word that can denote the diaphragm, the muscular membrane that separates the heart and liver from the lower viscera. The *phrenes* were sometimes thought of as a container into which perceptions could fall.[55]

Passages in historiography and oratory never specify whether pity affects the *enkephalos* or *phrên*; rather, it is vaguely attributed to the *psukhê* with no precise location given. According to Herodotus, Kambyses subjects Psammenitos to the sight of his condemned son and enslaved daughter in order to test his *psukhê* (Hdt. 3.14.1). Demosthenes, in *On the Crown*, excoriates Aeschines for lack of feeling (18.291): "He did not cry, nor did he experience any such thing in his *psukhê*." The speaker in *Against Polycles* recollects for the jury his feelings upon learning that his mother is dead, his wife sick, his farm wrecked by drought, and his creditors at the door (Dem. 50.62): "When I heard these things by the account of people who came and also through letters from relatives, what *psukhê* do you think I had and how many tears do you think I shed . . . ?"

Ancient Greek intellectuals might have been surprised to learn that Paul Ekman, in his neo-Darwinian quest for "basic emotions," has nothing to say about pity. It perhaps lies hidden within his category "sadness." Other evolutionary biologists and psychologists, attempting to explain altruism, point to the fundamental importance of sympathetic responses within human society,[56] but few scholars today would argue that specific concepts such as "pity" and *eleos* or *oiktos* are universal rather than culturally constructed. Rather, their cultural specificity is what makes them interesting to us. Yet ancient folk theories about the locus of pity in the human body suggest that the Greeks, while aware of cultural difference, were inclined to think of emotions as universal. For them, all human beings possessed consciousness, and apparently all were capable of pity. In typical fashion, this finer psychological point emerges most clearly in the pages of *The History*. As Edith Hall points out, Herodotus depicts a Persian empire that encompasses nations of barbarians whose diverse customs are, on the whole, more bloodthirsty than those of the Greeks.[57] Athenians prided themselves on their clemency and protection of the oppressed yet, paradoxically, most scenes of compassion in Herodotus put at center stage a barbarian: Croesus, Cyrus, Kambyses, Psammenitos. Herodotus seems to insist, especially through the story of Xerxes, that every human being, no matter how brutal, can feel pity.

DISTRUST OF PITY

It is impossible to know definitively why pity was not considered a virtue in Classical Athens – as compassion would be in the Christian era – but one reason surely was the status of pity as an emotion. Modern psychological research shows how emotion primes us for action (Frijda 1986), and the ancient Greeks noticed this as well. But if correct actions depend upon correct decisions, and those decisions depend on feelings as well as on dispassionate reflection, the fact that pity can be played upon so easily is a problem. Aristotle recognized this in the *Rhetoric*, where he warned that emotions like anger or envy or pity can distort a *dikast*, juror, so that he will serve no better than a warped ruler (1.1, 1354a24–26).[58] More than twenty oratorical passages reveal how a litigant might elicit pity from the jurors in order to win a favorable verdict,[59] as in Lys. 27.12:

> *And the most extraordinary thing of all is that while in private suits the wronged shed tears and are pitied, in public suits the wrongdoers are pitied and you, the wronged, pity them. Even now, perhaps, both fellow-citizens and friends will do the very things they have been accustomed to doing before: crying for [the defendants] to be let off by you.*

The manipulation of emotion, including pity, is twice termed a *tekhnê*. Demosthenes, railing against Meidias, has just ridiculed his tears and now offers ironic praise for his *tekhnê* (Dem. 21.196). Aeschines in *On the Embassy* condemns weeping as a device (2.156), placing it among the "unholy arts of rhetoric which [Demosthenes] makes known to the young and even now is using against me." This particular *tekhnê* is, as Aeschines suggests, a subset of the better-known *tekhnê* of rhetoric. Thrasymachos of Chalcedon, a late-fifth-century sophist and rhetorician who serves as interlocutor to Socrates in the first book of Plato's *Republic*, is said to have written a treatise called the *Eleoi* that told orators how to stir pity in their listeners; it may have focused on techniques of delivery.[60] Aristotle, as we have seen, devoted a substantial section of his *Rhetoric* to the analysis of various emotions, including pity, as an aid to orators.[61]

Pity was an emotion that jurors were often warned to resist, as demonstrated by the "banish pity" motif that occurs in about 20 percent of the one hundred or so extant speeches. Dinarchus urges that pity not be allowed to threaten the public interest (Din. 1.109). In a similar vein, Lycurgus exhorts jurors to condemn Leokrates without pity because he fled Athens after the Battle of Chaeronea (Lyc. 1.150). One function of forensic oratory was to educate the public, and pity was not supposed to prevent the guilty from being held up as negative examples, as in *Against Ergocles* (Lys. 28.11).[62] About the same percentage of speeches contain appeals to pity (21 percent) as injunctions to avoid it (19 percent),[63] and whether pity was invited or discouraged the arguments boil down to the same thing: pity was supposed to be subordinated to considerations of justice, on the one hand, and piety on the other. Justice was the stronger of the two considerations, and the preoccupation with the manipulation of pity as a *tekhnê* of oratory must not obscure the point that in their attempts to sway the emotions of jurors, litigators usually couched both negative and positive appeals within the context of reason and justice. They either said, "This man deserves pity," or "Don't pity him, he doesn't deserve it."

On one level, Athenians accepted the need for pity in human society. On another level, though, they rejected pity on the grounds that it was an emotion. As such it could be easily manipulated and was therefore untrustworthy; unless subordinated to considerations of justice and piety it might lead to undesirable consequences. Aristotle's view that pity accrued only to the deserving proves doubly problematic. Some fates, especially collective disasters like the plague, were so terrible that nobody deserved them. And in other contexts the would-be pitier *should* judge, but pity itself could confound one's judgment. Beliefs influenced emotion, but emotion influenced beliefs.[64] So despite its cognitive aspects, pity lacked intellectual rigor. Clearly it was not a virtue one should cultivate but an impulse one should govern, for it could prove dangerous. As we have seen, pity caused assassins to spare the infant Kypselos. But since Kypselos was spared he grew up – into a murderous tyrant.

◨◉◧

ENDNOTES

1. I would like to thank Neil Bernstein, Tom Falkner, Don Lateiner, Keith Oatley, and Anna Wierzbicka for reading and commenting on this chapter. Thanks are due also to various other friends on whom I have imposed, as well as the anonymous referees, whose criticisms were bracing and helpful.

2. Wierzbicka rejects the extreme position of cultural and linguistic relativism represented by Edward Sapir and Benjamin Lee Whorf. Her cross-cultural investigations into discrete emotions include Ifaluk *fago*, which anthropologist Catherine Lutz glosses as "compassion, love, sadness." Greek *oiktos* and *eleos* are more recognizable to us than Ifaluk *fago* owing to the continuity of Western culture. Since we are intellectual heirs to the Greeks, their idea of pity can be traced from Homer through classical and Hellenistic philosophy and into the Christian era, as Konstan (2001) has done.

3. Griffiths 1997: 1; cf. the "folk theories" discussed by Kövecses 2000: xiii.

4. Demosthenes, in *On the False Embassy*, assumes that most of his audience pitied the Olynthian war captives who were brought to Athens for prostitution (Dem. 19.309): "When I mention that Philokrates brought the women, all of you, even the bystanders, know what happened next, and I know well that you pity these unlucky and miserable beings, whom Aeschines did not pity." This episode may be compared with and perhaps explored through *The Trojan Women* of Euripides, but it is historical rather than legendary or fictional.

5. Rhetorical arguments for and against pity appear frequently in oratory and also in Book Three of Thucydides, with the Mytilenean debate and the Plataian appeals for pity. A good example of philosophizing about pity is found in Xenophon's *Oeconomicus* 2.2–7.

6. The expressive *splankhnizomai*, used in the New Testament, did not exist in Attic Greek.

7. For complete results of this lexical study, based on computerized word searches in the Thesaurus Linguae Graecae (TLG) and Perseus, see Sternberg 1998: 11–58. The analysis is guided by Zgusta 1971 and Zwicky and Sadock 1975.

8. "Compassion" has more positive connotations but is less satisfactory than "pity" for two reasons. First, Christian compassion is a virtue, and we know that *oiktos* and

eleos were not. Second, compassion in the strict sense requires that the compassionate person share the emotional state of the sufferer; yet *oiktos* and *eleos* are sometimes felt for individuals who are blissfully unaware of their impending misfortune. Compare Wierzbicka's contrasting definitions of pity and compassion expressed in semantic primitives (1999: 100–3).

9. Arist. *Eth. Nic.* 2.6, 1106b18–21; *Rh.* 1.1, 1354a16–18, and 2.1, 1378a19–22.

10. Pity and hatred (*misos*) are contrasted at Dem. 24.196 and Lys. 2.14. A stock contrast between the two emotions of pity and envy (*phthonos*) is drawn about a dozen times: Hdt. 3.52.5; Thuc. 7.77.4; And. 2.6; Lys. 2.67, 20.15, 21.15, 24.2; Isae. 11.38; Dem. 21.196, 28.18, 29.2. Aristotle (*Rh.* 2.9, 1386b8 and 16–17) says pity is opposed to indignation (*nemesis*) and envy.

11. Compare Dem. 21.185.

12. Compare Din. 1.92, 1.108, 1.111.

13. Hdt. 4.167.1: *tote de houtos ho Aruandês katoikteiras Pheretimên didoi autêi straton ton ex Aiguptou hapanta.* Compare Hdt. 1.45.2, 3.14.11, 3.52.3, 3.119.13, 5.92c3; Xen. *An.* 7.2.6, *Cyr.* 7.1.41 and 7.2.26, *Hell.* 1.5.19; Lys. 2.67 and 18.12; Dem. 49.17, 53.8, and 59.83; and Din. 1.20.

14. Compare *eleêsai* at Isae. 2.44, in the epilogue of *On the Estate of Menecles*, where Dover (1974: 196) finds that "'pity' is tantamount to 'a just verdict in accordance with the evidence.'" Yet much of the speech was calculated to draw the jurors into a state of sympathy with the speaker.

15. In *Against Timocrates*, the defendant is expected to claim that he pities people who suffer terrible things (Dem. 24.196). Compare Dem. 24.201 and Lys. 18.12. For other examples in which either *paskhô* or *pathos* or *pathêma* is linked to pity, see Thuc. 3.67.4; Xen. *Cyr.* 5.4.32 and *Ec.* 2.7; Antiph. 1.27.

16. Those defeated in war: Hdt. 1.165.3, 3.119.13, 3.14.11; Xen. *Apol.* 18; Xen. *Cyr.* 6.1.47, 7.3.14, 7.1.41, and 7.2.26; Xen. *Hell.* 1.5.19; Lys. 2.67; Dem. 19.309 and 53.8; Din. 1.20. The sick, the old, or the emasculated: Thuc. 2.51.6; Xen. *An.* 7.2.6; Xen. *Cyr.* 5.4.32; Isoc. 12.232. Wrongdoers: Hdt. 1.45.2; Xen. *An.* 1.4.7; Lys. 10.22; Dem. 59.83. The financially strapped: Xen. *An.* 3.1.19; Dem. 49.17. Babies, children, or adult offspring: Hdt. 3.52.3, 5.92c.3; Lys. 18.12. Three cases resist categorization: Hdt. 4.167.1, 7.46.2, and Dem. Ltr. 3.7.

17. *Rh.* 2.8, 1386a7–11. Aristotle in the same passage also mentions lack of nourishment, lack of friends, ugliness, weakness, and disablement.

18. Xen. *Apol.* 18; Xen. *Hell.* 1.5.19; Lys. 2.67; Dem. 19.309, 53.8; Din. 1.20.

19. Antiph. 3.2.11; Lys. 20.35; Dem. 19.283, 24.201, 25.84, 49.17.

20. For example: Lys. 6.48, 27.9–10; Dem. 20.18, 21.98, 21.213–16, 45.67, 57.36. See Rosivach 1991.

21. *Rh.* 2.8, 1385b13–16. Konstan's translation is found in his illuminating appendix on Aristotle's view of pity and pain (2001: 128–36).

22. Compare Cyrus' pity for Gadatas, who did not deserve to be emasculated (Xen. *Cyr.* 5.2.28 and 5.4.32).

23. Compare Din. 2.11, where Aristogeiton failed to pity his own father, who in exile was reduced to starvation. Two contentious references to pitying one's own wife and

children are found at Lys. 21.24 and 28.14. In the first, the speaker says he bravely risked his life in battle without pitying his wife and children: *oudepôpot' êleêsa oud' edakrusa oud' emnêsthên gunaikos oude paidôn tôn emautou.* In the second, *Against Ergocles*, the speaker urges that Athenians would be more justified in pitying themselves, their children, and their wives than in pitying men who abused power.

24. Compare Aeschin. 1.188 and Din. 1.110. An interesting case of false self-pity is found at Hdt. 3.156, where Zopyros horribly mutilates himself in order to trick the Babylonians and deliver their city to the Persians. He goes to their assembly with nose and ears cut off and bewails himself. Since his bewailing is pure pretence accompanied by false explanations (*phas*), we can be certain that in this context, *katoiktizeto* does not mean that Zopyros actually felt sorry for himself.

25. Burkert (1955: 36) and Scott (1979: 6–9) argue the case in Homer, Johnson (1980: 8) in fifth-century tragedy.

26. Compare Antiph. 1.21–27; Isoc. 14.52; Hyp. 2.9.

27. Noted by Burkert 1955: 35–36.

28. The most common trope, which conveys the notion of "deserving pity" and uses some form of *axios* or *axioô*, is formulated sixteen times (89 percent) with *eleos* words and only twice (11 percent) with *oiktos* words. Similar proportions, only slightly more balanced, occur in the expression for "obtaining pity" (82 percent and 18 percent) and in the envy-pity motif (71 percent and 29 percent). Meanwhile, the notion of "proper or befitting pity," using some form of *prosêkei*, is invariably formulated with *eleos* words and never once with *oiktos* words; several other stock phrases follow the same pattern.

29. Because ancient sources criticize the orators for their manipulation of pity (see Arist. *Rh.* 1.1, 1354a16–18 and 24–26), it is easy to forget that pity is often invoked with an overt emphasis on reason rather than emotion.

30. Pitiers inspired by *oiktos* often take mitigating action: Croesus spares Adrestos (Hdt. 1.45.2); Kambyses tries to halt the execution of Psammenitos' son (Hdt. 3.14.11); Periander takes back his son (Hdt. 3.52.3); Darius accedes to the pleas of Intaphrenes' wife (Hdt. 3.119.13); Aryandes gives Pheretime an army (Hdt. 4.167.1); assassins spare the life of Kypselos (Hdt. 5.92c3); Kleander nurses sick Persian soldiers (Xen. *An.* 7.2.6); Cyrus treats Panthea kindly (Xen. *Cyr.* 6.1.47), spares Egyptians (7.1.41), and restores Croesus' household (7.2.26). But pitiers inspired by *eleos* also act: Athenians release Dorieos (Xen. *Hell.* 1.5.19); Athenians fight war to aid Corinthians (Lys. 2.67); jurors acquit Theomnestus (Lys. 10.22); Pausanias acts kindly toward nephews of Nicias (Lys. 18.12); Pasion loans Timotheos money (Dem. 49.17); Apollodoros lends Nicostratus money (Dem. 53.8); the Areopagus Council acquits Theogenes (Dem. 59.83); and Arcadians are ready to fight because they pity the Thebans (Din. 1.20).

31. Orwin (1994: 9) cites Karl Reinhardt, David Grene, Hans-Peter Stahl, Colin Macleod, and Hugh Lloyd-Jones among the Thucydidean scholars who have found in the *Peloponnesian War* a humanity that transcends the ancient historian's harsh realism. Compare de Romilly 1974.

32. *Metaph.* 1.1, 980a21–24.

33. Padel also notes a shift in the conventions of contemporary painting, as the old-fashioned ground line that used to link human figures was abandoned in favor of the meeting gaze. Allen (2000: 79) elaborates on the idea that sight in ancient Greek culture was considered a "two-way exchange between seer and seen." Hartog (1988: 261–62) analyzes sight as a source of knowledge about the world.

34. See Lys. 20.34–35; Dem. 19.281–83, 19.310, 21.99, 21.182, 21.195, 25.84, 53.29; Lyc. 1.141.

35. Compare Dem. 19.65, which contains a similar scene of defeat at Delphi in the 340s that Demosthenes and the other envoys actually saw. Hyperides, in his *Funeral Oration* of 322 during the Lamian War, says that seeing the destruction at Thebes spurred the Athenians to fight (Hyp. 6.17). For other examples of the figurative usage of *horaô* in close association with a pity word, see Isoc. 4.132; Dem. 28.18, 49.17.

36. Compare Xen. *Cyr.* 2.2.13, where a captain of Cyrus says that some authors, inventing pathetic incidents in poems and stories, try to lead people to tears.

37. Compare Dem. 36.58: "For you see for yourselves and you hear from the witnesses what kind of man he shows himself to those in need."

38. See Diels 1954: 2.290. For a full-length treatment of this theme, see de Romilly 1975.

39. This anecdote, retold by Aristotle (*Rh.* 2.8, 1386a20–22), supports his point that pity requires a certain minimal distance between the pitier and the pitied.

40. See Kennedy 1994 and Solmsen 1975.

41. Fortenbaugh 2002: 9–18. See also Cooper 1999: 406–23.

42. Plato's Socrates (*Phdr.* 267c) discusses the use of tearful speeches to arouse pity. Compare *Leg.* 949, where he would outlaw "womanish sobbing" in court.

43. Ten times: Hdt. 3.14.11; Xen. *Cyr.* 2.2.13; And. 4.39; Lys. 27.12, 32.18; Isoc. 4.168; Dem. 19.309, 19.310; Lyc. 1.33; Din. 1.110.

44. Compare And. 1.48, where Andocides and other suspects in the Mutilation of the Hermes are thrown into prison and their female relatives join them in lamentation.

45. To express the idea that Amasis did not pity his own son, Aristotle says he did not weep (*Rh.* 2.8, 1386a20–24). For another example of *eleeô* and *dakruô* in tandem, see Lys. 21.24.

46. Isocrates later corroborates this reading by referring to Cyrus' start in life as pitiable (5.67).

47. Kövecses 2000 analyzes the figurative language, especially metaphor and metonymy, that people ordinarily use in describing emotion.

48. They happened to be at once his grandchildren and his nephews and niece, because all three were born to his daughter, whom he had married off to his brother, now deceased (Lys. 32.4).

49. de Romilly (1988) pursues the theme of the beautiful captive in this episode and two others: Alexander the Great's treatment of the wife of Darius and Scipio's treatment of the wife and daughters of Mandonios at New Carthage. See also Gera 1993: 221–45.

50. *Rh.* 2.8, 1386a34. Compare *Rh.* 2.8, 1386b7, *kai en ophthalmois phainomenou tou pathous.* Also the definition once again at 1385b13: *estô dê eleos lupê tis epi phainomenôi kakôi phthartikôi ê lupêrôi.*

51. See, for example, Frijda 1986 and the very accessible explanations in Damasio 1994.

52. His "philosophical psychology" is explored in Durrant 1993.

53. *Phd.* 86c, discussed by Sorabji 2000: 254.

54. Some early Stoic philosophers in the century after Aristotle defined their four basic emotions in terms of physical contraction (distress), expansion (pleasure), reaching (appetite), and leaning away (fear). Zeno himself is supposed to have said that emotion is a movement of the soul, also a *ptoia,* a fluttering (Sorabji 2000: 34).

55. Padel (1992: 20–23) explores the attributes of *phrenes* in Homer and tragedy. Compare Pelliccia 1995.

56. Sober and Wilson 1998 pursue the evolutionary question; Eisenberg, Losoya, and Spinrad 2003 sum up current psychological research on empathy and prosocial behavior.

57. Hall 1989: 158–59. Though Greeks can be vicious, certain crimes are reserved for the barbarians, such as impalings, mutilations, live burials, cannibalism, and the use of human hides.

58. Fortenbaugh (2002: 82–83) offers a separate explanation for why Aristotle never identifies any moral virtue equivalent to Christian mercy. The philosopher, he says, regarded pity as a nonpractical emotion that did not necessarily entail action and therefore could not invite virtue.

59. Antiph. Frag. D1; And. 4.39; Lys. 6.55, 20.34, 27.12; Isae. 11.38; Dem. 21.99, 21.186–87, 21.194–96, 21.204, 27.53, 37.48–49, 38.27, 39.35, 40.53, 45.88, 53.29, 54.43; Aeschin. 3.209–10; Lyc. 1.33; Din. 1.92, 1.108–11.

60. Kennedy (1963: 68–70) reviews the evidence for *Eleoi.* For the suggestion that the treatise encompassed delivery, he cites Arist. *Rh.* 3.1, 1404a14–15 and Quint. 3.3.4.

61. See also Kennedy 1959. Solmsen (1938) provides detailed *testimonia* on contemporaries of Aristotle who took an interest in pity and other emotions.

62. Hunter (1994: 108–11) discusses the creation of both positive and negative stereotypes.

63. Complete data in Sternberg 1998: 52–58.

64. Frijda, Manstead, and Bem 2000 deal with this issue, shortchanged in the psychological literature until recently.

PITY AND POLITICS

DAVID KONSTAN

◎▣◎

IN THUCYDIDES' REPORT OF THE DEBATE OVER THE FATE OF Mytilene, which rebelled against Athenian hegemony near the beginning of the Peloponnesian War, Kleon accuses his fellow Athenians of being naively disposed to pity in their treatment of allied states (3.37.2). Pity, he continues, is ruinous to empire, and is wasted on those who are one's natural enemies (3.40.2–3). Kleon, as Thucydides represents him, is a hard man, not so much dispassionate as angry and vengeful. It is left to Diodotos, in his reply to Kleon, to insist that the decision of the assembly should be based, not on considerations of justice or sentiment, but solely on advantage (see Konstan 2001: 80–82).[1] In the *Rhetoric* (1.3, 1358b20–29), indeed, Aristotle stipulates that the object or *telos* of deliberative oratory is precisely the consideration of "advantage and harm" rather than justice, which is the province of forensic rhetoric. So too, in Plato's *Greater Alcibiades*, the title character observes (114d): "I think, Socrates, that Athenians and other Greeks rarely deliberate about what is more just or more unjust, for they believe that such matters are self-evident. And so, letting that pass, they look to which will be of advantage to their affairs."[2] What place does pity have in the cold and calculating arena of political debate?

In this chapter, I examine how the relationship between pity and politics is represented on the tragic stage, with particular attention to dramas of supplication. For tragedy sometimes permits us to glimpse the interaction between public and private motives in a way that is normally eclipsed in the historians and orators, where for the most part speakers self-consciously restrict their appeals to the tropes of public discourse. They do so in tragedy as well, to be sure, when characters

48

engage, as they often do, in formal debates over matters of state. But tragedy also reveals unofficial attitudes, for example, those of women and other characters at the margins of politics, which do not normally find expression in the public record. Such scenes provide a contrast to the uses of pity in more or less official deliberations.

HISTORICAL SUPPLIANTS: THE PLATAIANS

I begin with a brief look at two supplicatory speeches drawn from genres other than tragedy, specifically historiography and oratory, in which the petitioners make an appeal to pity. These examples indicate the nature and limits of such pleas in formal contexts. In both cases, as it happens, the suppliants are Plataians, inhabitants of a small town in Boeotia, to the northeast of Athens. The first is reported by Thucydides, the second was composed as an exhibition piece by the fourth-century orator Isocrates.[3]

At the beginning of the Peloponnesian War (431 BCE), Plataia, which was sympathetic to Athens, was penetrated by a contingent of Theban hoplites (Thuc. 3.53–59). The Plataians overcame the attackers and took a substantial number of prisoners, whom they later put to death. Subsequently, the Spartans forced the surrender of the last defenders of the city. These men then made their case before the Spartans for being spared, while the Thebans argued in favor of their execution. The Plataians appeal chiefly to the Spartans' own advantage, in the manner characteristic of speeches before a deliberative body. In their peroration, however, they represent themselves as suppliants (3.59.2), appeal to the common laws of the Greeks (*ta koina tôn Hellênôn nomima*, 3.59.1), and entreat the Spartans to be moved by reasonable pity (*oiktôi sôphroni*, 3.59.1). To this, the Thebans retort that pity is due only to those who have suffered unjustly: "those people are worthy of pity who have suffered something unsuitable, whereas those who have suffered justly, like these men, on the contrary deserve to be gloated over" (3.67.4: οἴκτου τε ἀξιώτεροι τυγχάνειν οἱ ἀπρεπές τι πάσχοντες τῶν ἀνθρώπων, οἱ δὲ δικαίως, ὥσπερ οἵδε, τὰ ἐναντία ἐπίχαρτοι εἶναι). The Plataians' fate, they add, is precisely *ennoma*, that is, within the law (3.67.5). The Thebans' argument wins the day.

Plataia was restored in 386, but was again destroyed by Thebes in 373 (it would be refounded once more, many years later, by the Macedonians). In the same year, Isocrates wrote the tract called *Plataïcus*, in which the Plataians are represented as speaking before the Athenian assembly, urging them to take vengeance on Thebes. In the course of their argument, the Plataians adopt the posture of suppliants (1, 6, 52, 53, 54, 56). Toward the end of their speech, moreover, they once again make an appeal to pity, alleging that it is not reasonable (*eikos*) that individuals are pitied if they have suffered unjustly (*para to dikaion*), while an entire city that is being wrongfully destroyed (*anomôs diephtharmenên*) should fail to win any pity at all (52; cf. *oiktron*, 56).

In both speeches, the Plataians reserve their appeal to pity for the peroration, a strategy that was characteristic of forensic oratory.[4] What is more, both times they link their claim to pity to the justice of their cause (cf. Hogan 1972: 244). This is in accord with the prevailing view of pity in Classical Greece, which was that pity is due not to suffering as such but rather to unmerited or illegitimate suffering. In fact, the practice of placing the appeal to pity at the end of a discourse is not unrelated to the connection between pity and desert. For speakers must first demonstrate, or attempt to demonstrate, that their case is just; only then can they appeal to pity on the grounds that they do not deserve the penalty or punishment that is proposed for them (fuller discussion in Konstan 2001: 34–43).

ARISTOTLE ON PITY

The Greeks in the classical period, then, did not perceive the same tension between pity and justice modern jurists do, when they exclude appeals to the emotions in the verdict phase of a trial on the grounds that they impede a fair and impartial appraisal of the evidence (Konstan 2001: 28–30). True, the Stoics rejected pity on the grounds (among others) that it corrupts judgment, and their view was anticipated by Aristotle in the first chapter of the *Rhetoric*, where he asserts that "one ought not to warp a juror by leading him to anger or envy or pity" (1.1, 1354a24–25), for that, Aristotle says, is like bending the ruler with which one takes a measurement. But Aristotle immediately comes round to endorsing the relevance of appeals to the emotions, including pity, to oratory, and devotes several chapters of the second book of the *Rhetoric* to an account of how to rouse and assuage them. This apparent change of view has been read as a naked inconsistency in the treatise as we have it (e.g., Kennedy 1991: 28; Barnes 1995: 262; Frede 1996: 264–65; Wardy 1996: 115–16). But perhaps we can understand the shift, at least in respect to pity, as a function of Aristotle's recognition that pity is a response not to any misfortune, or to misfortune that one has brought upon oneself, but only to undeserved hardship, for precisely this proviso provides the link between pity and justice. Thus, Aristotle defines pity as "a kind of pain in the case of an apparent destructive or painful harm *in one not deserving to encounter it*, which one might expect oneself, or one of one's own, to suffer, and this when it seems near" (*Rh.* 2.8, 1385b13–16). So too, the *Rhetoric to Alexander* (ascribed by some scholars to the pre-Aristotelian rhetorician Anaximines) advises (34.4–6):

> *we shall be capable of rendering things pitiable whenever we wish if we*
> *are aware that all people pity those whom they suppose to be*
> *well-disposed toward themselves and whom they believe to be*
> *undeserving [anaxioi] of misfortune. One must show that those whom*
> *one wishes to render pitiable have these qualities, and demonstrate that*
> *they have suffered or are suffering or will suffer wrongly [kakôs], unless*
> *the hearers help them. If this is not possible, then you must show that*
> *those for whom you are speaking have been deprived <or are being*

deprived or will be deprived> of goods that all or most others
have a share in, or have never obtained or are not obtaining or
will not obtain a good, unless those who are now listening pity
*them /*oikteirôsin*/.*

Far from being incompatible with a verdict based on the merits of a
case, pity depends upon a belief in the petitioner's innocence.

Does a judgment influenced by pity, then, differ in no way at all from
a dispassionate evaluation of the facts? Surely it does. Aristotle, indeed,
characterizes the emotions or *pathê* in the *Rhetoric* (2.1, 1378a19–22) as
"all those things on account of which people change and differ in regard
to their judgments [*kriseis*], and upon which attend pain and pleasure,
for example anger, pity, fear, and all other such things and their opposites." This account has been deemed defective as a definition or *logos*,
although in my view it is defensible in Aristotelian terms. However
that may be, it accords broadly with popular Greek ideas on the effects
of the emotions on judgment. To take a couple of examples more or
less at random, in Sophocles' *Oedipus the King*, the chorus, seeking to
explain to Creon why Oedipus has accused him of having conspired
to slay Laius, the former king, asserts (523–24): "this was indeed the
charge, but perhaps it was compelled by anger rather than the mind's
judgment (*orgêi biasthen mallon ê gnômêi phrenôn*)." Later, when the report of Polybos' death reassures Oedipus that his fear of the oracle was
exaggerated, Jocasta says to him: "Didn't I keep telling you this from the
beginning?" to which Oedipus replies: "You did, but I was led astray
by fear" (973–74: *egô de tôi phobôi parêgomên*). Pity too, for all that it involves an assessment of the sufferer's deserts, has the capacity to affect or
modify the verdict that one might have delivered on the basis of reason
alone.

The relation between pity and justice thus seems to be bidirectional.
An appraisal of desert is a precondition for pity, but pity, once elicited,

in turn conditions how one judges. To illustrate the double movement, we may again cite a case involving anger from *Oedipus the King*, in which Oedipus first reproaches the seer Teiresias: "Who wouldn't be angry at you upon hearing such words, with which you are now dishonoring the city?" (339–40), and then, further provoked to anger (*orgê*) by Teiresias' stubborn silence, jumps to the conclusion that Teiresias is not only withholding information but in fact himself conspired in the murder of Laius (345–49).

There remains a paradox here: if pity can induce jurors to judge differently than they would otherwise have done about a defendant's guilt or innocence, on what basis was the pity itself evoked? Perhaps the cognitive condition for pity is weak or variable. Sometimes, signs of extreme suffering may stimulate pity, or perhaps one should say proto-pity, irrespective of merit; then one may subsequently judge in such a way as to justify or rationalize the prior sentiment. Aristotle himself notes that such painful but ethically neutral conditions as death, old age, and disease are pitiable (*Rh.* 2.8, 1386a4–9), and in the *Poetics* he acknowledges that, even when the moral conditions for tragic pity are absent – for example, when a character slays an enemy who presumably deserves his fate – the sheer pain or *pathos* of the event may still be pitiable (13, 1453b17–18; cf. Gorg. *Hel.* 9, 32, but contrast 7; Thrasymachus fr. 6 Diels-Kranz).

But it may also be that severe illness, premature death, or being reduced to slavery never seem truly to be earned, except perhaps by profoundly evil people. In particular, when suffering is inflicted in a way or to a degree that violates social norms or *nomoi*, it is likely to appear exaggerated or unjust, whatever the sins of the sufferer. In our own time, for example, no one is deemed to deserve torture; in ancient Greece, where torture was sometimes acceptable, putting an entire population to death, as in the case of the debate over the fate of Mytilene, might seem to exceed customary limits on cruelty and hence arouse pity, and this sentiment in turn might affect one's judgment of the nature of the offense. Conventional ideas of what counts as lawful (*nomimon*), then, are not irrelevant to the emotion of pity. But pity predicated on such norms is nevertheless foreign to political deliberation, insofar as such deliberation is restricted to considerations of self-interest or "advantage and harm," as Diodotos, Aristotle, and Plato's Alcibiades maintain. In such a context, the only way to introduce a concern for what is right is to argue that defending the *nomima* or conventional laws is itself in the community's interest. This complex relationship between pity, law, and interest may be observed in motion on the Athenian stage in the tragedies involving supplication.

THE SUPPLIANT WOMEN OF EURIPIDES

Euripides' *Suppliant Women* opens with a tableau in which Aithra, the mother of Theseus, stands before the temple of Demeter at Eleusis, pronouncing a prayer for the welfare of her son and her city. Before her kneels the chorus of Argive women, whose sons lie unburied at Thebes, and Adrastus, the king of Argos, who sponsored the unsuccessful attack; a second chorus of boys, the sons of the fallen Argive warriors, also sits or lies on stage. The old women (*graus*, 9) bear a suppliant bough (*hiktêri thallôi*) and have suffered, Aithra declares, a dreadful misfortune (*pathos pathousai deinon*, 10–11). Now, supplication does not in itself entail an appeal to pity: the gesture alone was ritually significant, and besides this, suppliants might also promise compensation (*Il.* 21.75–80), invoke former services (Eur. *Hec.* 271–78), or claim a personal bond with the beseeched (Eur. *Or.* 665–79). But the prostrate posture of the suppliant, enhanced by rent garments and unkempt hair (what the Romans called *squalor*), was designed to seem pitiable as well as humble (on humility, cf. Gould 1973: 94), all the more so when the appeal came, as in Euripides' tragedy, from powerless figures such as women, children, and the aged. Thus, Aithra is moved to "pity [*oiktirousa*] these childless, gray-haired mothers of sons," while at the same time she "reveres [*sebousa*] their sacred garlands," that is, the symbols of a ritual petition (34–36).

The misfortune that prompts Aithra's pity is a double one. On the one hand, she is sensitive to the women's childlessness as a result of the war to restore Polynices, a son of Oedipus, to the Theban kingship (11–16; *polias apaidas* in 35 answers *apaides* in 13); on the other hand, she regards the fact that the rulers of Thebes will neither bury the corpses of the fallen nor return them to their mothers as a violation of divine law (*nomim'atizontes theôn*, 19; cf. Eur. *Hec.* 799–801 for the gods as guarantors of *nomos*; Hogan 1972: 247ff.). Because Aithra considers the Thebans' behavior to be illegitimate, her pity for the women is motivated by a moral appraisal based on the nature of their affliction: the Argive mothers are being treated wrongly, irrespective of any complicity of their own in their suffering.

Of course, Aithra's disapproval of the Thebans' impiety also stands on its own, irrespective of her pity for the women: the Thebans' breach of practices sanctioned by the gods is one of the arguments with which she will later encourage Theseus to intervene in the Argives' behalf. Aithra, however, not only sees the women's suffering as unjustified, but she is also sensible of the similarity between herself and them, which Aristotle lays down as a condition for pity (*Rh.* 2.8, 1386a25–27; *Poet.* 13, 1453a2–6). Thus, the chorus will appeal to Aithra's pity by observing that she is aged, as they are (42), and that she too has a son (54–58; cf. Eur. *Hec.* 339–41). Indeed, Aithra's initial prayer for the well-being of Theseus and Athens (1–7), while it speaks to her concern for the practical interests of her city, at the same time suggests that the women's fate has reminded her of her own vulnerability as a mother.

As for the weeping figure of Adrastus, Aithra remarks coolly that it was he who launched the unfortunate expedition against Thebes (20–23), and hence he bears the responsibility for its failure (that women do not decide on war perhaps mitigates their culpability). Adrastus' plea that Athens take up his cause (24–28), she adds, is strictly a political matter and thus men's business (40–41); she can do no more than summon Theseus so that he may consider whether to expel the Argives and their grief from the land or else, by delivering them from their plight, perform a holy action for the gods (36–40). Though pity and piety coincide for Aithra, she is well aware that for Theseus, the Argives' suffering counts for nothing, and that if he helps them, it will be only in order to uphold divine law.

In their opening ode, the chorus touch on the several themes raised by Aithra in the prologue: they come as suppliants (42, 67), their case is pitiable (*oiktra*, 48, 67), they are, like her, old women (50), and their cause is just (*endika*, 65).[5] Theseus arrives on the scene alarmed by the wailing of the women who surround his mother and are, he observes, shedding pitiful tears from their ancient eyes (95–96). Aithra explains that they have come as suppliants, and when Theseus asks about the man who is groaning pitiably (*oiktron*, 104) at the temple door, she identifies Adrastus. Theseus then bids Adrastus uncover his head and tell his story. The two mentions of *oiktron* do not imply that Theseus feels pity: he recognizes the grief-stricken comportment of the suppliants, but he withholds judgment, and hence an emotional response, until he has inquired into the facts of the case.

Adrastus begins by affirming his status as suppliant (114; cf. 130) and recounting the Thebans' refusal to allow the bodies of the besiegers to be buried. Theseus acknowledges that what Adrastus demands of the Thebans is holy (*hosia*, 123), and asks about the circumstances leading up to the disastrous campaign against Thebes. He is none too convinced of the wisdom of Adrastus' alliance by marriage to Polynices (cf. 220–25), but the crucial reservation is a religious one. "Did you approach any seers and watch the sacrificial flame?" he asks, to which Adrastus replies: "Alas, you are pursuing me where I most tripped up." "You didn't march forth, it seems, with the favor of the gods." "Worse than that: I marched forth against Amphiaraus' will" (155–58). Adrastus blames his action on the pressure of young hotheads in Argos, but Theseus is dismissive of his excuse (159–61). At this point, Adrastus grasps Theseus' knees in the traditional gesture of supplication (165), and begs for pity for himself and the aged mothers of the dead (168–69), reminding Theseus that those who are well off should look to the pitiable fortunes of others (179). Adrastus concludes his appeal by affirming that Athens is both strong and has regard for what is pitiable (188–90), and the chorus add their voices to his in beseeching Theseus' pity (*oiktos*, 194).

Theseus responds with a lecture on the gods' rational arrangement of the cosmos and the need for humility, together with a defense of the decisive importance of the middle class for the well-being of the polis. With that, he sends Adrastus packing (246–49). Although his speech may seem to be a showpiece of Euripidean didacticism – a kind of tragic parabasis – it in fact bears directly on Adrastus' petition. Adrastus revealed his contempt for the gods by ignoring the omens when he marched into battle, and his failure as a civic leader by yielding to the pressure of the young, who hanker after war regardless of justice – Theseus compares their role to the influence of the mob or *plêthos* in a democratic state (232–37). Since the fault lies with Adrastus and his city, there is no reason why Athens should become implicated in their woes. Adrastus does not deserve to be helped or pitied, because he has brought his misfortune upon himself. Theseus evidently recognizes no likeness between himself and the aged, reckless king of Argos, such as his mother had sensed with respect to the Argive women.

Adrastus sees nothing for it but to submit to Theseus' decision, but the chorus, weeping, throw themselves at Theseus' feet and again beg for pity (280–81). The women make no allusion to the wisdom or justice of the war against Thebes: their appeal is based wholly on their terrible plight. There is no reason to suppose that they will succeed in moving

Theseus where Adrastus has failed, and they do not. But Theseus perceives that his mother is weeping and groaning (286–91), and hears her
exclaim: "O wretched women!" (292). With this, Aithra presents the
case for supporting the Argives' cause, on the grounds that it is right to
honor the gods (301–2) and that it will bring honor (*timê*, 306) to Theseus if he prevents violent men from confounding the laws of all Greece
(*nomima pasês Hellados*, 311). Besides, she observes, if Theseus does not
undertake to right this wrong, he will gain a reputation for cowardice
(314–19). Aithra affirms that she herself is unafraid, since Theseus will
set out with justice on his side (328). Theseus replies that he stands by
his former opinion concerning Adrastus' fault, but he nevertheless sees
the force of his mother's arguments: it is not in his nature to avoid
difficulties; rather, he is ever the chastiser of evils (338–41). He will,
nevertheless, present the case first to the people for a vote, bringing
Adrastus with him to support his arguments (350, 354–55).

As the reader will have noticed, there are no references to pity in this
exchange, and in fact it is not mentioned again in the play. Nor is there
any hint that Theseus' change of heart has been inspired by pity. He has
been convinced to help the Argives on the grounds that doing so will
enhance his reputation and that of Athens, and will also vindicate a
divinely sanctioned custom of the Greeks. This is a politically sober, if
high-minded, motive, and Theseus is sure that the people will endorse
it. That Adrastus foolishly went to war for Polynices' sake and brought
disaster upon his city is irrelevant to Theseus' purpose, although it sinks
Adrastus' claim to pity. Theseus' arguments, moreover, are precisely
those that Aithra used in persuading him to help the Argives, even
though she, unlike her son, did respond with pity to the plight of the
chorus.

Aithra, as we have observed, is the same age as the Argive women
and is conscious of her own vulnerability as a mother. In addition,
she believes that the Thebans are violating divine law, and so regards

the women's suffering as undeserved or at least unwarranted, despite Adrastus' failings. She is thus moved to pity for reasons that involve an assessment of desert, as Aristotle stipulates, or at least of justice. Her pity, in turn, disposes her to help convince Theseus to reclaim the unburied Argive corpses at Thebes. She does so, however, not with arguments based on the women's misery but by appealing to Theseus' reputation for valor. It is a sensible tactic, since she knows that Theseus pities neither Adrastus nor his city, and she also understands that political decisions are based on interest, not sentiment and justice. But if Aithra makes her case on pragmatic grounds, she nevertheless reintroduces the motive of justice by appealing to Theseus' renown as a champion against evil, thereby identifying Theseus' interest, and by extension that of Athens, with the defense of an ethical principle. Although pity drops out of the equation, Aithra at least opens a space for considerations of right and wrong in deliberative discourse, and she does so in the only possible way: by translating the moral question into one of self-interest.

Aithra, I suggest, is a case study in the dynamics of pity and its relation to political decision making. She initially pities the Argive women because she recognizes her similarity to them and regards their misfortune as unjustified, or at least contrary to what custom (*nomos*) permits. Her pity, in turn, conditions her decision to defend their cause before Theseus: emotion, as Aristotle says, is just that on account of which people differ in their judgments. In recommending a political course of action, however, Aithra respects the canons of deliberative rhetoric by casting her arguments in terms of advantage rather than sentiment. But she subtly unites interest with justice by insisting on the practical necessity of upholding sacred customs.

I have suggested that Aithra's pity has an oblique relation to the question of the Argives' desert. If no one may be justly prevented from burying kin, then it is not right that the Argives suffer this misfortune, irrespective of their responsibility for initiating the war. This is not quite the same as the view Aristotle advances in his definition of pity: his attention is on the responsibility of the sufferer for her or his misery, not its relation to a universal standard of right. This latter conception is akin to the modern doctrine of human rights, which now too has served as a motive for intervention in disputes between foreign powers. Although the emotion of pity does not enter into the political discussion, it nevertheless finds common ground with the argument based on norms, and thus provides the link between Aithra's private sentiment and her advice to Theseus. The connection between interest, the common beliefs of mankind, and a capacity for pity will emerge clearly some three centuries later in the history of Diodorus Siculus (13.20–27; see Konstan 2001: 75–95). But the problem was in the air when Euripides' *Suppliant Women* was staged, probably around the year 423 and thus shortly after the debate over the fate of Mytilene in 427, and the tragedy may be read in part as a commentary on the role of pity, interest, and justice in international politics.

THE SUPPLIANT WOMEN OF AESCHYLUS

Aeschylus' *Suppliant Women*, produced about forty years earlier, resembles Euripides' in structure. The chorus of Danaids, accompanied by their father Danaus, have come to Argos seeking refuge from their Egyptian cousins, who desire to marry them. Like Euripides' Argive women, the Danaids bear boughs of supplication (21–22) and lament piteously (58, 63), and they further call upon the pity and sympathy of the gods (*oiktire*, 210 [Zeus]; *sungnoiê*, 215–16 [Apollo]; cf. *oiktizomena*, 1031 [Artemis]). They too regard their cause as just (78 et passim; cf. Turner 2001: 33), although the Argive king Pelasgos is initially inclined to believe that Egyptian law, rather than Argive, is applicable to their case (387–91). When Pelasgos balks, like Theseus, at undertaking a war in their defense, they respond that Justice will protect him (342–43); we may compare Aithra's similar confidence in Theseus' campaign against

Thebes (328). Again like Theseus, Pelasgos declines to treat the Danaids as personal suppliants at his own hearth (*ephestioi*, 365), but insists on presenting their appeal before the entire citizen body (365–69; contrast the Danaids' cry at 370: "You are the city!").[6]

Nevertheless, Aeschylus' tragedy maintains no clear distinction between pity and practicality as motives for aiding the Danaids. When the Danaids succeed in intimidating Pelasgos with the threat of hanging themselves and thereby polluting the land, the king claims to fear the wrath of Zeus of Suppliants (478–79), and directs the maidens to place their boughs on the altars of local gods, so that the people will not blame Pelasgos but may pity them (*oiktisas*, 486), since everyone bears goodwill toward the weak (489). When they learn that the Argives have voted to defend them, the Danaids ascribe it to pity (*ôiktisan*, 639) as well as to reverence for suppliants protected by Zeus (641; contrast the pitilessness of the Egyptian herald, 904).

In a recent article on "perverted supplication" in the Danaid trilogy, Chad Turner (2001: 28) argues that:

> The Danaids' claim of victimization axiomatically depends upon the justness of their suppliant cause. The suppliant may be in the right by virtue of striving toward a socially accepted goal (e.g., burial of the dead, as in Eur. Supp., or ritual purification, as in Aesch. Eum.), or, more vaguely, by simply suffering hardship from a position of weakness (e.g., as in Soph. OC; Eur. Hcld.). The Danaids fail to meet either of these criteria. Consequently, their assumption of the suppliant's role is invalid.

This is, I think, to confuse supplication with the appeal to pity. Unlike the claim to pity, supplication, especially at an altar, has a ritual component, the efficacy of which is independent of a prior evaluation of right and wrong. As Manuela Giordano (1999: 190–91) notes, "The inviolability of refugees extends not only to those who are truly in need, that is, the classical types of Homeric supplication, but also to murderers and those condemned to death, and to criminals of every kind. Supplication at a sanctuary turns, in the end, into the possibility of finding asylum."[7] The Danaids' avowal that their petition is just is of course compatible with their posture as suppliants and is integral to their claim to pity. In addition, they are convinced that marriage to their cousins violates divine law – it is not *themis* (37, 336–37, 360) – and hence that Pelasgos is bound to vindicate them, without relating this motive specifically to pity.[8] Finally, the Danaids' threat of polluting the city engages the issue of the Argives' interest, but not in the reasoned way characteristic of political deliberation. The several strands of pity, supplication, right, and interest are thus intermingled in Aeschylus' play, at least in comparison with Euripides' handling of them in his *Suppliant Women*. It is plausible to suppose that at the time the play was produced, which was perhaps earlier than the now accepted date of 463 (see Scullion 2002: 87–101), the conventions of political and supplicatory discourse had not yet congealed in the more structured form they were to acquire in Euripides' time.

THE *HERACLIDAE* OF EURIPIDES

The argument of Euripides' *Heraclidae*, like that of Aeschylus' *Suppliant Women*, hangs on the due treatment of suppliants who claim asylum at an altar of the gods. As Iolaus exclaims when the herald of Eurystheus attempts to seize Heracles' children: "O you who dwell in this land since time immemorial, help us! We are suppliants of Zeus of the Marketplace, but are being subjected to force and our garlands are being polluted – a disgrace to the city and a dishonor to the gods" (69–72). The chorus recognizes that "one must revere suppliants of the gods, and they must not abandon the seats of divinities by dint of force, for Lady Justice will not permit it" (101–4). When Demophon, the king of Athens, arrives on the scene, the chorus express their pity (*hôste m'ekbalein oiktôi dakru*) for the way the suppliants have been treated by the

herald, who has attempted to drive them from the altar and has gone so
far as to trip old Iolaus (127–29); since the chorus consists of old Athenian
men, they recognize more readily their own similarity to Iolaus.

Demophon declares the herald's behavior worthy of barbarians,
though he wears Greek attire (130–31); so too, Pelasgos accused the
Egyptian herald of barbarism. Eurystheus' herald replies that Iolaus
and the others have been condemned to death by the laws of Argos,
which has jurisdiction over them (141–43) – again, this recalls Pelasgos'
doubts about whether Argos had the right to judge the case of the
Danaids. Not even the Heraclids, the herald alleges, would expect
Demophon to be so foolish as to pity them (150–52; cf. *môria*, 147),
the idea being that, whatever their plight, the Athenians would be
more circumspect than to protect suppliants when it means risking
war with Argos. With this, the herald shifts the terms of the argument
to the issue of material gain and loss (cf. *kerdaneis*, 154) and cautions
Demophon against "going soft by looking to their arguments and their
pitiful complaints" (158–59), for this will lead to war, all for the sake of
a foreign old man and some children.

Iolaus responds in the idiom of international diplomacy, adduc-
ing the kinship between the Heraclids and the house of Theseus (on
kinship as a basis for alliance, see Jones 1999) and Athens' debt to Heracles
for having rescued Theseus from Hades, and he concludes with a re-
minder of the disgrace (*tod' aiskhron*, 223) entailed in surrendering the
young suppliants to their enemies. The chorus are moved to pity by
Iolaus' plea (*ôiktir'*, 232), since children of a noble father have fallen
from prosperity and are suffering undeservedly (*hoide gar patros / esthlou
gegôtes dustukhous' anaxiôs*, 234–35): a dramatic change of fortune was one
of the commonplaces of the rhetoric of pity. Demophon, taking his cue
from Iolaus, rather pedantically enumerates exactly three reasons for
not expelling the Heraclids (*trissai m'anankazousi sumphoras hodoi, Iolae,
tous sous mê parôsasthai xenous*, 236–37): (1) first and foremost (*to megiston*,

238), the fact that they are suppliants at an altar; (2) then their kinship with his own family and his obligation to reciprocate Heracles' service to Theseus; and finally (3) the disgrace (*to t' aiskhron*, 242) involved in yielding up suppliants to force. There is, appropriately, no reference to pity in a statement of policy that will lead directly to war with Argos, and the question of justice (*to dikaion*, 254) pertains only to the sacrosanct status of the suppliant, who must not be removed by force. In the denouement, when Eurystheus has been defeated and captured, he appeals to the *nomoi* of the Greeks that forbid slaying a prisoner of war (1009–13, esp. 1010–11: *toisin Hellênôn nomois/ oukh hagnos eimi tôi ktanonti katthanôn*, i.e., I shall bring a miasma to the one who slays me). Eurystheus is above pleading for his life (1026, to Alkmene: *ktein', ou paraitoumai se*) and invoking the commonplaces of pity, but his attitude confirms the emphasis throughout the play on respect for common norms as the foundation of relations between states.

CONCLUSION

In a paper on the role of emotion in international politics, Neta Crawford (2000: 154) points out that "recently, several scholars have argued that actors follow normative prescriptions for emotional reasons." On the one hand, human attachment to social norms is emotional in character; on the other hand, "sympathy is an important element of decisionmaking" (Crawford 2000: 154 n. 126, referring to Sen 1990), even in the political sphere. The Athenians recognized the influence of emotion, and of pity in particular, on judgment; pity, moreover, was conceived of as based on desert, and hence involving justice. In the political climate of the 420s, however, when Euripides most probably produced the two tragedies of supplication discussed earlier, it appears that the Athenians were beginning to separate out the canons governing forensic discourse, to which the question of justice was central, from those of political deliberation, which was now seen as being properly restricted to the issue of advantage versus harm. Appeals to pity might still be made, of course, and citizens were not so callous as to be insensible to them, but they were likely to be dismissed as irrelevant to the hard realities of international relations. However, where the claim to pity could be linked to a violation of *nomoi*, or widely accepted principles of right or holy behavior, then the argument from pity might be given a special twist. For the petitioner could then appeal to the practical need and religious duty to uphold such laws, and thus shift the grounds of the argument to a form of self-interest – and hence a theme proper to deliberative rhetoric.

But while pity was marginal to formal decisions, it retained a place in the preliminaries. It was Aithra's pity that inspired her to insist on the divinely sanctioned right to bury the dead, and the old Athenians' pity for the Heraclids set the stage for Demophon's defense of a suppliant's rights. The Athenian theater thus showed how pity as a personal sentiment did indeed affect politics: if it was not itself a basis for policy, its implicit influence might nevertheless be manifested in a judgment favorable to the unfortunate. As Aristotle says, the emotions are "those things on account of which people change and differ in regard to their judgments."

Endnotes

1. Diodotos does not entirely ignore considerations of right; as Orwin (1984: 492) observes, "From the depths of Diodotos' argument pipes the still, small voice of justice."
2. Alcibiades continues: "For I do not think that what is just and what is advantageous are the same; on the contrary, many who have committed great wrongs have profited from them, while others who have performed just deeds have reaped no advantage"; cf. Chrysothemis in Soph. *El.*, 1042: "there are times when even justice brings harm." Socrates, of course, dissents from the common view; see Denyer 2001: 132–34.

3. For fuller discussion of pity in these genres, see the chapters in this volume by Donald Lateiner and Angeliki Tzanetou.

4. Macleod 1977: 227, 234, 236–67, reads the entire speech as an example of forensic oratory (227); cf. 236: "59.1 explicitly evokes pity, and the whole speech aims to create it." But he too recognizes that the Plataians chiefly cast their argument in terms of the Spartans' interests (234).

5. Perhaps there is a reference to justice also in 43–44, if the unintelligible *anomoi* conceals a reference to unlawful treatment of the corpses, as Campbell (1950: 123) and Kovacs (1995, in the critical apparatus) have suggested, rather than an expression such as *ana moi* vel. sim., adopted by the OCT.

6. Contrast the situation at the beginning of Sophocles' *Oedipus the King*, in which the priest, speaking on behalf of the children and elders of the city (15–17; the latter perhaps constitute the chorus), supplicates Oedipus personally to save the city; Oedipus sees himself as the one most affected by the city's affliction (60–64), and he responds with pity (*katoiktirôn*, 13; cf. *ô paides oiktroi*, 58) to the sad spectacle of the suppliants (*hiktêriois*, 3, *hiketeuomen se*, 41). The priest makes it clear that he is making his appeal at Oedipus' own hearth (*tois sois bômois*, 16; cf. *ephestioi*, 32). If indeed the old men are present on stage (so Sheppard 1920 and Jebb 1883; Dawe 1996 and Lloyd-Jones 1994 take *hoi de* in 17 as a poetic plural), the resemblance to the opening scene of Euripides' *Suppliant Women* is striking.

7. "L'inviolabilità dei rifugiati si estende non solo a soggetti veramente bisognosi, ai soggetti classici della supplica omerica, ma anche agli assassini, ai condannati a morte, e a criminali di ogni tipo. La supplica al santuario diviene insomma la possibilità di usare una zona franca."

8. Turner argues that the Danaids refuse marriage as such, not just with their cousins, and that "this absolute rejection of marriage and all that goes with it . . . is hardly on a par with burying the dead or seeking protection from tyranny" (32). This is perhaps psychologically true, but it is not their own stated view of the matter.

The Pitiers and the Pitied in Herodotus and Thucydides

Donald Lateiner

◎▣◎

GREEK TEXTS IN EVERY EPOCH, STARTING FROM AND THEN responding to Homer,[1] weigh with interest the power and limitations of pity. It has but a small role, at best, in public decision making in the heroic world. Nor does the exiguous evidence remaining from 700 to 450 BCE suggest that pity increased in Athenian public political debate. The two extant historians writing from the second half of the fifth century tell the same story. Related questions arise: what price does pity exact, and how do others value the person who expresses it in word or deed? Is pity for the Greeks an obligation or a privilege, and can others coerce it, or its appearance, from the unwilling? Can one be bullied into pity? And, in ancient Athens and Lesbos, could a group as a group experience this emotion or passion? Does the expression of pity put the pitier in a superior position, since not all pitied individuals have asked for, or welcome, or accept the "favor"?[2] Does pity promote solidarity with others or emphasize a painful de facto situational hierarchy?

Pity remains difficult to categorize. Like a virtue and unlike an instinct or a raw emotion, it involves calculation. It requires at least a one-way social interaction. To supplicate for pity poses personal and interactional problems (cf. Homer's Priam and Hecuba in Euripides), but to grant it is also problematic. Pity can respond to a debt (Dem. 19.310, Eur. *HF* 1236–38), recognize clear merit, or react to a great fall.[3] Modern analyses of pity address the role of cognition, detached appraisal, impulse, and physiological reaction (Konstan 2001: 10). Contemporary psychologists struggle to grasp the nature of any emotion, behavior, or action laden with and shaped by values from various religions, ethics,

and ideas about noble or ignoble human nature. Pity follows sorrow
(a passion) and sometimes precedes mercy (an action).

One cannot grasp the archaic experience of relatively simple, visible phenomena such as colors – *polios*, gray, or *oinops*, "wine-dark,"
or *aithops*, "shiny dark – or shiny bright." *A fortiori*, Aristotle's bold
attempt – even though he was a contemporary – to define amorphous
ancient Hellenic (Athenian, Ephesian, or Spartan) concepts of "pity"
verges on audacity,[4] and ours – 2,400 years later – on foolishness. As
Ionic and Doric ethnic perceptions of loyalties and interests differed,
as the many autonomous cities' calendars, laws, altars, and coins differed, so too these various Hellenic cultures' head and heart responses
to suffering differed.[5] The classical constructions of *pathos* and *oiktos*,
suffering and pity, will mirror local tolerance and intolerance of experiences and expressions of weakness and vulnerability. Recall how
invidiously and cruelly the Spartan warriors of the archaic and classical eras treated those who came home without their shields and not
on them. Ponder the reputed painful penalties and derisory stigmas
recorded by Plutarch (*Lyc.* 21), and the specially charged word reserved
for their dishonor: they were the "tremblers," οἱ τρέσαντες (Hdt. 7.229–
32).[6] Pity for affliction here shades into caustic cruelty or contempt for
those who have not properly earned it in heroic, warrior-focused value
systems. There, public honor and shame inhibit gentle qualities like
pity, and the same is true for a more open society like the Athenians'.

The Hellenic vocabulary for pity includes *oiktos* and the arguably
different *eleos*. In Homer's poetry, *eleos* appears more active, the giving of pity, as opposed to *oiktos*, the more passive feeling of pity,
a restraint from inflicting further shame.[7] The *oikt-* root is rare in
the fictional world of Homer,[8] while the *ele-* root is reasonably frequent. The fifth-century historians, describing a world in which the
exercise of pity has little scope, inversely favor *oiktos* over *eleos*. The
Attic orators, at least, in the next generation, pleading for (or against)

significant actions of pity in the law courts, again reverse the preference to *eleos*.

In Homer, pity is frequently requested but infrequently granted (Alastorides: 20.465, Lykaon: 21.74–106).[9] Pity, praised by many but practiced by few, never leads to a bad result,[10] as well it might. Consider Odysseus' and especially Patroklos' arguments (*Il.* 9.301–3, 16.30–35), and the sympathies of warriors, for example, Patroklos' and Asteropaios' sentiments concerning their helpless comrades (11.814–48, 15.397–404, 17.35; cf. 5.561, 610; 17.346). Pity is a gentle and respectful value against which we read the dreadful violations perpetrated in the bellicose and brutalized world of *Iliad* Year Ten. It should be allied to active mercy and the profitable ransom of captives, but is subverted and abandoned due to institutionalized Achaean war goals, berserker states of aggression, and individual exasperation (war psychosis: e.g., Achilles at 24.3–18).[11] Both cooperative norms among Achaean and Trojan allies and the protocols of "fair play" between adversaries – for pity exists in both venues – are repudiated and rejected in the results-oriented war situation. Sanctions for acute violations of *noblesse oblige* and for the abuse of the unprivileged and unprotected have been attenuated.[12] Achaeans have changed their thin tune about pity, and Achilles, their high-strung canary, most of all. But he who recently (six days ago?) broke bread with his captive Lykaon and will break more with his enemy Lord Priam (21.76, 24.618–19; cf. the pitiable Iphidamas 11. 241–44) is no inexorable killer. He conforms to Homeric ideals of shame and honor, personal relations and corporate obligations. Owing to Agamemnon's outrageous violation of community protocols and insulting nonheroic "compensation" (Wilson 2002: 75–107), Achilles is temporarily[13] extruded from the host and from the normal web of give-and-take – including pity. No one wins, but – in books 19, 23, and 24 – loss is palliated.

Only two isolated eccentrics in Homer's world – Achilles and the brute Cyclops Polyphemos, neither an ordinary mortal – are ever described as "pitiless" (νηλεής: *Il.* 9.632, 16.33, 204; *Od.* 9.272 – usually an epithet for bronze, as at 4.743). Yet Achilles had presumably agreed to honor the suppliant Chryses, had certainly shielded the weak seer Kalchas, had spared the dead hero Eëtion's armor for his corpse, and had ransomed live supplicants (1.22; 1.85–91, 6.416–27, 21.75–80). He indeed does pity, if only twice explicitly: bellicose Patroklos and defenseless Priam (16.5, 24.516). He withholds that response when it is imperiously or disingenuously requested (9.302, cf. 9.497, 632). However one reacts to their previous heroics, angry sulking in tents and rolling in muck while lamenting, Homer's most feeling heroes – the eloquent Achilles and suppliant Priam – show us the force of pity in *Iliad* 24. This culminating confrontation explores the pity of mortals and gods.[14] Achilles, reflecting on a decade of human slaughter, articulates clearly (24.549–51) the fragility he shares with the once mighty King of Troy.

The *Odyssey* repeatedly illustrates pitying gods and heroes. For instance, consider the Ithakan assembly, Athena, Calypso, Ino, Nausikaä, Circe, Eumaios, Odysseus, and Penelope (2.81–83, 4.828, 5.191, 5.336, 6.175, 10.399, 14.389, 19.210, 19.253, and 19.543). The Ithakan example is unique, for in that congregation "pity (*oiktos*) gripped the whole crowd." Note that the restraint that keeps heroic manhood from mocking Telemachos does not produce restorative action (Scott 1979: 8). The pitiers, although inhibited from further damage, do not try to put things right. Those who feel or show no sympathy or pity are condemned, or at least are not approved, for example, Polyphemos, Melanthios, Antinoös especially among Penelope's suitors, and Poseidon (23.313, [17.215–53], [17.459–87];[15] 2.84; Poseidon: 1.19–20, 68; 13.182). Zeus, the god who guards what little pity is admitted, and feels pity on several occasions, moralizes the story and the "good guys" win.[16]

Homer's fictions allow justice and merit to be rewarded and the vicious and greedy heroes to be curbed, blinded, or exterminated. The gentler virtues are thus vividly validated. In the historians' texts, however,

Herodotus' Hellenic triumph is compromised by civic division, new imperial inclinations (Spartan and Athenian), and the never-ending recycling of greatness and decline. Thucydides' Hellenic catastrophe proves a bullying teacher (βίαιος διδάσκαλος) both within the *polis* and outside it in the so-called leagues or alliances, as well as between adversaries. The gentler virtues are repeatedly neutralized, as we shall see, by Persian and Hellenic autocracies, by *stasis* or civil war, and by the unleashing of berserker blood-lust – synecdochized by Xerxes' beheading of Leonidas and the Corcyrean butchery (Hdt. 7.238; Thuc. 3.81). The classical historians rarely observed the phenomena of pity and (consequently) hardly employ the words. This chapter examines that noteworthy absence of pity in their two lengthy texts.

Heroic and then Archaic pity may be expected to differ from both Classical and Hellenistic expressions of pity, as the conditions of war, the state, the citizen, and the slave, and their concepts of *aretê*, self-aggrandizement, and generosity evolved. Aristotle, later and perhaps eccentrically, describes the poetics of pity, an audience response arising from composed evocations of pity or fear (*eleos, phobos*) experienced in theatrical *mimêsis* (*Poet.* 11.4–13.2, 1452b–53a: ἔλεος ἢ φόβος). This pity was theatricalized in the atypical, dramatic *anagnoriseis* and *peripeteis* (sudden recognitions and sudden reversals of fortune). In that controlled and ritualized "stop-time" context, Aristotle describes it as an elicited reaction, one that surely varies significantly from "real-life" historical reports, such as military pity found on the battlefield, political pity developed in the Spartan or Athenian assembly (as Kleon observes, Thuc. 3.38.2–5), and even from pity provided in historiographical anecdotes. Classical pagan concepts, *a fortiori*, may well not conform to later Christian ideas (recall the Catholic mass's resonant plea *Kyrie eleeson!*) or to post-Christian pity protocols.

The fifth-century Hellenic historians' general abstention from, and avoidance of, the usual scenes, vocabulary, and even the subject of pity, an issue that frequently appears in heroic epic and Attic tragedy, leads us to explore several questions posed by the presence and absence of pity in early historiography. Certain scenes of human suffering (including humiliation) in Herodotus and Thucydides have elicited comment from internal observers or the external narrators. They react to represented intense suffering and sometimes encourage the audience to react with pity and/or compassion.[17]

Dionysius of Halicarnassus (*Pomp.* 1.3) praises Herodotus above Thucydides for his generous sympathy for others' misfortunes (διάθεσις . . . τοῖς δὲ κακοῖς συναλγοῦσα). Dionysius recognizes Thucydides' own superiority in scenes evoking pathos, even when the word is absent. He invented for him a verb, to "tragedize" (*De imit.* 2.3, *Thuc.* 28: ἐπιτραγωδεῖν). The rhetorician (*Pomp.* 1.3; *Thuc.* 42) further praises Thucydides' portrayal of emotions and his Plataians' speech above all others. Pitilessness is monstrous. But since pity involves moral judgment and interventionist responses, weaker states like Mytilene and Plataia rarely enjoy the experience of that luxury in international affairs. The pressures (ἀνάγκη, *anagkê*) of time and place constrain their choices and their emotional options.

Only rare circumstances draw these two earliest historians to scenes in which they experienced and/or aroused pity. After Homer, but long before Aristotle, they realized that narratives that arouse fear and pity in the audience may win attention and appreciation. No reader ever denied that Herodotus and Thucydides provide scenes richly woven with pathos and other dramatic elements, however we define those slippery terms.[18] Historians dwell on emotional reactions: Thucydides devotes more papyrus to the spectators' emotions watching the battle in the Great Harbor than he does to the tactical reasons for the outcome, the Syracusan victory.[19] The questionable pleasures of "tragic history," the later subgenre, may be deemed the creation of Phylarchos, or pre-Aristotelian Ktesias, or post-Aristotelian Douris of Samos, but the element of *pathos* in historical narratives, hence the arousal of a reader's pity, originated in the classical historians.[20]

Modern historiographers need to distinguish (explicit) pity experienced by and noted for characters in the text from (implicit) pity aroused in the reading audience. For an epic prototype, Homer's Lykaon supplicates the berserker Achilles for mercy (*Il.* 21.34–135) – again, a second time, when cornered after Patroklos' death. He is rejected implacably; he is unsuccessful in beseeching pity because his vanquisher Achilles satisfies both of Aristotle's (*Rh.* 1386a) mutually exclusive definitions of two categories of those who cannot feel pity. "Pitiless" Achilles claims that he has nothing left to live for, nothing to lose after Patroklos' death. Somewhat contradictorily, he is above misfortune, insolent and harsh in his present indifference to death. In this instance, the blood-spattered, heroic character remains unmoved. The audience, however, feels great pity for Lykaon, the very young, very unfortunate, cruelly taunted, and soon decapitated Trojan.[21] Herodotus and Thucydides also provide examples of this arousal of audience pity from speech and act, without any character's experiencing it; it is left implicit in the circumstances.[22] I note passages in which pity words appear and others in which the words are absent, but where characters in the text nevertheless experience an author's warranted pity.

Although history may be popularly understood as the "unvarnished truth," critical readers know that every half-wit taleteller and also historians apply several kinds of perpetuating finishes. We allude here, briefly, to affective vocabulary, the personal selection of incidents, the length of their narration, organization of events with compositional patterns, juxtapositions, and sequences, and the insertion of retardatory speeches and anecdotal subnarratives. Changing points of view in a battle narrative or debate further affect our readings, such as an often-admired Thucydidean description of military defeat and departure when the vanquished Athenians and their allies despair and decamp after the final battle in Syracuse Harbor in 413 BCE. Both *wie-es-eigentlich-gewesen* historical information (*WEEG*, Alan Griffiths' acronym in Buxton 1999: 169) and evaluative reflection through instructional *mythoi* and pointed anecdotes enrich the two historical narratives. To return to pity, one also experiences a peculiar pleasure in their rare but powerful extended scenes of merited and unmerited suffering. The guilty pleasures afforded by Herodotus are so great that his reputation as an historian has never been high. He looks too good to be true.

HERODOTUS

In an examination of the functions and social context of Attic drama,[23] Jasper Griffin (1998) drew a parallel between Attic tragedy and fifth-century historiography concerning their debt to epic and their portrayal of the use and abuse of power. Although not looking at issues of pity as such, he drew attention to scenes of *pathos*, mentioning certain of Herodotus' stories of crime and disaster – Gyges, Adrestos, Periander, and Kambyses – and to Thucydides' stories of Pausanias' and Themistokles' suppliancy, and catastrophes at Corcyra, Ambrakia, Plataia, Delion, and Melos. That pity is explicitly mentioned in all three genres is not, after all, surprising. History and tragedy as genres share certain origins in Homeric military and civic subject matter and moral purposes. The two intersect interestingly at the end of Herodotus' account of the Ionian Revolt (6.21), where the public behavior of the Athenians and Sybarites is contrasted with respect to the fall of Miletus, c. 494/3. The passage concerns public displays of *penthos*, grief. Milesian males had all cut their hair, perhaps shaved their heads, in sympathy (or pity?) upon hearing of the earlier capture of Sybaris and the exile of its citizens, c. 510. Yet, the Sybarites did not display reciprocal grief when the Persians expelled the Milesians from *their* city, although no two cities shared deeper *xeniê*, according to Herodotus. In contrast, the Athenians emphasized their sympathy, ὑπεραχθέντες, "hypergrieving," at the sack of Miletus. They did so in many other ways and not least by their response to Phrynichos' tragic drama, the Homeric-sounding *Capture of Miletus*. First, the Athenian viewing public wept at his tragedy, and then the Athenian assembly fined Phrynichos one thousand drachmas for reminding them of *their own* proper woes (οἰκήϊα κακά). Finally, they prohibited productions of this spectacle. Here we have historical notice taken of three spontaneous community-shared or state-sponsored gestures of grief and pity. Herodotus depicts the Milesian show of grief, the Sybarites' failure to repay (as expected) their brethren's similar suffering, and the Athenians' communal sorrow and angry response to a representation of the disaster. Their pity engendered disapproval of vivid remembrance. Aristotle's distinction between responses to our own and to others' woes is exemplified over one hundred years earlier. The Athenians fined Phrynichos for the *Capture of Miletus* because his drama collapsed the distance between myth and history, between pity for others and horror and fear for oneself.[24]

"Pity" as noun and verb and the adjective "pitiful" (meaning "worthy of pity") appear fifteen times in Herodotus' *History*.[25] On fourteen of these occasions, pity words characterize Eastern potentates (10) or Corinthian tyrants (4).[26] These last four examples concern two endangered Corinthian boys in the tyrant's line: baby Kypselos and Lykophron, the father-bullied, teenaged son of Periander. The sight of a helpless baby or close family relation (such as a son) who may be killed or spared induces pity: Cyrus, Lykophron, the wife of Intaphrenes, and Kypselos (1.112, 3.52.3, 3.119, 5.92c3–4). Half of the examples of pity appear in speeches, *oratio recta*. Nearly all of them appear in that capacious category of events that we label "anecdotal." They lack, that is, corroborating external evidence, although they attest to the impressive power of oral tradition. Verbs for pity emerge in dramatic contexts, depicting helpless and despairing people on the verge of destruction or disaster, facing unopposable power. Great personalities confront striking choices that vitally affect people of inferior means and mobility. Gruesome criminal opportunities and dangerous temptations invite men to transcend selfish interests or accede to their passions.

The despots are connected to pity words most often because the consequences of their humiliating, nasty, and brutal whims engender potential pity. Therefore, the value of their occasional pity is small or nil. Zopyros is mistakenly pitied by the Babylonians because they assume that Darius' despotic savagery was responsible for the shameful mutilating of his face. Intaphrenes' wife evokes Darius' thin pity when he himself has arrested all her male family in order to execute them (3.119.3, 3.156.2).[27] Pity leads some few, who can act on responses, to mercy, but the results seem ironic – impermanent or unimpressive. Pity can enter (or arise in) the body and restrain an autocrat's will, and then, his overwhelming power. Responses evoked by pity include passive sympathy such as tears, or active reaction in words, or, finally, intervention in deeds (Sternberg 1998: 32, Table 6). We can categorize the types of incidents in which pity is portrayed in the historians; examine what motivates its consideration or appearance; determine whether Herodotus mentions pity only for monstrous and horrible suffering or gruesome crimes, or whether he evokes it for quotidian misfortunes. My research shows that pity in Herodotus emerges in unexpectedly few and limited contexts.

Xerxes provides, as so often, the paradigm *and* the limiting case of despotic pity stories. The hospitable Pythias of Lydia, the second richest man in the world, fed the entire Persian expeditionary army at Kelainai in rich Midas' Phrygia. Xerxes richly rewarded his voluntary generosity. Later, however, at Sardis, Pythias requests one favor from his new guest-friend: "Pity me in my old age and release my oldest son from your army. Take the four others." Xerxes waxed wroth at this Anatolian *chutzpah* and had the son chopped in half and mounted for display so that his army could march between the slices (7.27–29, 38–39). The request for pity here emphasizes an acute disparity in power. He who can show mercy may well choose not to. Xerxes' logic is sound; why should "number one" son remain safe when Xerxes himself, his sons, and brothers advance to the battlefront? His unpredictable responses to his subject's initiatives show a generosity in material goods and a brutality to bodies that is paralleled elsewhere in the *History*. Xerxes assumes that his subjects' lives and bodies are always at his disposal.

Soon after this, in the last appearance of pity in the *History*, Xerxes reviews his forces at Abydos. Suddenly, his volatile mood dramatically shifts from joy to tears. Uncle Artabanos, a Solonic wise advisor, inquires the reasons for the inexplicable mood swing (7.45–46). Xerxes replies that he pities the ephemeral life of all men, none to see the sun one hundred years hence. Artabanos, leveraging the key word pity, responds, "We suffer in other ways more pitiable (οἰκτρότερα) than that in this life." Life is short, yet no one is so happy as not to wish to die, often and not just once (πολλάκις καὶ οὐκὶ ἅπαξ – a Homeric, indeed Indo-European, echo and a polar positive and negative expression).

Artabanos continues with the panoply of Herodotean pessimism: accidents, diseases, and troubles. Thus, the divine offers only a taste of sweetness but grudges any more. This makes death the "most desirable refuge" from troublesome life: θάνατος μοχθηρῆς . . . ζόης καταφυγὴ αἱρετωτάτη.[28] In brief, pity articulates Herodotus' essential awareness of all mortals' vulnerability. Herodotus highlights not the pity associated with action that we can, if we are powerful, extend to the weak, but pity for the limited capacities "enjoyed" by all human beings. Xerxes ends this dialogue with a brusque "Right you are – but enough of that."

Pity first appears, like many motifs in Herodotus, in the reaction-shaping "Lydian" *logos*. Only Croesus pities twice in Herodotus' *History*.

Croesus represents, for the *Weltanschauung* of Herodotus, unlimited good fortune as Lydia's tyrant; unlimited bad fortune as poster-boy victim of Persian imperialism and of his self-delusion. He also embodies "man's narrow learning capacity."[29] Croesus pities Adrestos son of Gordias, his son's unwitting murderer, who begs the ruler to cut his throat like that of a sacrificial victim and end his wretched life. Herodotus notes (1.45.1–2) that Croesus pities him "despite his own overwhelming disaster," blaming – in his own helpless misery – some divinity for the disaster (θεῶν κού τις).[30]

The most elaborated drama of pity in the *History* again concerns the now ex-tyrant and intermittently wise advisor Croesus, a "catalyst of instability" (Stahl 1975: 33). He and Kambyses, now the Great King of the Persians, come to experience pity for the defeated Egyptian pharaoh Psammenitos (3.14). Beginning one of those royal tests, in which coercive autocrats torture the helpless to investigate human endurance or divine favor,[31] Kambyses tests his humiliated opponent. First, the pharaoh's own daughter, now enslaved with other formerly noble girls, is led past him as a lowly water carrier. Next, his son, enchained like an animal with a bit in his mouth, is walked to his execution with many other (two thousand?) humiliated noble boys. Whereas the victims and the other parents moan and grieve at the sight of each procession, Psammenitos without a sound or other obvious sign of grief bows deeply down to the ground. Assigned Egyptian guards communicate to Kambyses his repeated response to this parade of *pathos*.

The final act of this passion-testing drama in the suburbs of Memphis sends forth one of Psammenitos' drinking friends, an elderly gent expelled from his estate and reduced to public begging. Now Psammenitos weeps aloud as he has not before, calls on his friend by name, and beats his own head – a Herodotean gesture that only *one other individual* performs.[32] Kambyses is surprised by this greater grief expressed for a mere friend, *not* a relative. Psammenitos explains that "my own family's (τὰ μὲν οἰκήια) disasters are greater than any wailing (ἀνακλαίειν), but my friend's grief deserves tears, having fallen from prosperity to beggary at the threshold of old age."[33] This variation on the Homeric and widespread folkloric "ascending scale of affection"[34] motif elevates friendship to the highest level, while indicating the limits and the proper objects of pity itself. Aristotle cites precisely this Herodotean story (*Rh.* 2.8, 1386a) to illustrate that terror drives out pity and arouses something opposite (it is not specified; anger perhaps?). Pity requires some distance. Even Kambyses the sadist, after this explanation, experiences pity for Psammenitos, but it is already too late to save his poor son, who had been first to be executed.[35] The Herodotean type scene describes the fallen king's dignity and the successful conqueror's untrammeled opportunities for experimental observation. The horror inflicted on the weak and the autocrat's pity both emphasize the humble human condition. No sanctions infringe the Great King's ability to harm the helpless (including widows and orphans). Those who cannot defend their household and kin are pitiable (e.g., Priam, Telemachos, Psammenitos here).

Expressions of grief are prominent in Herodotus, again from the mouth and gestures of despots. Lamentation, moans, wailing, and weeping punctuate sudden realizations of the "too late," anagnoristic variety. Kambyses grieves for his dead brother; Croesus groans, remembering Solon's wisdom, Kleomenes because of the grove named Argos (like the *polis*), Hippias for his missing tooth at Marathon (3.64.2 [*bis*], 65.7; 1.86.3; 6.80, 107.4). Some examples describe ritual mourning for the dead:[36] the expected mourner for the decapitated Egyptian thief, for Kambyses, and for the Persian aristocrat and general Masistes. There are two unusual collectives that express grief: all the Spartans mourn loudly for every deceased Spartan king, and the Persian nation wails as one for the specific disaster at Salamis (2.121γ1, 3.66.1 [*bis*], 9.24, 6.58.3, 8.99.2).[37]

The only remaining example of pity exhibits a quasi-Thucydidean awareness of power politics. Pheretime of Cyrene comes to Persian

Aryandes, Satrap of Egypt, to supplicate him for assistance. She wants revenge for her son Arkesilaus' assassination. She also wants her son's royal power (4.162–67, 200.1). Herodotus reports that, "*taking pity*" on her (κατοικτίρας), the satrap lent her an army and navy to besiege Barka in North Africa. Herodotus then says conclusively that this murder investigation was only a pretext for both rulers. The queen wanted a god-forsaken revenge (4.205), and Aryandes' real motive was African conquest (4.167): "Now this reason was the revealed pretext but the expedition was sent, as I see it, for the subjection of Libya" (αὕτη μέν νυν αἰτίη πρόσχημα τοῦ λόγου ἐγίνετο, ἐπέμπετο δὲ ἡ στρατιή, ὡς ἐμοὶ δοκέειν, ἐπὶ Λιβύων καταστροφῆι). In short, Herodotus recognizes that expressed human sympathy may be a cynical fabrication for selfish state policy. Here he anticipates Thucydides' analysis of the alleged and the truest causes of the Peloponnesian War (1.23.5–6).

The pity of autocrats like Kambyses mainly serves the *literary* theme: to highlight their limitless power and willingness to use it. Croesus' pity for Adrestos and Periander's for his unwashed and unfed son did little good. Babylonian and Corinthian authorities who pity the mutilated enemy and a condemned baby cause only the pitiers' communal misfortune. Phokaian self-pity led to their enslavement by the Persians. Xerxes rewards and punishes Pythias the descendant of deposed tyrants as Kambyses had punished and rewarded his deposed Egyptian subject. The only net gainer is Intaphrenes' caterwauling wife. Darius' pity, while conditioned by the necessity to eliminate retaliation, inclines him to allow one woman to save two lives.

THUCYDIDES

Thucydides asserts that he will avoid the partisanship and exaggerations of naive observers, untruthful poets, and sensational logographers (1.21–22). Further, he suggests that his *History* through its τὸ μὴ μυθῶδες, perhaps translatable here as "lack of fictional structures and language," may *perhaps appear* less pleasure-producing, ἀτερπέστερον. The language hedged with litotes suggests that Thucydides believes that the intended reader will find pleasure enough, if of a peculiar sort. He certainly acknowledges that pleasure is a literary value and that he desires a very prolonged period of readership. Thucydides cannot mean that his work lacks suspense, or elaborate discussion of the causes, costs, and effects of failure and success, or intense παθήματα, sufferings (1.23) with crimes and punishments – because all those virtues abundantly appear in his text. Remember, for example, Brasidas' dash, the Athenians' improbable victory at Pylos, and cliff-hanging passages leading up to "So near did Mytilene come to disaster."[38]

Although he has often been thought to aim his historiographical criticisms at Herodotus' minidramas, more likely candidates are Homer's epics and the tragedians' spectacles. If he also intends Herodotus, his superiority emerges only in his sparing use of inserted, not entirely germane, dramas. Certainly the biographical narratives of the suppliants Kylon, Pausanias, and Themistokles are noticeably Herodotean in their story-telling details and dramatic features – and they are not unique.[39] Many of his other narratives command attention because of the moral issues, suspenseful emotional tension, lives in question, and both powerful and defenseless individuals and communities who briefly dominate the scene.

Eight of the ten occurrences of Thucydidean pity words appear in Book 3 in two contiguous and decisive incidents, each furnished with antilogies, sets of opposed speeches (3.36–50, 52–68). And although Herodotus' speakers barely mention pity, these Thucydidean speakers consider it a useful *topos*: a clay pigeon to toss out and shoot down. Thucydides employs the noun οἶκτος and the verb οἰκτίζομαι. He employs the noun *oiktos* seven times, *eleos* (ἔλεος) but once.[40] The juxtaposed and parallel antilogies early in Book 3 discuss adult male extirpation for surrendered Mytilene and Plataia. Nameless Athenians

afflicted by plague, Kleon, Diodotos, surrendered Plataians, exultant
Thebans, self-massacring Corcyreans, cornered Melians, and Nicias
(their former besieger: 3.91, 4.53) speak of pity and act or suffer in critical
situations. These persons and their situations evoke and invoke sympathy and terror, fear and pity. The compound verb ἀντοικτοῦντας,
"show pity in return," *hapax legomenon* for all extant Greek texts, occurs in Kleon's pitiless speech. The demagogue claims that Athens' subjects cannot reciprocate generosity, show such compassion in return.[41]
Thucydides invites the reader to compare the two superpowers' decisions by juxtaposing these two ferocious debates.[42] The Athenians moderate their earlier decision for committing atrocity at Mytilene, but the
Spartans scarcely listen to the Plataians' pleas. Thucydides barely mentions quite comparable later atrocities, such as the Athenians' killings
at Skione (5.32.1).

The Athenian assembly decided to reconsider their blanket condemnation to death of the disloyal male Mytileneans. In response
to their humane discomfort, Kleon condemns that particular vote
and any inclination to act on pity in interstate politics. Kleon's diatribe assaults the very mechanisms of the democratic Athenian body
governing the empire (3.37.1–2). The "change of heart" (or mind;
μεταμέλεια or μετάνοια; cf. 36.4), he declares, suits only theatrical
spectatorship, not real-world imperial survival. Pity brings no benefit to the Athenian polity. The moralizing demagogue describes pity
as one of any empire's three most unfortunate failings. These three
are pity, enjoyment of impressive speeches, and reasoned humaneness
(ἐπιείκεια).[43] These "attitudes" are irrelevant and incompatible with
prudent tyrannical exploitation. Diodotos, his adversary, recognizes
human obstinacy and desire for autonomy as ineradicable; even Kleon
acknowledges that punishment will not prevent other subjects from
revolts (3.45.3, 39.3; Stahl 1966: 121–23). Moreover, only parties of equal
standing deserve pity, and, more precisely, equals who may return the

favor of pity, not permanent foes. The rejection of pity is a forensic *topos* (Macleod 1978: 72), here manipulated in a formally symbouleutic context.

Diodotos' arguments respond pointedly to Kleon's. His conclusion also explicitly and equally emphatically rejects the momentary "pity" and more enduring "humanity" that Kleon referred to (3.48.1; cf. Macleod 1978: 72–73). But he argues that the Athenians should limit the proposed executions to the guiltiest rebels – purely for the sake of expediency. So, however much Thucydides and we admire the unknown Diodotos' successful effort,[44] we cannot find therein an open endorsement of gentleness or pity or justice. The manipulative rhetoric, the weapon that persuasive Kleon justly feared, finally finessed his more murderous proposal. By one-upping Kleon's harshness and by his own (perhaps) deceptive dismissal of justice, Diodotos captures not the moral high ground but expediency's middle ground.

Thucydides makes clear in his own framing remarks (both before and after the two reported *logoi*) that Kleon's opponents viewed the situation differently. Diodotos and the others who addressed the assembly condemn Kleon's misguided ferocity. Conceivably the massacre of all adult males on Lesbos led some to pity. Kleon is characterized as the most "violence-prone" citizen, and here is an item of evidence.[45] The debate had been reopened because the Athenians experience a calculated remorse, *metanoia* (μετάνοια), at their previous "raging" ruthlessness (ὑπὸ ὀργῆς ἔδοξεν). They recognized that their resolution was "savage," *ômon* (ὠμόν). The trireme sent to Paches moved slowly on its "monstrous" errand.[46] The deadpan pseudo-closer, "so near to danger came Mytilene," is dramatic and emphasizes the nearness of catastrophe in two ways.[47] The second trireme arrived in the nick of time, and the vote concerning whether to limit the killing to the most responsible Mytileneans remained, after all, "nearly equal," *ankhômaloi* (ἀγχώμαλοι; thrice, only here of an assembly).

So, Athenian pity, such as it was in summer 427, emerges only after initial fury and condemnation, gains only denunciation by both sides actually reported in the debate,[48] and still permits the execution of one thousand leading men of Lesbos, if the questioned number stands. Thucydides allows pity to peep through some cracks, but when the proposed shocking genocide is reduced to mass murder and confiscations, he does not credit the Athenians with impressive pity or mercy. The sentiment of pity is only indirectly attributed to the Athenians. However much Thucydides and we share it (and how do we determine whether he did?), the altered decision is based on other factors, Kleon's punitive and Diodotos' preventive calculus.

The Plataian-Theban antilogy poses fewer interpretive problems for the student of pity – because no such sentiment emerges. The Plataians, on capital trial and *in extremis*, speak for themselves much like defendants in a conventional Attic capital criminal trial.[49] With a flurry of religious terms,[50] creating images of *pathos* (four references) in the "tombs-ancestors" package, they repeatedly call on the Spartan judges' deceased fathers as well as on their own (all such men who fought against the Persians there). Their emotional peroration supplicates for pity and self-restraint from the victors of the moment. They face the erasure of their community "deserted and unprotected" (57.4). They thus urgently appeal to the gods, the vivid and present sight of the graves of the Spartans' fathers, and the Plataians' annual rituals repeated on the hallowed spot (58.4). No stone is left unturned. "It is not Greek custom, *nomos*, to kill those who surrender hands out!"[51] With pathetic irony, they call the Spartans in one breath their potential "saviors" and "the Hellenes' liberators" (59.4). The trial itself tragically travesties legal forms (Macleod 1977: 242) since, *inter alia*, the flustered accused must defend themselves before their accusers rise (53.2).

Point by point, the Theban prosecutors' refutation (ἔλεγχος) carefully addresses both Plataian defense arguments and their self-praise

for the great days of yore (ἀπολογία καὶ ἔπαινος, all 3.61.1) and also
responds to their accusations (κατηγορία) against the Thebans. The
Theban plaintiffs' "brief" has seemed unpersuasive to readers of every
generation, arguably disrespectful of traditional Spartan values, and
rhetorically incompetent.[52] We "eleologists" note that their epilogue
responds to the Plataian epilogue discussing pity. "Let no profit ac-
crue to the accused arising from appeals to pity and wailing[53] over the
graves of the Spartan judges' fathers and their own extirpation." The
malevolent Thebans *counter*appeal – with cruel echoes – for their own
fathers' revenge on the Plataians (67.3: [our ancestors] "supplicate you
that [these Plataians] suffer vengeance"; ἱκετείαν ποιοῦνται τούσδε
τιμωρήσασθαι). They theorize the circumscribed appropriateness of
classical pity before Aristotle was born. They think that undeserved suffering is worth pity, but justly suffering men earn only the opposite –
their own punishment and their foes' deserved rejoicing.[54]

The painful farce soon concludes (3.68). In any case, the Spartan
judges had already been bribed to condemn the prisoners (53.4). The
self-appointed judges eventually repeat their original murderous query.
They proceed to the shambles as if there had been no hearing at all. Few
men ever persuade the Spartans (cf. 1.88). Mercy, shame, and pity – the
aim of "the whole speech" (Macleod 1977: 237, citing Isoc. 16.48) – seem
irrelevant and unwelcome.[55] Again, Thucydides softly speaks his mind.
He regards the Lakedaimonians' cold-blooded actions as "unfeeling"
(68.4: ἀποτετραμμένοι, *hapax*), based solely on the perceived utility of
the Theban alliance. The Spartans execute the prisoners of war already
in hand (225+ men), enslave the women, raze the city to the ground,
and rent the land – to the Thebans.

The closing formula of the next sentence, dating the Plataian erad-
ication to the ninety-third year since their often-mentioned, late
sixth-century alliance with the Athenians, manages to arouse the
reader's indignation against both the present Spartan killing squads

and the absent Athenian allies.[56] Gomme (*ad* 3.67.4) acutely observed that the Boeotians "do not exactly win our sympathy. There is no palliation in Thucydides." He ignores, however, Thucydides' intent here: to provide two *paradeigmata* of hegemonic pitilessness, or better, of the shrinking or nonexistent space for pity between political communities. Paradoxically, savage Kleon, the vindictive Thebans, and the endangered Plataians all mention the need for or danger in sending this clear message about uncompromising imperial force (3.40.7, 57.1, 67.6; cf. Diodotos at 3.44.2–3). Thucydides thus underlines the intransigent and callous nature of imperial conquest. The historian allows the existence of rules in the Hellenic international community but describes the absence of enforceable sanctions.

After Book 3, as Thucydides reflected (3.83), the old manners and vocabulary rapidly retreated before a depraved morality, κακοτροπία. Nicias shouted his antiquated *parakeleusis* or battle exhortation to the demoralized Athenian troops attempting to escape the encircling Syracusan forces. The general describes the Athenians' unjustified invasion of a land far, far away as merely human nature and an aggression undeserving of any further suffering imposed by gods. Their suffering to date, deserved or not, has been sufficient and barely endurable – "so enough, already." Whatever the crime, we have suffered enough – he thinks. The all-too-human sufferer remembers his Herodotean Amasis who avers that the gods by nature are resentful of human good fortune, *to theion . . . phthoneron* (τὸ θεῖον . . . φθονερόν, Hdt. 3.40.2). But he forgets the horrific punishments that Herodotus' arrogant and aggressive Pheretime endured before death (Dover in Gomme et al. *ad* Thuc. 7.77.3). After cheering references to incalculable lucky "breaks", ἔλπις, εὐτυχία, τὸ εἰκός, he asserts (7.77.4) that "we may expect to meet gentler[57] treatment now from the gods *because* we are now worthier of their pity than their resentment."[58] This bizarre encouragement misconceives divine calculus, especially divine interference, most especially that of the *Greek* gods. Even though Thucydides makes the ailing, desperate Nicias pitiable to us, the historian's unflinching presentation and the plain narrative of the next eight days with its thousands of other deaths, render this deluded man's words *about pity* empty, vapid, actually repulsive. Nicias had now become another blinded Herodotean Xerxes.[59]

Appeals to the gods, or to hope, or for pity, in Thucydides' text foreshadow and perhaps ratify an imminent death sentence. The Plataians, Melians, and Nicias make such hopeless appeals.[60] An appeal for pity signals weakness in the Thucydidean world of *Machtpolitik*. In Thucydides' architecture, Book 3 marks the kinetic exit of mercy, moderation, fairness, and appeals to past norms and justice.[61] The arrival of Hesiod's Iron Age (*Op.* 200) similarly had witnessed the departure of *Nemesis* and *Aidôs*, archaic names for similar dames. Inside the *polis* at Corcyra and outside it for Mytilene and Plataia, both rational and sentimental appeals for pity and to traditional practices evaporate without a trace. Later, the Melians and Nicias more briefly reinvoke the dead letter, of course, but Thucydides presumably intends to show how such clueless appeals to gods – their justice or their pity – were now desperately "out of time," thus pathetic intellectually and circumstantially.

The uniquely *self*-revealing case arises in the historian's account of the plague. Thucydides only once explicitly takes near ownership of an emotional state – and that is pity. He describes how those Athenians who had recovered from the disease showed the most compassion toward the dying and the sick (2.51.6: ᾠκτίζοντο). Since he has told us that he himself was so afflicted and saw others suffering (2.48.3: αὐτός τε νοσήσας καὶ αὐτὸς ἰδὼν ἄλλους πάσχοντας), Thucydides perhaps for once describes his own feeling of pity.[62]

Pity, whether we think it a natural or culturally induced response, becomes regarded as a sentimental reaction, or an impeachable refuge. On it and on awareness of human reversals (3.59.1, fin.), moral and legal conventions have been constructed. Thus, the Geneva Convention's somewhat dependable rules for the treatment of prisoners of war have slowly emerged among nations. In the Peloponnesian War, Thucydides saw the collapse of such humane, civilized conventions and perhaps their ultimate futility (Macleod 1977: 244). Thucydides' speakers and voters in Athens, Corcyra, and Melos laugh down pity as an antiquated response, no more useful than the "old time religion." The *kala onomata* or "fair words" had lost their (traditional) meanings at Corcyra (3.82.4, 8) and any remaining currency at Melos (5.89*, 111.3*), but Nicias imagined otherwise when the tables were turned on him.[63] The Athenians (1.76.2*) decry the weaker parties' use of self-serving morality ploys. Atrocities replace sympathy or compassion, if we can assume they ever were a practiced norm – as opposed to an acknowledged morality. Thucydides' thought (to paraphrase Stahl 1966: 127, 140, 156) transcends the political sphere; results make a mockery of plans; his facts of war constitute a portrait of human fallibility and limits. The entire war evokes our head-shaking *pity* for men's misreadings of every motive and event.

CONCLUSION

Thucydides' speakers pay brief lip service to pity arising from unmerited misfortune (3.39.6, 40.7, 59.1, 67.4). Macleod (1977: 246) notes that victorious states and speakers can disguise their hatred as justice and their self-interest as essential expediency. The reader then pities the hopeless or the suppliant victims twice over: in response to the appeal crafted in the narrative and in response to the pitiless response that they encounter. The historian stands at a remove describing the pressures on each party, suggesting pity for others, but showing that one can never expect it from combatants in the heat of war.[64]

Those who deny that Herodotus comprehends *Machtpolitik* or *Realpolitik* and think him mostly stuffed with charming superstition and tear-jerking folktales will discover to their surprise this absence of tear jerking by the author or his characters. Pity is entirely absent from the factors he mentions that influence city-states and nations. No Herodotean figure engaged in international diplomacy, war, or *raison d'état* even mentions it. The absence is historically significant, while in Thucydides' work, Kleon fears its presence in the Athenians, the Plataians request it from the Spartans, and the Spartans ignore the thought of it.

Each historian only once evokes the participants' explicit pity and drags along the reader's pity. Herodotus' broken pharaoh Psammenitos and Thucydides' broken remnant of the imperialist Athenian army appear helpless and forsaken as they are forced to forsake others. The action and diction and the reported passion convey fear and despair amid wretched appeals. The mortified losers cannot help the dead and almost dead. Degradation and humiliation multiply guilt, grief, fear, and tears in the evocation of pity (cf. Sternberg 1998: 83–85). In Memphis and Syracuse, the sights and sounds of the victims (and even a dramatic example of haptics, clinging touch, for Thucydides) evoke pity within the text. The few pitiers in the text focalize our attention. At a safer distance, the reader pities both the pitied and the pitier.

Such rejection of brutality and evil seems equally manifest in his highly abstract analysis of human nature at Corcyra. Thucydides generalizes that "peace and prosperity promote better inclinations and motives (γνώμας), while war strips away material assets and drives men's characters (ὀργάς) down to the level of animal necessities."[65] But pity, at his remove and, more so, at ours, never produces a better outcome. In war, pity never determines the policies of his *poleis*. Pity never appears as a viable justification offered for state policy or action (as in Vergil's questionable prophecy *ex eventu*: "spare the conquered," *parcere subiectis*). Later readers' subsequent pity, however genuine, leads to – nothing.

A survey of semantics and even of ordinary language's periphrastic constructions for pity risks missing other evidence of the experience of pity. If it were to appear embedded in different vocabulary, situations, and institutions, we *might* incautiously discount its salience in ancient Greek life.[66] To illustrate, recall a mere page, the forgettable massacre at Boeotian Mykalessos (Thuc. 7.29–30). This was a "nowheresville" cross-roads, a tiny town far from any frontline. The Thracian irregulars had come too late to Athens to join the fleet's sail for Sicily. Consequently, they were dispatched northward, home from Athens, with orders to attack any conveniently located Athenian enemies. Commanded by the Athenian Dieitrephes, they fall without warning on this strategically insignificant hamlet and sack it.

Further, they kill both old and young men, "and children and women, and further even pack animals and anything breathing." Thucydides deploys polysyndeton (καί appears five times in thirteen words), hyperbole, the more usual litotes and superlatives, and another Homeric "polar" expression: "disaster less than none, greater than others." The final detail of the total slaughter – the butchery of young Greek scholars just chancing to enter their school house or *didaskaleion* – darkens the *pathos*. The Thracians show no pity or mercy. The Thebans, motivated by alliance and obligation to the unguarded town of dilapidated walls, march too late to protect their dependents. Pity is irrelevant to any of the participants: the absent Athenian paymasters, the thuglike Thracian killers, the little Mykalessians killed, and their Theban allies who arrive too late to save a soul. Pity is elusive, scant, indeed irrelevant to this terrible war too, but pity afflicts any reader of these Thucydidean paragraphs.[67] Clearly, overwhelming power raised issues of pity; clearly, Thucydides wishes to evoke it in several spectacles; presumably, he himself shares the response.

Mercy or *epieikeia* (ἐπιείκεια), the cousin of pity, does not figure prominently in the two earliest Greek historians.[68] I conclude that although pity is often entreated, commonly invoked, and arguably central in Attic *tragedy*[69] and in the Athenian *courts*, pity meant very little, if anything, in interstate Mediterranean policy or even intrastate fifth-century Hellenic politics and thus in the narratives of the two first preserved historians. Had the facts been different, they would not have disregarded the potent literary opportunities. The exercise of selfless humanity through pity has a restricted sphere.

Augustine asked, some 850 years later (*Conf.* 3.2, well cited by Macleod 1983: 8, 14), whether we should be appalled that we find pleasure in pitying others' woes and suffering in literature and history.[70] Can we morally defend that enjoyment from a charge of self-indulgence? Augustine denies the authenticity of our compassion (*insania*) for staged fictions and for events long past. More incisively, he notes the paradox that the greater our experienced sadness of a theater narrative, the greater our enjoyment. He endorses compassion only for suffering experienced by those whom we know and those whom we *can* help. Compassion for imaginary beings or long dead historical figures does not qualify, although the tough Bishop Augustine does not claim that pity exists in only limited supply.

Can we disagree? Humanity's common weaknesses and our sensitivity to suffering perhaps justify both our humility and instinctive, sympathetic respect for others in pain. With these attributes, maybe we *can* legitimately pity personalities of myth and history as well as our current neighbors. When we contemplate victims in recent history – for instance, the European Gypsies and Jews of the Nazi Holocaust, the Tutsis of African Rwanda, Native American tribes, even the Bosnians of the former Yugoslavia – moral agents imitating Augustine should consider whether the desirable response of pity leads us to *change* the situation. Thus, pity, ancient and modern, seems unexpectedly problematized.

◨◉◧

ENDNOTES

1. Burkert's Inaugural Dissertation discusses the two principal terms and their meanings in part I, the *Iliad* more than the *Odyssey* in the interpretive part II. See pp. 99–107 for his discussion of *Iliad* 24, discussed below. Herodotus and Thucydides barely appear in his study (1955: 51–52). Scott distinguishes Homeric *oiktos*, an impulse that restrains one from increasing another's shame and humiliation, from *eleos*, an active "positive impulse in favour of someone in trouble" (1979: 13).
2. Perikles explores the economy of generosity for Athenians at Thuc. 2.40.4–5.
3. Pity is usually spontaneous, although Plato and Demosthenes (*Men.* 294e, Dem. 24.171; Dover 1974: 200) claim patriotically that pity for the weak is an Athenian characteristic.
4. Aristotle, *Eth. Nic.* 1105b, incidentally discusses pity – a passion and not a virtue or a mental faculty, as William Fortenbaugh noted in discussion at the Rutgers conference on pity. Aristotle recommends it in moderation (at the right time only! the theater?) while acknowledging lack of choice in experiencing it or other passions. In *Poetics* 1449b, pity provokes *katharsis* of pain (cf. *Pol.* 1342a, *Rh.* 1385b). *Poet.* 1453b states that pity arouses pleasure. Yet it is akin to fear (*Rh.* 1385b, 1386a; *Poet.* 1451a–b, 1453b). Aristotle may represent, in rational and argued form, the common views of his age, or – more pertinently for his fifth-century texts – the views of a century earlier. Alternatively (as I would guess), his treatment of pity in the theater unexpectedly analyzes a topic that few had previously pondered.
5. Some examples of heroic pain and suffering seem richly deserved and some others undeserved; this calculus affects Hector's and Odysseus' (and later Kleon's) limited willingness to sympathize with others' shame and loss.
6. See Loraux 1977 and David 1989 for the institutions and educational mechanisms for approved Spartan social policies. A dissertation might develop a sociology of Hellenic pities as well as an epistemology for identifying the phenomenon among different value systems.
7. Homer repeatedly portrays suppliants of gods and of victorious warriors deploying this *elee-* stem to evoke pity for themselves.
8. Four appearances only: adjective: 11.242 (Antenor for Iphidamas), 22.76 (Priam foreshadowing hypothetical Priam); verb: 23.548 (Antilochos crediting Achilles with pity

for Eumelos!) and 24.516 (Achilles for Priam). See also Burkert 1955 and Scott 1979 on Homer's vocabulary; the latter seems unaware of the former.

9. Contempt is more common than pity: Telemachos' humiliation might gain pity but never respect from both his bullying "guests" and even his local sympathizers (van Wees 1992: 117–18). Konstan's Aristotelian paradigm does not work well for Homeric phenomena.

10. Zanker 1994: 23 n.47, on, for example, Menelaos 5.561; Lykomedes, 17.346. Meleager (*Il.* 9.590–99) yields to his heart and necessity. Pity is not explicitly mentioned.

11. Agamemnon the corporate voice and occasional monster: 6.45–62; the practical Odysseus: 10.42–57, "that was then, this is now": 11.99–112. Shay (1994: 32–38) and Zanker (1994: 47) discuss warrior estrangement and changes in personality and values after ten years of war.

12. Grudging Agamemnon: 1.224–31, 275–76, 293–303; Zeus: 15.184–99; dead men, live women and children, similes of animals selflessly nurturing their young, for example, 9.321–27, 11.113–19, 17.133–36, 18.318–22.

13. Some may be surprised to learn that Books 1 through 19 occupy at most twenty-seven days. Of these, twenty-one consist of two very brief passages on the pestilence (nine days: 1.50–54) and the gods' African vacation (twelve days: 1.423–25, 493–95).

14. Eleven occurrences: ἐλ- stems: 19, 23, 44, 174, 207, 301, 309, 332, 357, 503, 504 (comparative adjective). οἰκ- stems once only (516), final, and uniquely Achilles'. *Eleos* is spoken four times by Priam and spoken two times to him. On the other five occasions, twice gods feel pity for dead Hektor, Apollo claims strongly once that Achilles has lost pity (44), and Zeus twice expresses pity for Priam (174, 332), responding to the king's anxious prayer and anticipating Achilles' response. Although no *eleos* word falls from Achilles' mouth or describes him, he does finally pity Priam and his gray age (516: οἰκτίρων), when pity last appears in the poem.

15. The brackets indicate that no pity word actually appears but the context makes its absence clear. The rule-proving exception, 17.367, where the other suitors unusually give with a generous hand (from another's larder!), prepares and emphasizes pitiless Melanthios and Antinoös' offensive greed. Note Telemachos' absence from the list of known pitiers – he is too angry.

16. See *Il.* 16.431–32, 17.441; 19.340; 24.332; *Od.* 1.19, 12.445–46, 13.213, 17. 484–86. Odysseus' pitiless slaughter of the suitors is carefully justified. They have forfeited any right to consideration or sympathy by endless and repeated violations of Homeric hospitality protocols. To pity them is to read Homer unhomerically.

17. Obviously, the pity word *eleos* or *oiktos* need not appear to cause the reaction to register in others.

18. See Lateiner 1989 on Herodotean patterns of transgression and autocrats (127–40, 170–85); Lateiner 1977a and 1977b on *pathos* in Thucydides, for example, 3.113, 4.98.6, 7.29, 7.87. Macurdy 1940: 140–70, a chapter devoted to the historians, provides only a summary of "merciful" incidents. De Romilly 1961 has little on the historians and that little ignores pity; her 1974 article discusses the vocabulary well. Pearson 1962 finds oddly little to say about the ethics of popular pity in any classical genre.

19. A point made with some irritation by W. S. Ferguson in *CAH* 5 (1927) 308 and noted by Walker 1993: 360 n.14.

20. I may consider the intermediate place of the fourth-century Xenophon in another study. Douris mentions μίμησις and ἡδονή. Walbank 1955: 6 distinguishes tragic from rhetorical history. Walbank 1960: 221–26 distinguishes history from epic, tragedy, comedy, and theatrical elements of *muthos* (Thucydides' anxiety, 1.21.1). Fornara 1983: 120–34 attempts to sort out the filiation and the issues of tragic history, a project bedeviled by the exiguous relevant texts, even in fragmentary form, and the hostility of our chief source, the polemical and unsympathetic Polybius (e.g., 2.56.7–12). Wiseman 1979 usefully discusses Roman theory and practice concerning justified color and invention in historical texts. Levene 1997 examines the treatment of pity in one Tacitean incident.

21. Zanker 1994: 103–6. "Pitiless" (*nêleês*) describes him at 9.632, 16.33, 16.204 (Achilles puts words into Myrmidon mouths!).

22. The ancient critics remark τὸ παθητικόν (*to pathêtikon*) in Thucydides' text, and they often refer to passages at the end of Book 7. This chapter does not dissect the two historians' emotional power, their rhetorical art of *pathos*-production in audiences; cf. Lateiner 1977b.

23. Griffin 1998: 56–59; cf. French 2001 and Scheff 1994 for non-Greek materials on vengeance. Although Herodotus was not an Athenian citizen, no reader should be surprised to find his provocative evidence (much of it gathered in Athens) included in this predominantly Athenian volume.

24. Macleod 1983: 3 makes this subtle point based on Gorgias and Arist. *Rh.* 1385b 32–33. Gorgias notes that tragedy examines the "misfortunes of others" and makes them our own (*Helen* 9). This distinction also illuminates the behavior of Pharaoh Psammenitos later. Roisman 1988 discusses authorship, date, and *Tendenz* of this drama and argues correctly that the Athenians may have been compassionate but they were *not* remorseful (18). Pelling (1997b: 19) argues a similar line for Aeschylus' *Persai*.

25. Twelve times only, if we excise the compounds of *oiktizomai*, since they connote "complain" and "grieve/lament" (1.114.4, 2.121c1, 3.156.2). Herodotus employs οἰκτ-, οἶκτος (3), οἰκτείρω (4), κατοικτείρω (4), οἰκτίζομαι (3) with ἀπό- (1) and κατά- (2) compounds. Herodotus employs the unique adjective οἰκτρότερα once. Ἔλεος and the adjectives and verbs formed from it never appear.

26. Anger is the vice of Herodotean tyrants and kings, rarely of Greek men, according to Harris 2001: 175. The single exception concerns the gypsy Phokaians. Soon after swearing curses and the ritual dropping of iron in the sea to seal their oaths, they lose more than half their ships to their fellow citizens' ineradicable nostalgia: a certain πόθος τε καὶ οἶκτος for the city and its ways draw the oath-breakers home. The unique hendiadys, "passionate pity" or "pitiable desire," must have resonated with the exiled Ionian author.

27. Darius allows her to save one male. She chooses her brother and Darius throws in her oldest son in admiration of her unexpected choice. The rest die. Cyrus as a

boy bullwhips and mutilates an apparently higher born boy who piteously whines (1.114.4).

28. The vocabulary is striking here, even if the thoughts seem familiar. Nowhere else in Herodotus, and rarely before him, do these words appear: "more pitiable" (*Od.* 11.381), "most desirable," "refuge," and even the celebrated word for a "grudging" god elsewhere appears only in the mouth of Croesus and the pen of Amasis (1.32.1*, 3.40.2*).

29. Stahl 1975: 29. How could the Lydian tyrant not have become the stuff of legend (cf. Bacchyl. 3)?

30. This regal mercy cannot prevent the outcast murderer from committing his follow-up suicide on his young victim's grave.

31. Compare 1.86.2–3, Cyrus mounts living Croesus on a pyre; 1.117–19, Astyages tests Harpagos; or Kambyses 3.16, 35–36. See Christ 1994.

32. 2.121 δ2, the deceptive fraud performed by the thief of Rhampsinitos; 6.58.3 offers a Spartan community parallel.

33. *Il.* 22.60, *Od.* 15.246, 23.212 contain the last metaphor; cf. Falkner 1989.

34. Kakridis 1949: 28–33, 49–53, 152–64 (the last on Hdt. 3.119).

35. Kambyses treated Psammenitos gently henceforth – until he was caught planning rebellion.

36. Conversely, the Getans cry at the birth and rejoice at the death (5.4.2), like certain American Christian black communities, such as New Orleans, where Jelly Roll Morton mentioned the practice to the ethnomusicologist Alan Lomax.

37. For completeness in cataloging the "grieving" terms such as ὀλοφυρ-, οἰμ-, ἀναστεν-, -κλαι-, see Sethos (2.141.3), Syagros at Syracuse (7.159, metaphorical), and Amasis' distraught foreman (2.175.5).

38. Also 3.49.4, 7.2.4 (Syracuse), 8.33.3 (Astyochos); ignored by Gomme, Dover, and Andrewes 1956–1981, although not by Hornblower's 1991 commentary.

39. 1.126–38: "here the lion smiled," a scholiast remarks at 1.126.3, thinking of the more relaxed style of Herodotean story-telling.

40. Since it follows the default word *oiktos*, Poppo-Stahl sense mere variation, *prorsus non differe*. Stevens (1944: 3, 14, 25) explores Thucydides' debt to Thrasymachos' *Eleoi* (*Commonplaces of Pity*) and the *ekbole eleou* topos, "banishment of pity," in Homer, Aristophanes, Antiphon (1.25–26), and Aristotle (*Rh.* 1386b–87b). The scholiast at 3.67 marks the appeal to pity and its refutation.

41. Compare 3.40.5: he fears that Athenians might "appear less aggrieved," *analgētoteroi*.

42. Sheets, ably arguing against those who see appeals in Thucydides to Hellenic *nomoi* (customary law) as merely "pious platitudes," specious excuses, or ineffectual defenses, must admit that Thucydides or his speakers often hold such pessimistic views as these (1994: 59). Nevertheless, the "friends" of Mytilene and all the speakers at Plataia refer to recognized principles of international law. Even more powerful opponents often concede that such *nomoi* exist (57–59, 63–64). Edward Harris drew my attention to this article.

43. Compare Diodotos' cuttingly responsive 3.48, the only other Thucydidean appearance of the noun, when it means generosity.

44. Ostwald 1979 on his identity; Orwin 1984 on his humanity; Connor 1984: 83–89, on his slippery ambiguities; Konstan 2001: 80–83, esp. 82 on *timôria* as both vengeance and punishment.

45. Compare his later decisive role in the similar punitive devastation of Skione (4.122.6, 5.32.1: the land given to the Plataians!).

46. ἀλλόκοτον is *hapax* in Thucydides, although his work boasts of many other unheard of horrors (1.1, 23.1–3; 3.83–84, etc.).

47. 3.36.2: ὑπὸ ὀργῆς; 36.4: ὠμὸν τὸ βούλευμα; 36.6: ὁ βιαιότατος; and 49.4, the *epiphonema*.

48. Thucydides admits to suppressing other points of view (3.36.6), perhaps including some that dilated (to his disapproval?) on pity.

49. See Pl. *Apol.* 34d; Ar. *Wasps* 568–74, 975–84; Lys. 20.34. Konstan (2001: 34–43) distinguishes appeals for mercy for the guilty and remorseful from appeals for pity for undeserved misfortune.

50. 3.59.2: θεοὶ ὁμοβώμιοι, ὅρκοι, ἱκέται, οἱ πατρῷοι τάφοι, κ.τ.λ. Compare Macleod 1977 for the parallels, Hornblower 1991 *ad loc.*, and Debnar 2001: 125–35. Macleod (1977: 243) observes that Thucydides recognized that the Athenians were more concerned to punish the Lesbians than to save the Plataians (3.36.1). The collocation of the two incidents is significant, and of course the noted coincident time (3.52.1).

51. The Thebans score points reminding the Spartan "court" that the Plataians had committed this crime *paranomos* (3.66.2; Sheets 1994: 57).

52. Debnar 2001: 136–45, Hornblower 1991–, 1.445.

53. Wailing (ὀλοφυρμός) appears five times, thrice for Athenians at Syracuse. Perikles twice rejects piteous grief: 1.143.5, 2.44: ὀλόφυρσις.

54. 3.67.4: ἐπίχαρτοι, *hapax*. Gomme et al. 1956–1981 *ad loc.* note that this word is the *vox propria* for reacting to an enemy's just deserts.

55. Nor, unsurprisingly, do mercy, pity, or sympathy appear in Adkins' (1960) index.

56. The next bridge paragraph (3.69), between Plataia and Corcyra, describes the fumbling failure of the Peloponnesian fleet, too late for the Lesbians, chased by the Athenian ships, scattered by a storm and eager to intervene in a civil war in the upper Adriatic.

57. De Romilly 1974 suggests that the word is out of place, here, but so is Nicias.

58. τά τε ἀπὸ τοῦ θεοῦ ἐλπίζειν ἠπιώτερα ἕξειν (οἴκτου γὰρ ἀπ' αὐτῶν ἀξιώτεροι ἤδη ἐσμεν ἢ φθόνου).

59. "No other city in Sicily could easily handle you, if you attacked it" (7.77.4). On his appeals to divine pity, cf. his earlier shouted speech (7.69) and Thucydides' critical evaluation of it (with Lateiner 1985).

60. 3.58–59*; 5.104–5*, 112*; 7.69, 77*. Thuc. 4.98.6 describes the flexibility of divine forgiveness for humans under duress.

61. Nevertheless, seven of the nine Thucydidean examples of *epieik-* nouns and adjectives are surprisingly Athenian.

THE PITIERS AND THE PITIED 97

62. No incident better proves the inadequacy of prior calculation (Stahl 1966: 80, 77). Perikles had no clue to the misery to come and the anger and pity that would envelop Athenians. Thucydides here anticipates Aristotle (*Rh.* 2.8.9, 1386a), who refers to pity arising from another's disease, because pity is especially expectable from survivors who understand the suffering.

63. Asterisks after references indicate passages in direct speech, *oratio recta*, in the ancient historical texts.

64. One can never *rely* on generosity. Recall the Homeric "rule" of supplication (five examples), a salvific possibility existing only to be rejected in the *Iliad's* battlefield examples. Ferocious Agamemnon states the Achaeans' genocidal intentions (6.42–62, 11.123–47).

65. Hornblower *ad loc.* (1.482) correctly asserts that Thucydides here morally evaluates states by rules that also apply to individuals. War is "a violent teacher," a famous metaphor, perhaps here suggesting *pathos* for the paradoxical collocation of nurture and murder, as at Mykalessos. The word *didaskalos* appears four times. Orwin (1994: 133–36) discusses "the dissolution of Greekness itself."

66. Cairns (1999: 171–73) raises these issues while considering the parallel problems of ancient remorse.

67. The epilogue observes that, despite its size, the Mykalessian *pathos* was "less than none in worthiness of lamentation" (7.30.3: οὐδενὸς ὡς ἐπὶ μεγέθει τῶν κατὰ τὸν πόλεμον ἧσσον ὀλοφύρασθαι ἀξίῳ). Obviously, *pathos* is related to pity but derives from another root.

68. Other Herodotean scenes, both barbarian and Greek, present characters showing self-control and restraint, particularly Hellenic recognition of human limitations. Recall Croesus' forgiveness of Adrestos, Harpagos' self-control (1.118–19), and Pausanias' behavior after the battle of Plataia. He refuses to maltreat the Persian general's Koan concubine or Mardonios' corpse (9.76, 79) – although he had the Persian precedent of Leonidas' mutilation. Herodotus views his courteous acts as proper Hellenic code, not mercy or pity.

69. Tragic plots revel in pity, especially when altars are conveniently nearby. See the complementary chapters by Konstan, Tzanetou, Johnson and Clapp, Falkner, and Kosak in this volume. Even Thucydides, a writer ambivalent at best about religion in his more cynical age, reports various suppliants rushing to altars: 1.126.10–11, 3.28.2, 3.81.5 (notable but not unique violation), 5.60.6, and 8.84.3. Hogan 1972, arguing against Adkins in favor of Euripides' engagement with pity, cites parallels between the Plataian-Theban antilogy and the *Hecuba*.

70. *Dolor ipse est voluptas.* I thank audiences at Rutgers University and the University of Pittsburgh for helpful comments, and most especially the muse and editor of this collection, Rachel Sternberg, for her invitation to the conference and many useful improvements.

A GENEROUS CITY: PITY IN ATHENIAN ORATORY AND TRAGEDY

ANGELIKI TZANETOU

– for Apostolos

◎▣◎

ATHENIAN TRAGEDY AND ORATORY SYSTEMATICALLY CULTIVATED the image of Athens as a generous city that offered unwavering support to the weak and the oppressed. The expression of pity for the suffering of non-Athenians allowed playwrights and orators to represent compassion as a collective trait of the Athenians. Athenian claims to humanitarianism are documented through recurrent mythical examples of supplication, notably the help that Athens lent to the Argives for the burial of the Seven and the protection of the children of Heracles. These episodes find their place in funeral and in display speeches that regularly focused on the praise of Athens. And such paradigmatic stories also formed part of the tragic repertoire of Athens' mythical past. In addition to Euripides' *Suppliant Women* and *Heraclidae*, Athens is portrayed as assisting exiles such as Oedipus in Sophocles' *Oedipus at Colonus*.[1]

This chapter argues that pity was linked to power in Athenian democratic ideology and served to conceal political motives of self-interest and advantage. My discussion focuses on the representation of pity as a collective emotion and explores how its evocation in contexts of political decision making benefited the public image of Athens. The comparison between oratory and tragedy extends Nicole Loraux's treatment of the praise of Athens in the context of the funeral oration.[2] The similarities and differences that emerge from this comparison illuminate different facets of the city's generosity toward outsiders. Close examination of certain mythical *topoi*, especially in tragedy, reveals that pity and power had become ideologically charged after the 470s.³ The intimate relationship between the two can be shown to underlie the very belief that Athens was open and compassionate toward non-Athenians. I argue that pity became associated with power when Athens acquired an empire. Oratory and tragedy called attention to Athens' considerate treatment of suppliants and outcasts, aiming to reinforce Athens' self-image as a compassionate city. In this context, power emerges as the *other* face of pity and offers a window into the dynamics of Athens' new double role as a democracy and as an empire.⁴

David Konstan argues persuasively in his chapter that pity is ordinarily juxtaposed to self-interest in the realm of Athenian politics. This juxtaposition, also amply illustrated in Donald Lateiner's chapter, is subsumed in the encomia of Athens in oratory and tragedy, thereby masking the dissonance between the two. Within the ideal self-portrait that orators and dramatists promote, pity and self interest become fused. In tragedy, however, the rhetoric of pity does not eclipse Athenian power and expediency altogether.⁵

MYTHICAL *TOPOI* AND SUPPLICATION IN ORATORY

I begin with oratory and the tradition of the funeral oration, where we find pity associated with the civic praise of Athens. The Athenian funeral oration formed an integral part of the public funeral for the warriors who had fallen fighting for the city. This ceremonial speech aimed to celebrate the democracy and extol the city on behalf of which many young men had sacrificed their lives. The praise of Athens' past was a central aspect of the funeral oration. The orator exalted the city's present exploits through a catalog of her past victories, including those in mythical wars. Two examples stand out: The wars that Athens fought against Eurystheus and against Creon in Thebes. These are included in the praise of ancestors along with the Trojan War and the wars against the Amazons and Eumolpus. Each contributed to the representation of an ideal moral and political outlook and emphasized the pursuit of excellence (*aretê*).[6] Among these exploits, the war against Eurystheus and Creon highlighted the Athenian virtue of pity toward suppliants and defined the Athenians as compassionate toward the suffering of others.

These two episodes, which came to embody Athenian pity and generosity, in outline tell a similar story: a group of suppliants turns to Athens for help against a powerful and unjust opponent; Athens respects their rights as suppliants and puts herself at risk by fighting against an evil foe. Thus, the children of Heracles, persecuted all over Greece by Eurystheus, find refuge only in Athens. The Athenians protect them by fighting against the hubristic Eurystheus and vanquish him. In the episode of the Argives' suppliancy, Adrastus or the Argives request that the Athenians intervene to help them recover the bodies of the Seven who fell in the battle against Thebes. The Athenians fight against the Thebans and succeed in recovering the bodies of the Seven for burial.

And yet one of the earliest mentions of the two mythical exempla, namely, the help that Athens offered to the children of Heracles and to the Argives against the Thebans, is found not in a funeral speech, but in the speech of the Athenians before the battle of Plataia in Herodotus (9.27). The Athenians argue that they are worthy of the place of honor in the battlefield. They offer as proof of their military superiority the wars they fought on behalf of the children of Heracles, the Seven against Thebes, and the Amazons, as well as their more recent victory at Marathon. It is difficult to speculate on the antiquity of the exempla, but they probably became part of the ideal image of Athens as liberator and protector of Greece in the years following Athens' victories at Marathon and Salamis in the Persian Wars.[7] Apart from Herodotus, the fifth-century record includes Euripides' *Heraclidae* and *Suppliant*

Women in the 430s.[8] And it is reasonable to assume that these episodes were also celebrated in the fifth-century funeral speeches that are no longer extant.[9] These provided the model for the praise of Athens that we find in the fourth-century funeral speeches, in Lysias 2 and in Plato's *Menexenus*, as well as in Isocrates' display speeches, notably, his *Panegyricus* and *Panathenaicus*.[10]

Through their inclusion in the catalog of the ancestors' praise, these stories highlight the exemplary moral and political judgment that Athens exercises by going to battle against an unjust enemy. Accounts of the Argive episode emphasize the Athenian respect for law and custom (Isoc. 4.55–56; Isoc. 12.170–1; Lys. 2.9).[11] The Thebans' violation of ancestral custom explains why Athens intervenes in Theban affairs and justifies the city's going to war (Lys. 2.10; Isoc. 4.58; Plato, *Menex.* 239b and especially Eur. *Supp.* 167–75, 186–92, 277–85).[12] The role of Athens as protector of the weak figures prominently in the suppliancy of the children of Heracles. Orators usually pose a clear antithesis between the weakness of the Heraclidae and the power of their enemy, Eurystheus. The inequality of power between Athens and the suppliants has moral ramifications. The suppliants face an unjust opponent and their suffering is presented as unjustified. This explains why Athens, though powerful, takes up their cause. The city protects the weaker party by choosing to defend justice (Lys. 2.12: "and they thought it proper to fight for the weaker party on the side of right [*huper tôn asthenesterôn meta tou dikaiou diamakhesthai*] rather than favor the powerful by handing over to them those who were being wronged by them").[13]

Although the Athenian response to the suppliancy of the children of Heracles and of the Argives became a byword for Athenian pity,[14] pity is explicitly addressed only in the more detailed version of these episodes, which survives in Lysias' funeral speech (2.14): "they undertook such great perils, pitying those who were wronged and hating those who were insolent (*tous men adikoumenous eleountes, tous d' hubrizontas misountes*) and attempting to impede the latter and thinking it proper to assist the former." The connection between pity and undeserved suffering (*tous men adikoumenous eleountes*), which we see in this passage, demonstrates that pity is not incompatible with political decision making, provided that it operates in conjunction with moral values.

In his discussion of Aristotle on pity, Konstan (2001: 128–36) has emphasized that it was not conceived of as a raw emotion, but rather as an emotion that presupposes the exercise of reason and ethical judgment.[15] As the examples drawn from the political and ceremonial speeches indicate, pity reflects the self-definition of the Athenians as morally and politically superior to their opponents. Accordingly, the emotions that are attributed to the Athenians, namely, the pity they display for those suffering unjustly and the hatred against their aggressors, reveal a concrete correspondence between emotions and ethical valuation. Pity for undeserved suffering is translated into action: the justified punishment of the offender. As a result, in ideological terms pity becomes both the proof of Athenian moral superiority as well as the justification for action, especially war.[16]

Whether pity is explicit or implicit, the moral principles that arouse pity in the Athenians and validate Athenian military action remain unchanging and unmistakable: Athenians are always represented as helping the wronged and punishing the unjust. Gorgias sums it up (82 B 6 D-K): "giving help to those unjustly afflicted and punishment to those unjustly flourishing, . . . insolent with the insolent, decent with the decent, fearless with the fearless, terrible among terrors."[17] In Plato's *Menexenus* (244e), the city is characterized as "prone to pity (*lian philoiktirmôn*) and favoring the weak." And, according to Demosthenes (24.170–71), the proper Athenian character (*to tês poleôs êthos*) consists in "pitying the weak (*tous astheneis eleein*) and preventing the strong and powerful from behaving insolently."[18]

In describing the relationship between the pitier and the pitied, David Konstan (2001: 131) briefly notes that the former is in a stronger material or military position than the latter. This perceived inequality is accented in the examples from Athens' distant past. These narratives represent Athens as more powerful in relation to her foreign friends and enemies. Isocrates suggests that the help that Athens lends to the suppliant children of Heracles and the Argives offers a proof of her character and strength (4.54): "One would recognize both the character and the strength [of the city] from the suppliancies (*gnoiê d' an tis kai ton tropon kai tên rhômên ek tôn hiketeiôn*), which already some had made to us." The orator renders explicit what is implicit in the previous examples, namely, that the Athenians' response to the suppliants offers proof of the power that the city possessed. Isocrates points out that the children of Heracles chose to come to Athens rather than any other city because they considered her the most powerful city in the Greek world (4.56): "And [the children of Heracles] ignoring the other cities, since they were not strong enough to help them in their own misfortunes and thinking that our city alone was able to return the favor for the benefactions (*tên d' hêmeteran hikanên nomizontes einai monên kharin apodounai*) that their father bestowed upon mankind." For the Athenians, the retelling of these patriotic stories affirmed belief not only in the moral conscience of their city, but also in Athens' military supremacy (4.57): "From these things it is easy to understand that the city also at that time held the position of a leader (*hoti kai kat' ekeinon ton khronon hê polis hegemonikôs eikhe*)." Similarly, in Herodotus (9.27) the Athenians in their speech before the battle of Plataia use the examples of the help they lent to the children of Heracles and the Argives in order to claim the leadership in the upcoming battle for themselves.

Pity, therefore, overtly or covertly asserts the prominence and superiority of Athens over those she helps or opposes. Again, the collocation of pity and moral values serves to illustrate the ideal alignment between emotions, morality, and politics in the context of Athenian ideology. The representation of groups of suppliants seeking assistance from the Athenians constitutes a recognition of the city's power and places her in the role of a benevolent and generous protector. Suppliants are weak; Athens is strong. Pity is an appropriate response on the part of the strong to the suffering of the weak and the defenseless. Accordingly, power creates a different outlook on pity. The help that Athens extends in helping others offers requisite proof of her political and military effi-cacy. In the two mythical episodes, less powerful groups, the children of Heracles, or Adrastus, seek help from Athens against a powerful enemy, Eurystheus or Creon. The former recognize Athenian superiority; the latter oppose it, but are defeated. The image of a pitying Athens also contains a cautionary message, namely, that Athens helps those who recognize her political and military superiority and punishes those who do not.

PITY AND EMPIRE?

Pity, as I have argued so far, became a salient trait of Athens' civic self-image by the middle of the fifth century. Athenians, however, presented different and contrasting motives to describe their actions in their panegyrics and in their political speeches, as we see in the works of Herodotus and Thucydides. Lateiner in his chapter notes that the "absence [of pity in historiographical narratives] is significant" and argues that pity did not play a role in the realm of *Realpolitik*. The question I address briefly in this section is a historical one: when did pity emerge as a prominent aspect of Athens' civic self-image?

I suggest that the characterization of Athens as pitier of the weak and punisher of the insolent emerged from the historical experience of Athens as leader of the Delian League. Founded in 478/7 BCE, following the end of the Persian wars at the request of the other Ionians and with the consent of the Peloponnesians, the league constituted a defensive alliance against the Persian threat (Hdt. 1.165.3; Thuc. 1.95–96, 3.11.4; Meiggs 1972: 42–49). The victory of Athens in the Persian wars had earned the city her reputation as liberator of Greece.[19]

As Sophie Mills (1997: 34–42) argues, the conception of Athens as civilizer and protector of Greece antedates the Persian wars and the formation of the alliance. The significant victories of Athens at Marathon and Salamis strengthened the image of Athens as protector and liberator of Greece. In the *Histories* of Herodotus, Athens is represented as promoting democratic freedom, following the rule of law against tyranny and despotism (e.g., 8.142; Raaflaub 2004). But once Athens becomes recognized as the leader of the alliance, the image of Athens as liberator of Greece is complemented by her depiction as helper of those suffering unjustly. For example, Athens goes to war in order to protect justice and freedom not only against the Persians, but also against other Greeks (Plato, *Menex.* 239b: "believing that it is necessary to fight for freedom (*huper tês eleutherias*) both against Greeks in defense of the Greeks and against the foreigners on behalf of all the Greeks").

Athenian representations of pity point to the *specific* nature of Athenian hegemony, whose imperial and expansionist agenda is seen as arising out of Athens' role as leader of the alliance. By the middle of the fifth century, pity is associated with the Athenians' character and with their democracy, which was considered milder than other constitutions.[20] In light of the absence of evidence from Athenian literature for the development of concepts of pity, this argument remains speculative. The evidence from the fifth century, however, indicates that the growth of the Athenian empire contributed to Athenian ideals of pity and compassion. The ideology of pity reflects in positive terms Athens' new role as ruler of the empire. Even after they acquired an empire, Athenians continued to view themselves as liberators and protectors. They never presented their influence in terms that openly admitted domination or overtly indicated their power in the context of civic ideology. The discourse of pity in oratory and tragedy often disguises the Athenians' pursuit of power and self-interest in the realm of the empire. But in the context of politics, the two were incompatible. As Kleon argues in the Mytilenean debate before his fellow Athenians, their empire is more akin to a tyranny and giving into pity for the allies would be dangerous for Athens' rule (3.37.2–3) and most disadvantageous for her empire (3.40.2).

The ideology of pity projects an idealized version of the Athenian empire and masks the unequal structure of power that existed between Athens and her subject allies.[21] Pity is always couched in terms that present Athens as rejecting her own self-interest, and the orators offer feigned criticisms of Athens for being overly compassionate and choosing the weaker allies against the city's proper interest.[22] Thus, in Isocrates 4.53: "this is why some accuse us of not deliberating correctly, because we [the Athenians] repeatedly choose to help the weaker party against our own interest (*para to sumpheron*) rather than to join with the stronger in committing wrongs to our own advantage" (cf. also And. 3.28, Dem. 20.3, 15.22, 16.15, Plato *Menex.* 244e). In celebrating Athens' civic self-image, Isocrates reverses the terms of pity and self-interest by suggesting that Athenians incurred loss instead of benefits by helping others. Admittedly, following upon the aftermath of Athens' defeat in the Peloponnesian War and the erosion of her power, the fourth-century speeches address a different historical reality than do the fifth-century examples.[23] And yet, as Loraux (1986) argues, these mythical examples are already part of a fixed tradition that celebrated Athens' military achievements.

To illustrate, finally, how distinctively Athenian the ideology of pity is, one may contrast it with Anchises' famous dictum in Vergil's *Aeneid* 6.853, *parcere subiectis et debellare superbos*, which expresses the ideal of Roman conduct in Augustan imperial ideology. Anchises advises

Aeneas to show mercy toward the defeated and to fight against the insolent. This appears to be a close variation on the Athenian theme of pitying the weak and punishing the unjust, captured by Demosthenes (24.170–71): *ton gar huper tês poleôs prattonta ti kai praon humôn teuxomenon to tês poleôs êthos phainesthai dei echonta. touto d'esti ti? tous astheneis eleein, tois iskhurois kai dunamenois mê epitrepein hubrizein* (for the one who does something good for the city and who will obtain your clemency must be shown to possess the moral character of the city; and what is this character? To pity the weak and prevent the strong and powerful from behaving insolently). Both Demosthenes and Vergil articulate a similar ideological stance: they base war on moral principles. Nonetheless, each author reflects the respective nature of Athenian or Roman imperialism. Anchises emphasizes mercy for the defeated *enemy*, while the orator underscores pity for the weak and the oppressed. Anchises boldly outlines the role of the Romans as leaders of an empire and their attendant responsibilities. The Athenian version, on the other hand, disguises the hierarchy of power that existed between Athens and her allies and suggests that the empire plays a protective role. Though Athenians benefited greatly from their empire (as many of the allies also did), they did not overtly define themselves as its leaders.[24] Rather, they sought to justify their imperial practices through recourse to democratic ideals.[25]

I have tried to illustrate that the ideology of pity reflects the role of Athens as a league-empire by relating the inequality between the pitier and the pitied to the unequal balance of power that existed between Athens and the other states within the alliance. It is not possible to include a survey of the transformation of the league into empire nor do justice to the complexity of the issue of how Athens treated her allies.[26] I am only proposing a connection between the historical moment of the emergence of the ideology of pity and Athens' role as the leader of the alliance. A fuller treatment would necessitate careful consideration of Thucydides, who undermines the ideal of Athenian compassion in his account of Athens' rule.[27]

TALES OF CIVIC GLORY: TRAGEDY

Tragedy offers important insights as to how pity was deployed in Athenian democratic ideology. The fourth-century orators note that the patriotic stories have been handed down to them from tragedy: "who does not know or has not heard from the tragic poets at the Dionysia of the misfortunes that befell Adrastus at Thebes?" (Isoc. 12.168 and also Dem. 60.9; Plato, *Menex.* 239b). Both tragedy and oratory aim to cultivate pity as an emotion appropriate for Athenians in the context of ceremonial occasions that reinforced civic consciousness and heightened national pride. The funeral speech was part of the public funeral for the dead, who were buried at the city's expense; performances of tragedy were part of the City Dionysia. Both were organized by the city of Athens, addressed the Athenian community, and constituted important political occasions. The funeral oration and tragedy functioned as official channels for pro-Athenian ideology; the cross-genre comparison allows us to understand some of the ways in which the ideology of pity was disseminated. As Loraux argues, the *topos* of Athenian pity and compassion is the same in tragedy and oratory (1986: 67):

> That the tragic writers exalt this generosity whereas the orators criticize
> it or at least pretend to do so cannot conceal the fact that the project is
> obviously the same: to show that Athens is fighting on the side of the
> right. Because they cannot tolerate a Greek who violates a Hellenic
> law, the Athenians take up arms to force Creon to submit; because they
> welcome the suppliant Heraclidae, they feel obliged to punish their
> persecutors. Thus, generosity leads to a sort of perpetual military activity,
> and militant compassion becomes belligerency.

Though the similarities are unmistakable, there are also differences in the manner that tragedy and oratory explore Athenian generosity. Orators praise the city's military activity by focusing on the moral motivations, which characterize the undertaking of past and present battles. In tragedy, however, the praise of Athens does not aim at underscoring Athens' military glory, but rather its *civic* glory; this is fitting in the context of a festival that celebrated civic membership.[28] The political nature of the City Dionysia was particularly accented in the predramatic ceremonies, which projected the power of Athens: generals poured libations; the city honored her civic benefactors; the tribute from the allies was displayed; and orphans of war, who had been raised at the city's expense, participated in a procession.[29]

These ceremonies displayed the city's power as an empire and also cast the relationship between Athenians and non-Athenians positively. Unlike the Athenian assembly, where only citizens could participate, the City Dionysia was open to noncitizens.[30] The festival in effect constituted the community broadly by acknowledging the presence and contributions not only of citizens but also of noncitizens and foreigners seated among them. Ritual occasions were often more inclusive than the political community. The plays also offered a forum for exploring the relationship between Athenians and foreigners because they often addressed the place and status of foreigners in Athens.[31] In particular, plays that dramatize the *topos* of Athenian pity and generosity examine the idealized openness of Athens against the reality of foreigners' secondary status in Athenian society.

With the exception of Euripides' *Suppliant Women*, Athenian piety and compassion is exemplified through the inclusion of non-Athenians who come as suppliants to Athens.[32] Sophocles' *Oedipus at Colonus* and Euripides' *Heraclidae* explicitly invoke the discourse of Athenian compassion, offering insights into the relationship between foreigners and Athens in the second half of the fifth century. In both plays, exiles or fugitives, namely Oedipus and the children of Heracles, arrive as suppliants in Athens.[33] Theseus' and Demophon's decisions to protect the suppliants by fighting a defensive war against their aggressors, Creon or Eurystheus, accord well with my preceding analysis of the praise of Athens in fourth-century oratory. Moreover, Athenian compassion as it is enacted within the theater highlights the moral and political principles that democracy guarantees (e.g., justice, freedom, equality of participation, absence of violence).

In Sophocles' *Oedipus at Colonus*, Thebes is characterized by tyranny and strife over the succession (e.g., 372–81, 1342–43). Creon uses violence to serve his own interests. Theseus opposes him and defends Oedipus by invoking democratic ideals, justice, and the law (913–18): "seeing that you came to a city that abides by justice and decides everything according to the law (*hostis dikai' askousan eiselthôn polin/ kaneu nomou krainousan ouden*) and then flouted this land's authorities when you made your incursion to take away all that you wished and subjugate it by force (*paristasai biai*). You thought my city had no men or was enslaved, and I counted for nothing!"[34]

Euripides' *Heraclidae* also poses an antithesis between the tyrannical measures of Eurystheus and Athens' democratic demeanor: *bia*, represented by the herald's intent to violate the rights of the suppliants and drag them back to Argos (59–60, 63, 67–68, 105–6, 267), versus Athenian *eleutheria* (e.g., 111–13: "Should you not have spoken to this land's ruler before taking this bold step rather than forcibly dragging these strangers from the gods' sanctuary? That would have shown respect for this land's sovereignty [*alla mê biai xenous/ theôn aphelkein, gên sebont' eleutheran* and cf. also 243–46]). The *topos* of pity and generosity in tragedy is also related to the inclusive character of Athenian democracy.[35] In tragedy, then, Athens' self-definition as a compassionate city is more readily associated with the praise of democracy than in oratory and is exemplified in her readiness to admit into the city exiles and refugees who have been unjustly cast out of their native cities.

Orators use the *topos* of pity and compassion to justify the city's going to war and support enthusiastically Athens' empire; playwrights affirm Athens' military achievements, but also praise her democracy. In tragedy, the city's democracy and her empire become interconnected.[36] The political superiority of democracy over tyranny, which is celebrated in both plays, benefits Athens' imperial image. The claim that Athenian democracy is better and preferable to the tyrannical regimes of mythical Thebes or Argos suggests that Athenians and non-Athenians alike would not fare well if the empire were to fall into the hands of Athens' opponents.[37] Athens' civic self-image as open toward foreigners, however, must be set against the negative image of Athens that her opponents promoted (e.g., Thuc. 1.68.3, 1.121.5, 1.122.2, 1.124.3; 3.31.1, 3.63.3, 3.64.3, 3.70.3, 3.71.1; 4.92.4). The speech of the Corinthians in the first book of Thucydides, for instance, exemplifies that Athens' power was regarded as threatening by other Greeks (e.g., Thuc. 1.38–43).

POWER AND THE SUFFERING OF OTHERS: ATHENIAN LESSONS IN CIVIC IDEOLOGY

The playwrights' representation of the reception of foreigners in Athens demonstrates concretely the pitying and compassionate nature of the Athenians.[38] The proof of Athenian compassion lies yet again in action, namely in the defensive wars that Athens takes up on behalf of the suppliants in both plays. But the enactment of pity in the theater also offers insights regarding its limits by focusing upon the relationship between the Athenians and the suppliants as foreigners. I focus upon the relationship between pity and power or, more specifically, the inequality between the pitier (Athens) and the pitied (non-Athenian suppliant exiles). Pity is less prominent in plays that treat the reception of suppliant exiles in Athens because Athens imposes limits and conditions upon their reception. In tragedy, exiles are accepted into the city if they can return the favor of Athens' protection. Suppliants, like Athens' allies, become Athens' dependents, and they too receive protection from a powerful city in return for their contributions.

Tragedy offers important evidence that Athens' relationship toward foreigners was an important issue during the Peloponnesian War – the date for Euripides' *Heraclidae* falls in the years between 430 and 427 BCE and the latest date for the composition of Sophocles' *Oedipus at Colonus* is 407/6.[39] Both plays praise Athenian compassion and generosity by focusing on the city's openness toward foreigners. The ideal of democratic openness is well-illustrated in Perikles' pronouncement in the funeral oration (Thuc. 2.39.1) that the city of Athens is open to foreigners (*tên te gar polin koinên parekhomen*) and that, unlike the Spartans, Athenians are not in the habit of driving foreigners out of the city (*xenêlasiais*).[40]

In Sophocles' *Oedipus at Colonus*, the chorus upon meeting Oedipus first ask him to depart from the grove of the Eumenides because he is treading upon sacred ground (166–69) but are willing to treat him as befits a suppliant (176). Upon the revelation of his identity (220–22), they shrink back in horror and ask him to leave the city altogether (226). Antigone's plea toward them to display *aidôs* toward the suppliant fails to change their mind. They respond (254–55): "Why know, child of Oedipus, we pity you and him alike for your fortune (*all' isthi, teknon Oidipou, se t' ex isou/ oiktiromen kai tonde sumphoras kharin*), but fearing what may come from the gods, we cannot speak to you further than what has already been said" (254–57). In this case, fear of Oedipus' pollution compels the chorus to drive the suppliant away, even though Oedipus' appearance as an old blind beggar is more than deserving of their pity.[41]

Oedipus retorts by invoking the *topos* of Athenian help toward the weak (258–63) and criticizes the chorus for failing to show the traditional piety and compassion toward a suppliant.[42] Oedipus goes on to argue that the chorus have misunderstood his identity "fearing only my name" (265) and at the end of his speech argues that he is "sacred, reverent and one who brings a special benefit for the citizens" (286–87). Oedipus is referring to his future status as a savior hero, since after his death his secret tomb at Colonus will protect Athens against a future attack of the Thebans (576–82, 616–23).

Furthermore, after Ismene brings news of Creon's impending arrival from Thebes, Oedipus offers his own account of his banishment and argues that he is a political exile (427–44). Immediately after, the chorus express their pity for Oedipus' suffering anew (461–64): "you deserve pity (*epaxios* . . . *katoiktisai*), Oedipus, both yourself and these your daughters; and since in your speech you offer yourself as a savior of this land, I wish to advise you on what will be beneficial for you." In the first instance, pity is expressed in words, but not in action. In the second, the chorus are ready to help Oedipus and prove their compassion in deed. There are many factors at work here, but I suggest that the shift in attitude brings us back to the issue of the balance of power between the pitier and the pitied. As an outsider, old beggar, and blind exile, Oedipus is deserving of pity.[43] Oedipus' first entreaty is rejected not only due to his pollution but also because he is a noncitizen.[44] Foreigners did not possess citizen status in Athens, and naturalization was a rare occurrence in the fifth century. Through his request for entry in the city, he claims a share in it and threatens the status quo according to which Athenians and foreigners were never on a par.[45] The difficulties surrounding Oedipus' reception reflect political reality: the exclusion of foreigners from citizenship challenges the message of Athenian openness toward foreigners that the play promotes.

In his speech of defense, nonetheless, Oedipus formulates his request for admission in a manner consonant with the city's practices and institutions regarding the reception of foreigners: his promise of benefits casts him as a suitable candidate for naturalization in Athens.[46] His claim thus acquires new validity. Meanwhile, the limits of pity reflect the inequality of status between Athenians and non-Athenians. Pity and openness toward foreigners are carefully manipulated in tragedy. The praise of Athens is subsequently validated,[47] not only by the chorus' change of attitude but also by the depth of Theseus' compassion and understanding (*kai s'oiktisas*, 556).[48] Theseus asks no questions and welcomes Oedipus because he too has experienced life as an exile (560–68). As the protector of exiles and refugees in tragedy, he embodies Athenian pity and generosity. He proves his compassion in deed by accepting Oedipus in the city as a citizen (*empolin katoikiô*, 637).[49] Practical concerns regarding a foreigner's integration into the city no longer clash with the ideology of Athenian generosity. Theseus' decision to help Oedipus reveals his flexibility, kindness, and depth of moral understanding. Yet, it is also based on an assessment of the benefits that Athens reaps by receiving Oedipus, a polluted exile, who will soon become a powerful savior of the city.[50]

Similarly, in Euripides' *Heraclidae* a group of suppliants, the children of Heracles who are fugitives from Argos, seek protection in Athens from the tyrant Eurystheus, who seeks to enforce violently their return to Argos. The fugitives pose a threat to the rule of Eurystheus, an usurper, and may soon seek to punish him for the misfortunes that he inflicted upon their father (1000–4). Demophon's decision to receive the suppliants underscores the city's democratic character. The Athenians define themselves as purveyors of freedom and justice and fight against violence and tyranny.

My interpretation of the reception of the suppliants differs from Konstan's treatment of the play in that I view the discourse of Athenian generosity as serving Athenian interests rather than as working against them. The decision to support the cause of the suppliants by Demophon, Theseus' son, is accompanied by the expression of pity (cf. Lys. 2. 14). Their unjust persecution by Eurystheus, the Argive herald's demands that they be handed over, and Iolaus' entreaties arouse feelings of pity in the chorus "My lord, I have listened and I pity these (*ôktir' akousas tousde*) for what has befallen them . . . suffering undeserved misfortune (*dustukhous' anaxiôs*)" (232–35; cf. also 127–29). Demophon decides to protect the suppliants and fight a war against Eurystheus, who is about to attack Athens in order to force the city to give up the suppliants. Piety, justice, but also Athenian sovereignty (*eleutheria*) are at stake (111–13, 197–98, 238, 243–46, 286–87). Athens in this case too exhibits compassion by helping the weak and punishing the insolent. The decision to shelter the suppliants projects the ideal combination of emotions with moral and political imperatives.

And yet a crisis erupts that impedes the suppliants' reception. Just before the battle, Demophon announces that oracle(s) instruct him to sacrifice a maiden to Kore for the sake of victory (406–10). Demophon's perspective shifts away from the suppliants' just cause against Eurystheus because the reception of the suppliants now endangers the well-being of Athens. Seeking to protect the citizenry, Demophon declines assistance to the suppliants. Bereft of the help of the receiving city, Iolaus expresses pity for Alkmene and the children for their undeserved suffering (445–46):

> *My children, I do not know what I am to do for you. Where shall we turn? What god's altars have we not garlanded? To what land have we not come for refuge? We are doomed, my children, now we shall be given up! I do not care for myself if I must die, unless my death gives pleasure to my enemies. It is you I pity and weep for, my children (*humas de klaiô kai katoiktirô tekna*) and Alkmene your aged grandmother.*

The chorus, unlike the chorus of Sophocles' play, no longer express pity, but seek to protect the city's reputation against the accusation of betraying the suppliants: "Old Sir, do not lay this charge against the city. For though it may be false, it would still be a shameful reproach, that we betrayed strangers" (*hôs xenous proudôkamen*) (461–63).

Once again the limits of pity are drawn; the relationship between the pitier and the pitied, Athenians and non-Athenians, cannot be rendered equal.[51] Athens extends its help to those who have benefits to offer to the city. Initially, the children of Heracles have nothing to offer; instead their protection places great demands upon Athens. Isocrates (4.63) in his *Panegyricus* captures it best: "it is not ancestral custom for foreigners to place themselves over those born of this land . . . nor those who are refugees over those who received them." Similarly, Demophon's rejection of the suppliants demonstrates that Athens does not extend help to others without expectation of benefits. For the audience of its day, the message of the play is cautionary and is aimed against the Spartans, who failed to recognize the generosity that Athens had shown to their ancestors. Once the unnamed daughter of Heracles offers her life for the sake of victory, the Athenians fight successfully against Eurystheus and the praise of Athens resurfaces again in the third *stasimon* (748–83). At the end, Eurystheus is captured and Alkmene, the aged mother of Heracles, vouches to avenge all the wrongs that he has committed against her family (941–60). Eurystheus, the former aggressor, falls victim to the wrath of Alkmene, whose revenge is harsh and savage (1045–52). But there is a final twist in the plot. Eurystheus is paradoxically accepted into the city, while Heracles' children return home to the Peloponnese.[52]

Before his death, Eurystheus announces a prophecy according to which he too, like Oedipus, will become a saving hero of Attica (1032–37): "I shall lie for all time beneath the earth, a foreign visitor who is kindly to you and a protector of the city (*kai soi men eunous kai polei sôtêrios/ metoikos aiei keisomai kata khthonos*), but most hostile to the descendants of Heracles' children when they come here with a great army, betraying the kindness you showed them (*kharin prodontes tênde*).

Such are the guests you have protected." We have come full circle: Athens pities those who will pity the city in return, as Kleon aptly remarks in his speech in the Mytilenean debate (Thuc. 3.40.2–3). History has taught the Athenians that the children of Heracles were ungrateful; their descendants became Athens' enemy. Eurystheus, like Oedipus, defines his standing as a hero after his death as a benefaction for the city to which he will now belong. Eurystheus, the unlikely hero, becomes a better candidate for admission in the city; for his contribution will be more lasting than those whose cause Athens championed.

Conclusion

Both plays represent pity and power as interconnected. Tragedy, as I have argued on the basis of these two suppliant plays, offers a unique standpoint for examining how and why pity became such a significant aspect of Athenian self-representation. Plays that focus closely on the theme of the reception of exiles and refugees offer a far more nuanced negotiation of the ideology of pity than oratory does, against Thucydides' portrait of the cold reality of Athens' imperial politics (e.g., Strassburger 1958: 17–40; Meiggs 1972: 375–96; Mills 1997: 79–86). The praise of the ancestors in fourth-century oratory is formulaic and emphasizes Athens' military glory. By focusing upon the reception of non-Athenians, tragedy problematizes Athens' compassionate stance at a time when the empire still stood supreme. By reading the plays against Athens' engagement with foreigners at the time, we can see the rhetoric of pity operating in concert with self-interest. The double identity of Athens as a democracy and as an empire allowed her to put the very paradox of her political identity to good use: the ideology of pity that Athens consistently projected served to conceal the fact that she had become an imperial power and to mask, however thinly, her hegemonic tactics. In that respect, Athens too, like America, may be characterized as a furtive empire,[53] and the comparative dimension of ancient and modern political practices of two systems that have as many similarities as differences may serve to illuminate the operation of power both then and now.

In conclusion, pity and power are integrally related in Athenian democratic ideology. The praise of Athenian compassion in tragedy promotes important civic ideological lessons – the city's openness toward foreigners as well as the privilege of belonging to the Athenian democratic community. The theme of Athenian pity and generosity in oratory, by contrast, justifies the city's interventionist politics by highlighting the ethical considerations that motivate her going to war. These differences in the articulation of the *topos* constitute variations of the same ideological position, for Athens consistently relied on its self-definition as compassionate toward the suffering of others. Thus, the city that promoted its military superiority by emphasizing its compassion and pity should not be seen as inconsistent with the city that boasted of its democratic tradition by invoking humanitarian causes.[54]

ENDNOTES

1. In addition to Euripides' *Suppliant Women* and *Heraclidae*, the same pattern surfaces also in Aeschylus' *Eumenides*, Sophocles' *Oedipus at Colonus*, and Euripides' *Medea* and *Heracles*.

2. Loraux 1986: 66–72. My discussion draws on that of Loraux, who examines the construction of a collective Athenian civic identity within the context of encomiastic literature. Her analysis of the funeral oration as a whole sheds light on some of the complexities and contradictions that characterize Athenian democratic civic ideology. On the definition and discussion of different aspects of pity, see Burkert 1955; Stevens 1944: 1–25; Sternberg's chapter in this volume; Konstan 2001.

3. See Tsitsiridis 1998 on 244e2–3. For a detailed discussion of civic pity in the orators, see Konstan (2001: Ch. 2) and Sternberg (1998: 87–117), who also treats historiography.

4. The bibliography on the Athenian empire is extensive; I refer selectively to Meiggs 1972 and the chapters by P. J. Rhodes, D. Lewis, and A. Andrewes in *CAH* 5². More recently, see Boedeker and Raaflaub 1998. For an analysis of democratic contradictions in tragedy, see Dougherty 1996. On different aspects of pity and power in Greek literature, see David Konstan's and Donald Lateiner's contributions in this volume.

5. Johnson and Clapp in the following chapter, by contrast, maintain that the ideal self-image of Athens imparted notions of compassion and understanding toward the suffering of others among Athenian citizens in the audience. The psychological and didactic force of tragedy is indisputable. Indeed, one cannot deny that Athenians may have viewed themselves as more compassionate than the Spartans and their allies. This, however, does not eliminate the inconsistency between the ideal and the reality of Athenian conduct in the political arena. The self-representation of the Athenians as responsive toward the suffering of non-Athenians, in particular, may have invited a variety of responses, ranging from national pride and self-justification to questioning and skepticism. Though Athenians may have gained lessons in empathy, the plays continued to serve an important ideological function and offered a sophisticated commentary on the complex relationship between pity and power.

6. Loraux 1986; Mills 1997: 43–78.

7. Kierdorf 1966: 89–95. See also Boedeker (1998: 195–96), who also cites Hdt. 7.161 and Thuc. 1.73–74. She rightly points out that the Athenians emphasized their contributions in the Persian wars as a means of justifying their hegemony.

8. For the treatment of both these episodes in oratory and other genres, see Heath (1987: 65 n. 52): "(i) Burial of the Seven: Hdt. 9.27; Pl. *Mnx.* 239b; Xen. *Hell.* 6.5.46; Lys. 2.7–10; Isocr. 4.54–65, 12.168–74. (ii) Heraclidae: Hdt. 9.27; Pl. *Mnx.* 239b; Xen. *Mem.* 3.5.10, *Hell.* 6.5.47; Ar. *Rhet.* 1396a; Lys. 2.11–16; Isocr. 4.54–65, 5.33–4, 6.42, 12.194. Note Isocr. 12.168: 'Who does not know, or who has not heard from the tragedians . . .' – this of (i); Pl. *Mnx.* 239b claims that both (i) and (ii) are commonplaces in the poets . . . " Aeschylus also wrote plays on both topics; neither his *Eleusinians* (frag. 53a, 54 Radt) nor his *Heraclidae* (frag. 73b-77 Radt) is extant.

9. On the dating of the funeral oration, see Loraux (1986: 56–75), who argues for a date in the 460s.

10. Loraux 1986: 64–65.

11. Isoc. 4.55–56: "nor that ancestral custom and law (*palaion êthos kai patrion nomon*) be abolished"; Isoc. 12.170–1: "that the city will not allow that they [the Thebans] transgress the common law of all the Greeks (*ton nomon ton koinon hapantôn tôn Hellênôn*)"; Lys. 2.9: "[the Seven] after not being granted the ancestral honor (*patriou timês*) and deprived of the Greek custom (*Hellênikou nomou*)."

12. The explicit expression of pity in relation to the burial of the Seven occurs in Euripides' *Suppliant Women* (e.g., 167–75, 187–90, 277–85). On the psychology of pity, see Sternberg in this volume.

13. See Naiden (2000: 259–65) on the difficult question of how to reconcile pity with justice in the context of supplication. Justice and pity, by contrast, are not at variance in these

examples of political supplication that reflected the standard of Athenian conduct in encomiastic literature. For pity displayed toward suppliants, often because of their secondary position toward the supplicated, see Aesch. *Supp.* 481–89. The Danaids are granted protection and residence (609–12).

14. Loraux 1986: 67–68; Mills 1997: 55, 77–78, 105–6, 109–10; Sternberg 1998: 103–6; Konstan 2001: 81.

15. Sternberg's chapter in this volume considers pity to be closer to a raw rather than a complex emotion; Konstan (2001: 1–25) places greater emphasis on the cognitive processes involved in evaluating pity as an emotion.

16. This is a variation on the pity and anger motif; see Allen 1999: 194.

17. Translation by G. Kennedy in Sprague 1972.

18. See also Eur. *Supp.* 339–41.

19. See Kierdorf (1966: 90–95) and, most recently, Forsdyke (2001: 329–58).

20. De Romilly 1979: 97–112.

21. Oakley in his chapter acknowledges the potential influence of the increase of Athenian power on the representation of pity in classical art, which also coincided with the heyday of tragedy.

22. On the connection between pity and interest, see Naiden's (2000: 261–64) comments on Diodotos' speech in the Mytilenean debate: "Here, then, is an argument for pity that disguises itself as an argument for profit or advantage (*to sumpheron*), but it is in truth an argument about grand strategy, a thoughtful imperialist's argument" (264).

23. Dem. 10.46–48, for example, blames the Athenians for neglecting their ancestral role as helpers of those treated unjustly in view of the current threat from Macedon.

24. See Rachel Sternberg's introduction in this volume.

25. Loraux (1986: 79–98) also argues that the funeral oration justifies the imperial power of Athens by disguising it as the pursuit of excellence (*aretê*). See also Shapiro 1996: 221.

26. See n. 4 above.

27. See Strassburger 1958: 17–40; Mills 1997: 79–86; and Donald Lateiner's chapter in this volume. Lateiner argues that Thucydides explicitly denies that Athens acted out of pity. Perhaps the strongest renunciation of pity by the Athenians comes from the Melian dialogue, where the Athenians argue that the strong prevail while the weak are forced to yield (Thuc. 5.89).

28. The ideal of *polupragmosunê,* which is associated with Athens' military activity and the praise of Athens in the funeral orations (e.g., Thuc. 2.40.4), is refashioned in tragedy: Athens fights defensive wars on behalf of the protection of suppliants and exiles. On *polupragmosunê,* see Ehrenberg 1947: 46–67; Bond 1988 *ad* 1163, who also cites Eur. *Supp.* 576; and Dodds 1960 *ad* 389–92. See also Blundell 1993: 300–1 and Mills 1997: 1–78.

29. Goldhill 1990: 58–76.

30. Pickard-Cambridge 1988: 58.

31. Ober and Strauss 1990: 235–40.

32. The pattern has been noted by Heath (1987: 64): "A recurrent pattern may be observed: Athens magnanimously receives a suppliant, and successfully defends his cause; in

consequence, the city receives some benefit, so that the glorious deed becomes by way of aetiology, an affirmation and celebration of the city's present well-being: an augury of prosperity for the city in the words of the Aeschylean *Life*." See also Kearns (1989: 50–53), who notes that savior-heroes in tragedy were predominantly non-Attic in origin.

33. On supplication, see most recently Naiden (2000), who explores systematically the definition of supplication as a *nomos*.

34. For Athens as represented by *nomos*, see Soph. *OC* 1382 and Eur. *Supp.* 430–31. For *nomos* as an expression of Athenian democracy, especially in literary sources, see Ostwald 1986: 83, 250, 252, 258, 273. Note Theseus' concern for law also in Eur. *HF* 1322–23. Translations for Sophocles' *Oedipus at Colonus* are from Lloyd-Jones 1994 and for Euripides' *Heraclidae* from Kovacs 1995.

35. See Isoc. 4.41. On *eleutheria*, see Raaflaub 2004.

36. I note briefly that Kleon in the Mytilenean debate argues that democracy is incompatible with ruling over others (Thuc. 3.37), though I cannot discuss in detail the problems and contradictions arising from Athens' character as a democratic empire.

37. Democracy was characterized as milder compared to other constitutions (e.g. Dem. 22.52, 24.170–71; Isoc. 4.47 [due to philosophy], 7.20). Athenian laws were established with a view toward alleviating human misfortune (Dem. 23.69–70) or for the benefit of those who are unjustly treated (Thuc. 2.37.3). See further Mills 1997: 56–78.

38. For the most recent treatment of *asulia* in Greek tragedy, see Grethlein 2003. For the differentiation between asylum and supplication, see Naiden 2000: 51–53 with ample bibliography.

39. On the dating of Soph. *OC*, see Edmunds 1996: 87–88. On the relationship between tragedy and history, see most recently Pelling 1997b, and on history and ideology, see his conclusion (1997b: 213–24). On definitions of ideology in general, see Eagleton 1991: 1–31.

40. Thuc. 2.39. Gauthier (1988: 24) notes, however, that the expulsion of foreigners was practiced only under exceptional circumstances.

41. On pity and sight, see Sternberg 1998: 61–68.

42. Compare the Plataians' address (Isoc. 14.1–2) that includes some of the same *topoi* (e.g., Athens' reputation for helping others, Athenian piety and justice); see further Naiden 2000: 206–9. Sternberg (1998: 88–96) argues that pity is associated with virtues, but is not a virtue itself.

43. On the object of pity, see Sternberg 1998: 30–40.

44. Vidal-Naquet 1990: 329–59.

45. On foreigners, see more recently Baslez 1984; Lonis 1988. On foreigners in tragedy, see Vidal-Naquet 1997: 109–119.

46. On naturalization in Athens, see Osborne 1983.

47. On the praise of Athens in Sophocles' *Oedipus at Colonus*, see Knox 1964: 154–56; Blundell 1993: 287–306; Vidal-Naquet 1990: 335–39; Zeitlin 1990b: 130–67.

48. See further Mills 1997: 164–85. On Theseus' exile, see Jebb on 562, 563, 564; Mills 1997: 172. Sophocles is referring to the epic story of Theseus' childhood in Troezen and his return to Athens where he acquired the throne. On the praise of Athens in the play, see Knox 1964: 154–56; Blundell 1993: 287–306; Vidal-Naquet 1990: 335–39.

49. The issue of whether Oedipus acquires citizenship in Athens is a vexed one. The case against citizenship, to which I do not subscribe, is made by Vidal-Naquet in his now classic essay, "Oedipus between Two Cities" (1990: 329–59). Naiden (2000: 253) notes that suppliants as a rule were not granted citizenship.

50. There are numerous references to the "benefit" that Oedipus will bestow: *onêsis* "benefit" (288, 452), *kerdos* "profit" (72, 92, 578–79, 1421), *ôphelêsis* "benefit" (401), *arkesis* "help" (73), *dôron* "gift" (577), and *alkê* "protection" (1524). Oedipus is also cast as *sôtêr*; see 457–60, 463. For a political interpretation of *sôtêria*, see Edmunds 1996: 142–46.

51. See most recently Mendelsohn 2002 for an interpretation of politics and ideology in connection to issues of gender in this play.

52. For a discussion of the historical interpretations of the play, see Allan 2001: 43–46. On the enemy-hero, see Visser 1982: 403–28. Wiles (1997: 193 and 195 with notes) discusses in detail the supplication of Zeus Agoraios by the Heraclidae at Marathon. For the tradition associating the Heraclidae with the Altar of Pity, see Wilkins 1993: xix, 52–53, 60. For a discussion of the historical interpretations of the play, see Allan 2001: 43–46. On the enemy-hero, see Visser 1982: 403–28.

53. Ferguson 2003.

54. I would like to thank warmly Rachel Hall Sternberg for comments and observations that have greatly improved this chapter, and for organizing with Corey Brennan a most inspiring conference on the topic of Pity at Rutgers University in March 2002, where this chapter was originally presented. Further thanks are due to Danielle Allen and the seminar group on Plato's *Menexenus* at the University of Chicago for the stimulating discussion on pity as an emotion in political life. This chapter is dedicated to my brother Apostolos with thanks for his strength, wisdom, and generosity.

Athenian Tragedy: An Education in Pity

James F. Johnson and Douglas C. Clapp

◎▣◎

THE ABSENCE OF PITY FROM THE POLITICAL SPHERE OF ATHENS AT its imperial height, as argued in this volume, contrasts sharply with the centrality of compassion in the tragedies that helped define Athenian civic culture. For David Konstan, tragedy teaches that pity must yield to politics. Donald Lateiner can find little pity in Herodotus and finds only denials of its efficacy in Thucydides. To Angeliki Tzanetou, compassion in certain suppliant dramas represents for Athens little more than an ideological commitment to appearing generous. We contend, on the contrary, that a wider survey of tragedy shows compassion to be a powerful response to human suffering, a response that transcends narrow political considerations.

With his famous conclusion that a successful tragedy must evoke pity and fear in its audience, Aristotle leaves no doubt about the close relationship between the tragic enterprise and the compassion it evokes.[1] Pity also plays a significant role within the action of many plays, as all three of the great Athenian tragedians inform their plots with explicit references to pity.[2] Both the plots and the language constructing those plots draw attention to the response of one human being to the suffering of another.

Such a powerfully moving performance was also, in the words of Edith Hall, "shaping and shaped by" the civic ideology of the Athenian democracy.[3] This connection has been well documented.[4] If Aristotle was right about the pity, and if modern scholars correctly adduce the ideologically complex nature of the City Dionysia and its tragic competition, then a connection exists between the cathartic relief of emotional

release and the radically democratic and unapologetically imperial political identity of an Athenian citizen. It is this very connection, according to Stephen Salkever, that lies at the heart of the conflicting
views of tragedy held by Plato and Aristotle.[5] Plato wanted to protect
the audience of citizens from the emotional excess of tragedy, while
his contrary student Aristotle wanted that same audience to receive
a *katharsis* from its emotional intensity. For both, the key lay in the
education of the *dêmos*, the people of Athens.

This was a people that constructed its self-image, according to
Tzanetou, to appear compassionate and selfless, even when the actions
of the city belied this careful pose. We might, therefore, conclude that
the intensity of the tragic festival affirmed an essential and yet illusory
element of the Athenian identity. The male citizens of Athens wanted
to believe in their compassion, and tragedy provided convincing evidence of it. Having experienced the *katharsis*, the Athenians could get
back to work ruling their empire with an iron fist. This interpretation
suggests a superficiality to the whole tragic enterprise, a superficiality
seemingly consistent with the emotional distance that scholars have
assumed necessary for experiencing pity.[6]

The following analysis shows that the compassion depicted in Greek
tragedy is anything but superficial. One who pities must reflect on the
nature of the human condition, must realize the reciprocal obligations
of human relationships, and must move beyond words and respond
with deeds. Pity was not a fleeting emotion derived from an engross-
ing form of entertainment; it was, rather, the very stuff of the moral
education expected of tragedy. We do not know what the Athenians
learned, but we can say with certainty that the tragic festival annually
confronted them with lessons full of compassion.

In order to isolate the compassion portrayed for the tragic audience,
this chapter focuses on the interaction between characters on stage
rather than on Aristotle's notion of pity as a tragic emotion that affects

the spectator. Our close textual readings examine the words and actions that signal the presence of compassion. We are not looking for the empty sentiment now implied by the English word "pity." Tragic *oiktos* or *eleos*, as our study of its depiction on the stage demonstrates, cannot be divorced from action.

Nor do we follow the modern tendency to equate pity with "altruism" and to conceive of it as "moral" behavior of a modern, post-Kantian sort. The Athenians did not act compassionately solely out of an abstract sense of "right" or out of a notion of "selflessness," as we moderns tend to idealize such behavior. They instead characterized even acts of compassion in terms of reciprocity.[7] We shall see in Athenian drama how reciprocity and self-interest functioned in appeals for compassion and in the acts of compassion answering those appeals.[8] We begin with a close look at Sophocles' *Ajax* and Euripides' *Hippolytus*, two classic plays that exemplify contrasting extremes of compassion's operation in tragic drama. Then we step back for a broader survey of tragedy to establish the consistent presentation of pity by the Athenian playwrights. In the course of our analysis, we examine the reflective and reciprocal nature of tragic compassion. Finally, we conclude with an extended argument against Plato's charge that tragedy encouraged thoughtless overreaction. Pity stands out in high relief as a virtue in the tragic performances, and this should reflect the significance accorded to compassionate behavior by the Athenians.

MODES OF COMPASSION

Ajax by Sophocles and *Hippolytus* by Euripides offer a dense matrix of meanings.[9] We do not argue that compassion is what drives these plays. We contend, rather, that because pity and its lack inform the action, the plays open a window onto Athenian modes of compassion. Both Sophocles and Euripides imbue their dramas with a subtle consideration of compassion and construct a lesson in the proper reaction to human frailty. The authors, however, teach compassion in very different ways. In *Ajax*, compassion is conspicuously present; in *Hippolytus*, it is conspicuously absent.

The audience's journey into the realm of pity and fear begins immediately in the two plays, as vindictive goddesses loom over the openings of both: Athena eagerly awaits the chance to expose Ajax's humiliation to Odysseus, while Aphrodite pronounces the coming destruction of Hippolytus. The ominous presence of these Olympian divinities at the outset of the tragedies sets the tone for what follows.[10] William Barrett pointed out that Euripides' depiction of Aphrodite "serves to induce our sympathy with the victim."[11] Likewise, compassion is the correct response to Ajax.[12] From the outset of both plays, then, Sophocles and Euripides encourage sympathy in the audience and so establish a sensitivity to compassion in the dramas. The tragedians diverge, however, in how they fulfill these expectations. In Sophocles' *Ajax*, compassion between the human characters counterbalances the pitiless power of divinity. In Euripides' *Hippolytus*, only a final, fleeting moment of humanity relieves the relentless cruelty of the drama. Both force the audience to confront not only human suffering but also human responses to that suffering.

When Athena greets Odysseus in front of Ajax's tent, she holds all the cards. She is invisible. She has watched Odysseus in his dogged pursuit of Ajax. She knows that Ajax is guilty, that he is in his tent. And yet she asks Odysseus his purpose. Sir Richard Jebb's "touch of divine irony" is more than "dramatically useful."[13] Athena relishes her superior position, and she very much wants Odysseus to learn what she knows (13). The goddess will unveil Ajax in his madness in order that Odysseus may inform the other Greeks (66–7). When Ajax emerges, Athena mocks his blindness. Her attitude exemplifies the proverbial expression she had used in her efforts to convince Odysseus to enjoy the spectacle (79): "Is not laughing at one's enemies the most delightful kind of laughter?'"[14] As Mary Whitlock Blundell has shown, Sophoclean tragedy complicates this adage uttered so blithely by Athena by blurring the distinction between one's friends and one's enemies.[15] In Ajax, Odysseus has an ally who is also an enemy (78).[16] His harm should be Odysseus' delight.

It is not. Odysseus, confronted by the spectacle of Ajax raving mad, takes no pleasure in his enemy's plight. As Athena brags about her power (118), Odysseus responds with compassion (121): "I pity him." He immediately explains his reaction, presumably because Ajax and his grotesque behavior hardly seem worthy of such sympathy. Odysseus can pity Ajax, despite the latter's crimes, because he realizes that such a downfall can strike any person at any time.[17] Compassion, then, is premised on an understanding of the common inheritance of suffering shared by all human beings. It results from reflection leading to an enlightened sense of self-interest. The pity felt by Odysseus does not correspond to a hierarchical concern for superiority.[18]

Odysseus' compassion is for an equal, a fellow member of the Greek warrior elite. It is also for a personal enemy. Interestingly, his pity emerges when Ajax is helpless – possessed by a god-given madness. We are presented with a paradox: Odysseus pities a madman who at that very moment is showing no pity to the captive he believes is Odysseus (105–6). But Odysseus, too, feels helpless, and compassion elides the boundaries used to construct his identity as a Greek warrior with friends to help and enemies to harm.

Sophocles underscores this lesson by reminding the audience of Odysseus' newly acquired wisdom: the chorus explicitly but wrongly expect that Odysseus will delight in Ajax's suicide (955–60).[19] And Sophocles brings Odysseus and his sympathy back on stage to conclude the play. The drama finds resolution because Odysseus acts on his compassion to persuade Agamemnon to allow the burial of Ajax' body.[20] Odysseus' pity begins and ends this drama. Since Sophocles has constructed this sympathetic ring around the tragic action, we should also pay careful attention to the dynamic of pity running through the heart of the play – a dark play coursing with hatred, dripping with images of slaughter.[21]

The Ajax who receives Odysseus' sympathy is stained with blood. The gruesome appearance and maniacal behavior he exhibits during his madness lie in tension with the compassion expressed by Odysseus.[22] Sophocles preserves this tension through the first episode. The chorus and then Tekmessa enter the stage grieving for their lord and master (172–207). Their own suffering coupled with their concern for Ajax offer the audience an indirect yet convincing picture of a noble hero whose madness has shocked those closest to him. The apprehension shared by Tekmessa and the chorus reminds the audience that Ajax is a human being who has the affection of others. This validates Odysseus' readiness to see Ajax's humiliation as an emblem of the human condition.

Even the recovered Ajax, however, belies the sympathy his plight has aroused. His harsh treatment of Tekmessa, when added to his previous ranting before Athena, would seem to undermine this compassion.[23] Ajax fails to display his humanity when he rejects both Tekmessa's plea for him to pity their child (510) and a similar plea from the chorus (525–6). A frustrated and apparently heartless Ajax declares that women want too much pity; Sophocles uses the rare superlative *philoiktiston* (580). Such disdain for compassion, in light of Odysseus' lesson that suffering demands pity, demonstrates that Ajax remains ignorant of the human condition.

He enters his hut ready to commit suicide. Having forcefully declared his intent, Ajax creates every expectation that the report of his death will soon follow.[24] Such a report, however, would be unsatisfactory. As John Moore rightly hypothesizes, "if at line 646, instead of Ajax' entrance, a messenger were to come out of the tent and announce his death, the result would be mere confusion and dismay."[25] That is due to the unresolved tension between his unsympathetic behavior, on the one hand, and, on the other, the sympathy accorded to Ajax in the perspectives of Odysseus, Tekmessa, and the chorus. The audience wants to pity Ajax because, as Gregory Dobrov points out, the audience shares Odysseus' position as spectator and so may adopt his perspective.[26] Consequently, Ajax has become an object of sympathy even when he seems utterly repulsive.[27] The pity is for a human being destroyed by fate, but the victim refuses to be human.

Ajax does not then kill himself. Instead, he returns to the stage with self-awareness and compassion. After a poignant examination of the changes wrought by time, Ajax offers sympathy to Tekmessa and Eurysakes (651–2). Although this passage lies at the enigmatic heart of the play's meaning, scholars generally agree that the profession of sympathy reflects the true feelings of Ajax.[28] Like Odysseus before him, Ajax becomes capable of compassion when he recognizes the ephemeral nature of human existence, and his experience of pity marks his return to humanity.[29] Ajax has learned the lesson that Odysseus faced in the prologue, even though his reflection has not altered his heroic character.[30] Instead, Ajax' musings on change lead him to reciprocate Tekmessa's concern for him. He pities her, and his kind words spoken in her presence fulfill the action demanded by tragic compassion. Since Sophocles renders compassion as a noble quality in Odysseus, Ajax too achieves a nobility hitherto absent. The tension regarding his suicide thus dissipates, not because Ajax will live, but because he will not die as an inhuman monster. Instead, he will die as a human being destroyed by the bitter realities of life.

Sophocles presents the wisdom first shown by Odysseus and now realized by Ajax as the only source of meaning amid human suffering.[31] Such meaning does not, of course, obviate the suffering. Rather, incomprehensible pain is recast in the comprehensible terms of compassion for that pain. What befalls Ajax admits of no explanation,[32] but Odysseus' pity can be explained: compassion is tied inextricably to understanding. Agamemnon and Menelaos, who lack both compassion and understanding, provide proof by counterexample.[33]

The inhumane Atridae would feel at home in *Hippolytus*, for there one can find little understanding. Euripides' play, like *Ajax*, opens with a display of divine ferocity. Aphrodite wants recompense for Hippolytus' refusal to grant her the honor due a divinity.[34] She has authored the plot that follows to illustrate this lesson (6): "I lay low all those whose thoughts toward me are proud." Although this axiom presents standard Greek theology,[35] the language of the goddess compels compassion for the suffering she causes Hippolytus, Phaedra, and Theseus.[36] Despite her claim to the contrary (20), Aphrodite certainly sounds spiteful toward Hippolytus,[37] and we sense foreboding at the careful planning that lies behind her revenge (23–4, 28): the hard work has been completed, so now she can sit back and admire her handiwork.[38] As for Phaedra, Aphrodite states explicitly that the queen's death carries little weight (47–50). Nor does the goddess display any compunction about using Theseus to kill his own son (43–6).[39] Then there remains her mysterious pronouncement (42): "I shall reveal the matter to Theseus and it will come to light." Since Aphrodite does no such thing, Barrett concludes: "Euripides is not being straightforward."[40] I would suggest that the plot's other author, Aphrodite, is not being straightforward and so underscores Theseus' role as an additional victim. The playwright further emphasizes Aphrodite's lack of compassion through the contrast with the prayer of Hippolytus' older servant (114–20), who begs the goddess for understanding and forgiveness. We already know that Aphrodite's plans are fixed,[41] so the servant's prayer highlights its certain rejection.[42] His voice stands almost alone in the play as an attempt to mitigate the harsh realities of human existence.[43] His brief echo of the ethos displayed by Sophocles' Odysseus quickly fades away amid the rising clamor in which every action engenders a pitiless reaction.

The brutal reality begins to unfold behind the door that initially muffles the angry shouts of Hippolytus (565–600). Neither Phaedra nor the audience needs to hear his words to know the reason for his wrath but they also know that the queen does not deserve such scorn, as she herself is a victim.[44] The audience, like Phaedra, realizes that the nurse has betrayed her mistress. Hippolytus does not. Considering only the affront to his chastity, he does not give a moment's thought to Phaedra's condition. It is in ignorance, then, that Hippolytus responds with condemnation. His harsh diatribe against women underscores his lack of understanding (616–68).[45] Phaedra, in turn, prepares a pitiless response of her own.[46] Her renewed resolve to commit suicide (599–600) becomes a plot against Hippolytus (715–31).[47] Despite her own suffering, Phaedra offers no understanding for the lot of Hippolytus. Her rationale shares Aphrodite's cruel sentiment (47–50): one life will not stand in the way of preserving her honor (720–21). The fierceness of her wrath fails to acknowledge human limits as she unknowingly emulates the goddess's merciless attitude.

Aphrodite's final victim, Theseus, returns home to news of Phaedra's death. As soon as he discovers Phaedra's note accusing Hippolytus, the expected outpouring of uncompromising wrath bursts forth. So Hippolytus assailed the Nurse and Phaedra; so Phaedra reviled the Nurse and plotted against her stepson. The anger of Theseus takes the form of a curse in Poseidon's name and of banishment in the name of the state (887–90, 893–98). The audience can only second the chorus' fruitless attempt to stop Theseus (891–92).[48] The king rejects their suggestion that he should wait and learn. Theseus' final words as he casts his son out of the palace confirm the tenor of this unrelenting drama (1089): "No pity for your exile moves my heart."[49]

This is, in fact, one of only two occurrences of the root *oikt-* in *Hippolytus*[50] – not because Euripides does not know or like the word, but because the tragedian chooses to make this a pitiless drama.[51] It is, of course, more than compassion that is absent from Hippolytus' tirade, from Phaedra's trick, from Theseus' curse. Miscommunication and misunderstanding rule the day and lead to the misapplication of helping friends and harming enemies.[52] This failure to communicate parallels the failure to reflect. All three characters lack the awareness of human frailty that moved Odysseus in *Ajax*. Odysseus waited and learned and, as a result, could no longer despise his personal enemy. Such patience, such an effort to understand another human being, is absent from *Hippolytus*. It is this failure to consider the human condition that leads to the pitiless responses.

Since compassion has been distinctly absent from the play's action, it seems fitting that Artemis will move the tragedy toward its resolution with a promise of merciless vengeance. But a moment of forgiveness does arise, as Hippolytus' patron deity effects a reconciliation between father and son. Critics have disagreed as to the proper interpretation of this reconciliation. George Dimock admires the "height of understanding" that Artemis brings to Theseus and Hippolytus,[53] while Bernard Knox and David Kovacs emphasize the divine departure, an exit that leaves the mortals free to understand each other.[54] Hans-Peter Stahl takes a dimmer view. He finds the reconciliation inadequate, as the brief connection between father and son is lopsided and short-lived.[55] All the readings, however, posit a vacuum of compassion; they differ in their conclusion as to whether and how that vacuum is filled. Euripides may or may not be offering his audience a "happy ending," but in either case he sets before his fellow citizens and their guests an evocative portrait of human suffering. No less than Sophocles, Euripides constructs a positive valuation for compassion. In Sophocles, pity helps resolve the problem of suffering.

In Euripides, the problem of suffering is aggravated by the lack of pity.

THE TRAGEDIANS' GOAL

Ajax and *Hippolytus* reflect the tendency of tragic theater to promote and reinforce the Athenian public's deep valuation of compassion. That Athenian audiences expected to be stimulated in this way is shown, most obviously, by the fact that the Greek tragedians themselves used so many techniques for arousing strong feelings of sympathy in their audiences. Aristotle, of course, has analyzed the ways in which the manipulation of the plot can arouse and intensify such feelings. There were also the abundant laments and expressions of compassion made by various characters, as well as frequent cries of pain or sorrow by the sufferers themselves.[56] These later became sources of Plato's objections to tragedy, as we shall see, but they were regular features of tragedy which suggested to the audience that sympathy was the appropriate emotion to feel. A common type of statement in tragedy that especially tended to encourage identification and sympathy in a member of the audience was the gnomic utterance that expressed the common frailty of humanity, the brevity of life, and mankind's relative lack of power and knowledge, usually in contrast to the gods'.[57]

The occasional explicit statement in tragedies that the civilized or humane person tends to feel compassion coincides with the tragedians' goal of arousing compassion in their audience and provides further evidence that development of compassion was an important element in tragedy's civic education. Aeschylus' Pelasgos (*Supp.* 489) acknowledges that all properly feel "kindness" (*eunoia*) toward the weak. In *Prometheus Bound* (242–44), the chorus at one point say that one who "does not sympathize" (οὐ συνασχαλᾷ) with Prometheus' suffering is "iron-minded and made of stone." But such statements are especially common in the late fifth-century poet Euripides. Euripides has the chorus of his *Cyclops* call Polyphemos "Pitiless" (*Nêlês*) for sacrificing the suppliants at his hearth (369–70).[58] In *Iphigenia among the Taurians*, the Hellenic Iphigenia is uncomfortable with the pitiless barbarity that is imposed upon her because she must sacrifice humans while among the Taurians (225–26) and then with her own incipient savagery after she hears of her brother's death (344 ff.). In Euripides' *Electra* (294–95), Orestes remarks that the wise and educated (*sophoi*) tend to feel *oiktos*, whereas the ignorant do not. In *Heracles* (299–301), Megara contrasts *sophoi* and nobly reared enemies, who are disposed to show *aidôs* ("reverence"), with the stupid (*skaios*) enemy, who is not so disposed. A similar idea is expressed in Frag. 407 of Euripides: "It is a lack of refinement (*amousia*) not to shed a tear for pitiable things (*oiktra*)."[59] Aristotle (*Rh.* 2.8.4, 1385b27) later will say that the educated (*hoi pepaideumenoi*) feel pity because they are properly foresighted (*eulogistoi*). The examples from tragedy show that Athenian tragedians (especially Euripides) often explicitly associated feelings of sympathy with wisdom and civilization in contrast to the barbarity or crudeness of the pitiless.

We can now return to the depiction of compassion in the interaction of characters on the tragic stage. A common plot that involves the exhibition of compassion by one character toward another is built around the suppliant theme.[60] In suppliant plays, the focus of interest and sympathy is placed in large part on a character who might be called the "saving hero," in contrast to the "suffering hero" of many better-known, prototypical tragedies, such as *Oedipus the King*.[61] When the "saving hero" is an Athenian king – a legendary hero and ancestor – he represents the *dêmos* and expresses the Athenian sense of cultural and political identity. Such "saving heroes" are role models: they exemplify ideal Athenian qualities and behavior. By showing Athenian kings as compassionate leaders, the tragic poets promoted compassionate behavior.[62]

Since David Konstan and Angeliki Tzanetou, in earlier chapters, have already dealt with suppliant dramas, our limited purpose here is to argue that compassion in them is not negated by considerations of interest or reciprocity. Rather, these may coincide and mutually reinforce one another. Typically, the suppliant's appeal for compassion was based on commonplace beliefs about the fragility of fortune but could also adduce ties of kinship or the mutual benefits and obligations of *xenia* or *philia*. All these relationships contained elements of reciprocity, and indeed the suppliant was expected to reciprocate, if possible, for his or her salvation at the hands of the champion.[63] Also, a champion might be asked to show compassion or might offer compassion on his own on the grounds that someday he might be in a similar state of vulnerability. Even this last has an element of reciprocity, in that the champion looks to a kind of return, but it is indirect, since such a reversal of fortune may never occur and since the present recipient of compassion may not be the one to offer such compensatory salvation.

In Euripides' *Children of Heracles*, Iolaus employs traditional appeals for compassionate aid when he invokes family ties, reciprocity, and the defenselessness of the Heraclidae (181–231). Although Demophon does not explicitly cite compassion among the reasons why the city should protect the suppliants, it is implicit in his acceptance of their request.[64] Iolaus had asked for rescue from the aggression of Kopreos (223–31), and the chorus of Marathonian men had expressed their pity in response (ᾤκτιρ'), acknowledging that the children's suffering was undeserved – and thus appropriately pitied (232–35). Demophon's assertion of support for them flows directly from this sequence of events (236 ff.), while the protection of suppliants is presented as a form of *aretê*. Iolaus then elaborately praises Demophon for his exhibition of compassion, calling him εὐγενής ("noble," "well-born"), ἐξ ἐσθλῶν . . . φύς ("descended from the best"), and one who preserves his father's glory (320–28). Demophon is being commended for nobility, valor – and his exhibition of compassion in honoring the suppliants' appeals. Of course, a suppliant praising his champion is somewhat like a starving man complimenting the chef, but Iolaus' accolades clearly link nobility and the compassionate protection of suppliants.

This positive outcome is problematized when Demophon discovers that oracles demand the sacrifice to Persephone of a young daughter of a noble father. Still, it is notable that Demophon persists in his determination to find a way to fulfill his pledge of compassionate assistance.[65] That Demophon's compassion does not continue to be mentioned does not mean that it does not continue to function as part of his motivation until the rescue of the children is accomplished. This is part of the linkage between compassion and action that stems from the heroic tradition of Homer: the suppliant does not appeal merely for the champion's sympathetic sentiment toward him or her, but for the saving action or rescue that heroic compassion entails.[66] Once the appeal for compassion is made and accepted by the champion, any response toward the satisfaction of that appeal can be assumed to involve compassion on the part of the champion, whether or not the champion continues to acknowledge it as a motive. In Demophon's persistent compassion in this play, Euripides provided his Athenian audience with a model worthy of emulation.

The connection between the persistent compassion and the *aretê* of the Athenian protector is continued in Euripides' *Suppliant Women*. The Argive mothers of the Seven are suppliants appealing to Athens as a "city which knows misery when she sees it" (190); Theseus, its leader, is called *esthlos* ("noble," 191). The chorus of Argive women appeal to Aithra for compassionate aid based on both their common old age and on the natural empathy between mothers. But when Adrastus, who has come in common cause with the mothers, appeals to Theseus, the Athenian king is at first unwilling to assent (195–249). The chorus therefore intensify their appeal, and when Theseus sees his mother weeping for the women, he acknowledges that a feeling has come over him as well: κἀμὲ γὰρ διῆλθέ τι ("Something shot through me as well!" 288).[67] It is pity and grief for the women's suffering that Theseus feels here. The chorus have explicitly appealed for his compassion just before (263–85, esp. 280–81). Aithra then makes an appeal to her son in which she warns of the gods' vengeance if Theseus should fail to honor the suppliants and calls his attention to the great prestige that Theseus and Athens would gain by upholding the commonly accepted right of burial (297–331). Theseus agrees to become the women's champion, since these arguments justify his compassionate assistance.[68] Indeed, the fact that he later personally and with great emotion oversees the burial of the dead strongly suggests that compassion continues to function as at least part of his motivation. The messenger uses the verb *agapaô* ("to show loving care for the dead") to describe Theseus' attitude toward the deceased warriors (764–66).[69] Then, as Theseus presents the ashes to the mothers and sons of the fallen, he asks them to remember and honor Athens for its good deeds to them. Adrastus assures him that the Argives will remain grateful and seek to return action with action (1165–79). Note the expectation of reciprocal benefit here and Adrastus' easy acceptance of it: it is something expected by both parties and easily dealt with by both.[70] The goddess Athena requires that the Argives swear an oath to defend Athens' interests in the future.[71] As we saw in *Children of Heracles*, the valor of the city and the nobility of the leader who protects and honors suppliants are emphasized. Especially in *Suppliant Women*, compassion itself is depicted as a strong personal emotion that motivates the protector. It is also persistent: as in *Children of Heracles*, the fact that pity is not the explicit focus of argument does not negate its importance as Theseus' ultimate motive.

The play that perhaps best typifies Athenian idealism and the ideal of Athenian compassion from an Athenian perspective is Sophocles' *Oedipus at Colonus*. Oedipus is clearly the protagonist of this play, but an Athenian watching it would see Theseus, the greatest legendary Athenian hero, as representing his culture's ideal. Sophocles presents Theseus in this play as a man of virtue (1124–27), an ideal hero-king who possesses wisdom, decisive leadership, and courage.[72] As such, he serves as a model for Athenian civic education. Our argument here is that Theseus' compassion, as shown by his treatment of Oedipus and his family, is an integral part of the ideal qualities he displays and a major part of Sophocles' instruction of his fellow citizens.[73]

The suppliant in this play, Oedipus, presents special problems,[74] since he has committed both patricide and incest with his mother. Do the expectations of supplication apply to such a suppliant? Can such a suppliant claim divine protection? These considerations can be seen in the anxious reaction of the Old Men of Colonus.[75] What is most striking about Theseus' entrance at 551 ff. is that he immediately expresses his pity for Oedipus and gives assurance that Oedipus' request will be granted *in advance of* even hearing that request.[76] Theseus' first words in greeting this stranger merit close attention (551–59):

> *Hearing from many in the past the story of the bloody destruction (τὰς αἱματηρὰς . . . διαφθορὰς) of your eyes, I have recognized you, son of Laius, and now seeing you after this journey, I even more thoroughly understand your situation. Your rags and your miserable (δύστηνον) head show clearly who you are, and pitying you (σ᾽ οἰκτίσας) I wish to learn with what request of the city and of me you have appeared – you and your unfortunate helper (δύσμορος παραστάτις).[77]*

Theseus shows an awareness of the outcast's past sufferings that is heightened by the vision of Oedipus now. He goes on to say that he would *never* turn aside from rescuing *any* exile (560–68):[78]

> *Teach me. For you would speak of some terrible undertaking (δεινὴν . . . πρᾶξιν) for me to refuse to take part in it – I who know*

that I myself (ὅς οἶδά γ᾽ αὐτός) was reared as a foreigner (ξένος), just like you (ὥσπερ σύ), and how in a foreign land (ἐπὶ ξένης) I, alone of men, struggled with many dangers to my life, so that I could never turn aside from someone who was a foreigner (ξένον), just like you are now (ὥσπερ σὺ νῦν), and not save him. Because I know well, human being (ἀνὴρ) that I am, that I have no more a share of tomorrow than you do.

His compassionate response to Oedipus' suffering is based on his own experiences as a foreigner and on his deep understanding of the instability of human prosperity.[79] Does Theseus expect a return benefit from Oedipus? If so, he doesn't mention it.[80] Theseus' assurances entail a deeper notion of reciprocity: mutual assistance will make the world a better place. He acts in the implicit hope that if he were in such a circumstance, someone would rescue him.[81] We may note that since Theseus is a mature hero, unlike Neoptolemus in *Philoctetes*,[82] he readily shows the requisite compassionate response and the appropriate heroic behavior that flows from it. Indeed, in *Oedipus at Colonus*, Sophocles presents the complete Athenian hero, whose response to suffering is emotionally warm and humane as well as being behaviorally effective. Theseus is not a cold, dispassionate *pater patriae*,[83] but a hero who, for Sophocles, represented the best of Athenian qualities and embodied the city's best hope in the critical final stages of the war with Sparta.[84] Theseus' compassion was at the core of those qualities.

The other side of the coin is that leaders who refuse to honor a suppliant appeal are often depicted as cowardly or corrupt. Euripides gives us many examples of these. We will look at one. Euripides' Hecuba (in the play of the same name) meets with a sophistic refusal of compassion when she begs Odysseus to intercede for Polyxena, who must die to honor the grave of Achilles. Hecuba reminds Odysseus of the debt of reciprocity that he incurred when she spared his life in Troy. Odysseus responds that he is obligated only to save Hecuba's life and not that of her daughter (299 ff.). He then seeks to justify the girl's sacrifice as an honor due to the dead Achilles. Later, when Polyxena herself refuses to beg her life from Odysseus, who exhibits fear that she will do so (342–45), she is praised by the chorus for her nobility (379–81); Odysseus, by contrast, seems less than noble. Still later in the play Hecuba asks Agamemnon to show compassion by taking a just revenge on Polymestor, the murderer of her son (786–863). Agamemnon's hesitancy to honor the request of the suppliant openly and his agreement to provide only passive support may be contrasted with the heroic behavior of nobler characters in other plays.

Nevertheless, the Athenian tragedians did not always depict compassion as appropriate or desirable behavior. Because the suppliant had such powerful persuasive forces at his or her disposal – religious sanctions as well as claims of reciprocity – and because compassionate action was greatly reinforced by praise, the appeal for compassion also contained the potential for abuse. There was always the risk that a treacherous suppliant would arouse pity to perverse ends. This caused anxiety and ambivalence on the part of Athenians, reflecting their belief that they were especially subject to being moved by such appeals. What if the person asking for compassion was treacherous or intended harm to those he or she appealed to, or had other devious plans?[85]

Euripides, ever the "realist," explores this possibility in *Medea*. Here we see a treacherous appeal used not once, but twice. First, after Creon has announced Medea's banishment from Corinth, Medea assumes the suppliant pose and begs Creon the king to allow her to stay one day to make provision for her children; she strengthens this appeal by noting that Creon himself has children (271–347). Creon has already expressed twice his fear of Medea and his need to expel her before she can harm him (282–91, 316–23). When her supplication causes him to relent, he again expresses anxiety, remarking how his *aidôs* has harmed him in the past and showing a momentary prescience of the harm to come (348–51).

After Creon leaves the stage, Medea confirms the deadly duplicity of her suppliant stance (370–75) and sets her plan in motion.[86] Later in the play, Medea makes a second supplication: she begs Aegeus to give her asylum in Athens and promises to end his childlessness in recompense (708–18). Aegeus agrees, swears an oath demanded of him by Medea that he will protect her from her enemies, and in turn is praised by the Chorus as being *gennaios* ("noble," 762). Aegeus, as king of Athens, was no doubt intended to remind the Athenian audience of Athens' heritage as the sanctuary of suppliants (cf. 824 ff.). But any flattery that the praise of Aegeus may have reflected upon the audience was undercut by their recollection of the tradition of Medea in Athens: how she would later plot the murder of Theseus. Medea also sends the children as suppliants bearing gifts to the princess, gifts that will work the latter's gruesome death. Creon, in his attempt to save his daughter, only ends up sharing her death.[87] All attempts to show compassion in this play sooner or later recoil upon the one who pities.[88]

Treacherous appeals for compassion, however, are rare in tragic drama and alien to most people's concept of the "tragic." Indeed, because it portrayed so well the frailty of human beings' predicament and the ever-present possibility of calamity, tragedy in general tended to promote compassion as an appropriate response – both to the fates of the characters on its stage and, one would think, to the fates in life of their friends, families, and, perhaps occasionally, even enemies.[89] Tragedy as a public institution of the democratic state thus tended to promote responsible compassion in Athens' citizens.

PLATO'S CRITIQUE OF TRAGIC PITY

On the whole, then, we can say the tragedians taught the Athenians that compassion or pity was a good thing, provided it was applied appropriately to a worthy recipient. Tragedy's promotion of pity, however, was not universally appreciated in the Greco-Roman philosophical tradition.⁹⁰ Early in this tradition, not long after tragedy's golden age in fifth-century Athens, Plato or rather his character Socrates carried on what Plato characterizes as the "ancient quarrel between poetry and philosophy" in Books 2–3 and Book 10 of *The Republic*.⁹¹ We take the time to consider Plato's critique of tragic pity here since he was such an influential philosopher and since his arguments against tragic pity would seem to oppose the argument we have presented in the first two sections of this chapter, that tragedy, in promoting responsible com-passionate behavior, did serve to educate beneficially the Athenian audience of the fifth century. We should note here also that our re-sponse to Plato will be in terms of the tragic genre generally rather than specifically in terms of fifth-century Athenian tragedies. We do this because Plato constructs his argument in general terms: his arguments against tragedy, while specifically meant to apply to the conditions he creates in his ideal state, have been taken by readers (and probably were intended by Plato himself) to apply to the tragic genre generally, both as practiced in fifth- and fourth-century Athens and as practiced in other places and other times.

In Book 2 (376e ff.) of *The Republic*, where the subject is the best education for the Guardian class, Socrates' objections to tragedy are twofold: (1) that tragedy and epic show the gods as sources of evil in the world, whereas they are rightly shown only as sources of good, and (2) that these genres show heroes wailing and lamenting. These two objections are not unrelated in that the hero's laments are sometimes portrayed as being the result of his unjust suffering at the hands of a god or a god's agent. Still, the first objection is based on a fundamental belief about the gods: that they are always just and should not be shown doing immoral or disreputable things, such as deceiving one another or human beings or engaging in conflict with fellow deities, as they do in Hesiod's *Theogony*. Plato argues that such stories set bad examples for young people and lead to the loss of religion. Also subject to this type of objection are stories in which good people turn out to be miserable while the unjust prosper (392a–c). In response to this objection, we would suggest that a worldview that allows the tragic does not necessarily require that the gods be evil, but does require that misfortune and suffering exist in the world.

The second objection (387b–388e), however, is more pertinent to our subject here: that heroes should not be depicted as wailing or lamenting over their misfortunes. The examples Plato gives are both Homeric: (1) Achilles, son of a goddess, tossing back and forth on his bed, unable to sleep, or wandering on the shore and lamenting the loss of Patroklos (388b, cf. *Il.* 24.3–13), and (2) Priam, near to the gods by kin, supplicating and rolling in the dung at the sight of his son's corpse being abused by Achilles (388b, cf. *Il.* 22.407–15). Partly, this objection is based on Plato's assumptions about the character of heroes: that they should be shown to be self-sufficient and lacking fear, and, furthermore, that they should bear personal losses patiently, without lamenting. Instead, such laments should be given to men and women of lower character, that is, to sorts that the Guardian students would disdain to imitate. Also, gods should not be shown as lamenting, such as when Zeus laments the fated death of his son Sarpedon. Again, the problem is with modeling and the tendency of the young to imitate their models. In Plato's ideal state, the values of piety, courage, and self-control are primary virtues for the Guardian class, and he excludes stories that do not promote these values.

In Book 10, Plato takes up these issues again, particularly the emotional appeal of tragedy. His first type of argument there, however, has to do with tragedy's representation of reality. Socrates sets up an analogy between the artist and the poet and argues that the works of both are representations of the world of appearance, which itself is a poor representation of the world of ideas, the world of higher reality. Thus, for Plato, the world of a painting or that of a tragedy is a poor copy of life, which itself is a poor copy of the ultimate reality experienced by the philosopher. This type of argument is a complex one best left to philosophers and aestheticians, such as Aristotle, who are better qualified to argue it at length.[92] A counter-argument from history and literary tradition, however, should suffice to convince most people, if not everyone, that tragedy is more than a third-rate representation of reality: Homer and the Greek tragedians, along with many other artists and writers of other times and cultures, have stood the test of time as artists who represent life as most of us experience it in deep and significantly meaningful ways, including the portrayal of human suffering, grief, and compassion.[93]

Plato's major argument against tragedy, however, relates to its appeal to emotion. In the course of this discussion, Socrates presents a series of arguments (604b ff.) on why we should bear misfortunes "reasonably," that is, as quietly as possible and without resentment. First, Socrates argues that we can never be sure that what appears to be a misfortune may not turn out to be a blessing. Although this is certainly true sometimes in life, and we can all think of examples, most of us would deny that this is always or even often the case when severe misfortunes occur. In fact, the two examples from Plato cited earlier, Achilles' loss of Patroklos and Priam's loss of Hector, did not turn out to be "blessings in disguise" for either Achilles or Priam. One might argue that they gained immortal fame through these losses, but that prospect did little to minimize their sense of personal loss and pain at the time of their losses or even for the rest of their lives as portrayed by tradition.

Socrates' second argument is that nothing is gained by bearing misfortune badly. This, again, is true to the extent that grief becomes excessive, but expressions of grief seem by common consent to be natural and psychologically salutary responses to the deep personal loss of a close friend, lover, or family member. It is true that the degree of expression may differ among different cultures, with some cultures accepting, even expecting, an open, public display of grief, whereas in other, more reserved cultures a person may feel uncomfortable with anything more than a modest, mostly private expression of grief. Plato would seem to advocate the latter type of culture in his ideal state; indeed, grief should not be felt at all.

Socrates' fourth argument (we reserve his third argument for last) is that grief may hinder us from seeking help that is needed in an emergency situation. This again is a reasonable argument, if grief or its display is so excessive that it allows further damage to occur through inaction. A crisis requires effective thought and action despite losses; grief properly comes later, after the crisis has been resolved. But this, again, is a special type of circumstance and does not apply to the examples Plato has given or to other well-known situations of great, irremediable losses in tragedy, such as Oedipus' discovery of his true identity and his mother/wife's suicide, or Heracles' grief after he has killed his wife and children. Indeed, in the *Iliad*, the heroes at times moderate their grief or encourage limits to it. In the course of Priam's supplication in *Iliad* 24, Achilles tells Priam not to "mourn without end," since doing so will not bring back his son (549–50), and Priam himself in response shows an impatience to get on with the ransoming of his son's body.

Socrates' third argument is the most revealing: that nothing human is of any great importance (οὔτε τι τῶν ἀνθρωπίνων ἄξιον ὂν μεγάλης σπουδῆς, 604b12–13). Here is perhaps the crux of the matter, where the poet's and the Platonic or Stoic philosopher's fundamental perspectives are most at variance. The philosopher with his or her rational, highly detached view of things may reason that an individual's suffering in the great scheme of all time and space is a passing phenomenon of little significance, or, in a specifically Platonic sense, perhaps, that it does not partake of the real world of reason and eternal ideas, the things of ultimate reality. The poet, on the other hand, an earthbound witness of life's great transitions and a person highly sensitive to human feelings, both his or her own and those of others, responds with his or her art to reflect that experience. Indeed, by valuing the artistic reflection of life and the pleasure it brings to him and his audience, the poet necessarily values highly the experiences of life in the here and now. Actually, both perspectives are valuable – both the detached perspective on life promoted by rationalist philosophers and scientists and the graphic portrayal of joy and suffering presented in the works of poets, dramatists, artists, and musicians. These different perspectives fulfill different needs, and both are beneficial for a culture to promote as part of its life and learning. In summary, Socrates' arguments against the expression of grief have limited persuasiveness and do not apply to all cases and situations.[94]

In particular, Plato's argument against tragedy has to do with its detrimental effect on character. This is especially important in regard to its educational effect and whether it should form part of the education of the state's leaders or whether it should be consigned, as Socrates argues, to only a small and highly select group of mature individuals (378a). Plato's fear of tragedy has to do with its emotional appeal, the powerful pleasure it arouses within the spectator. One basis of his fear of this appeal is that it engages what he calls the unthinking part (*to anoêton*) of the human psyche, which he associates with elemental fears and desires, rather than engaging the reasoning, calculating part (*to logistikon*) of the psyche, the intellect. Socrates says (*Rep.* 605b):

> *The dramatic poet implants a pernicious governance individually in the soul of each person, gratifying its unthinking part, which distinguishes neither the greater from the lesser, but supposes the same things to be at one time large, at another time small; and he fashions images which are very far removed from reality.*

Certainly spectators[95] from antiquity to today have enjoyed tragic theater and gotten pleasure from it, but that pleasure is more than an unthinking one. In the course of watching or even reading a tragedy, spectators sympathize with characters, a more complex emotional response than simple fear of impending danger or desire for food, drink, or sex. Also, they are challenged to understand the characters' situations and to comprehend and interpret the choral songs, speeches, and events presented by the playwright. This pleasure engages, we dare say, the intellect, the spirited part, and the desiring part of Plato's tripartite soul. Furthermore, in contrast to other forms of theater that involve greater spectacle or simpler forms of language and thought, tragedy seems in particular to appeal to the intellect. This is not to say that tragedy appeals to these parts of the psyche in the same way that Plato envisions. His goals of promoting piety and courage are better met through the use, respectively, of hymns and patriotic songs. On the other hand, the unthinking part of the psyche that Plato fears is more directly engaged by stories that depict sex and violence more graphically than ancient tragedy does (for example, modern horror films, action flicks, and pornography). In comparison, tragedy is relatively tame in its appeal to the desires and fears of the psyche.[96] More importantly, even when tragedy presents taboo relationships, such as incest or infanticide, it portrays them as tragic rather than as desirable or worthy of emulation.

Part of Plato's objection to tragedy's appeal to the spectator's pity has to do with his association of pity and pitiable behavior with women rather than with men. Socrates says (*Rep.* 605d):

> *Whenever personal trouble comes our way, you know that we take pride in the opposite, if we can keep quiet and put up with it, as this is the part of a man, whereas that which we were praising then [in a tragic representation of sorrow] is that of a woman.*

What he characterizes here as womanish are the wailing and laments of heroes, including, presumably, those of Oedipus, Ajax, and Heracles in both *Trachiniae* and *Heracles*. Women, we know, tended to funerals in ancient Greece and performed public laments for the deceased. But Plato here is praising a stoic, perhaps even Spartan type of self-control and consigning any powerful display of grief or sorrow, even by heroes who are the epitome of masculine *aretê*, to the feminine realm.[97] Brian Vickers, citing the examples of both the grieving Ajax and the groaning Heracles in Sophocles, asserts the following (1973: 68–69):

> In both cases, Sophocles invokes the Stoic principle[98] in order to draw attention to the fact that two supremely heroic characters have found it to be unworkable. Experience disproves the Stoic consolatio; in tragedy, strong men weep. The uninhibited expression of their suffering is natural, right, inevitable.

Plato's concern is that, by watching tragedy and indulging their pity for its tragic characters, the spectators themselves will be corrupted by the pleasure of the emotion so that in their own misfortunes they will become self-pitying lamenters rather than the manly, self-controlled types Plato would have them, or rather his Guardians, become. Plato sees this corruption taking the form of a loss of self-control (something typically associated with women in Greek culture, as feminist scholars have demonstrated). Tragedy, he suggests, arouses pity to such an extent that reason loses control. The emotion takes us over! The spectators' enjoyment from watching and sympathizing with a noble character who is suffering and grieving will carry over into their own behavior. Socrates (606b) asserts that few reckon that the pity (*to eleinon*) that they enjoy yielding to in the theater as they view the sufferings of others will be hard to restrain (*katekhein*) in regard to their own sufferings.

This, apparently, is the crux of Plato's objection. By watching tragedy, spectators (including theoretically his Guardians to be) will consequently allow self-pity and grief to take control of them in times of great loss because they have had the experience in the theater of feeling deep pity for the sufferings and losses of great heroes. A corruption will take place – a feminization, no less – which will result in their giving vent to their emotions rather than keeping them under the cool control of the rational part of their psyche. Lest tragedians and their audiences feel themselves the exclusive targets here, Plato also extends the criticism to comic representations that arouse laughter and to any others that arouse powerful emotions and desires of whatever kind. The kernel of these objections is that any art form that arouses emotions so powerfully that they overwhelm and take control of the rational part, *which should be in control*, is inherently objectionable because of that very upsetting of the philosophic apple cart, no matter how temporary or how harmless in its behavioral consequences. Plato distrusts the emotions as guides of behavior because, according to his system, people can be happy only when their reason is in firm control of their emotions.

The most serious problem with this exclusion of powerful art from Plato's or any other educational system is that reason alone is not necessarily a sufficient determinant of good, compassionate behavior, although it is probably necessary as a "practical" guide. Plato sees reason as always superior to the emotions in its apprehension of reality and in its decision-making function. But in seeing a scene of suffering in life or as represented in the theater, or in hearing a tragic *mythos*, one's senses trigger both an intellectual prehension of the situation and an emotional response to it, partly conditioned by the mind's estimation of the factors involved.[99] Presumably, one can be trained to respond with great emotion or with no emotion or with some degree of emotion between these extremes. What type of response is best? Plato would seem to suggest as little emotion as possible. Tragedy, on the other hand, would seem to promote sympathetic emotional response to undeserved suffering. We submit that an emotional response – if it is a sympathetic response to undeserved suffering – is a good thing to develop, since emotion provides a stronger impulse for beneficial saving action than does a cold, emotionless response. In fact, what is the guarantee that reason will always be a reliable guide, if the spectators' emotions are not cultivated so as to provide an almost automatic positive response when they perceive an innocent in pain or danger? At a critical time, might not the compassionate impulse be a quicker and surer guide to appropriate behavior than an elaborate reasoning process?[100]

There is no doubt that at times people's emotions, especially the violent ones of anger and fear, can lead them to act in ways that they will later regret, but pity or compassion, provided it is not applied wrongly toward one who should not be pitied, rarely has such an outcome. Still, might not pity lead them to take risks potentially harmful to themselves and even to their loved ones? Yes, but there the decision becomes one of fundamental importance: does one seek to save another person at the possible expense of his or her own life, or does he or she let the other person perish? Isn't one's own life worth more than the other person's? A case where one decided otherwise would be one that we, as moderns, would tend to label as altruistic: we sacrifice ourselves or risk sacrificing ourselves for the greater good of the other person or for that of the larger society. In a sense, this is what soldiers, police officers, firefighters, and other rescue workers today do as part of their jobs. The mythic hero who intervenes to save a suppliant from aggressors likewise puts himself at risk. In cultures, however, such as that of the ancient Greeks, where rewards for compassionate behavior were considered natural and appropriate, he will win accolades and rewards if successful or, at least, he will have a good reputation if he dies trying. In life, such situations are among the most difficult we encounter. It seems reasonable to conclude, therefore, that both the reason and the emotions must be educated, respectively, by sound philosophic argument and by powerful, humane art that shows human suffering, human connections, and human sympathy in ways that lead people to want to help one another, as well as knowing rationally that they should do so.

In contrast to the simplistic triumphs of Rambo and the Terminator, who wreak revengeful violence on thoroughly evil enemies, tragedies and other stories that emphasize the suffering of noble, sympathetic characters, such as Oedipus, Achilles, and Priam, encourage in spectators a respect for human life and a sympathy for others who suffer in life.[101] Furthermore, as Thomas Gould has argued, to the extent that sympathy for tragic characters causes us to be more tolerant of our own sufferings and to be less harsh in judging both others and ourselves, the effect on our own psyches should also be beneficial. Plato, on the other hand, fears a breakdown of courage and discipline from this effect, an outcome that possibly may happen, but would seem to require an extreme situation in which the person affected already lacked self-control or discipline. Gould raises the contrary example of an individual who is overcontrolled by a hyperactive, punishing super-ego, a phenomenon not uncommon in the modern world. For such a person, permission to feel grief or to sympathize occasionally with his or her own failings would seem to be salutary.

Finally, Plato does not raise what would seem to be the most natural transference to come from feeling pity in the theater: that people become more sympathetic with others around them – their family, friends, and even strangers that they might encounter. To see in the theater the sympathetic representation of undeserved suffering should naturally lead spectators to question whether the suffering they see in others is deserved or not and should incline them to feel sympathy for those they judge to be suffering undeservedly. This, more than a tendency to excessive grief or self-pity, would seem to follow from spectators' experiences of compassion in the tragic theater. Also, provided that they do not sympathize with characters who do not deserve sympathy, their morality, contrary to Plato, should remain intact; indeed, it should be enhanced.[102]

Having said this much about Plato's concern with the effects of tragedy on the spectator, we should point out that in regard to compassionate behavior in real life (or, Plato's prescriptions for what we call real life), other writings of his suggest that he held a position not inconsistent with traditional Greek views on the subject. In speaking of the Guardians' temperament in *Republic* 375c, Socrates says that they should be gentle (*praioi*) to their friends, but dangerous to their enemies.[103] Such gentleness would presumably include compassionate behavior when fellow citizens need it. In speaking of the unity of citizens (462–63), Socrates advocates the sharing of pleasures and pains by fellow citizens. Furthermore, in the work of his maturity, the *Laws*, Plato advocates a very traditional observance of pity toward alien suppliants: "For the foreigner, being alone without companions or relatives, is more worthy of compassion (*eleeinoteros*) from both human beings and gods" (729e). The suppliant here, as in traditional texts from Homer on, has the protection of Zeus of Guest-Friendship and, consequently, a claim on human reverence and compassion. Plato's objection, therefore, doesn't seem to be to compassion per se, but rather to the display of heroes' suffering and lamentation on the tragic stage and to the criticism of the gods that sometimes accompanies such suffering. We should, however, accept such lamentations and their portrayal in tragedy as a valuable part of our human experience.

In this chapter our goal has been to show how Athenian tragedy sought to promote a compassionate sensibility in its audience. As is clear in the case of the representation of the noble Theseus, King of Athens, who wins honor and prestige for his *polis* through his compassionate action, such action represented a cultural ideal for the tragedians. Pity, according to Athenian tragedy, results from an awareness of membership in the human race. Compassion is grounded in and integrally connected to a tragic understanding of life as inherently unstable and liable to reversal, especially to negative reversals from prosperity to misery. This perspective on life derived in part from Homer (e.g., the myth of Zeus' jars of good and evil in *Iliad* 24) and was nourished in the Greek Archaic age, a period of great uncertainty and chaos.[104] It is applied to individuals or groups who exhibit such a fate by those who fear such a fate themselves. The response to such an exhibition of suffering is a strong feeling of compassion that prompts action to remedy that suffering. This expression of compassion is generally considered a sign of full humanity and its lack a deficiency.

Not that compassion was required of the Athenians in all circumstances and for all persons. As Aristotle understood, pity was felt and compassion displayed only for those whose suffering was judged to be undeserved and who themselves were thought to be worthy of compassion. Compassion was not applicable toward enemies, especially in times of war; the ethic was "no mercy for those who have shown no mercy," a form of negative reciprocity.[105] But since the Athenians were especially prone to feel and show compassion, they experienced some anxiety when they perceived that the desert or intentions of a suppliant were in question. This very anxiety, however, demonstrates that the Athenians did expect themselves to be moved by compassion – that it was an ingrained cultural tendency they needed to guard themselves against at times.

The displays of human suffering and concomitant displays of compassion for that suffering were enacted for Athenian citizens in a festival conducted under the auspices of the state. Nicole Loraux rightly rejects a narrowly political reading, as the plays were not produced in order to illustrate political positions.[106] Owing to the depth of treatment and differences among plays and playwrights, a simple "moral" does not emerge. It is difficult to deny, however, that the emotional impact of tragedy could have consequences for the *polis*. Since pity occupied a central place in the ethical content of tragedy, and since the ethical content of tragedy helped shape the perspective of the Athenian citizen, compassion emerges not as a posture assumed by the people of Athens but as a key element in their understanding of human existence.

This compassion, set in the heroic age, operates beyond the bounds of political ideology. Because of this, Loraux can conclude that the tragic performance will "arouse [the spectator] to transcend his membership in the civic community and to comprehend his even more essential membership in the race of mortals."[107] That is a membership we share, and that is why Greek tragedy can share its lessons with us, even if we do not worship Dionysus or witness the presentation of the tribute in ceremonies of the Athenian tragic festival.

◻◉◻

ENDNOTES

1. Arist. *Poet.* 6.1449b.
2. Stanford (1983: 23) writes, "The supreme tragic emotion, to judge from the surviving tragedies, is *eleos* or *oiktos*." Words based on these roots appear in every extant tragedy; Aeschylus averages six such words per play; Euripides, eight (excluding *Alcestis, Rhesus,* and *Cyclops*); and Sophocles, ten. These figures are based on word searches in *Thesaurus Linguae Graecae* and *Perseus Digital Library.* See also Kim's discussion of pity in Homer (2000: Ch. 2). In this chapter, we use both "pity" and "compassion" as English equivalents for Greek *oiktos* and *eleos.* Our understanding of the history of the two Greek words is that *oiktos* in Homer and early writers tended to emphasize lamentation and the emotion of pity proper whereas *eleos* tended to entail responsive action, much as English "compassion" tends to do. In tragedy, the *oiktos* cognates tend to dominate and to be used in both senses of a sorrowful, sympathetic emotion felt and of a sympathetic emotion that arouses a behavioral response; possibly tragedy may prefer *oiktos* because of tragedy's emphasis on lamentation; cf. Burkert 1955: 49–51. Aristotle then reverts to the use of *eleos* in his discussion of the pity of the tragic spectator. Since our chapter is focused on the interaction of characters in tragedy, our interest is in acts of compassion more than in the sentiment of pity, such as that felt by a theatrical spectator. We therefore tend to prefer "compassion" to "pity" for both *eleos* and *oiktos*, especially when the situation

involves a behavioral response or a request for such a response. We also find that Greek *oiktos* and *eleos* in epic and tragedy lack the demeaning assertion of inferiority that English "pity" often conveys. This makes "pity" problematic as an English equivalent for the Greek words, but as the traditional translation for Aristotle's *eleos*, it persists as the preferred equivalent in classical studies. Compare Stanford 1983: 23–27.

3. Hall 1997: 100. Also emphasized by Cartledge 1997 and Goldhill 1997, in the same volume.

4. In this volume, see the chapter by Tzanetou; also Loraux (2002: 19) who, although writing to overturn political readings of tragedy, nevertheless summarizes the political elements of tragedy.

5. Salkever 1986: 278.

6. Vernant and Vidal-Naquet (1990: 246): The events of tragedy "touch and concern us, but only from a distance."

7. On this issue with regard to Achilles' pity for Priam in *Iliad* 24, cf. Gill 1998: 312–13; also cf. Seaford 1998: 5–6, on the general issue of reciprocity versus altruism. Compare Konstan 2000a on altruism, especially in Aristotle and later writers, and Schopenhauer 1840/1995 on altruistic compassion as the basis of what he terms "morality." Johnson 2002 shows pity operating reciprocally between friends in Euripides' *Heracles*.

8. Our focus on compassionate action and reciprocity differs from that of Konstan in this volume, who focuses on the emotion of pity and its role or lack of a role in public political discourse.

9. We compare these two because of similar structural elements: an introduction from a hostile divinity and a bipartite structure divided by the suicide of a central figure. The juxtaposition of the Sophoclean Athena with the Euripidean Aphrodite is a commonplace: Jebb 1907: *ad Ajax* 15; Kovacs 1995: 119; Knox 1961: 130 with n. 36. See Szlezák 1982.

10. Regarding *Hippolytus*, Zimmermann (1991: 98): "It can be shown, however, that it is just this divine frame that imparts meaning to the intentions and actions of the characters in this play."

11. Barrett 1964: 155. Presumably Barrett's victim is Hippolytus, though at 1403–05 Hippolytus and Artemis mention three victims: Hippolytus, Phaedra, and Theseus. Kovacs (1995: 120) comments on Hippolytus and Phaedra: "there is no reason to sympathize with one of them to the exclusion of the other. Both are victims of Aphrodite, as is Theseus."

12. See Knox 1961: 130, and Garvie 1998: 124.

13. Jebb 1907: *ad* 12.

14. Lloyd-Jones 1994: 39. All translations in this section are from the Loeb Classical Library.

15. Blundell 1989: 261. See, too, the discussion of Goldhill 1986: 83–85. Knox (1961: 128): "But the Sophoclean presentation of the old code in action makes the simple point that it is unworkable."

16. Garvie 1998: *ad* 1–3.

17. See Knox 1961: 130; Garvie 1998: 15 and *ad* 121–6.

18. As suggested by Tzanetou, Chapter 4.

19. Garvie 1998: *ad* 955–60, notes their surprise.

20. Knox (1961: 129): Odysseus "restores some measure of dignity." Mahoney 2001 recognizes that the opening scene provides "the necessary bridge between the two halves of the play, before and after the death of Ajax, because it is this drama that causes Odysseus to pity Ajax and, finally, argue for his burial."

21. Knox 1961: 125 and 128; Moore (1977: 58): "from one end to another it is an unrelieved nightmare of madness and blood." Tyrrell (1985: 156) sees *thusia* as a central theme.

22. Here we think Garvie (1998: *ad* 1–133) overstates the case when he sees a consistently positive picture of Ajax: "From the very beginning we are meant to admire him."

23. Kitto 1956: 183.

24. Garvie 1998: *ad* 596–645; Golder 1990: 19; Stevens 1986: 329; Knox (1961: 135): "In the previous scene he made it perfectly clear that he intended to kill himself, announced his decision firmly, refused to argue the matter, and brutally silenced Tekmessa's attempt to dissuade him."

25. Moore 1977: 58.

26. Dobrov (2001: 64 and 67), however, twice calls Odysseus' state of mind "disoriented."

27. Moore (1977: 58): "We are already predisposed in Ajax' favor, and have been from the very first."

28. For views of Ajax' speech, see Garvie 1998: *ad* 646–92. Jebb 1907: Intro. 12, "He does feel pity." See Stanford 1963 and his appendix on the speech of Ajax. Knox 1961 and Sicherl 1977 understand this speech as the climax and make it the starting point of their studies. Ajax's claim to pity is a point affirmed despite the debate: even scholars advancing the idea of deception acknowledge it as true sentiment; see Moore 1977: 50. Rosivach (1976: 53 n. 12), however, ascribes little significance to Ajax' profession of pity.

29. Sicherl 1977: 91 n. 101 and 92 n. 105; Knox 1961: 138.

30. With Garvie 1998: *ad* 642–96.

31. Knox 1961: 150–51; Sicherl 1977: 76 (Reinhardt); Knox 1961: 138 calls it a "beam of light in darkness."

32. That is why, despite the emphasis of Tyler 1974 on Athena's wrath, the goddess's role is so small. The play is not about *hubris* leading to destruction. It is about a broken person in a broken world.

33. Knox 1961: 149: "they are incapable of the tragic sense that world demands. . . . The ignobility of their attitude is emphasized by the tragic humility of Odysseus, who abandons the traditional code."

34. Halleran 1995: *ad* 5–6 calls attention to the workings of reciprocity between gods and mortals, which stand in stark contrast to the reciprocity behind a compassionate response for a fellow human being.

35. As the messenger in *Ajax* makes explicit in lines 758–83, Ajax had angered Athena with excessive pride. Athena, however, tells Odysseus what has passed with no reference

to her personal anger: Aphrodite, on the other hand, directly addresses the audience with an explicit reason for her anger.

36. See note 11 and Norwood 1954: 74.

37. Barrett 1964 *ad* 20–22.

38. Compare Halleran 1995: *ad* 28.

39. Aphrodite emphasizes Theseus' role by uttering his name five times: lines 34, 42, 45; lines 10 and 50 use his name to identify Hippolytus. On names, see Segal 1993: 124.

40. Barrett 1964: *ad* 42. See Halleran 1995: *ad* 42.

41. And her role never fades from view; it becomes explicit again when Artemis explains the disaster to Theseus.

42. Barrett 1964: *ad* 114–20, rightly emphasizes the contrast between the servant and Hippolytus, but does not mention the contrast with Aphrodite. See Halleran 1995: *ad* 114–20, and Dunn 1996: 88.

43. In his efforts to place Hippolytus in a good light, Kovacs (1980: 132–33) discounts the value of the servant's prayer.

44. So Davies (2000: 67): "we find a sympathetic heroine."

45. Kitto 1939: 203; Davies (2000: 61–65) offers a thorough discussion of the scholarly divide over the acceptability of Hippolytus' diatribe. But it is enough to note that Hippolytus is critical, and critical toward an innocent party, whether or not he is pathologically so.

46. In such a situation, it would be preferable, with Parker 2001, for Phaedra to have heard the bitter remarks of Hippolytus.

47. Devereux 1985: 113.

48. Unlike Theseus, Sophocles' Oedipus yields to the chorus and does not act on his wrath toward Creon (*OT* 671–72).

49. Kovacs 1995: 229.

50. The first was a reference by the chorus to women grieving for Phaethon (740). About which, Segal (1993: 25): "aesthetic framing of grief by metaphor is reinforced by the combination of embedded myth and geographical distance."

51. See note 2. According to the *Perseus Digital Library*, the Euripidean corpus contains thirty-five nouns, forty-one verbs, and fifty-one adjectives based on the root of *oiktos*.

52. On miscommunication, see Halleran 1995: *ad* 565–600.

53. Dimock 1977: 254.

54. Knox (1952: 228): "a human act which is at last a free and meaningful choice . . . man's noblest declaration of independence." Kovacs (1995: 121): "Mortals, perhaps because they are subject to loss and death, exhibit a sympathy with misfortune and a loyalty to each other of which the gods are incapable. The reconciliation of father and son at the play's end is a demonstration of such sympathy and loyalty in the face of disaster." Of the present authors, Johnson prefers Kovacs' reading.

55. Stahl (1977: 167): "ever since exchanging 'goodbye' with Artemis (1437; 1440), Hippolytus has been wishing to take leave of his father, too (already in 1444 darkness approaches

him), but has been kept from doing so because of his promise to Artemis (1442) and Theseus' own repeatedly expressed desire for absolution and reconciliation." Others read the reconciliation hesitantly: Schenker 1995: 9–10; Goff 1990: Ch. 5. This is the interpretive stance adopted by Clapp.

56. Cf. Loraux 2002 *passim*.

57. Examples include Soph. *Aj.* 121–26; Aesch. *Ag.* 1327–30; Eur. *El.* 1329–30, *Or.* 976–81, and *Hec.* 488–91. Outside of tragedy, similar statements can be found, such as Hdt. 1.86 and 7.46. Democritus (Frag. 107a) says "it is fitting for human beings not to laugh at the misfortunes of their fellow men, but to lament (*olophuresthai*) them" because of the instability of life. Similarly in Euripides' *Andromache* 421, the chorus says, "misfortunes, even of a stranger, are pitiful to all mortals" (cf. also Eur. *El.* 290–91). That these sentiments were also to be found in Greek aristocratic literature, such as Pindar's epinician odes, suggests their universality in the Greek worldview.

58. Compare *Il.* 9.629–30, where Ajax calls Achilles "cruel," one who has made his heart "savage" (ἄγριον), for his refusal to show compassion to his *philoi* in need; in *Od.* 9.475–79, 23.312–13, Odysseus and his men repay the barbarous Cyclops for eating his guests rather than pitying them.

59. The quotation continues with the philanthropic sentiment that "it is evil, when there is abundant wealth, to benefit no mortal out of base stinginess."

60. Compare discussions of supplication by John Gould 1973: 85–90; Kopperschmidt 1971; and Vickers 1973: 438–94. Also, for treatments of supplication in Homer, see Pedrick 1982 and Crotty 1994. Not all supplications involved appeals for compassion; also, *aidôs* ("reverence, shame") was typically aroused or sought by the suppliant as well as pity (cf. Kim 2000: 18). In most supplications between humans, however, the suppliant was in a condition of weakness and desperation and consequently sought compassion or mercy from the supplicated champion; cf. Cairns 1993: 49. The examples we analyze here are of this type.

61. It is, of course, with the latter that Plato is so concerned in the *Republic*; see the later section on Plato.

62. In his provocative essay, Griffin (1998: 51) argues that in plays featuring Athenian kings, imperial power is treated unsympathetically and furthermore that "Athens herself never interferes except to right some grievous wrong and then promptly withdraws (*Heraclidae, Suppliant Women, Oedipus at Colonus*)." Also, he concludes: "Nowhere do these edifying Athenian rulers show a trace of imperialism" (51 n. 46).

63. Compare J. Gould 1973: 92–93; Belfiore 1998: 146.

64. Conacher 1967 interprets the play in terms of *kharis* (reciprocal favor) rather than pity or compassion. There is some necessary overlap here, in that appealing to a *philos* for compassion also entails an appeal based on *kharis*; the two motives reinforce one another.

65. Earlier in this volume, Konstan, in contrast, denies pity a role in Demophon's motivation here; Tzanetou emphasizes the limitation of Athenian pity in the play.

66. As Kim (2000: 67) has analyzed it in the *Iliad*, *eleos* prompts one to avenge one's fallen comrade, to rescue friends in danger on the battlefield, to seek to heal a friend who is wounded, or to give proper burial to a dead friend. Pity, in other words, entails behavioral assistance or compensatory action, that is, *aretê*. Adkins (1960: 157) cites lines 285–87 of this play, Demophon's last words to Kopreos, as illustrating the continuation of the *aretê* of the Homeric warrior in the fifth-century king who protects suppliants.

67. Compare Vickers 1973: 90–91, 459.

68. Compare Zuntz 1955: esp. 7–10, who also sees *oiktos* ("compassion") and *logos* ("reason") working in harmony to motivate Theseus here. Burian (1985: 133–35), to the contrary, argues that Aithra's argument is not "a plea for pity at all," but since her arguments promote the same end as the mothers' pleas and reinforce those pleas, both are directed toward Theseus' performance of an act of compassion: the burial of the mothers' sons. As Zuntz (1955: 16–17) concludes, Athens is seen in this play as "prompted by compassion to succour the injured. . . . Their pity was active help." Heath (1987: 14–15) also sees compassion as motivating Theseus here. Again, contrast Konstan's discussion of Euripides' *Suppliant Women*.

69. See Scully's introduction (1995: 11–12) to the new Oxford translation for further discussion of these lines.

70. Compare Mills (1997: 167), who discusses Athens' idealization as a city that "will always take risks, and be rewarded for doing so."

71. Vellacott (1975: 30–32, 157–59) rightly accords Theseus high praise for his restraint in not pressing the Athenian victory over Thebes and sacking the city, but he is troubled that Theseus does not rebuke the sons of the fallen Argives when they pledge to someday avenge their fathers. But when Athena then predicts that the young boys will take vengeance (1213–26) and encourages them to do so, Theseus must accept this as the standard Greek ethic of "harm your enemy" and as the working of fate. Shaw (1982: 10) also notes Theseus' admirable restraint in not sacking Thebes, and argues (16–18) that Theseus' and Athena's views at the end of the play are compatible.

72. See, for example, recent book-length studies of Theseus by Walker (1995) and Mills (1997), both of whom present insightful treatments of his mythic career.

73. See Irwin (1977: passim, esp. 54–56, 86–90, 134–36 and 206–8) on Plato's concepts of the inseparability and unity of virtues.

74. Compare Burian 1974 on Sophocles' adaptation of the conventions of the suppliant drama in this play.

75. Compare later pp. 140–41 on Athenian anxiety regarding unworthy or treacherous suppliants. Here the chorus' fear seems to stem from the possible pollution that Oedipus may carry, according to Blundell 1990: 30 n. 31; cf. Jebb 1907: *ad* 235–36. Although they initially resist Oedipus, the chorus eventually develop a relationship of *xenia* with him based on mutually beneficial acts and promises. Few scholars seem to have noted the moderation of the chorus' resistance to Oedipus after they have heard

his story and his promise of benefit to Athens. Tzanetou, in this volume, is one of those few.

76. Compare Mills 1997: 171.

77. Translations in the second and third sections of this chapter are our own, except as otherwise noted. The complete Greek text of *Oedipus at Colonus* 551–68 (Lloyd-Jones and Wilson 1990) is as follows:

> πολλῶν ἀκούων ἔν τε τῷ πάρος χρόνῳ
> τὰς αἱματηρὰς ὀμμάτων διαφθορὰς
> ἔγνωκά σ', ὦ παῖ Λαΐου, τανῦν θ' ὁδοῖς
> ἐν ταῖσδε λεύσσων μᾶλλον ἐξεπίσταμαι.
> σκευή τε γάρ σε καὶ τὸ δύστηνον κάρα   555
> δηλοῦτον ἡμῖν ὄνθ' ὅς εἶ, καί σ' οἰκτίσας
> θέλω 'περέσθαι, δύσμορ' Οἰδίπους, τίνα
> πόλεως ἐπέστης προστροπὴν ἐμοῦ τ' ἔχων,
> αὐτός τε χἠ σὴ δύσμορος παραστάτις.
> δίδασκε· δεινὴν γάρ τιν' ἂν πρᾶξιν τύχοις   560
> λέξας ὁποίας ἐξαφισταίμην ἐγώ·
> ὃς οἶδα γ' αὐτὸς ὡς ἐπαιδεύθην ξένος,
> ὥσπερ σύ, χὤς εἷς πλεῖστ' ἀνὴρ ἐπὶ ξένης
> ἤθλησα κινδυνεύματ' ἐν τώμῷ κάρα,
> ὥστε ξένον γ' ἂν οὐδέν' ὄνθ', ὥσπερ σὺ νῦν,   565
> ὑπεκτραποίμην μὴ οὐ συνεκσῴζειν· ἐπεὶ
> ἔξοιδ' ἀνὴρ ὢν χὤτι τῆς εἰς αὔριον
> οὐδὲν πλέον μοι σοῦ μέτεστιν ἡμέρας.

78. The word *praxis* here is somewhat ambiguous: it could refer either to Oedipus' past activity, which Theseus might shrink from supporting or, what is more likely, to the hardship or danger Theseus and Athens might incur in meeting Oedipus' request. We take the word to refer to Oedipus' request or, rather, the action implicit in such a request rather than to Oedipus' past experiences. So also Kamerbeek (1984), contra Jebb (1889), who interprets it as "fortune."

79. In regard to the former, note the emphasis Theseus places on his own life experiences (ὃς οἶδά γ' αὐτὸς, 562), the parallelism he perceives between his upbringing in a foreign land and that experienced by Oedipus (ὥσπερ σύ, 563), and his emphasis on Oedipus' present participation in the class of *xenoi* (ὥσπερ σὺ νῦν, 565), a class that Theseus says he would never refrain from rescuing. Compare Burian (1974: 415), who writes of "Theseus' spontaneous assertion of a common human bond between himself and his suppliant." Burian notes that, unlike the chorus, who are horrified by Oedipus' past, Theseus sees Oedipus as merely "ill-fated" (557). Also, compare Reinhardt 1979: 207–8; Mills 1997: 172–73.

80. Oedipus has told the chorus that he bears a benefit for Athens, but Theseus does not know it. This will be the subject of the conversation between them. Compare lines 288–90 and Jebb's note on 309. In lines 307–8, in reference to the benefit he is bringing, Oedipus comments on the noble's tendency to benefit himself by helping others. We might, indeed, note the common expectation of the noble man's behavior: that it will be appropriate and beneficial both to others and to himself (and his own). Jebb comments: "The generous man, though he acts from no calculation of self-interest, actually serves himself by making zealous friends."

81. In Monroe's *The Heart of Altruism* (1996), a study of rescuers of Jews from Nazi persecution in World War II and other life-risking rescuers, her modern "heroes" deny that any sense of self-interest motivated their actions, and Monroe carefully concludes that their behaviors should be called "altruistic." What they seem to share with Theseus here, however, is a deep sense of common humanity. Monroe writes (206): "Altruists have a particular perspective in which all mankind is connected through a common humanity, in which each individual is linked to all others and to a world in which all living beings are entitled to a certain humane treatment merely by virtue of being alive. It is not any mystical blending of the self with another; rather, it is a very simple but deeply felt recognition that we all share certain characteristics and are entitled to certain rights merely by virtue of our common humanity. It constitutes a powerful statement about what it means to be a human being." The Greeks did not explicitly express such a value of universal humanity, although something close to it seems implicit in the phenomenon of supplication and in the Greek understanding of the fragility of life shared by all human beings.

82. Johnson (1980: Ch. 3) provides a detailed analysis of the theme of compassion in *Philoctetes*.

83. Indeed, at points he shows some anger and impatience. He, for example, chides Oedipus at 592–94 and at 1208–9, although in both instances he quickly moderates his response.

84. Compare Blundell 1993: 299–300, 305–6. Although ancient testimony indicates that the poet did not live to see the play produced and, furthermore, that its first production occurred after Athens had lost the war with Sparta, still the play depicts an Athens undaunted and full of hope for the future.

85. Another source of anxiety would be a suppliant who was polluted or who otherwise might bring harm to the polis, even unknowingly. As we have seen in *Oedipus at Colonus*, this is the problem that the chorus has initially with the suppliant Oedipus.

86. J. Gould (1973: 85–86) discusses Medea's supplication of Creon in terms of the religious significance of the ritual act: Medea's taking of Creon's hand, along with the lowering of her demands, forces the king Creon to consent. Compare Cairns 1993: 277–78.

87. Rachel Sternberg, the editor of this volume, pointed out this irony to us.

88. Another example of a treacherous appeal for compassion in Euripides is that by Electra to Hermione in *Orestes* (1337 ff.). Also, cf. the charge against Alcibiades in And. 4.39, that he is ruthless in bringing about the death and exile of others, but ready to use supplications and appeals for pity on his own account.

89. Isocrates (4.168) protests the discrepancy between Greeks weeping over the sufferings created by the poets and their callous disregard for the suffering resulting from civil strife in the real world. His negative tone suggests that the strife has corrupted the good sensitivity that tragedy provided. Compare Lada (1996: 407) on this discrepancy.

90. Hellenistic and Roman Stoic teachings, for example, sought to suppress such emotions in favor of emotional detachment and virtue. See Konstan (2001: 48, 113) for examples concerning pity; also Nussbaum 1994: 428, n. 38; 495–97. Nussbaum (2001: Ch. 7) defends compassion against the arguments of the Stoics and their modern successors, Kant and Nietzsche.

91. See Halliwell 1996 for an interpretation more favorable to Plato's critique of tragedy. The contrary arguments offered here, although expressed in different terms, seem to us to be in general accord with Aristotle's refutation in *Poetics* of Plato's critique of tragedy. See Nussbaum, "Interlude 2" (1986: 378–94), for an interpretation of *Poetics* with which we generally agree; cf. Nussbaum 2001, Ch. 6, esp. 350–53. Also, see Iris Murdoch 1977 and Thomas Gould 1990: *passim*, esp. Ch. 6, for still different critiques of Plato.

92. See, for example, *Poetics* 1451b. Belfiore (1983) attempts to tackle these issues and relate them to Plato's larger argument against poetry in Book 10.

93. In discussing the difference between Platonic dialogue, with its search for a single form of truth, and tragedy, which is characterized by more open-ended conflict and debate (*elenchos*), Nussbaum (1986: 134) writes: "The tragic *elenchos* does not present itself as part of an ongoing search for *the* correct account of anything . . . the force of tragedy is usually, too, to warn us of the dangers inherent in all searches for a single form: it continually displays to us the irreducible richness of human value, the complexity and indeterminacy of the lived practical situation." Murdoch (1977: esp. 76–89) also presents an insightful analysis of the differences between art and philosophy.

94. An objection has been made to our argument here that for Plato and Socrates the only truly bad thing that can befall a person is to be a bad person, that is, to do wrong; that in comparison to this, the objects of people's grief are not truly evil. We will grant that doing wrong oneself is a worse evil than losing a loved one, but our view is that the latter is still a formidable evil for most people. Furthermore, we argue that sympathizing with the suffering of tragic heroes can in fact make spectators or readers better persons (see later pp. 149–52). Is it not as bad (or, almost as bad) to fail to educate ourselves to be actively good as to fail to educate ourselves not to do wrong? We grant that Plato may provide the latter kind of virtue, but by excluding tragedy, we suggest that he may fail to provide a fully adequate foundation for active goodness.

95. We use "spectator" in this section to refer to either the spectator of a tragedy in performance (whether live theater or on screen) or the reader of a tragic play.

96. Again, cf. Aristotle's *Poetics* (see earlier, n. 91).

97. See Falkner's contribution in this volume concerning Sophocles' use of feminine imagery in depicting Heracles in *Trachiniae*. Johnson's colleague, Rod Stewart, points out that Plato's "Spartan" self-control here is in keeping with "the 'lean' and 'minimal' model of the just polis that begins in Books 2 and 3"; also, he notes the irony of this, given Athens' experience with Sparta in the Peloponnesian Wars. See Rubidge (1993: 247–76) for an account that emphasizes Plato's overriding concern with training the spirited element of his warrior-guardians.

98. That is, the notion that we can bear our pain with dignity (see Vickers 1973: 67).

99. Compare Else (1967: 374–75), who argues that "the emotions are not merely irrational, as Plato had made them out to be, [but that] they also have their rational side or at least are amenable to reason."

100. Compare Lada (1996: esp. 403–4) on the contribution of emotion as aroused by Greek tragedy to one's "access to the truth," "understanding of others," and "self-realization"; also, Lada 1993: 114–16. Monroe found that the rescuers, whom she interviewed (cf. n. 81), saw their actions as virtually spontaneous (210–13). Her subjects, whom she calls "altruists," described their actions as being based on an impulse to help, rather than on "a conscious process in which reason subjugated the passions" or calculated the costs and benefits of acting. Instead their behavior resulted, according to their accounts, from a deep sense of the common humanity which they shared with those they rescued. "Humanity plus need: This is the only moral reasoning, the only calculus for altruism," she writes. See Frank 1988 and Damasio 1994 for modern analyses of how our emotions, including compassion, are necessary components of "rational" decision making and success in life. For example, Frank (1988: 255) writes: "Developmental psychologists tell us that moral behavior emerges hand-in-hand with the maturation of specific emotional competencies. The psychopath fails not because of an inability to calculate self-interest, but because of an inability to empathize, a fundamental lack of emotional conditionability." Damasio, arguing from a neurobiological perspective, makes similar points, especially in chapters 7 and 8.

101. Compare T. Gould 1990: 281, 294–95.

102. Compare Lada (1996: 407): "the overflow of emotions at the stage dramas should ideally transmute itself into altruistic action"; also, cf. Halliwell 2002: 228–29. Also, see Janko's interpretation of *katharsis* in Aristotle's *Poetics* (1987: Intro. Sec. 5, xviii–xx): tragedy promotes the education of our emotions, especially pity and terror, so that we feel them in proper measure and in appropriate circumstances. "By responding emotionally to the representation, we can learn to develop the correct emotional responses." Thus poetry has an "educative and moral function, that is, it helps to form character" (xviii). Tragedy, through *katharsis*, provides, like music in general, both education and entertainment.

103. Compare Isocrates' characterization (15.20) of the Athenians as "most compassionate and most gentle."
104. Compare Johnson 1980: Ch. 1, pp. 19, 42; Dodds 1951: Ch. 2.
105. Konstan (2001: Ch. 3) provides an overview of the behavior typical of ancient warfare.
106. Loraux 2002: 13.
107. Loraux 2002: 93.

ENGENDERING THE TRAGIC *THEATÊS*: PITY, POWER, AND SPECTACLE IN SOPHOCLES' *TRACHINIAE*

THOMAS M. FALKNER

"Woman is, to be sure, a creature
most inclined to pity (philoiktiston*)."*
– Ajax 580

◎▣◎

THE FOLLOWING CASE STUDY – HERE OF *TRACHINIAE* BUT ALMOST AS easily of any of the plays of Sophocles – asks a number of questions about Greek tragedy that are relevant to a discussion of pity and power and that measure the difficult terrain between the two. The first has to do with the nature of tragic pity (*eleos, oiktos*) in its most familiar, which is to say, Aristotelian context: as the emotion that, together with fear (*phobos*), tragedy evokes or seeks to evoke in the audience.[1] I am interested in particular in the relationships of power that are embedded within the very nature of theatrical experience. In what sense does tragic discourse assume a differential between the power, status, and privilege of the audience and that of the object of its pity? The second has to do with the importance of the visual dimension of tragedy to the evocation of pity – the text in its formal and visual display before a collective audience. The Greek *theatron* is itself, of course, a place for seeing (*theasthai*), a point that cannot be urged too often on classicists, with their fixation on the written word and persistent undervaluing of the importance of sight in Athenian tragedy. Although performance criticism has focused in important ways on the stagecraft of the plays, their material resources, and the scenic conventions they employ, less attention has been paid to tragic viewing itself as an act of spectating, to what it means to *see* and *be seen* in a tragic context, and how this is related to the civic context of the theatrical production.[2] A third question relates the nature of tragic response to the subject of gender. In one sense it asks: What gender was the audience of Greek tragedy? – not as yet another inquiry into the composition of the historical audience at the City Dionysia, but rather into the nature of the experience that the tragic audience is offered and the subject position it is invited to assume. In another it asks: What is the gender of the object of our tragic pity? That is, gender as one of the primary metaphors through which the audience is encouraged to regard the objects of its pity, and the relationship between this metaphor and other aspects of tragic and civic ideology.

Sophoclean tragedy is remarkable for its attention to the process of spectating, for the frequency with which it discusses the concept of sight and seeing, and for the number of scenes in which the idea of spectacle is itself literally "theorized" and characters are represented in the act of beholding.[3] Sophocles repeatedly exploits dramatic form to represent the idea of theater itself, creating internal representations of the theatrical situation to establish a self-conscious discourse on tragedy, despite the proscriptions against explicit self-reference in Greek tragedy.[4] Such "intratextual" scenes are in part functional, one of the rhetorical strategies that serve in the construction of their actual audiences by modeling the spectator, offering him a subject position, instructing him in how to see in new and unfamiliar ways. In Sophocles, I would suggest, the theatrical situation is consistently described in terms that suggest the potential power, privilege, and security of the spectator (*theatês*) over and against the suffering, vulnerability, and even humiliation of the object of sight, and Sophocles expresses this superiority through conceptual oppositions of power and control that are fundamental to the Greek social order: god over mortal, male over female, free over slave, citizen over exile, ruler over suppliant. These texts implicitly recognize the power the *theatês* enjoys by virtue of his position as spectator – social superiority here becomes a metaphor for theatrical superiority. Yet at the same time, we repeatedly see in these plays a process of inversion whereby one "kind" of spectator describes his or her experience not in terms of superiority or authority but from the perspective of the sufferer, offering expressions of pity and sympathy and drawing affinities between his or her situation and the sufferer's. This position is crystallized in what might be called "protocols of pity," scenes in which the potent gaze of the public spectator is subverted by an equally profound private sympathy. By presenting these spectators in ways that are sympathetic or otherwise attractive, or by discrediting others as ignoble, vindictive, or in some way excessive, the text valorizes the one as more authentically "tragic" and so guides the response of the audience. *Trachiniae* provides a striking example of Sophocles' predilection to "theorize" the *theatês* through a range of internal scenes of spectacle – public and private, on-stage and off-stage, actual and "virtual."[5] In these embedded scenes of spectacle, *Trachiniae* directs our own response as spectators, attempting to create the kind of disposition and sensibility the playwright asks for his own work.

This discourse on pity, power, and spectacle is fundamentally intertwined with the play's treatment of gender. If *Trachiniae* is, as R. P. Winnington-Ingram says, "a tragedy of sex,"[6] it is equally a tragedy of gender, one that examines gender in itself and uses it as the primary category of analysis of its other concerns.[7] Indeed, it might be hard to identify a play in which gender is more thoroughly dichotomized than *Trachiniae*. As Heracles epitomizes the questing male hero, Deianeira achieves archetypal status as the female who waits, is indeed defined by a lifetime of waiting and watching. As if to sharpen their power as critical tools, the play defines male and female and the social and cultural worlds they inhabit so exclusively that their two primary representatives are kept from meeting face to face. Male and female constitute parallel universes so opposed that they can be presented on stage only sequentially and not simultaneously: the entrance, exit, and death of the one must be completed before the entrance, exit, and death of the other may commence.[8] In less critical circumstances, the marriage bed provided a space where the two worlds overlapped, however infrequently and temporarily (31–33). But in the bifurcated world of this play that place of union has itself become divided, as the *lekhos . . . kriton* (27) of Deianeira finds its double in the *kruphion . . . lekhos* (360) of Iole, and is then in turn gendered, with the off-stage bridal bed that Deianeira invokes in death inverted in the on-stage sick bed from which Heracles instructs Hyllos in his marriage. Although these two worlds are separate, they are not hermetically sealed. Communications between them are mediated by figures who are themselves liminal in nature, and who might otherwise be able to operate in the interstices. Yet in *Trachiniae* these exchanges break down and these figures lose their ability to mediate effectively. Hyllos, *pais* but not yet *anêr*, is sent to gather information. But just as the play provides for him in compressed form a rite of passage to manhood, he becomes in his successful transition an extension of his father and the vehicle of his misdirected hatred of Deianeira. And the herald, in his mendacious account of Heracles' activities, exceeds his charge and becomes the creator rather than the reporter of the news he bears. In his failed attempt to negotiate the complexities of the situation, he becomes the carrier of fatal diseases that poison communication between husband and wife: first in the *nosos* of Eros that he brings with Iole, and then in the *nosos* of the Centaur's blood that he delivers to Heracles. The failure of these attempts at mediation, the breakdown of the proper boundaries and protocols, reflect a collapse of the larger system of gender in which male and female can neither coexist separately nor define a space where difference can be negotiated.

In *Trachiniae*, I would argue further, spectating subject and object themselves become gendered roles, defined as "masculine" or "feminine" independent of the character who occupies them in any particular scene or moment, in ways that correspond to different kinds of seeing and different kinds of situations. Sophocles uses gender as the primary metaphor by which tragic and nontragic spectacle are to be distinguished, and consistently characterizes tragic spectacle as "feminine" in terms of both the subject position of the spectator and the object position of the suffering protagonist. That is, where "masculine" or nontragic spectacle presents a performative hero to an audience that is correspondingly empowered by its superior status, perspective, and knowledge, "feminine" or tragic spectacle is characterized by the way it exposes the vulnerable and suffering protagonist to the gaze of others and in the sympathetic and nonhierarchical disposition the spectator is required to assume. *Trachiniae* describes tragedy as a form of experience that requires that we *see* and its protagonists *be seen* as female, drawing out the gendered infrastructure of the genre and bringing into the foreground a set of associations that permeate Athenian tragic discourse and go to the center of its ideology.

That there is a larger and even essential connection between tragedy and the feminine has been argued by Froma Zeitlin, who describes the way in which the feminine is fundamentally implicated in such basic theatrical categories as body, space, plot, and mimesis. As she goes on to suggest, Plato's critique and repudiation of tragedy "darkly confirms the inextricable relationship between theater and the feminine," and so poses a threat to the rehabilitated patriarchy he seeks to promote.[9] An examination of the patterns of gender and spectacle in *Trachiniae* thus may tell us something not only about this play but also about the cultural poetics of tragedy in general. These associations present a set of paradoxes for a theater whose performers are male, whose intended and actual audience is predominantly or exclusively male, where tragedy is a central part of the civic discourse and education of its male citizenry,[10] and whose official ideology claims that its intellectual life is enjoyed without compromise of its masculinity: *philosophoumen aneu malakias*, as Perikles boasts (Thuc. 2.40.1). It is perhaps not appreciated often enough just how ironic, even counterintuitive, is the institution of tragedy by the Athenians, and that a culture so thoroughly agonistic, patriarchal, and devoted to the acquisition of power and prestige should provide regular opportunities at state expense for its citizens to pity the sufferings of others. Yet elsewhere in this volume James Johnson and Douglas Clapp rehearse the high value that the Athenians put on pity and compassion, regarding the tragedies not only in evidence for this valuation but also for their crucial role in the moral and ethical education of the polis regarding the proper exercise and expression of pity; and this education in turn had practical value, reflecting the "real-life experiences of the exercise of power by states and their agents."[11] By defining more carefully the subject position that the Athenian audience was invited to assume, and by appreciating the extent to which it involved the adoption of a perspective that might more naturally be regarded as feminine, we can understand better the cultural effort and achievement that Athenian tragic spectatorship required.

The Masculine *Theatês*

The masculine *theatês* is epitomized in the parodos, in which Heracles commands no less an audience than the Sun, and the chorus implores the god to use his powerful vision to determine the hero's location (94–102):

> *Helios, you whom the quick-moving night brings forth when she is slain,*
> *you whom she lulls back to sleep when you are burned out, this I ask of*
> *you, Helios, Helios: herald forth news of the son of Alkmene. Where, oh*
> *where, I ask, does he dwell, you who blaze forth with brilliant flashing:*
> *at the channels to the Black Sea, or leaning upon the two continents?*
> *Speak, you who are powerful for your eye.*

Helios provides at the cosmic level a masculine audience equal to this hero who bestrides the world, an eye in the sky for whom earthly affairs from east to west provide a kind of theater and whose power is reflected in his splendor and panoramic vision. As such, he offers an idealized masculine image of the spectator, distant and detached, perfect in his vantage and unerring in his knowledge, and the questing and conquering Heracles offers a display of sheer performative power to match. As pure spectator, Helios has as it were no subject position, no cultural location or personal experience to influence what and how he sees. Able to see things simply as they "are," he suggests a beholding that is free of the need for mediation or interpretation. His heralding (*karuxai*), unlike that of his mortal counterpart Lichas (*kêrux* 188), is without duplicity or motive.

Yet the chorus' description of the Sun and this simple and clear-cut equation of sight, power, and masculinity are on closer examination ambivalent and potentially tragic: in the counterbalancing power of a female night (*nux*) who in maternal fashion brings forth and puts to bed (*tiktei kateunazei te*) the exhausted god and on whom his power is thus dependent; and in the danger inherent within the beams of the Sun himself, which generate not only light but also heat, and with it the power to destroy that upon which it looks, anticipating the fatal role that the sun will play in activating the dark poisons on the robe. In a kind of literary version of the Heisenberg principle, we will be shown that the spectator cannot look without in some way affecting what he sees.

The female *theatês* is similarly intimated in Deianeira's opening description of her "courtship" by Heracles and Acheloös. Here too we have a display of male strength, which Deianeira describes as an *agôn* (20) presided over by Zeus *agônios* (26). Yet her perspective complicates this scene of masculine prowess, and she must direct us elsewhere for the details (21–25):

> *As to the nature of their struggle, I could not tell you, for I do not know.*
> *Whoever (*hostis*) sat there fearless at the spectacle – he (*hode*) might*
> *tell you. I sat dumbstruck with fear that my beauty would only bring me*
> *pain.*

The hypothetical male spectator is defined by his ability to take in such a sight *atarbês* and to report the outcome unequivocally. Deianeira's fear (*phobôi*) makes her an unwilling spectator, indeed unable to watch at all, and she reports the outcome ambiguously: *kalôs, ei dê kalôs* (26–27). The ambivalence of her experience is captured in the language of spectacle. Those who watch the show (*theas*) are properly seated (*thakôn*), terms appropriate to the appreciation of public spectacle. Deianeira is seated (*hêmên*), but *hêmai* unlike *thakeô* describes a sitting still or idle. The word *ekpeplêgmenê* has strong dramatic resonances, with *ekplêxis* often referring to the astonishment the tragic poet produces, but here it describes the fear that made her unable to look on.[12] Ironically, this same fear makes her tragic for us, precisely in its representation of her subjectivity and vulnerability – in this case her consciousness of her own implication in the situation. Just as Deianeira sees this physical spectacle from a perspective that reflects its tragic dimension, it is she rather than the contestants who becomes for us a tragic focus for the complexity and subjectivity of her position.

As if in response to Deianeira's invitation to "ask someone else" about the duel, the chorus provides in the first stasimon a "virtual" first-person account, speaking "like a spectator" (*thatêr . . . hoia*, 526)[13] and in a way that reflects their status as *parthenoi*. Like Deianeira, they refer to the event as *agôn* (506), but for them it is not Zeus but Aphrodite (*eulektros . . . Kupris*, 515) who comes down in person to umpire (*rhabdonomei*, 516). As these young women "watch" the encounter, the struggle of heroes is just a chaotic mêlée of noise and dust, blows and inarticulate groans (see 517–22). The true object of their attention is revealed in the final stanza (523–30):

> But the delicate girl with the beautiful face sat on the far-off hill, waiting for the one who would be her husband – I speak as a spectator would. The girl they fought over waited with pitiful (eleinon) gaze for the end. And suddenly she was gone from her mother, like a calf left all alone.

In contrast to the "action scene" on which the male audience is fixed, the female chorus offers a rival spectacle in the image of Deianeira, the unwilling spectator, seated alone on the hillside, for whom they become an imaginary audience. This counterimage becomes an interpretive gesture that gives expression to the *meaning* this contest has for them. Where the duel of Heracles and Acheloös offers a display of physical agony, the suffering of the woman who waits alone to learn her fate is more tragic in character and makes her the object of their pity (*eleinon*). As she is marked by the more complex subjectivity, the chorus directs the reader accordingly.

The chorus' ability to empathize with the situation of the maiden Deianeira is the result of not only the spectacle but also their own subject position, as constituted by their age, sex, and life experience. Deianeira addresses this directly in her earlier exchange with them, where ironically she challenges their ability to understand her situation. As they enter in the parodos, they express sympathy for her tear-filled vigils and declare their kind regard; they counsel against despair, advising her to trust in the cyclic nature of fortune and in Zeus' mindfulness of his children. Deianeira is touched by their support but declines their advice, pointing instead to the limits of their understanding. In the process she articulates a theory of sympathy that underscores the subjectivity of tragic response (141–52):

> *You are here, I imagine, because you have learned of my suffering. But*
> *may you never come to know from your own suffering how my heart is*
> *torn. Now you are inexperienced. For young life is nurtured in such*
> *places of its own, afflicted neither by the heat of the sun-god, nor the*
> *rain, nor the winds, and grows its life in trouble-free pleasure; until the*
> *time when she is called a woman instead of a maiden, and she gets her*
> *share of worries at night, fearful for her husband or her children. Then*
> *someone might see for herself, by looking at her own situation, the ills by*
> *which I am crushed.*

In describing her situation as a *pathêma* (first occurrence of the root *path-*), she declares its tragic character and exploits the semantics of the word: they cannot fully understand (*ekmathois* – a key term in the play[14]) her *suffering* (*pathêma*) because they have not had the necessary *experience* (*pathousa*). Deianeira describes such knowledge as more than mere awareness: the chorus may know of her pain, but it cannot understand how she suffers, since as *parthenoi* they lack experience (*apeiros*). Deianeira does not suggest that they need to have suffered the *same* experiences as she but only experiences of the same order – any *gunê*, she suggests, will come to know what it is to be "fearful for her husband or for her children" (150). Tragic understanding becomes a process of extrapolation: by "looking at" one's own affairs (*tên hautou skopôn praxin*), one can then "see for oneself" (*eis idoito*) the sufferings (*kakoisi*) of another. Deianeira's remonstrances to the chorus describe a model of tragic experience that involves a dialectic between sympathy and subjectivity. It suggests how the audience is to draw upon its own experience of suffering to enter into the tragic predicament of another, even as it shows the boundaries that may limit our readings and preclude full understanding.[15]

This pattern is dramatized most fully in the spectacular entrance of Lichas and the captive women. The episode takes on a markedly self-referential character by the way in which it plays against the familiar conventions of the messenger speech and problematizes the scene-type:[16] doubling the figure of the *angelos* in the old man and Lichas, embedding their competing *logoi* one within the other, with the "first messenger" (180, cf. 191) openly vying with the second (348) to win Deianeira's reward and favor. In its repeated use of verbs of seeing, the scene draws attention to the extravagant spectacle that Deianeira beholds.[17] In the exposition that follows, Lichas functions not only as messenger but also as a kind of poet and performer, a creative artist who presents the fiction he has constructed to Deianeira. This is the domestic counterpart to his more public "show," which is marked by its theatrical and performative character,[18] and he presents it with equal flair and conviction.

Even as Lichas' opening report secures the news of Heracles' imminent return, the visual dimension of this spectacle begins to impress itself. As Lichas directs her attention to "the women you see before your eyes" (*horais en ommasin*, 241), she begins to take in the larger mise-en-scène (242–43): "And they, by the gods, who are they, and who is their master? For they are pitiable (*oiktrai*), unless their misfortune deceives me." Deianeira's expression of pity (*oiktrai*, the first occurrence of this root word in the play) suggests the powerful impression they have made upon her and the distance between the herald's and her reading of this scene: where she sees a group of wretched women and seeks after their identity, he presents them as so much human cargo, "choice possessions for himself [Heracles] and for the gods" (245). In his account of the sack of Oechalia, the women are relegated to a minor role (two lines out of forty-two) in a larger story of moral principles, hubris, divine retribution, and inherited guilt (283–85): "The women you see (*eisorais*) here come to you from being prosperous to find an unenviable life."

For Lichas, their plight is so much narrative raw material to exploit, and it is significant that he uses *pathos* in reference only to Heracles' suffering (256, 261), not theirs. Deianeira's reading of the spectacle opposes his almost point for point (293–302):

> How could I not rejoice, and have every right to do so, when I hear of the fortunate issue of my husband's work? How necessary it is that my joy keep step with his. But nevertheless those who are circumspect feel apprehensive for the man who fares well, lest he be tripped up. For a terrible pity (oiktos deinos) comes over me, friends, as I look upon (horôsêi) these unfortunate women, wandering homeless and without a fatherland to a foreign land. They were once perhaps children of free men, but now they have the slave's life.

Invited to enjoy this scene of suffering from a position of status, security, and knowledge, Deianeira demurs, despite the fact that she would be "perfectly justified" (*pandikôi phreni*, 294) to do so. She refuses to view the scene as a matter of a simple "justice," in the knowledge that "for those who consider well" (*toisin eu skopoumenois* – implicitly "for those who *behold* well") prosperity may be the harbinger of disaster. This awareness makes her apprehensive (*tarbein*) for the man who is successful and evokes pity (*oiktos deinos*) for those whose lives have been overturned. Where Lichas presents their situation dispassionately, her words suggest the pathos with which she regards them. Where he cites Zeus and justice, she sees fate and fortune (*duspotmous* 299, *dustalaina* 307, *talaina* 320; cf. *eutukhê* 293). Deianeira's sympathy is clearly related to her earlier comments to the chorus. Just as she had insisted that only someone who knew the anxieties (*phrontidôn*, 149) of womanhood could understand her situation, here too it is her concern for her own family that enables her to understand the suffering of the captives. Her fear (*tarbein*) that the prosperous may be "tripped up" (*sphalêi*, 297) applies as readily to her own husband as to these captive women. She prays such a tragedy may never befall her own children, again through the language of sight (303–6): "Zeus, god of victory, may I never see (*eisidoimi*) you coming to my family like this. Or, if you are going to do something, at least not while I live. That is my fear as I look at (*horômenê*) these women."

Her ability to extrapolate from personal experience allows her to reject the hierarchical perspective Lichas offers and to appreciate the tragedy of the situation. Again it is specifically the *sight* of these women that leads her to single out Iole for special regard (307–13):

> O poor girl, who of the young women are you? Are you unmarried, or a
> mother? For your nature has no experience (apeiros) with all of this,
> and you are noble. Lichas, to whom does this foreign woman belong?
> Speak out. For when I saw (blepousa) her, I pitied (ôiktisa) her most of
> these women, in that she alone knows how to feel.

The application of *apeiros* (143, 309) to both the chorus and the Oechalian maidens suggests the distance between them: the one a picture of idyllic youth untouched by suffering, the other a paradigm of the tragic. Deianeira directs the audience away from the moralizing account with which Lichas rationalizes their suffering. Although she is deceived as to the circumstances of the situation, she models the kind of sympathetic understanding the spectator is to bring to the tragic text, and in opposing her reading to the performance of Lichas, the text encodes the response in terms of gender. As tragic suffering is again represented through the metaphor of female weakness, vulnerability, and sensitivity, the kind of response it is to elicit is equally feminine. In a kind of triangulated arrangement that is frequent in Sophocles, Lichas and Deianeira become rival *theatai*: he regards the victorious display of the questing hero, she the tragic situation and tortured sensibilities of its victims. The tragic *theatês*, though placed in the position of empowered spectator, declines the invitation to take pleasure from his vantage of authority and control and assumes a subject position that sees from the object's perspective of suffering and powerlessness.

This multiple perspective has an interesting counterpart in *Philoctetes*, in a scene in which Neoptolemus, even more than Deianeira, finds himself overpowered by his pity for another. At the climactic moment the young hero, having confessed his true intentions to Philoctetes, finds himself unable to execute them. At last in possession of the bow that has been his goal, he balks, and tries to explain himself to a confused chorus (965–66): "A terrible pity (*deinos oiktos*) for this man has befallen me, not just for the first time now but for some time." Philoctetes replies (967–68): "O child, pity (*eleêson*) me, for gods' sake, and do not expose yourself to others with this reproach, that you have taken me by deceit."

In the preceding scenes, Neoptolemus has seen Philoctetes in the fullness of his misery – his abandonment by the Greeks, the squalor of his living conditions, the horror of his solitude, the agony of his illness. After gradually and cumulatively taking in the impact of these, like Deianeira he acknowledges that he has been overtaken by a *deinos oiktos*. Clearly it is not only the magnitude of Philoctetes' suffering that has brought on these feelings but also his ability to connect with and relate to this alien realm of experience. As removed as Neoptolemus is from the life that Philoctetes suffers, he has come to see in the hero a common exemplar of the human condition and a fate that could be no less his own. This again is exactly as Philoctetes had earlier begged of him (501–6):

> you *save me*, you *pity* (eleêson*)* me, *seeing how all things are dangerous*
> *and that men run the risk of doing either well or badly. When a man is*
> *not in trouble, he should keep an eye on the dangers, and whenever life*
> *is good he should most of all watch out not to be destroyed unawares.*

Again like Deianeira, Neoptolemus recognizes that present prosperity
is no safeguard against future misfortune, that indeed it may be the
prelude to subsequent disaster, and in his expression of *oiktos* he shows
that he has taken this lesson to heart. And just as Lichas is unable or
unwilling to make these connections, so too Odysseus, who has been
an off-stage spectator to this display, is unmoved – he runs on stage to
keep his shameful (*kakist' andrôn*) young comrade from acting on his
pity.

The paradigm of tragic response offered in both of these situations is
classic and humanistic in character. It is also recognizably Aristotelian.
It recalls the statements in *Poetics* that describe the best kind of tragedy
as that which is successful in arousing pity for the kind of protagonist who is undeserving of his misfortune and ethically like ourselves
(*peri ton homoion*, 1453a4–6). And it also resonates with Aristotle's definition of pity in *Rhetoric* (2.8, 1385b13–16) in which he emphasizes that
an additional precondition for the experience of pity is the recognition that the suffering of the person pitied is also one that we could
suffer ourselves.[19] That Neoptolemus acknowledges his *deinos oiktos* for
Philoctetes can thus be read as recognition that he has also come to see
Philoctetes' suffering in a larger context, a noble man's change in fortune from prosperity to misery and a principle that might apply to him
as well. And likewise, in beholding the suffering of Iole, Deianeira sees
someone who is equally like herself, not so much in her noble origins
(although she recognizes these) as in her recognition of a possible (and
ironically, actual) destiny for herself. Indeed, in her plea to Zeus that
"may I never see you coming to my family like this" she provides a
textbook example of Aristotle's claim that one pities an evil "which a
person might expect himself *or one of his own* to suffer."

Neoptolemus is closer in age to Hyllos than Odysseus, and for him
too the play presents a kind of coming of age. Although he is certainly
not "womanly" in his emotions, neither has he yet been fully inured to

the callous sensibilities of his older tutors. As such he is, like Deianeira, possessed of a sensibility and an emotional flexibility that enables him to sympathize with perspectives and experiences at odds with his own. Deianeira's ability to extrapolate from personal experience is not limited to her own gender. She shows herself able to "read across gender" and to use her experience to understand both male and female. Even when she discovers the truth of Iole's arrival, her knowledge of human nature (*t'anthrôpôn*, 439) allows her to sympathize with both her husband and with Iole. She says to Lichas (436–44):

> *I beg you . . . do not give me a deceptive speech. For you will not be speaking your words to a base woman, one who does not understand human nature, that people do not always take delight in the same things. Anyone who gets up like a boxer to oppose Eros is not thinking well. For he rules even of the gods whomever he will, and me too for sure. And how not others too beside me?*

Because she is no less ruled by love than her husband, it would be foolish to blame others who are in love's thrall. Deianeira's response is a function less of her individual character than of her experience as a woman: her vulnerability as a maiden, her fear for her husband's safety, her anxiety about her marital security and her family. Male characters in the play, on the other hand, prove consistently unable to read successfully across gender. Lichas' coldly moralistic reading of the suffering of the Oechalian maidens is aptly reflected in his misunderstanding of Deianeira herself. He claims that it was his concern for Deianeira's feelings that led him to misrepresent the situation, for fear his words would bring her pain (*algunoimi toisde tois logois*, 482; cf. 458). He patronizingly declares his surprise to find in Deianeira not only a woman but also "a human whose thoughts are human and not insensitive" (*manthanô thnêtên phronousan thnêta k'ouk agnômona*, 471–72).

INVERSIONS AND TRANSFORMATIONS

The second "half" of *Trachiniae* (the break is clear at 663) is structured as a series of inversions and transformations of the first. Deianeira
and Heracles achieve, respectively, full tragic status, and their deaths
become a structured sequence: from female to male, off stage to on
stage, domestic to public, narrated to enacted. Deianeira's death is offered as "virtual spectacle" by the *exangelos*, and it comments further
on the display of the Oechalian women. Just as Deianeira had provided a sympathetic audience to the suffering of Iole, her suffering
becomes a tragic scene for the spectating nurse. As if to underscore
this, the nurse repeatedly emphasizes her eye-witness status (*epeidon,
hôs dê plêsia parastatis*, 889), not just to strengthen her credibility but
to connect the visual experience to the scene's tragic character: "had
you been close at hand to see (*parousa plêsia eleusses*) what she did, you
would have pitied her greatly (*ôiktisas*)" (896–97).[20] The nurse watches
Deianeira, first as she "hid herself where no one could see her" (903),
then as she moved through various parts of the house, and finally as
she retreated into the marriage chamber, where the nurse hides her
face and looks on in secret (914). Her secret vantage reminds us of our
own invisible presence in the theater. Also like the tragic *theatês*, the
nurse is spared the actual scene of Deianeira's death, which happens as
it were "off stage" – she returns with Hyllos to see the corpse, not the
deed.

The nurse's narrative is remarkable for its careful coordination
of space, gender, and perspective, contrasting the female world of
Deianeira with the masculine world of Hyllos. As Deianeira goes
within the house, Hyllos proceeds to the outer courtyard. Where
Hyllos spreads blankets for his father's sick-bed, so Deianeira spreads
coverlets on her lonely marriage bed (902, 916). As son prepares to
leave the household altogether to join his father, Deianeira goes deeper
within, to say farewell to its altars, her servants, and her marriage bed.

The movement toward the tragic act is thereby coordinated with the penetration of domestic and feminine space, and with the exposure of its most private recesses comes the revelation of her most inner emotions in extravagant expressions of grief.[21] Tragedy here is given a thoroughly female face: the heroine, in the female space, in unabandoned grief, culminating in the feminine death par excellence, suicide.[22] And Hyllos, exchanging the outer court for the marriage chamber, is transformed into a tragic spectator (932): "And when the boy saw her, he groaned." The verb *ôimôxen*, which echoes the response of the crowd to Heracles' suffering (*oimôgêi*, 783), marks Hyllos' movement into the tragic space, and his status as a tragic spectator is coordinated with his own effeminization. As his mother had stricken herself in the side (*pleuran*, 931), he lies down side to side with her (*pleurothen pleuran*, 938–39), and his laments echo his mother's unrestrained grief.[23]

In similar fashion, the story of Heracles' death completes a gendered movement, from masculine, performative spectacle to female, tragic spectacle. Hyllos' account captures the theatricality of the hero's arrival at Cape Cenaeum, with its lofty setting, its large audience (795) and fulsome ceremony. Heracles officiates, glorying in his new *peplos* and sacrificing male beasts (760) to "Zeus of the fathers" (753). The process of transformation of this spectacle into tragedy is signaled by sudden changes in the relation between the hero and the audience. After his bloody murder of Lichas, "all the people cried out with a loud wailing" (*oimôgêi*, 783). A few lines later we hear how Heracles, rehearsing his ill-arranged marriage, "cried out in a loud wail" (*oimôgêi*, 790, also the same word to be used to describe Hyllos' response to the sight of his slain mother, *oimôgêi*, 932). It is precisely in the loss of his superiority, in the leveling of difference between performer and audience, that the scene assumes a tragic aspect.

Heracles' suffering is also associated explicitly with his exposure, weakness, and vulnerability. He begs Hyllos to remove him not only from the sight of those around him but also from the company of men altogether. Again, the language of sight predominates (794–802):

> Then rolling his eyes (ophthalmon) and raising them above the thick
> smoke hanging about him, he saw (eide) me in tears amidst the huge
> crowd. He looked at (prosblepsas) me and cried out: "Son, come here,
> do not run away from my pain, not even if you should have to die
> together with me. But lift me up and take me away, and best of all set
> me where no man shall see (opsetai) me. Or if you have pity (oikton)
> for me, then rather transport me from this land as quickly as possible,
> and let me not die here."

Unwilling to leave his father to die in some desolate place, Hyllos brings him home, only to be displayed to an audience that is large (1071) and feminine in its composition – apart from the anonymous old man, domestics, and attendants, the only male present is Hyllos.

The entrance of Heracles provides the crowning piece of the play's spectacle and completes the *nostos* that informs the play. As so often in tragedy, this *nostos* is concluded in ironic terms – the triumphant return of the hero becomes the occasion of his destruction, and the warrior who has vanquished his external enemies is overwhelmed by female forces from within his household. These inversions are again marked in the language of sight and spectacle. The woman who had most longed for his return abandons the stage when she learns that his appearance is imminent: "you shall see (*esopsesthe*) him at once, either alive or newly dead," Hyllos tells his mother (805–6), adding that she will not again see (*opsêi*) his equal (812); as she exits in silence, Hyllos prays for a wind to speed her from his sight (*ophthalmôn emôn*, 815). The chorus had earlier sung in jubilant expectation of his return home as a reunion of male and female and a kind of *hieros gamos*. His arrival was to represent a new marriage at which the whole house should ring out with joy, its men and women united in respective hymns to Apollo and Artemis (205–24). In the second stasimon they imagine his glorious arrival, laden with the spoils of victory and filled with new longing for his wife (645, 660–62). But with their prayers on the verge of fulfillment, they wish only that they could be spirited elsewhere, dreading that they will die of fear (*tarbelea*) at the mere sight (*eisidousa*) of him (955–58). Here the same word (*tarb-*), which repeatedly has described Deianeira's fear that she might *not* see Heracles (23, 176, 297), becomes the fear of what they will see when he arrives. They await the appearance of Heracles as an *aspeton theama* (961) – an "unspeakable spectacle" that cannot be expressed in words. This description proves to be literally the case. The mighty hero is carried on stage speechless (*anaudatos*, 968) in a procession so eerily silent (*apsophon*, 967) that the chorus cannot tell if he is asleep or dead. The spectacle is "unspeakable" for them, too – they speak only four lines in the three hundred of the exodus.

The arrival of the hero with his male entourage, before the equally large female audience that awaits him, is the culmination of the play's gendering of spectacle. One way to approach the ending of this difficult play, which has put off readers and critics, is precisely in terms of a conflict between the hero and the infrastructure of the genre, that is, of locating the male within a space that is intrinsically female and tragic. The tragic fulfillment of this play is presented as the establishment of a feminine space and the feminization of the hero who is placed in it. His life is made to conform to the laws and rule of that tragic space, and his suffering is an extension of the female suffering that has preceded it. The chorus, who define the space into which Heracles arrives, mark the tragic unity of the two "halves" of this tragedy in their inability to distinguish the suffering they have seen from that which they wait to see (947–52):

> *Which woes do I mourn for first, which woes next? Poor me, it is difficult to determine. Some of them we can see* (horan) *within the house, others we await in expectation. To have and to anticipate come to the same thing.*

Here, as with Oedipus' appearance at *OT* 1297ff., Sophocles uses the chorus as a surrogate audience to orchestrate the external response to a piece of supercharged spectacle.

This relocation is the proposition that is elaborated in the rest of the exodos: into what kind of space has Heracles been brought, and can he find a place in it? The ending of *Trachiniae* presents a hero who adamantly refuses to conform to the gender and power relations of tragedy. To try to fit this most "hypermasculine" of heroes, as Loraux calls him, into this genre is to drive a very square peg into a very round hole.[24] Heracles' finale represents his resistance at the prospect of becoming tragic, that is, of *being seen* in his humbled condition. His first reaction to his undoing at the hands of his wife had been to ask to be removed from human sight altogether. Now, when he is revealed to the audience that awaits him, he declares his effeminized status, and openly asks for pity (1070–75):

> *Come here, son, be brave. And pity* (oiktiron) *me, pitiable* (oiktron) *in the eyes of many, who have wept and cried like a maiden* (parthenos). *No one could say that he has ever seen* (idein) *me do this before, but in my pain I always kept myself from groaning. But now, from such a man as I was, I – poor me – have been found to be female* (thêlus).

Heracles' resistance to the role of tragic protagonist is replicated in his inability to empathize with the tragedy of others. Where he grudgingly asks others for pity, he pities no one but himself. He reacts to Hyllos' predicament and Deianeira's death, even after her innocence is declared, with utter indifference. Although some critics relate this to his self-sufficiency and imminent apotheosis,[25] the patterns of gender in the play suggest a larger concern with the relation between tragic response and masculinity itself. The model of masculinity embodied in the questing and philandering Heracles is devoid of the kind of experience that would afford the kind of tragic understanding modeled in Deianeira, for whom feminine experience has provided the capacity for tragic pity. This same kind of masculinity is mirrored in the story of Hyllos' initiation into manhood. In a sense, Hyllos goes through two initiations in this play, each involving the spectacle of human suffering and human response. As a witness to the death of his mother, he was initiated by the nurse into the mysteries of tragic response, and his response as we have noted is carefully coordinated with his emotional and even physical connectedness with his mother. At the same time, his dutiful obedience to his dying father initiates him into Herculean masculinity, a process that culminates in his participation (albeit reluctantly and under duress) in the exchange of Iole as bride, reaffirming masculine authority, the male subject position and the object status of the female.[26] At the end of the play Hyllos is required to disregard his feelings for his mother and his grief altogether, to choose, as it were, between being a man and being a tragic spectator, and is compelled to renounce the latter as part of the ties that bind him to his mother's world.

It cannot be emphasized too strongly that gender is being employed here as a metaphor and as a structural device to represent the range of human response to suffering. Moreover, as a representative of "extreme masculinity," Heracles can hardly be offered as a model of the typical male Athenian spectator. But in connecting the hypermasculine with an incapacity for tragic response, and in extending that incapacity to others such as Lichas and Hyllos in his final achievement of manhood, the play presents in gendered form one end of the spectrum of tragic response, as it correspondingly presents in Deianeira, the chorus, and even Hyllos prior to his final initiation to manhood models that link the feminine to a capacity for tragic response and in particular for pity. In this regard, the play reinscribes the familiar association of women with a disposition that offers pity even too readily and easily, as in the quote from *Ajax* 580 with which this chapter began – "woman is, to be sure, a creature most inclined to pity (*philoiktiston*)" – and Megara's apologetic words to her father-in-law at *Heracles* 536: "For the female of the species (*to thêlu*) is more compassionate (*oiktron*) than the male." To these are also associated the many references, usually critical, to women as more prone to tears and weeping.[27] That tragic pity involves a disposition that is in relative terms feminine is also implicit in the well-known words of Ajax, a hero who approximates the Herculean model of masculinity (*Ajax* 650–53):

> And I, who formerly was frightening in my obstinacy, like a sword that
> has been hardened by dipping, have become womanish (ethêlunthên)
> in my speech for this woman, and I feel pity (oiktirô) to leave her a
> widow and my son fatherless.

Whether offered sincerely or not, Ajax's words acknowledge that pity involves a softening of harder masculine responses – indeed, his words are in direct response to Tekmessa's plea at 594: "for gods' sake, be softened" (*malassou*, 594). It is significant that at the end of *Ajax*, Odysseus – who earlier in the play acknowledged his own profound sense of pity (*epoiktirô*, 121) at the spectacle of his humiliated enemy – cautions Agamemnon against an excessive hard–heartedness (*sklêran . . . psukhên*), and that Agamemnon associates this kind of softness and flexibility with cowardice (*deilous*, 1361–62), leaving the gendered associations of the hard–soft metaphor only implicit.[28]

This way of conceiving of theatrical representation in terms of gender and power resonates with contemporary theories that have examined questions of aesthetics and representation in relation to power and

hierarchy.[29] Feminist film critics, extrapolating from the representation of women in cinema, have argued that the genre is fundamentally
structured around a process of objectification and a mechanism that
is deeply gendered, by which the director creates a gaze that invests a
"male" looker with power over a "female" object, quite independent of
the gender of the party that occupies these positions in any given situation. Cinema itself is revealed as one of the multiple "technologies of
gender," to use Teresa de Lauretis' phrase, and is of its nature complicit
in gendering the reader in ways oppressive to women.[30] Others, most
notably Susanne Kappeler, have engaged in a more radical critique of
Western aesthetics to insist that the structure of representation itself –
the very categories of reader and text, spectator and spectacle – is based
on the exercise of power by the former over the latter; and that this
differential is implicitly and in some cases explicitly linked to gender,
such that the very notion of the aesthetic subject and object involves
and inscribes categories of power and gender.[31] Amy Richlin summarizes Kappeler's argument, by which high art and pornography both
participate in what is ultimately the same politics of representation
(1992: xvii):

> [Kappeler] argues that the process of representation is like the process of
> pornography in that both involve a relatively powerful viewer and a
> relatively powerless viewed, and that images and texts are
> crystallizations of this power relationship and are further used to mark,
> enforce, reproduce, translate, and trade in power.

Greek tragedy is particularly amenable to such an examination of the
"power dynamics" of the theatrical situation. Athenian tragedy puts
the lives and destinies of powerful individuals on display before the
powerful collective gaze of its audience at a ritual assembly of citizen

males on a state occasion. The act of spectating takes on an especially intense character in light of the social context of Athenian ethics, where mechanisms of shame and public scrutiny play so central a role in the shaping of behavior. Indeed, tragedy consistently uses metaphors of emasculation and effeminization to express the destruction of the tragic hero, in ways linked with powerful spectacle, exposing an impotent hero to the public gaze. In *Agamemnon*, Clytemnestra celebrates her appropriation of masculinity in exposing the corpses of Agamemnon ("the darling of the girls at Ilium") and Cassandra together. In *Oedipus the King*, Oedipus' self-blinding is a powerful symbol of his symbolic self-castration and emasculation, which is reflected also in his helpless dependency on Creon and even his children. Jason's pitiful cries to Medea, who towers over him with the bodies of their sons, represent his humiliation at the extirpation of his male lineage. And in *Heracles*, the hero's destruction is expressed in his muted cries as he is hidden under a woman's veil.

Trachiniae comes close to making explicit the relations of gender and power that constitute tragic spectatorship and provides a model that can be employed more generally in the analysis of tragedy. On the one hand, it gives us a hypermasculine protagonist who openly announces his own emasculation. On the other, it provides a theory of tragic response that suggests that the tragic spectator must become feminized in order to respond properly to tragedy. *Trachiniae* suggests that if we are to experience tragically, we must extrapolate from the stuff of our own lives and find in our subject position the comparanda that allow us to behold from a sympathetic and nonhierarchical perspective. But in this play only women seem to be able to do this, and only women's lives seem to offer the kinds of experiences that can be used in this way. In thus encoding and gendering successful and unsuccessful tragic spectators, *Trachiniae* suggests a conflict between masculinity and the capacity for tragic response. To the extent that *Trachiniae* invites its male audience to read Deianeira's situation sympathetically, it identifies problems in the construction of masculinity that work to preclude that very possibility.[32]

◻◉◻

ENDNOTES

1. *Poet.* 1449b; Aristotle discusses pity in the *Rhetoric* (2.8, 1385b13–16), defining it as "a certain pain at an apparently destructive or painful evil happening to one who does not deserve it and which a person might expect himself or one of his own to suffer, and this when it seems close at hand" (trans. Kennedy). The bibliography on Aristotle's statements regarding "tragic pity" is immense; see esp. Belfiore 1992: 179–253.

2. On the connection between pity and sight generally, see Sternberg (Ch. 1 in this volume).

3. For discussion and bibliography on the metatheatrical features in Sophocles and Greek tragedy in general, see text and notes in Easterling 1997: 165–73; Falkner 1998: 24–33 and 1999: 174–79; and Ringer 1998: 1–30.

4. Compare Taplin 1986.

5. Ringer (1998: 51–66) comments insightfully on various of the play's self-referential features. As will be clear, I take fundamental issue with his view of Deianeira as a failed or imperfect audience and "deprived of full knowledge of the objects and people brought to her perception" (57–58); on the relationship between deception, the theatrical illusion, and the tragic audience, see Falkner 1998: 43–46.

6. Winnington-Ingram 1980: 75.

7. See in particular the excellent recent studies of the *Trachiniae* by Wohl 1998 and Ormand 1999, which focus on the relation between gender, marriage, exchange, and male homosocial practice. Wohl (esp. 3–56) sees the play as an expression of the "tragic exchange of women" and in relation to Deianeira's object status; the play, "by staging Deianeira's struggle for subject status, questions this necessary drama of male subjectivity." Ormand (esp. 36–59) sees the play's issue in Deianeira's failure to understand that Heracles' relationship with her (as with Iole) is not primarily an expression of heterosexual desire: "Heracles views his wedding to Deianeira as he views virtually every other aspect of his life: as a relationship, whether antagonistic or friendly, with other men. It is an expression of male homosocial desire."

8. Segal (1981: 106) identifies this "tragedy of separation" in the "spatial divergence between the two protagonists, circle and line, inward and outward movement."

9. See Zeitlin 1990a: 90–96. To her discussion of *Republic, Gorgias, Laws* and *Symposium*, add *Apology* 35b where Socrates criticizes the "pitiful dramas" (*eleina dramata*) that some defendants produce in court as unbecoming and womanish. On the relation between Plato's objections to tragedy and his association of pity and pitiable behavior with women, see also Johnson and Clapp's chapter in this volume.

10. On the Great Dionysia and civic ideology, see especially Goldhill 1990. The kinds of tensions that Goldhill identifies between public ideology and certain texts (e.g., *Ajax, Philoctetes*) I here extend into the area of gender formation – an issue the more striking for the crucial role that the ephebes played in the Great Dionysia: their participation in the Procession (*pompê*) in escort of the sacrificial bull; and their attendance at the performances (seated together in the *ephêbikon*).

11. Johnson and Clapp's chapter in this volume.

12. Aristotle uses *ekplêxis* twice in *Poetics* of tragic plot, not performance, in connection with the "best kind" of recognitions (1454a4, 1455a17), and singles out *OT* in this regard, which he also commends for its ability to achieve the tragic effects entirely independent of performance. The term has strong Aeschylean associations: see *Frogs* 962 (and cf. 144).

13. Following Zielinski 1896 and Easterling 1982, who notes *ad* 526–28: "The Chorus can describe the blows and groans because they imagine the duel as if they had been spectators at the games; whereas D. simply waited in a piteous state of anxiety until it was over."

14. The theme of "knowing for certain" (*ek manthanein*) is introduced programmatically in 1–3, where Deianeira refers to the "old saying" that one cannot truly know (*ekmathois*) if someone's life has been good or bad until he is dead, and offers herself as the counterexample, assured already of the tragic character of her life; cf. 336, 450, 583, 694.

15. Deianeira provides a succinct expression of this later, when the chorus tries to ease her fears about the sending of the robe. Because her intentions were innocent, the anger against her might be softened (727–28). She again disqualifies their advice for their lack of experience: "these are the kinds of things a person would say who has no trouble of his own, but not one who has grief in his own household" (729–30). As in her more developed exposition, Deianeira suggests that only those who are acquainted with suffering can understand her situation.

16. See especially Heiden (1989: 53–64 and 67–71), who focuses on the epistemological implications of the conflicting reports.

17. The messenger emphasizes what Deianeira is about to see (*opsêi*, 199), Deianeira refers to Heracles' imminent return as an *aelpton omma* (203), and the chorus attempts to direct her vision (*blepein*, 224) as the procession comes into view.

18. Lichas' initial off-stage report was proclaimed to "all the people of Malis," who crowded about in a circle (194) in a meadow that was also the Trachinians' place of assembly (371–72). He holds forth before a crowd eager to learn (*ekmathein*, 196) from him.

19. On this point see especially Konstan 2001: 49–74.

20. As the chorus notes from the cries it hears (*kluô tinos oiktou*, 862–67), the pity is quickly shared by all within the house. On *oiktos* as implying audible grief or lamentation, see Konstan 2001: 53–54.

21. Compare Padel (1992: 9): "Physically, tragedy was itself a paradox of inside and outside, an open space making public that which was unseen, such as feelings, the past, the secrets of the 'house.'"

22. Compare Loraux 1987: 23–24.

23. *odurmatôn* (936), *goômenos* (937), *anastenôn* (939), *klaiôn* (941).

24. Loraux 1990. Compare also Ormand 1999: 49.

25. For example, Silk (1985), who sees a conflict between Heracles' essential *autarkeia* and the suitability of his character for tragedy.

26. See especially Wohl 1998: 11–16.

27. On Plato's criticism of tragic pity in *Republic* as involving feminization and a loss of self-control, see in this volume Johnson and Clapp's chapter. On the historical and cultural causes for the association of tears and grief with women and their subsequent stigmatization, see van Wees 1998 and the literature cited there: "When, by 580 BC, the dust settles, controlled and rational behavior has established itself as a vital ingredient of true masculinity" (45).

28. On the larger significance of the scene, see Falkner 1993: 38–39.

29. This approach was earlier developed in relation to *Ajax* in Falkner 1999: 178–79.

30. Mulvey 1975; de Lauretis (1984: 58ff. and 1987: 117–18) discusses the achievement and theoretical limitations of Mulvey's work.

31. Kappeler 1986, esp. pp. 56–58, 103–5, and 212: "The subject-object relation is at the core of [the] dominant way of seeing. The individualistic perspective of our culture has insistently focused on the necessity of this pair, denying any capacity of the human individual for collectivity and intersubjectivity. It is the fundamental axiom of the justification of inequality, domination and power." Rabinowitz (1992: 37–39 and notes) usefully discusses Greek tragedy in the light of Mulvey, de Lauretis, MacKinnon and other feminist work on representation.

32. This chapter first took shape in 1997 during a research leave at Cambridge University, and I wish to thank in particular P. E. Easterling, for wise counsel and support throughout. Earlier versions were presented at meetings of the American Philological Association and the Comparative Drama Conference, as well as at the Rutgers conference that inspired this volume, and the chapter has profited greatly from the responses of those audiences. I am grateful to the editor of this volume and to the anonymous readers for a number of helpful suggestions that I have adopted.

PITY IN CLASSICAL ATHENIAN VASE PAINTING

JOHN H. OAKLEY

◎▣◎

WHAT DOES ATHENIAN CLASSICAL VASE PAINTING TELL US ABOUT pity, an emotion that has been explored mainly from the literary side? And does vase painting in any way reflect the tension between pity and power that is the central theme of this volume? At first, these might seem to be straightforward and easy questions to answer, but in reality they are quite complicated. Not only does contemporary artistic convention make it difficult to determine when pity is being depicted, but in many cases one cannot tell whether a specific vase painting would evoke pity from all viewers, just some, or none. Similarly, the identity of the viewing audience for a particular vase painting and the setting in which it was viewed are often uncertain and could vary. Yet despite such difficulties, reasonable answers can be found. The thought process I followed to answer these questions provides the underlying structure for this chapter and will take us in several different directions. In addition, I want to stimulate further thought about what methodologies and parameters scholars should use when interpreting the emotions of a figure in ancient Greek art.[1]

That various emotions, sometimes conflicting ones, can be assigned to the very same image is not uncommon because scholars often have different readings for the same scene. For example, compare the following two descriptions of the boy Perseus on a lekythos by the Providence Painter in Toledo (Fig. 1), where he is shown in a large wooden chest before his mother Danae and wicked grandfather Akrisios. Cedric Boulter and Kurt Luckner in the first fascicule of the *Corpus Vasorum Antiquorum* from the Toledo Museum of Art[2] say of Perseus:

> *He looks towards his mother, and raises his right hand to salute*
> *her. . . . What is unusual about the Toledo lekythos is the central role*
> *played by Perseus, and his resolute, dauntless gesture.*

More recently, however, Ellen Reeder in the catalog to the exhibition *Pandora* describes Perseus as follows:[3]

> *Inside the chest can be seen the head and shoulders of Perseus, whose*
> *head is in left profile as he gazes up at his mother's face and stretches his*
> *arm to her, fingers extending and touching. . . . We are at the moment*
> *in the drama when the chest has been finished, the carpenter has left,*
> *and Perseus has already been placed within. . . . Dwarfed by its size, he*
> *turns to his mother for comfort, his gesture and gaze echoing other scenes*
> *in which young children appeal to their nurse or mother for solace.*

Thus, depending on whose reading the viewer accepts, Perseus is either resolute and dauntless, or afraid and upset. In other words, he acts either as one would imagine a young hero should or as a young child normally would.

Which reading is correct cannot be determined, for nothing in the composition allows us definitively to support one over the other. In classical Greek art, children usually are shown extending both hands to an adult when seeking aid and comfort, although occasionally they use only one, as here.[4] Yet in another depiction of the same scene, Perseus is shown in the chest with his mother facing Akrisios, and the child extends one hand to him – and certainly this is not because he seeks comfort from him.[5] Therefore, the pose and gesture of Perseus on the Toledo lekythos do not solve the problem of interpretation. Normally one would rely on them, since faces are mainly nonexpressive at this time, in accordance with contemporary artistic convention. What emotion Perseus displays remains in the eye of the beholder.

FIGURE 1.

Danae, Perseus, and Akrisios. Attic red-figure lekythos attributed to the Providence Painter (front), c. 470 BCE. Slip decorated earthenware, ht. 15¹⁵⁄₁₆ in. (40.5 cm), diam. of mouth 3⁵⁄₃₂ in. (8 cm), shoulder 5⁵⁄₁₆ in. (13.5 cm), diam. of foot 3¹⁵⁄₁₆ in. (8.8 cm). Toledo Museum of Art, purchased with funds from the Libbey Endowment. Gift of Edward Drummond Libbey, 1969.369.

With the understanding that it can often be difficult to determine exactly which emotions figures in classical art display, let us turn now to pity. A natural starting point is to ask whether there exists an actual figure of pity, a personification – that is, a human form given to this abstract emotion.[6] Personifications appear already in Athenian art in the sixth century, one of the most famous examples being the red-figure calyx-krater of c. 515 BCE by Euphronios that shows Hypnos (Sleep) and Thanatos (Death) lifting up the dead body of Sarpedon to carry him off to Lycia for burial.[7] The late fifth century was the heyday for personifications in Attic vase painting, when a wide variety of them appear, particularly on the works of the Eretria and Meidias Painters. The Meidias Painter's hydria in Florence with Phaon and Demonassa provides an excellent example because inscriptions identify all the figures.[8] The personifications represented are Pothos (a desire for what is lost), Himeros (a desire for a person or thing), Pannychis (all-night revel), Herosora (springtime), Hygieia (health), and Eudaimonia (happiness).

Literary evidence for pity as a personification does exist. A fragment from the *Synergika* of Timokles (*PCG* VII, fr. 33), a fourth-century poet of Middle Comedy, mentions the god Eleos (Pity) and contrasts him with the god Phthonos (Envy). *Eleos* and *phthonos* are often thought of as opposites in Greek literature, because pity involves pain caused by another's misfortune, while envy is pain caused by another's good fortune. In addition, later sources mention the Altar of Pity in Athens, which may well be another name for the Altar of the Twelve Gods in the Agora.[9] We know of several cases where people sought refuge at the Altar of the Twelve Gods as early as 519 BCE, when ambassadors from Plataia came as suppliants, requesting help against Thebes (Hdt. 6.108.4). Because of the many different personifications shown on classical vases, and because there is evidence for pity as a personification in classical Athenian literature, one might well expect to find a depiction of the personification of pity. Unfortunately, at present there is none known in ancient art, although one could appear on some vase or relief discovered in the future.

A track less likely to produce a positive result, but one that also must be considered, is whether there exists an inscription on a vase indicating that pity is taking place in a particular scene. On occasion, inscriptions on vases tell us more than just names. In the tondo of a cup in Boston by Douris, for example, a vertical inscription overlaps the bent-over couple making love. As if coming from the man's mouth, it proclaims ἔχε ἥσυχος — keep still.[10] Another example is the inscription emanating from a kottabos-playing *hetaira* shown on a psykter by Euphronios in St. Petersburg.[11] It says in Sicilian dialect: τὶν τάνδε λατάσσο Λέαγρε – I cast these dregs for you, Leagros. Apparently she and her comrades are casting for the affection of the ones to whom they are attracted. Sometimes an inscription can also refer to an emotion taking place in the scene, as *AIΔΟΣ* appears to do on a red-figure amphora by Phintias where Leto veils herself when attacked by Tityos.[12] Unfortunately, the two main Greek words for pity, *eleos* and *oiktos*, and their cognates are not to my knowledge found at all. Thus, there is no inscriptional evidence to indicate that pity is shown on any Greek vase.

But what about when we look at the pictures on the vases? Do we ever sense pity despite the lack of inscriptions? To answer this we must follow two different tracks. The first is to consider whether there are any pictures that evoke a sense of pity from the viewer, the second whether there are any pictures in which one person is shown pitying another. Let us start with the first.

The Evocation of Pity from the Viewer

Many common subjects found on Greek vases are not likely candidates for pictures that evoke pity from the viewer. From everyday life these include scenes of: (1) athletics, (2) music, (3) the symposium,

(4) work and play, (5) cult and ritual, (6) schooling, and (7) the household. There are other types of everyday life scenes that are equally unlikely candidates, but those very common ones I have listed are enough to demonstrate that most such scenes are not subjects that would arouse pity from the viewer.

That said, however, there is one clear and obvious exception to the rule, and that is the subject of death. Greeks experienced its effects at an earlier age and more often than we do today in North America and Europe. A much shorter life expectancy (c. forty-five for males and thirty-six for females), a much higher childbirth mortality rate for both mother and child (only half of all children reached adulthood), and the greater discrepancy in age at marriage between husband and wife (Aristotle [*Pol.* 1335a28–29] suggests thirty-seven and eighteen respectively as appropriate ages) are contributing factors.[13] Of all the situations that might evoke the emotion of pity, death is the most common, and because the Greeks used special types of figured vases in their funerary ritual, the images on them supply a number of pity-evoking images.

Many are found on white-ground lekythoi with polychrome painting atop a white slip, the primary source of funerary imagery in classical Athens.[14] Made specifically for use in Athenian ritual, they are a type of vase whose intended audience we know for sure; the vast majority of other Attic painted vases, by contrast, were exported all over the Mediterranean. The most common scene on the white-ground lekythoi is the visit to the tomb, and one of the most moving of all figures in Greek vase painting is the old man at the tomb on the Achilles Painter's masterpiece in Berlin (Fig. 2).[15] He stands before a large white stele holding his hand to his forehead. The pain he feels for his dead son, the warrior shown on the other side of the tomb, is evident in how the old man's partially closed eyes indicate that he is fighting off tears, the way his mouth is parted so as to let out a groan, and the wrinkled nature of his face, which is acerbated by the strain on his emotions. No

FIGURE 2.
Warrior and father at
tomb. Attic white-ground
lekythos attributed to the
Achilles Painter, c. 450–445
BCE. Antikenmuseum,
Staatliche Museen
Preußischer Kulturbesitz
Berlin, Inv. 1983.1. Photo:
Ingrid Geske.

pain is greater in human life than the loss of a child, and for a Greek, the loss of a son was even more painful, since he represented the continuation of the family. Any viewer of this picture, ancient or modern, would have to feel pity for this man.

This is also true of the picture on a lekythos by the Sabouroff Painter in Munich (Fig. 3), where the woman kneeling and mourning vociferously at the tomb would remind any viewer of the suffering due to the loss of a relative. So would the old Thracian nurse mourning her lost mistress on a lekythos by the Phiale Painter.[16] But figures such as these are not common, and most lekythoi have emotionless figures in their scenes. For example, the calm figures of a woman and youth on a lekythos at Oxford by the Achilles Painter (Fig. 4) are unlikely to induce pity, for they display a calm classical dignity.[17] Thus, even when the subject depicted on classical vases is connected with death, the emotion of pity is not always something that one necessarily feels when viewing the image.

Another major funerary subject on white lekythoi is Charon. About ninety white lekythoi show him waiting on the shore to take the deceased across the water. Few tug at the emotion of pity so greatly as does one in New York by the Painter of Munich 2335 (Fig. 5).[18] Standing on a rock in the middle, a nude young boy with long flowing hair in a headband waits, holding the pole of his toy-roller in his left hand. His body is poised toward Charon's ship, which is moored on the right, as he turns to face his mother behind him and extends his arm in a poignant gesture of farewell. She stands motionless, wrapped in her mantle, gazing down upon her lost son. They will not see each other on earth again.

About forty white lekythoi and several red-figure vases depict the prothesis, which had its heyday earlier in the Geometric and Archaic periods. This was an emotion-letting moment, particularly for women, who are mainly shown lamenting feverishly around the corpse. On

FIGURE 3.
Woman mourning at tomb
and youth. Attic
white-ground lekythos
attributed to the
Sabouroff Painter,
c. 450–440 BCE. Staatliche
Antikensammlungen und
Glyptothek München,
Schoen 76.

an unattributed red-figure loutrophoros in Munich of 430–420 BCE
(Fig. 6), two of them are dressed in black: the dead man's mother at
the head of the bed – she has white hair – and a Thracian slave at the
foot, her ethnicity indicated by the tattoos decorating her arms.[19] The
mourning, white-haired father stands at the head of the *klinê*. Behind
him another woman, distraught at the sight of the man's corpse, flees
right while looking back. One can't help but think that any viewer
would feel a sense of pity for this man who died before his time, and
for most of the dead shown on the classical vases with this subject.

FIGURE 4.
Woman and youth at
tomb. Attic white-ground
lekythos attributed to the
Achilles Painter, c. 440–435
BCE. Ashmolean Museum,
Oxford, 1896.41.

FIGURE 5.
Charon with boy and
mother. Attic
white-ground lekythos
attributed to the Painter
of Munich 2335, C. 430 BCE.
Metropolitan Museum of
Art, New York, 09.221.44,
Rogers Fund, 1909.

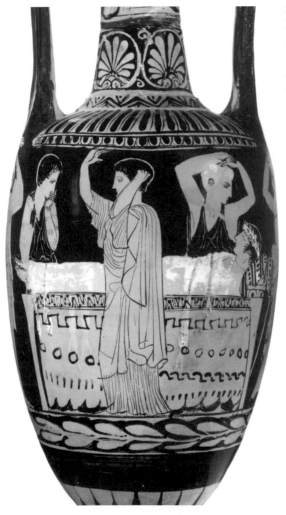

FIGURE 6.
Prothesis. Attic red-figure
loutrophoros, c. 430–420
BCE. Staatliche
Antikensammlungen und
Glyptothek München,
2688. Photo: Museum.

Let us now turn to the world of myth. As with the pictures of everyday
life, so also with myth there are many subjects that are inappropriate
for pity. Some of the more popular ones are (1) birth scenes, (2) deities
libating, (3) Dionysiac scenes, (4) most of the various deeds of heroes, and
(5) gods pursuing their loves. Scenes connected with death once again

FIGURE 7. Achilles and Penthesilea. Attic red-figure cup attributed to the Penthesilea Painter, c. 460 BCE. Staatliche Antikensammlungen und Glyptothek München, 2688. Photo: Hirmer Fotoarchiv, Munich.

are the best candidates for pity, although there is many a classical battle scene that, in my opinion, would not evoke pity from a viewer. Sanitized pictures of war, they do not show contemporary hoplite phalanxes in action and the massive bloody tangle that resulted from their clash; rather, they feature old-fashioned, idealized, and heroic one-on-one combat.

Some battle scenes, however, clearly do evoke pity. The name-piece of the Penthesilea Painter in Munich is one of the most moving (Fig. 7),[20] and it demonstrates how the power of one individual over another – a stronger male over a weaker female – helps create pity in the viewer. The eye contact the falling Amazon queen makes with the Greek hero, as well as the way her right hand limply grabs his chest and her left hand his right arm in an attempt to ward off the death blow, all indicate her seductive submission. There is no real struggle, for she appears to make only a weak attempt to survive; she is resigned to her fate at the hands of the superior hero who falls in love with her at this moment. Her weapons are nowhere to be found, rather our eyes are drawn to her jewelry, which is emphasized in relief, thereby underscoring the beauty that Achilles fell in love with.

The question arises, then, what causes some scenes to evoke pity from the viewer and some less so, or not at all? I may add here that I am fully aware there is many a scene where one could argue over whether it evokes pity or not. Nevertheless, there are some pictures, such as that on the Penthesilea Painter's name-piece, that I think all can agree upon. What separates those that do from those that do not?

One important element, I suggest, is the subject matter. Mortals or heroes, or their loved ones, must be suffering in some unusual way, often from an unwarranted affliction – death, disease, injury, and so forth. The degree of pity can be heightened by the power of one person over the other. Penthesilea, for example, is being killed by the one who loves her and is more powerful than she. These are special circumstances that make the situation tragic and arouse the viewer's pity.

Another element is the composition of the scene, including the gestures and poses of the figures. These are crucial to raising the emotional content of the picture. A subject depicted by one artist often does not evoke pity, or as much pity, as does a picture of the same story by another artist. Consider, for example, the Berlin Painter's depiction of Achilles and Penthesilea on a hydria in New York.[21] In contrast to the Penthesilea Painter's cup we just looked at, there is no sense of affection between the two: Achilles is rendered moving forward in a steadfast, purposeful manner, stabbing her in the thigh with his spear. She is just another fallen warrior.[22]

A third element is the time when the picture was produced. Drawing conventions, subjects, and compositions varied according to period. It should not be surprising, then, that vases from the Early Classical period (480–450 BCE) often are best at rendering emotion. This was the period when emotion and changing states of mind were of greatest interest to the artists, both those who painted and those who sculpted. It was also a time when dramatic content was a frequent goal. During this period Athenian tragedy – a natural breeding ground for pity – first matured, and the use of gestures to indicate emotion must be due partially to the influence of the theater. *Ethos* and *pathos* were also first explored in large-scale wall paintings at this time by the great Thasian painter Polygnotos – and *pathos* is often a trigger for pity. These characteristics contrast with those of the earlier stiff, formulaic, smiling figures of the Archaic period and the emotionless, god-like figures of the High Classical period.

Let us look at another example from the Early Classical period, a lekythos of 460 BCE by the Alkimachos Painter in Basel that shows the suicide of Ajax (Fig. 8).[23] Unlike most earlier Archaic depictions of this myth, in which the hero has already fallen on his sword, or Exekias' masterpiece[24] that shows the hero as he puts his sword, point up, into the ground, here we see Ajax in a frenzy, raising both hands as he looks heavenward a moment or two before he will fall on the sword and end his life. Note the expression on his face, which helps evoke pity from the viewer.

This is not to say, however, that Early Classical artists were the only ones drawing scenes capable of evoking pity, nor does death have to be the final result. There are two good examples from the High Classical period. The first is a hydria in Oxford of 430 BCE from the

FIGURE 8.
Suicide of Ajax. Attic
red-figure lekythos
attributed to the
Alkimachos Painter, c.
460 BCE. Antikenmuseum
Basel und Sammlung
Ludwig, Inv. BS 1442.
Photo: Claire Niggli.

Group of Polygnotos showing the blinding of Thamyras (Fig. 9).[25] The
Thracian bard had dared to challenge the Muses to a musical contest,
and his blinding was the penalty for his loss. Here he sits in the middle,
instrument by his side, gesturing wildly with arms extended to each
side, his head tilted down with closed eye indicating his blindness. The
emotional intensity of the scene is augmented by the figure of Argiope
on the left – his mother – who has raised both hands to her head and

FIGURE 9. Blinding of Thamyras. Attic red-figure hydria attributed to the Group of Polygnotos, c. 440–430 BCE. Ashmolean Museum, Oxford, G 291.

moves about with bent knees. One of the victorious Muses stands by with her lyre on the right.

The second vase is a poorly preserved double-register calyx krater by the Phiale Painter in Bologna of 440 BCE (Fig. 10).[26] The upper register

FIGURE 10. Odysseus and Circe. Attic red-figure calyx krater attributed to the Phiale Painter, c. 445–440 BCE. Bologna, Museo Civico, 298. Photo: after G. Pellegrini, *Catalogo dei vasi greci dipinti delle Necropoli Felsinee* (Bologna 1912) 140.

shows two moments in the story of Circe and Odysseus, the earlier of which has Circe holding her wand over one of Odysseus' companions, who is caught in the moment of transformation into an animal. She has clear power over him. His contorted, bent-over pose, with kicking leg and hands enveloping his head, indicates the agony of the spell and evokes pity from the viewer. Nor is he alone in his suffering. Note his comrade on the far left, who leans over at a forty-five degree angle, body and arms rigid, as he supports himself on the padded *diphros* before him. His attempt to shake off the spell's effect is not working.

THE DEPICTION OF PITY WITHIN SCENES

Let us now return to the fork in the road we took earlier, and take the other track – that is, to the scenes that show people pitying one another. These are extremely rare and very much dependent on how one interprets the gestures of the figures in view of the action taking place. The Penelope Painter's skyphos in Berlin of c. 430 BCE is a good example

FIGURE 11. Odysseus and the Suitors. Attic red-figure skyphos attributed to the Penelope Painter, c. 430 BCE. Antikenmuseum, Staatliche Museen Preußischer Kulturbesitz Berlin, F 2588. Photo: after A. Furtwängler and K. Reichhold, *Griechische Vasenmalerei* (Munich 1904–32) pl. 138,2.

from the mythological sphere (Fig. 11).[27] The subject is Odysseus slaying the suitors. On one side we see the suitors under attack. The suitor on the left has already been shot in the back; another kneels and hides behind a table he has picked up, while the third, stationed on a *klinê*, gestures with extended arms for Odysseus to spare him. On the other side of the vessel Odysseus is poised to shoot his bow once again. Behind him stand two female servants, undoubtedly two of those who had colluded with the suitors. Their gestures indicate a strong emotional reaction to the slaughter. One holds out both her hands clasped together in a prayerlike pose, while the other rests her left hand against her face, both arms drawn in tightly to the body. Do their gestures indicate compassion or sympathy for the suitors? Shock, or anxiety, or pity for their own situation? I think one could use any or all of these terms and, indeed, the modern definition of pity overlaps with the rest. *Webster's New Collegiate Dictionary* gives synonyms for pity that include sympathy, compassion, commiseration, and condolence, and indicates the relationship of pity to most of them. So, for example, "compassion implies pity coupled with an urgent desire to aid or spare."

FIGURE 12. Achilles and Memnon. Attic red-figure cup attributed to the Penthesilea Painter, c. 460–450 BCE. Ferrara, Museo Nazionale 44885. Photo: Hirmer Fotoarchiv, Munich.

The gestures implying pity and related emotions displayed by the on-lookers on this vase serve to raise the intensity of the action for the viewer.

The latter is also true of the picture of Achilles slaying Memnon on a very large cup by the Penthesilea Painter from Spina of 460–450 BCE (Fig. 12).[28] Eos runs to shelter her wounded son in the middle of the picture, while the gestures of two out of the three onlookers on the left, Memnon's side, indicate their emotional response to the situation – pity, sympathy, and so on. The bearded man nearest the hero holds his left hand to his forehead, while the last grasps the back of his head with both hands. The Penthesilea Painter, the most important Early Classical painter of cups, was a master at the use of gestures in his pictures, as is evident once again here.

FIGURE 13. Ransom of Hector. Attic red-figure hydria attributed to the Pioneer Group, c. 510 BCE. Cambridge, MA, Courtesy of the Arthur M. Sackler Museum, Harvard University Art Museum. Bequest of Frederick M. Watkins, 1972.40. Photo: Photographic Services. ©2004 President and Fellows of Harvard College.

There are several other vases, mainly those with scenes of supplication from the mythological world, that may imply pity, although the temporal relationship of the emotion to the moment depicted is unclear. One good example is the "Ransom of Hector," such as that shown on a hydria from the Pioneer Group at Harvard (Fig. 13).[29] Priam supplicates with extended arms to Achilles who reclines on his *klinê*. Hector's corpse is lying below. Like other depictions of the ransom of Hector in Attic vase painting, most of which are late archaic and not classical, this scene seem to focus on the moment of Priam's arrival and his initial plea to Achilles, who controls possession of the corpse.[30] The reclining hero normally holds a knife and piece of meat, as on the Harvard hydria, and sometimes his head looks away from Priam, suggesting he hasn't yet noticed his arrival. Part of the ransom is normally shown being carried by servants. The shortened version on the Harvard hydria omits this element, and it is omitted on other vases as well.[31] Thus, Achilles does not yet seem ready to experience the pity he will later show, as we know from the story told in the *Iliad* (24.516). This is interesting, since literary scholars have recently focused so much attention on Achilles' pity, while apparently the vase painters did not.[32]

Another scene that may depict pity is Orestes at Delphi, as shown on two column kraters of c. 440 BCE, one by the Duomo Painter in the Louvre, the other by the Naples Painter in San Antonio (Fig. 14).[33] In both cases, Apollo motions toward a pursuing Fury to indicate his protection of the kneeling Orestes. The god was moved by pity for the suppliant, but whether Apollo is experiencing the emotion at this moment or did so earlier is not possible to say.

Let me end with an example from everyday life, a remarkable black-figure oinochoe with bail handle of c. 500–490 BCE, which is at Bowdoin College and by the Sappho Painter.[34] It has the only known depiction of the corpse being placed in the coffin. The most important of the three groups of figures is centered on the main side, where two women and a bearded man lower the corpse of another bearded man into a coffin having the form of a wooden chest with legs. Behind the two women stands a bearded man who extends both hands toward the corpse; another stands behind him giving the valediction with his raised right hand while carrying an axe over his left shoulder, indicating that he is the carpenter who has made the coffin and will place its lid on shortly. Next to him a woman bends over, picking up a basket with four lekythoi. She makes ready for the funerary procession to the grave, the *ekphora.*

FIGURE 14. Orestes and the Furies at Delphi. Attic red-figure column krater attributed to the Naples Painter, c. 440–430 BCE. San Antonio Museum of Art, 86.134.73.

FIGURE 15.
Old man, women, and girl
mourning. Black-figure
bail-handle oinochoe
attributed to the Sappho
Painter, c. 500–490 BCE.
BCMA Accession #
1984.023. Terracotta,
14⅝ in. × 5½ in. × 4½ in.
(37.15 cm × 13.97 cm ×
11.43 cm). "Bowdoin
College Museum of Art,
Brunswick, Maine,
Museum Purchase with
funds from Adela Wood
Smith Trust, in memory
of Harry de Forest Smith,
Class of 1891.

The second group, consisting of four figures, is the one that concerns
us here (Fig. 15). An old man sits in the center on a block seat, head
bent over in mourning, as indicated by his raised right arm. Only
traces of his white hair remain. A young girl stands before the seated
man, reaching toward his lap, showing compassion and pity for him

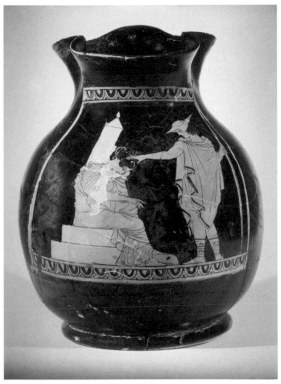

FIGURE 16.
Man and woman mourning
at a tomb (Orestes and
Elektra?). Attic red-figure
oinochoe, c. 430 BCE.
Antikenmuseum,
Staatliche Museen
Preußischer Kulturbesitz
Berlin, V.I. 3393. Photo:
Jutta Tietz-Glagow.

while consoling him. These figures probably represent the dead man's father and daughter. The woman standing behind the old man holds up an alabastron in her left hand, while raising the right to her face. She appears to be wiping away tears of grief, for a similar pose is found on a few other vases. Further supporting this interpretation is the woman shown above the man's bowed head. She commiserates with or shows pity for the crying woman by placing her right hand on the other's left shoulder. Here again, pity is one aspect of the action, although other synonyms of pity are also applicable. The final group consists of two short men carrying vessels on their shoulders, who move toward a woman with straggly hair facing them and standing by a *diphros*.

Pity in the form of sympathy is also depicted on rare occasions in funerary scenes on red-figure vases, such as on an unattributed chous in Berlin (Fig. 16) of c. 430 BCE.[35] Here a young man in traveler's attire (Orestes?) reaches out to touch the head of a woman (Electra?) seated on the steps of a grave. Apparently she is crying, for her head has sunk into her mantle-covered left hand, and he is trying to comfort her.

CONCLUSION

This completes our survey, and we can conclude that pity has no specific iconography in classical Athenian vase painting. There are no depictions personifying it, nor scenes labeled so as to indicate its presence. From a modern viewer's perspective, pity is evoked primarily by scenes connected with suffering and death, either real-life or mythological, especially where we see death's effects upon the living. Gesture, pose, and composition are key elements in evoking this pity from the viewer – not necessarily the subject of death or human suffering alone. Even fewer scenes, mainly those connected with death or supplication, have figures that appear to pity others. There is no specific gesture that indicates pity and pity alone; several are suggestive of it, but must be considered in context. Other synonyms of pity could be used to describe the action of the figures in these scenes, and in the case of supplication, it is always unclear whether the emotion is experienced at the exact moment illustrated on the vase, or indeed at all.

What, then, can classical Athenian vase painting add to our understanding of pity in the culture of Classical Greece? Probably not as much as one might hope, but it does show us that it was one of the emotions first explored in the Early Classical period, a time when Greek art reflects a great interest in emotional content. Other chapters in this volume have suggested that the years 480 to 450 were also a time when pity attracted the interest of Athenians because of their widening exercise of political and military power. It may well be that the vase paintings reflect a new social consciousness, although this cannot be proved. Nevertheless, we know that vase paintings can be highly reflective of political and social changes, and the power of one figure over another did augment the sense of pity in some scenes, so it is not illogical to postulate some connection here. Our search for pity has demonstrated just how precarious it can be to assign a specific emotion to a particular figure, so we should always think twice before doing so and take care to qualify our observations when necessary.

Before ending I do need to note that I have used the modern American sense of "pity" when viewing the vase paintings, which is not necessarily the same as the ancient meaning of *eleos* and *oiktos*, which varied over time and according to literary genre and social context.[36] Aristotle's definition of pity indicates that men pity those they know, but who are not very close kin, and that people suffering are pitiable when they are contemporaries, not those from the distant past or in the future (*Rh.* 2.8, 1385b13–16). If we were to use these requirements as a guide when searching the vases for pity, we might conclude that as viewers of the scenes, none of us would feel pity in the Aristotelian sense because we don't know the people. On the other hand, Aristotle does not say that we can't pity people we don't know, rather he is telling us the most likely scenarios in which pity would occur. Fifth-century Athenians did have strong emotional reactions when viewing tragedy – recall the punishment of Phrynichos for using the capture of Miletus as a theme for his drama (Hdt. 6.21) – and in fifth-century tragedy individuals do pity people they don't know, as long as they are deserving of pity. For example, Aithra pities the Theban mothers in Euripides' *Suppliant Women* (265–331). It is a well-known fact that art – both high art, and more common, less-privileged images, as those on the vases – can evoke strong emotions from a viewer, as several recent art historical studies have reaffirmed.[37] Thus, it is not too hard to believe that the pictures on the vases could evoke pity from their viewers, both modern and ancient.

◘◉◙

Endnotes

*Special thanks to Rachel Hall Sternberg and Corey Brennen for organizing the conference at Rutgers University and for the invitation to speak at it. I would also like to thank the following people for help in obtaining photographs and permission to publish them: V. Brinkmann, U. Kästner, S. Knudson, J. Latman, J. R. Mertens, G. Scott, V. Slehoferova, and M. Vickers.

Abbreviations

ARV^2 = J. D. Beazley, *Attic Red-figure Vase Painters, 2nd ed.* (Oxford 1963)
$BAdd^2$ = T. H. Carpenter, *Beazley Addenda, 2nd ed.* (Oxford 1989)
CAT = C. W. Clairmont, *Classical Attic Tombstones* (Kilchberg/Zurich 1993)
CVA = *Corpus Vasorum Antiquorum*
$LIMC$ = Lexicon Iconographicum Mythologiae Classicae (Munich 1981–97)
Paralipomena = J. D. Beazley, *Paralipomena* (Oxford 1971)

1. For the problem, see Woodford 2003: 57 and 171–75. Gloria Ferrari has recently attempted to identify figures wrapped in mantles as well as those with downcast eyes as displaying *aidôs*: 1990, 1997 (especially 5–12 and 38–39), and 2002: 54–56 and 72–86. Unfortunately, she does not clearly define the parameters for when a particular woman depicted on a vase should be interpreted as actively displaying *aidôs*, that is, experiencing the emotion. Rather, her point that "the enveloping mantle and the related image of the lowered gaze carry the idea of *aidôs*" (2002: 80) is a more general one and not helpful in determining the presence or absence of the emotion in a particular scene. Better on this problem is Cairns 1996, 2001, and 2002.
2. Toledo, Museum of Art 69.369; *CVA* Toledo 1 USA 17 p. 29 and pl. 44.
3. Reeder 1995: 271–72.
4. For example the late-fifth-century Attic gravestone of Mnesagora and Nikochares: Athens, National Museum 3845; *CAT* 1.610. For children in Greek art most recently, see Neils and Oakley 2003.
5. New York, Metropolitan Museum of Art 17.230.37: ARV^2 498,1; *Paralipomena* 381; $BAdd^2$ 251; Reeder 1995: 272–73.
6. The standard study of these is Shapiro 1993.

7. New York, Metropolitan Museum of Art 1972.11.10: *BAdd²* 404–5; Shapiro 1993: 133, Fig. 86.

8. Florence, Museo Archeologico Nazionale 81947: *ARV²* 1312,2; *Paralipomena* 477; *BAdd²* 361; Burn 1987: pls. 27–29.

9. Thompson and Wycherley 1972: 129–36.

10. Boston, Museum of Fine Arts 1970.233: *ARV²* 444,241; *BAdd²* 240; Buitron-Oliver 1995: pl. 111,233.

11. St. Petersburg, Hermitage B 1650: *ARV²* 16,15 and 1619; *Paralipomena* 509; *BAdd²* 153; Goemann 1991: 178–81.

12. Paris, Louvre G 42: *ARV²* 23,1; *Paralipomena* 323; *BAdd²* 154; Cairns 1996 with pl. 1.

13. Bisel and Angel 1985: 197–210; Pomeroy 1997: 6–7; Golden 1981: 327; Golden 1990: 83.

14. For the images on these now, see Oakley 2004.

15. Berlin, Staatliche Museen, Antikensammlung 1983.1: Oakley 1997: pls. 140b and 141.

16. Munich, Staatliche Antikensammlungen und Glyptothek, ex Schoen 76: *ARV²* 845,171; *Paralipomena* 473; Kavvadias 2000: pl. 120. Athens, National Museum 19355: *ARV²* 1022,139bis; *Paralipomena* 441; *BAdd²* 316; Oakley 1990: pl. 111.

17. Oxford, Ashmolean 1896.41: *ARV²* 998,165; *BAdd²* 313; Oakley 1997: pl. 118c–d.

18. New York, Metropolitan Museum of Art 09.221.44: *ARV²* 1168,128; *BAdd²* 338; Oakley 2004: figs. 75–76 and 108–113 for a list of scenes with Charon.

19. Munich, Staatliche Antikensammlungen und Glyptothek, ex Schoen: *ARV²* 1102,1; *AM* 53 (1928) Beilage XVIII, 116. For the *prothesis* on white lekythoi, see Oakley 2004: 76–87.

20. Munich, Staatliche Antikensammlungen und Glyptothek 2688: *ARV²* 879,1 and 1673; *Paralipomena* 428; *BAdd²* 300–1; Simon and Hirmer 1976: pls. 183 and XLII.

21. New York, Metropolitan Museum of Art 10.210.19: *ARV²* 209,169; *Paralipomena* 343; *BAdd²* 195; Richter and Hall 1936: pls. 16 and 172,14.

22. Another good example is the two scenes of Phineus and the Harpies compared by Woodford 2003: 132–33.

23. Basel, Antikenmuseum und Sammlung Ludwig BS 1442: Schefold and Jung 1989: 263, Fig. 239.

24. Boulogne-sur-Mer, Musée Communal 558: *ABV* 145,18; *Paralipomena* 60; *BAdd²* 40; Simon and Hirmer 1976: pl. 76. For depictions of the death of Ajax, see O. Touchefeu, *LIMC* I (Munich 1981) 328–32 and 333–36, s.v. Aias I.

25. Oxford, Ashmolean G.291 (V 530): *ARV²* 1061,152; *Paralipomena* 445; *BAdd²* 323; *CVA* Oxford 1 Great Britain 3 pl. 32,1.

26. Bologna, Museo Civico 298: *ARV²* 1018,62; Oakley 1990: pls. 42 and 43a, c, and d.

27. Berlin, Staatliche Museen, Antikensammlung F 2588: *ARV²* 1300,1; *Paralipomena* 475; *BAdd²* 360; Schefold and Jung 1989: 321, Fig. 280.

28. Ferrara, Museo Nazionale 44885 (T.18 C VP): *ARV²* 882,35 and 1673; *Paralipomena* 428; *BAdd²* 301; Schefold and Jung 1989: 255, Fig. 229.

29. Cambridge (MA), Harvard University Art Museum, Sackler 1972.40: *Paralipomena* 324; *BAdd²* 157; Buitron 1972: 80–81.

30. See Shapiro 1994: 38–45 and 186 with earlier bibliography.
31. Shapiro interprets the shortened version of the scene in the tondo of a cup in the Shelby White and Leon Levy Collection as depicting a later moment, because the full scene is shown on the exterior of the cup and the corpse is not shown on the interior. This seems unlikely to me, since Achilles still holds the knife and piece of meat on both and because the shortened version in the tondo of another cup (Paris Louvre G 153 and a joining fragment in Florence: *ARV²* 460,14; *BAdd²* 44; Kunisch 1997: pl. 61) shows only Achilles and the corpse and no Priam, thereby indicating that most likely the absence of the corpse is due to the lack of space and the shortened version of the image, rather than as an indicator of a later moment in the story: see Shapiro 1994: 42–45 and figs. 25–27.
32. Macleod 1982: 13–16; Crotty 1994: 3–23; Kim 2000: 62–63 and *passim*. I thank Rachel Hall Sternberg for bringing these to my attention.
33. Paris, Louvre K 343: *ARV²* 1117,7; *BAdd²* 331; Prag 1985: pl. 31a. San Antonio, Museum of Art 86.134.73: *ARV²* 1097,21bis; *Paralipomena* 450; *BAdd²* 388; Shapiro, Picón, and Scott 1995: 174–77 and pl. XI.
34. Brunswick (ME), Bowdoin College Museum of Art 1984.23: *Paralipomena* 247; *BAdd²* 126–27; Kurtz and Boardman 1971: pls. 37–38; Oakley forthcoming.
35. Berlin, Staatliche Museen, Antikensammlung Inv. Nr. 3393: *CVA* Berlin 3 Germany 21 pls. 146,4; 147,5; and 150,4.
36. Konstan 2001.
37. Freedberg 1989 is the most thorough; see also Brown 1996 and Elkins 2001, who concentrate more on high art.

THE CIVIC ART OF PITY

AILEEN AJOOTIAN

◎□◎

THIS CHAPTER ABOUT ATHENIAN ART AND ITS PUBLIC AUDIENCE MUST begin with Athenian society, where the manipulation of *eleos* or *oiktos* constituted an important aspect of forensic practice in the courtroom. The Aristotelian concept of pity was fully operative here: jurors who observed and pitied litigants whom they thought had suffered unjustly were rarely close relations of the sufferers.[1]

The role of *eleos* as the legitimate goal of a legal defense was also acknowledged, and represented, in Athenian tragic drama. Both contexts explored life experience and social custom, reflecting it back to Athenian citizens, and perhaps shaping their reactions as well. As Tom Falkner stresses in his contribution to this collection, the act of viewing, of being a spectator, was an essential aspect not only of Greek drama, but also of being Athenian. The role of the ancient fifth-century spectator can be understood in a broad, democratic context. City cults and civic activities alike were essentially performances, demanding the participation of citizen-viewers, whether the spectacle took place in court, at the Theater of Dionysus, in the Bouleuterion, or on the Pnyx (Goldhill 1999: 4–5). The city was the *theatron*, the citizens *theatai*.

Thus audiences at the Theater of Dionysus on the South Slope of the Acropolis (Traulos 1971: 537–52), along with jurors and spectators at an Athenian trial,[2] experienced the painful emotional state of *eleos* when they witnessed unmerited suffering from a distance. The architectural configuration of the theater or ancient courtroom established physical space between the pitiable scene and its viewers. The audience's separation can be understood to represent the emotional distance of viewer from sufferer, as Aristotle stipulated. Moreover, this distance symbolized an essential, underlying aspect of ancient *eleos*: the discrepancy of power between the viewer and the viewed, the witness of suffering and the sufferer. Watching from a distance implies a position of power that transcends class or rank. And other social mechanisms, as we shall see, demonstrated that the ancient experience of pity was essentially about power, or the lack of it.

The travails of the innocent were associated with a conditioned set of public emotional responses in various Athenian civic settings. It is likely that this same ensemble of situations and conditions may also have been worked out in other contexts and media, including contemporary art. The concept of *eleos* apparently was not personified, or identified by inscription in classical Greek iconography,[3] as John Oakley demonstrates in his chapter. Yet it may be possible to identify the ancient impact of this intellectual and emotional state reflected in fifth-century sculpture and vase painting, evoking similar culturally embedded and legislated responses from viewers. Although his interpretation of pity is not based closely on the Artistotelian conditions, Oakley suggests in his chapter that certain episodes and motifs in Attic vase painting, especially death scenes like the suicide of Ajax, could evoke pity in the viewer.[4]

Emma Stafford, in a chapter on the literary evidence for *eleos*, considers its formal uses in oratory and drama. She suggests that it "is both the practical mercy sought by a suppliant, either from a god or a mortal in a position of power, and the pity aroused in an audience by a tragedy, or in a jury by a skilful orator" (2000: 200). This perspective embraces *eleos* divine and mortal, involving situations and settings in many aspects of ancient life.

Using this model, let us consider a series of artistic test cases to determine whether or not some classical monuments set up in Athenian and other Greek public spaces were intended to re-enact scenes and elicit viewer responses of *eleos* that echoed or paralleled those of spectators in courtroom or theater, or in other forms of human interaction. We shall consider mythological episodes involving the family, the most intimate level of social organization – specifically, myths about mothers and children. The polyvalent manipulation of myth in fifth-century Athenian art, as in drama, explored the complex relationship between *oikos* and *polis*. It is important to note that in the last quarter of the century, the emphasis on family matters, inheritance, adoption, and the political implications of family life were reflected in large private grave reliefs and grave precincts throughout Attica (Oliver 2000; Humphrey 1980).

Prokne and Itys

Sophocles' tragedy *Tereus*, of which only fragments survive, explored a story known to Homer (*Od.* 19.518–23) and Pherekydes (3 F 124).[5] The date of the play is controversial; it must have been performed before 414 BCE, when Aristophanes parodied it in *Birds* (97–100).[6] Sophocles introduced the names Prokne and Philomela, and this version of the story appears to have become standard. Its outlines are well known: Thracian King Tereus, marrying a royal Athenian bride, Prokne, daughter of King Pandion, brought her back to his homeland. Later Tereus escorted Prokne's sister Philomela to Thrace. But things went wrong on the journey. Tereus raped his sister-in-law and then cut out her tongue, muting his victim and concealing the crime. The king's act was subsequently revealed through woman's *tekhnê*: Philomela wove an account of the assault for Prokne to discover. The climax of the family story, the transformation of sisters and king into birds, was preceded by infanticide (Forbes Irving 1992: 99–107, 112). To avenge Philomela, Prokne killed her young son Itys and served him up as dinner to Tereus.

Katerina Zacharia (2001) has convincingly argued that fifth-century perceptions of the Tereus myth, and possibly Sophocles' play, involved the themes of kinship, colonization, and diplomacy. A foreign king violated Athenian family life and parodied his own role as husband. Prokne, confronting her spouse's crime and her sister's violation, also abandoned her role as protective mother. She is often compared with another infanticidal mother, Medea, and one of her fragmentary speeches (frag. 583) resonates with similar awareness of her woman's lot.[7] But Prokne is an Athenian wife, not a foreign witch. In some ways, her act may have been even more complex and disturbing for the ancient city audience.

Along with its emotional impact, the political backdrop of this tale surely contributed to its meaning in Athens. Prokne was the daughter of Pandion, a Megarian hero and Athenian king, an important figure in the early history of the city: he was one of four Athenian kings preceding Theseus who were singled out as Eponymoi for the Attic tribes late in the sixth century BCE.[8] The Kleisthenic tribe Pandionis was named for him.[9]

Sophocles' fragmentary play does not preserve details of Prokne's vengeful plan or the actual murder of the child, but painted versions of this bloody scene on a small group of Attic vases predating the drama appeared by the end of the sixth century (Touloupa 1994: 527–29).[10] In the tondo of a kylix by Makron (Fig. 17), both sisters are present, labeled with their bird names – Khelidon, the swallow, and Aedon, the nightingale (Touloupa 1994: 527.1).[11] The mother lifts Itys off his feet, pulling him away from her sister, who raises both hands, with fingers spread, this unusual pose perhaps representing her attempt to communicate. At her side is the sword they will use to kill the boy.

Both women apparently participate in the slaying on a fragmentary cup attributed to the early work of Onesimos, c. 500 BCE (Fig. 18). Itys, named with an inscription, is suspended between the two (Touloupa 1994: 527.3).[12] The mother acts alone in another cup tondo decorated by the Magnoncourt Painter, around 510–500 BCE, where she is about to stab her son (Touloupa 1994: 527.2).[13] Inscriptions identify her as

FIGURE 17. Prokne and Itys with Philomela. Tondo of an Attic red-figure kylix attributed to Makron, c. 500 BCE. Paris, Louvre G147. Photo: Réunion des Musées Nationaux / Art Resource, NY.

Aedon, the nightingale, and the boy as Itys. She grips him by the hair and exposes his throat, mimicking the sacrificial gesture of priests slaughtering animals at an altar.[14]

These scenes of family violence appeared on Attic vases shortly after Kleisthenes' political reforms and the emergence of the ten tribes.[15] They predate the construction of the first, fifth-century, Eponymous Heroes monument in the Agora, with its ten bronze statues and message boards, or Pheidias' bronze group of Athenian eponymous heroes, Militiades, and gods at Delphi.[16] Apart from his probable appearance in these groups, Pandion rarely turns up in ancient art. He may be one of the white-bearded symposiasts on a rhyton attributed to the Triptolemos

Painter, c. 480 BCE (Shapiro 1981: 85–87, no. 32). And Pausanias (1.5.4) mentioned a statue of Pandion, well worth seeing, on the Acropolis, but provided no information about date or artist.

Decree inscriptions of the tribe Pandionis discovered on the Acropolis mention Pandion. The earliest stones date to the late fifth century BCE. They support the presence of a shrine for him on the east side of the summit (Hurwit 1999: 188–89; Brouskari 1996: 167–68; Lewis 1955: 22). Some critics identify the foundations of Building IV, filling the southeast corner of the Acropolis, as Pandion's heroön (Hurwit 1999: 188–89, 314, no. 4), though Robertson proposed a site closer to the precinct for Zeus Polieus, on the northeastern side of the citadel (Robertson 1996: 41; Hurwit 1999: 190–91, 314, no. 6). In addition, the tribe Pandionis celebrated an annual festival called the Pandia, honoring Zeus as well as the namesake king. Decree inscriptions indicate that a tribal assembly was associated with this event (Kearns 1989: 91–92).

More popular in ancient art and drama, as we have seen, was the story of Pandion's daughters, a myth focused on betrayal and rape initiating family violence that spiraled out of control. Both mother and father abandoned their nurturing parental roles, causing the civilized structure of the family itself to disintegrate. The most innocent family member suffered because the stabilizing framework of relationships collapsed around him. The early painted representations of Prokne, Philomela, and Itys focus on the horrifying climax of their undoing, a mother murdering her offspring. This dramatic moment may have been favored as the visual crystallization of the story, not only evoking the momentary pain of pity in the viewer, but also serving as a memorial to its impact. The abused sister, the mother's fateful decision, and her child's death were presented as a tableau of undeserved anguish. Within the family drama, the exposure of Tereus' crime in fact relied on a crafted object, a textile with the events legibly woven into it. The figured

FIGURE 18.
Prokne and Itys. Attic red-figure kylix attributed to Onesimos, c. 500 BCE. Herbert Cahn (HC 599). Photo: by kind permission of Adrienne Lezzi-Hafter and David Cahn.

weaving tells a story inside the story and thus Prokne herself witnesses her sister's bloody and cruel violation.

Although securely identifiable images of Prokne's story decrease in Attic vase painting by the mid–fifth century, a sculptural rendering of the theme, roughly contemporary with Sophocles' play *Tereus*, was installed on the Acropolis, according to Pausanias (1.24.3). He reports that Alkamenes, assumed by modern critics to be the prolific Classical sculptor, dedicated the composition (Ridgway 1981: 174–78).[17] But Pausanias, the only authority to mention this work, reveals neither the motive for this dedication nor its recipient. The attribution of the

FIGURE 19a.
Prokne and Itys. Sculpture group attributed to Alkamenes, c. 430–420 BCE. Athens, Acropolis Museum (Akr. 1358). Photo by the author.

statue group to the fifth-century sculptor Alkamenes rests on this single testimony.

The statue group Akr. 1358 (Figs. 19a–19c), now in the Acropolis Museum, has been connected with Pausanias' report (Triandi 1998: 403, figs. 420–21).[18] This group, carved in Parian marble, was found in several pieces near the west bastion of the Propylaia (Triandi 1998: 403). Many scholars, considering it the very work Pausanias mentioned, date it to 430–420 BCE, but some have argued that it copies a lost fifth-century original (Ridgway 1981: 175).

FIGURE 19b.
Detail of 19a. DAI Neg. 1975/426. Photo:
Hellner.

FIGURE 19c.
Detail of 19a. Photo by the author.

Although Pausanias did not record the votive occasion for the composition, he described it, focusing on Prokne's mental state, which seems to have been the work's outstanding feature. Pausanias reported that Prokne had made up her mind about Itys (1.24.3): *Proknên de ta es ton paida bebouleumenên autên te kai ton Itun anethêken Alkamenês.* The sculpture group did not depict a violent scene of bloodshed, as did the earlier vase paintings, but explored the mother's emotional condition.

We may now turn to the sculpture. The adult stands 1.59 m. high without head and neck; her original height should be around 1.95 m., so the installation was large and impressive. Based on findspot, and Pausanias' report, Gorham Stevens identified a cutting in bedrock near the northeast corner of the Parthenon as the statue's original site; the work was displayed atop a now lost base of unknown height.[19] The cutting is aligned with the third column from the east of the Parthenon's peristyle.

The woman wears a peplos, with a mantle pinned on her shoulders. Her costume and stance have been compared with the roughly contemporary Karyatids supporting the roof of the Erechtheion south porch, nearly opposite the spot where the statue probably stood.[20] But she is no ordinary Classical *peplophoros*. Most figures of this type tend to be static, standing frontally with arms lowered. The sculptor transformed a popular Classical form into a narrative vignette with the use of gestures and an added figure. Prokne raised her left arm, holding her hand up to her face, and lowered her now missing right hand, held close to her body, to just above the head of the child. In this hand she probably gripped an added bronze knife.

Pressed against her right leg, interrupting the regular pattern of drapery folds, is a little boy, naked, carved from the same piece of marble as the adult. His torso and head are broken away, but drilled holes for an added wreath survive. One can also observe how his left shoulder indented the woman's body, his left arm following the line of folds down the center of her dress. His complicated twisting pose, legs and feet carved free of the main block, contrasts with the adult's still, solid figure. The child's urgent torsional movement against his mother intensifies the kinetic quality of the composition. In fact, few other surviving fifth-century marble statue groups, apart from pedimental works, present this degree of physical interaction between separate figures, combined with an exploration and expression of the characters' state of mind.

Prokne's raised left hand can be linked with an iconographic gesture recognized in other fifth-century sculpture.[21] The Early Classical statues that filled the east gable of the Temple of Zeus at Olympia told a family story of discord, *agôn*, and retribution.[22] Pausanias (5.10.2–10) identified the still moment of the east gable. King Oinomaios and the hero Pelops were about to compete in a chariot race that would end in disaster for the king and victory for the young challenger. Looking back toward the apex of the gable in the north side sits an old man, probably the local seer Iamos.[23] He raises his hand to his chin in a gesture representing thoughtful contemplation and the inner working of the mind. Iamos perhaps sees the outcome of the race – the death of King Oinomaios and the curse on Pelops and his descendants. The Early Classical taste for representing the moment before the action of a narrative began was worked in three dimensions, with the figure of the seer functioning as a witness to the outcome of the myth.

So the sculpted Prokne stood on the Acropolis, hand raised to her face, symbolizing contemplation of what she was about to do and perhaps seeing, like Athenians who knew her story, beyond this last moment with her child. The killing was not reenacted, as in earlier vase paintings. Instead, the sculptor focused on the mother's internal struggle. He chose a temporal setting for the sculptural tableau just before the action began and relied on spectators to initiate and complete it in their minds. He manipulated the viewer's experience of the narrative and exploited, through a canon of recognizable gestures, the statue's potential to convey the impression of interior emotional activity.[24] Furthermore, the boy, wreathed like a sacrificial animal, would evoke in viewers the fear and horror of such an offering. Through this rather complex interaction of the sculpture and its spectators, *eleos* may have been generated by their own interior re-creation of the myth and the visual symbolism of the child about to be sacrificed.

Despite the composition's grim theme, it has been suggested that the statue group was erected as a victory monument commemorating Sophocles' winning play *Tereus* (Hurwit 1999: 231). But scholarship focused on the political and diplomatic triangulation of Athens, Megara, and Thrace embedded in the myth of Prokne and Tereus suggests that the function of the late fifth-century sculpture dedication on the Acropolis could have drawn in part on ethnic and regional identities and relations (Zacharia 2001: 91–112; La Rocca 1986). Sophocles' fragmentary drama appears to have emphasized the agonistic relationship of these regions through its main characters, setting Prokne/Athens/insider against Tereus/Thrace/other.

The uneasy historical relationship between Athens and Thrace goes back at least to the sixth century BCE, when Thracian mercenaries supported Peisistratus in his final and successful effort to control Athens. Subsequent relations swung back and forth between bloodshed – the Thracians' massacre at Drabeskos of ten thousand Athenians c. 460 BCE, for instance – and Athenian diplomatic efforts to shape alliances with Thracian kings. Yet by the late sixth century, Athenians had adopted elements of Thracian costume and culture (Cohen 2001: 247–48; Tsiafakis 2000), and Thracian gods like Bendis joined Athens' urban pantheon by c. 400 BCE (Tsiafakis 2000: 386–88) or even earlier.

In Attic vase painting, scenes of *dokimasia*, the registration process for the Athenian cavalry and their horses, depict horsemen wearing the distinctive foxskin caps and high boots recognized as Thracian military garb. Similarly dressed horsemen, most likely Athenian youths and not foreigners, are recognized later in the fifth century on the west and north sides of the Parthenon frieze. Symbols of Thracian military exotica were appropriated in an Athenian context and might be interpreted as evidence of cultural exchange between Thrace and Athens in the fifth century.

But the story has further regional complications. Pausanias (1.41.8) later stressed Tereus' and Pandion's links with Megara, locating Tereus' tomb and King Pandion's hero shrine there. The later Megarian association could reflect the historical links of her colonies near the Black Sea with Thrace. Eugenio La Rocca (1986) in fact proposed that the Prokne and Itys dedication on the Acropolis was connected with Megarian politics just before the beginning of the Peloponnesian War. The adoption of Pandion and Kekrops, for that matter, as eponymous heroes for the Athenian tribes can be seen as a way of stressing Athens' power over a traditional rival, Boeotia (Kearns 1989: 81).

Thus the choice of Prokne and Itys as the theme for this probable dedication, though no inscription survives, may have been quite nuanced. A political motivation for the statue group might account for the unusual motif. It was set up at a time of strained relations between Megara and Athens, perhaps in the wake of Sophocles' drama, where Athenian heritage and the tribulations of foreign travel were stressed. Its placement on the Acropolis undoubtedly contributed to this significance. If Stevens is correct about the ancient setting of the composition, it occupied a prominent spot (Stevens 1946: 10–11, no. 3, Fig. 3). Visitors to the Acropolis in the last thirty years or so of the fifth century BCE encountered it against the backdrop of the Parthenon itself. The group was probably set up shortly after the completion of Athena's temple in 432 BCE.

The Parthenon and nearby Erechtheion were both encrusted with sculpture programs unusually rich in sculptured mothers and children and themes of family and kinship (Neils 1999: 9). Athena's birth scene, dominating the center of the Parthenon's east gable, was framed by important divine families: to the south, Demeter and Kore (East E and F), and to the north, Aphrodite and Dione (East L and M: Palagia 1993: 20–22). Both mother-daughter groups expressed family ties through their intimate, engaged poses. In the west gable were other family groupings: Kekrops with his daughter (West B and C), plus figures D, an adult possibly related to E, a boy; P, Q, and R, a mother with two children; and U, another pair with seated woman supporting a youth in her lap (Palagia 1993: 42–44; Boardman 1985: Fig. 77).

The east frieze ornamenting the top of the Parthenon's cella presented Aphrodite seated among the other Olympian gods with her son Eros, depicted as a young boy (*pais*), leaning against her lap in a torsional pose (VI. 41–42), reminiscent of Itys. And Aphrodite links arms with Artemis (VI. 40), seated next to her, as if emphasizing the family relationship and the goddesses' ties with young mortals. Furthermore, Neils has identified the female standing behind Hera (V. 28–29), south of Aphrodite and Eros, as Hebe, youthfulness personified and Hera's daughter by Zeus (Neils 2001: 164–66; Neils 1999: 8). And finally, the center of attention on the east frieze is the boy bearing the folded peplos (V. 35). Neils most recently has supported the idea that the pairing of Athena and Hephaistos (V. 36–37), seated just to the right of the peplos scene, alludes to Erichthonios, their child by proxy, and that the youth standing next to them, the focus of the Panathenaic ritual, is the autochthonos king of Athens himself (Neils 2001: 175–77; Harrison 1996: 202–5).

The mother and child theme also appeared among the contemporary marble appliques of the Erechtheion frieze, which included a group with a child reclining across a woman's lap. The resonance of this iconography in the architectural programs of the Acropolis' Periklean monuments served specific ideological functions, but it also emphasized the summit as the site of Athenian origins, celebrating the autochthonos connections of Athenians with their city and its spiritual center.[25]

There are other ways in which the Prokne and Itys group interacted with monuments in the Acropolis landscape and drew its meaning from the sacred and mythological environment. The Acropolis' central zone, bracketed by the Parthenon and the Erechtheion, was filled with emblems of the city's ancient heritage, memorializing Erechtheus, Kekrops, and other mythical early rulers and ancestors, including Pandion. If the statue group is considered in the broader sacred landscape of the Acropolis, it may have derived at least some of its meaning from the installations surrounding it.

Knowing Prokne's story, perhaps having seen it dramatized in Sophocles' play, spectators understood the inevitable outcome – she would kill her child. But the scene enacted by the sculpture on the Acropolis drew viewers into the emotional world of the distraught mother contemplating the slaughter. The killing of Itys – an act horrible to contemplate – was always about to occur; spectators on the Acropolis completed the story initiated in marble. And the daughter of Pandion stood not far from her father's precinct and possibly near his statue as well. How the sculptural group may have interacted with the heroön cannot be determined, yet we have seen the importance of Athens' first royal families in the architectural sculpture program of the Parthenon.

The depiction of infanticide itself is a theme difficult to contemplate in any medium. But if the myth and its visual expression reflected fifth-century concerns, then we should consider the political implications of the dedication on the Acropolis. At the same time, ancient viewers reacted not only to that episode, but also to associated myths.

NIOBE AND HER CHILDREN

The myth of Niobe features another mother responsible for the death of her offspring.[26] This story also was reenacted in classical art in ways that focus on the innocent children's suffering. The mortal mother Niobe, bragging to the goddess Leto about her own, bigger family, unleashed the violence of Artemis and Apollo's punishment. The god and goddess shot down Niobe's many children, whose number varied in versions of the story, known as early as Homer.[27] But the emphasis in the *Iliad* (24.604) is not on the children's unwarranted suffering but on the mother's distress. Priam's inconsolable grief for Hector was equated with the unending, petrified mourning of Niobe for her children.

Classical versions of Niobe's story emphasized her foreign background. Daughter of Lydian Tantalus and Euyanassa, she married King Amphion of Thebes. So this story, too, involved outsiders and "mixed" marriage. When petrification transformed the grieving mother into stone, she became Mt. Siphylos in Lydian Magnesia. Sophocles' Antigone likened herself to Niobe, the "Phrygian guest" who became the endlessly weeping Mt. Siphylos.[28] Niobe's fatal affront to Greek gods could then be attributed to her barbarian persona.[29]

The Niobids died because of their mother. She was understood as a paradigm for mortal pride and the danger of challenging divine will. In the fifth century BCE, both Aeschylus and Sophocles explored her pride and loss. In the earlier playwright's fragmentary *Niobe*, the children were already dead, the mother mourning wordlessly over their grave through three acts.[30] Sophocles, however, re-created the slaughter, with Apollo and Artemis firing arrows at the Niobids from the rooftops.[31]

While fourth-century Apulian vase painting focused on the petrified image of Niobe herself, posing like Prokne as she contemplated her loss,[32] the earliest painted versions of the myth depicted the slaughter.[33] On the Niobid Painter's well-known name-piece calyx krater (c. 475–450 BCE), Apollo and Artemis shoot their victims in the back: arrows pierce their bodies, and they collapse on the ground and die while attempting to escape (Fig. 20).[34] We witness the slaughter of Niobe's

FIGURE 20. Artemis and Apollo slaying the Niobids. Attic red-figure krater by the Niobid Painter, c. 475–450 BCE. Paris, Louvre G341. Photo: Réunion des Musées Nationaux / Art Resource, NY.

innocent children as it occurs, in an uneven landscape setting that stresses the gods' unerring aim and the futile flight of their victims.

This scene was popular in various media. On the supports of the monumental throne for Pheidias' lost chryselephantine Zeus at Olympia (c. 430 BCE), Artemis and Apollo also attacked the Niobids (Lapatin 2001: 84).[35] Large three-dimensional sculptured versions of the dying Niobids, possibly from a Classical Niobid group (c. 430 BCE), found their way to imperial Rome. Associated with the Gardens of Sallust, their original setting is unknown.[36] But clearly, the statues, roughly contemporary with the Prokne and Itys group discussed earlier, were reworked and reused in a Roman setting. One of the figures, a collapsing female Niobid shot in the back with an arrow, attempts to pull it out as she falls (Fig. 21).[37] Among the earliest surviving nude females from the Classical period, she represents a sculptural tradition of wounded figures whose momentary and tortured poses express their pain. Another female Niobid, now in Copenhagen, is running away, shielding her back with the overfold of her peplos as she tries to avoid her sister's fate. Their brother, also in Copenhagen, has already been brought down and lies in a twisted pose, reaching behind himself for the arrow that has pierced his back (Boardman 1985: figs. 133.1–2, 134.1).

Wounded, fleeing, and dying, the three statues together present the inescapable sequence of divine retribution. Because of cuttings on the backs of the statues, most commentators have assigned the group to the pediment of an unidentified Classical temple, possibly for Apollo or Artemis, on the Greek mainland or in Magna Graecia.[38] Although the poses and scale of the statues may have been dictated by their place in the gable, one wonders whether they, like the painted Niobids on the calyx krater discussed earlier, could possibly have been part of a freestanding composition meant to occupy a specific landscape setting on the ground, rather than a pediment. In any case, the small two-dimensional drama portrayed by the Niobid Painter on his krater was also rendered in a large three-dimensional format that brought the Niobids' undeserved fear and suffering closer to the realm of human experience.

The spectacle presented to the viewer – in plays, sculptures, or vase paintings – emphasized the victims, their fruitless struggles, their final moments. Spectators, like Niobe herself, witnessed the children's unearned fear, pain, and death at the hands of the gods. Ancient viewers would also be able to review the decisions and reactions leading to their plight, explored remorselessly in marble. Niobe's false sense of pride and power as the mother of a large family unleashed the divine power of Artemis and Apollo against her children.

FIGURE 21.
Collapsing Niobid.
Pedimental sculpture, c.
430 BCE. Rome, Terme
72274. Photo: after
G. M. A. Richter, *The
Sculpture and Sculptors of
the Greeks* (New Haven
1929), fig. 5.

HERMES *KOUROTROPHOS*

But a third category of mythological children survived: defenseless and innocent babies hunted by an angry god. These infants, notably Dionysus, Heracles, and Arkas, had to escape Hera's or Artemis' vengeful pursuit. The birth of Dionysus became a popular topic in Greek art by the Archaic period, his babyhood and youth a paradigm for human childhood transitions.[39]

The classical iconography of Dionysus as infant and toddler was especially influential; his vulnerability as an infant symbolized the physical and spiritual dangers faced by mortal newborns.[40] Hesiod, in the *Theogony* (940–42), first told the story of Zeus and Semele and the birth of their child Dionysus. Neonatal scenes with Dionysus appear on vases from the late sixth century BCE, with Zeus himself carrying the baby to a foster home. A lekythos painted by the Alkimachos Painter around 460 BCE depicted Dionysius' second birth, his head emerging from Zeus' thigh (Fig. 22), a later iconographical development.[41]

Hermes, who served as a herald in early examples of these scenes, then took over as *kourotrophos*, or caretaker of a child, by the mid–fifth century BCE. Apollodoros (3.4.3), in the second century BCE, provided a full account of Dionysus' early years and was the first authority to mention a connection between the god of wine and Hermes. He reported that Zeus, having given birth to Dionysus, turned him over to Hermes, who brought the baby to the Theban King Athamas and his wife Ino.[42]

Infanticide dominates this story as well. According to Apollodoros, Hera punished Dionysus' foster parents by driving them mad. King Athamas actually killed one of his own children; his wife plunged the other son into a cauldron of boiling water and then leaped into the sea, where mother and child became the sea gods Leukothea and Palaimon. Human parents, driven mad by a god, killed their own offspring. Their home became, instead of a secure haven, the scene of the unthinkable, the murder of children. Hermes then rescued the divine foster child, survivor of Hera's ill will, and found a new home for him with nymphs living in the wild on Mt. Nysa.

On Attic vases just before the mid–fifth century BCE, Hermes began to take over Zeus' fatherly role, his destination either the court of King Athamas or the mountain home of the nymphs. The journey itself was apparently important to depict. On a hydria by Hermonax,

FIGURE 22. Birth of Dionysus from the thigh of Zeus. Attic red-figure lekythos attributed to the Alkimachos Painter, c. 460 BCE. Boston, Museum of Fine Arts 95.39. Photo: after J. D. Beazley, *Attic Red-Figured Vases in American Museums* (Cambridge, MA 1918), 135, fig. 83.

dated to around 460 BCE, Hermes delivers Dionysus to Ino (Fig. 23).[43] Although he sometimes brings the infant god to a female nurse, there were also male guardians, like Silenus, who waited to receive him, as on a white-ground calyx krater (c. 460 BCE) by the Phiale Painter (Fig. 24).[44]

Hermes' role as male caretaker rescuing infants from danger and transporting them across important boundaries developed in Greek painting at about the same time as depictions of family life in general. In addition, the intimate glance between child and guardian and the protective quality of Hermes' careful embrace of Dionysus were

FIGURE 23.
Hermes bringing the infant
Dionysus to Ino. Attic
red-figure hydria
attributed to Hermonax,
c. 460 BCE. Athens, Kyrou
Collection 71. Photo: John
H. Oakley.

FIGURE 24.
Hermes handing the infant Dionysus to
Silenus. Attic red-figure calyx krater
attributed to the Phiale Painter, c. 460
BCE. Vatican Museum 16586. Photo:
Hirmer Fotoarchiv, Munich.

FIGURE 25.
Hermes handing the infant
Dionysus to Silenus. Attic
red-figure phiale, Barclay
Painter, c. 450 BCE. Rome,
Mus. Naz. Etrusco di Villa
Giulia, 49002. Photo:
Christoph Clairmont.

emphasized, as on the Barclay Painter's pelike (c. 450 BCE) now in Rome
(Fig. 25).[45] In these journeys, the divine danger threatening the innocent
baby is imminent but unseen; the iconographic emphasis is on flight
to a home in a secret cave or hidden forest. The baby Dionysus appears
vulnerable and innocent even though he was a powerful god. This motif
may have evoked a kind of civic pity, too, since in this guise Dionysus
represented the young and helpless. His cult was available to Athenians
of all ages, even toddlers, who participated in the Anthesteria and thus
could be associated with their patron at an early age.[46]

As for sculpture, Hermes *kourotrophos* appears to have come into his own in the early fourth century BCE, along with an increased demand for sculptures of children set up as votives at sites like the sanctuary of Artemis at Brauron in southeastern Attica.[47] The earliest surviving sculptured versions of Hermes as guardian continue the tradition of the vases, embedding the *kourotrophos* in a narrative context. Hermes and baby Dionysus are featured on a votive relief (c. 330 BCE) now in the Agora Museum in Athens (Fig. 26), dedicated by a man called Neoptolemos, according to the inscription (Camp 1990: 200–1).[48] Framed by a rocky cave, Hermes hands over baby Dionysus to a waiting nymph. Gods and other nymphs witness the infant's safe arrival. Holding out the baby, Hermes steps up onto an object jutting from the cave floor. This detail has been interpreted either as a natural feature, emphasizing the rough cave setting, or as a rupestral altar (Shear 1973: 168–70; Thompson 1977).

If this second reading is correct, the altar symbolizes the sacred nature of Hermes' mission but also may allude to something more specific. Ancient sources, albeit none of them classical, mention an Altar of Pity somewhere in the Agora.[49] Individuals both mortal and mythological sought sacred refuge there, and the worship of Eleos as a divinity appears to have set Athenians apart from other peoples, according to the testimonia.[50] Located in a grove, the altar may have been made of stone. Once identified with the Altar of the Twelve Gods marking the center of the Agora (Wycherley 1954: 143–45), this elusive monument's location has been shifted east, toward the Roman market (Gadbery 1992: 478; Vanderpool 1974: 310; Thompson 1952: 52). Stafford, however, reconsidering the placement of the Altar, opts for the earlier link to the Altar of the Twelve Gods (2000: 211–22). She further argues that the Pity epithet refers not to a specific *daimôn* worshipped at the Altar, but instead pointed to a traditional place of sanctuary in Athens.

That there actually was an altar connected with *Eleos* in Athens as late as the second century CE is attested by a votive stele (*IG* II² 4786)

FIGURE 26. Hermes and the infant Dionysus. Votive relief, c. 330 BCE. Athens, Agora I 7154. Photo: American School of Classical Studies at Athens, Agora Excavations.

dedicated by Thracians. The text addresses the father of Eirene (Zeus) and states that the dedicants approach the altar of Eleos as suppliants.[51] The spelling *elaiou* instead of *eleou* used in the inscription has been explained as a regional variation, but Stafford proposes that *elaiou* might refer to the olive branches customarily carried and offered by ancient Greek suppliants, and thus would allude to the altar's function as refuge (2000: 208–9).

Let us return to the earlier Neoptolemos relief. If the rocky projection in the nymphs' cave is an altar, then perhaps it represents sanctuary as well as identifying a sacred spot. Hermes' act of turning over the innocent baby to the nymphs in the setting of a sacred refuge could then be perceived as the expression of *eleos* – not a helpless, painful reaction to the sight of innocent suffering, but an active, protecting role,

FIGURE 27.
Hermes handing the infant
Dionysus to Ariadne (?).
Attic red-figure pelike
attributed to the Chicago
Painter, c. 440 BCE.
Palermo, Mus. Arch.
Regionale, 2186. Photo:
after *Monumenti inediti
publicati dall' Instituto di
Correspondenza
Archeologica* 2 (1834–1837)
pl. 17.

acknowledging not only the dangers of childhood but also the role and
risks of being a parent. And just possibly the appealing gestures of the
babies, as they reach out to Hermes or their foster parents in many of
the painted and sculpted scenes, represented something quite serious,
part of the venerable tradition of supplication described in literature
and represented in art (Fig. 27).[52]

Classical Greek painted or sculpted imagery recalling scenes of undeserved suffering or innocent vulnerability may have been understood
in ancient times as a representation of that state, to be contemplated

and rewitnessed by viewers. These works had the ability to inscribe the experience of suffering on the public landscape and perhaps on the civic conscience. The issue of power, or powerlessness, that is always at the heart of unjust punishment and suffering – and is also an ingredient of *eleos* – could be thus contemplated, and represented, through the lens of art in Classical Athens.

⬛⊙⬛

ENDNOTES

Abbreviations

ARV² = J. D. Beazley, *Attic Red-figure Vase-Painters*, 2nd ed. (Oxford 1963)

CVA = *Corpus Vasorum Antiquorum*

1. Most 2003: 57–62; Konstan 2001; Dover 1974: 195–96. Also Stafford 2000: Ch. 7; Konstan 2000b: 125–45. Similar criteria for pity were recognized in Roman law as well, and could be employed to create a successful defense in court, according to Cicero (*Inv. Rhet.* 1.107–9).
2. On the architecture of Athenian law courts see Boegehold 1995: Ch. 15; Camp 1990: 101–8, 180–81.
3. Although other abstract ethical, moral, and emotional qualities and social concepts were depicted, including Adikia, Dike, Eirene, Harmonia, Eris, Eudaimonia, Eukleia, Eunomia, Eutychia, Himeros, Peitho, Pothos, Themis (Shapiro 1993: 26; see also Borg 2002).
4. Hurwit (1982) argued that even the trees in painted scenes of Ajax' suicide drooped sympathetically.
5. Kaufhold 1997: 66–71; Radt 1999: 4.435–45; Fitzpatrick 2001.
6. Burnett 1998: 177–91.
7. Lloyd-Jones 1994: 3.292–95.
8. King Pandion: Nercessian 1994; Kron 1976: 104–19.
9. Kron 1976; Mattusch 1994.
10. The earliest version of the scene appears on a terracotta metope from the Temple of Apollo at Thermon (Athens, NM 13410, third quarter of the seventh century BCE; Touloupa 1994: 527.1). On the myth and iconography see March 2000; Lyons 1997: 173, 226; Touloupa 1994; Wiemann 1986; Sparkes 1985: 29–33; Cook 1964.
11. Paris, Louvre G147, *ARV²* 472.211; Sparkes 1985: 31, pl. 35.

12. In the collection of Herbert Cahn (HC 599): Sparkes 1985: 31–32.

13. Munich, Antikensammlungen 2638, 9191; *ARV*² 456.1, 1654. Sparkes 1985: 29, pl. 34.

14. Detienne and Vernant 1989.

15. Pausanias (1.5.1–4) listed them.

16. Mattusch 1994: 73–81; Harrison 1979.

17. The dedicant, Alkamenes, is assumed to be the fifth-century Athenian sculptor to whom ancient writers attributed a statue of Aphrodite in the Garden (e.g., Paus. 1.19.2), among other important works. Several of Alkamenes' statues, according to the sources, were on the Acropolis and occupied significant spots near the Propylaia: a Hekate (Paus. 2.30.2) and possibly a Hermes Propylaios (Rolley 1994–1999: 2.143–49; Stewart 1990: 1.164–65; Ridgway 1981: 174–78). If proposed replicas of the Hermes, with their deliberately archaizing style, can be attributed to Alkamenes, they suggest that he had some interest in employing older artistic forms. The moment chosen by the artist of the Prokne and Itys, just before an event was about to happen, is generally associated with the *early* Classical period (c. 480–450 BCE). So the choice of temporal approach could be a clue linking the work with Alkamenes.

18. Akr. 1358: Kreikenbom 2003: 187–89; Rolley 1999: 2.147–48; Hurwit 1999: 206–7; Brouskari 1996: 237; Touloupa 1994: 528, no. 11; Stewart 1990: 1.164; La Rocca 1986; Ridgway 1981: 175–76; Knell 1978; Brouskari 1974: 165–66.

19. Stevens 1946: 10–11, figs. 3, no. 3, and 12–13.

20. Hurwit 1999: 206–7.

21. In the Neo-Attic three-figure reliefs depicting Medea, one of the Peliads appears to be a reversed version of the three-dimensional Prokne. She grasps a knife in her right hand, held up against her face (Ridgway 1984: pl. 88).

22. Ashmole and Yalouris 1967: 12–22; Ridgway 1970: 18–22; Osborne 2000: 233–34; Ridgway 1999: 17, 19, 20, 80; Kyrieleis 1997; Hurwit 1987; Tersini 1987; Simon 1969.

23. East Pediment N (Boardman 1985: Fig. 20.4).

24. On the function of gestures in Greek art and literature, see Boegehold 1999.

25. The emphasis on nurturing and autochthony north of the Acropolis appears to have continued into later periods. Just north of the Parthenon, along roughly the same line as the Prokne and Itys dedication, was a Hadrianic dedication to Ge that consisted of a statue possibly represented as emerging from bedrock (Hurwit 1999: 276).

26. There is a mythological connection between Niobe and Prokne, through a variant Theban form of the latter's story. Aedon, daughter of Pandareos and Himothea and wife of Zethos, had a son called Itylos. Aedon mistakenly killed her son instead of Niobe's and was then turned into a nightingale (*Od.* 19.518–23; Lyons 1997: 173).

27. Schmidt 1992; Wiemann 1986.

28. Soph. *Ant.* 823–33: Lloyd-Jones 1994: 2.80–81.

29. Gilby 1996: 41–47.

30. Lloyd-Jones 1971: 2.430–35, 556–62.

31. Lloyd-Jones 1994: 3.227–35.

32. For example, the loutrophoros in Malibu, J. Paul Getty Museum 82.AE.16, *CVA* California 4, pl. 183–85, 189.2; for this and other examples, see Schmidt 1992: 11–20.

33. On the iconography of Niobe and the Niobids: Geominy 1992. Archaic examples of the Niobid story are rare but they depict Apollo and Artemis attacking the Niobids; for example, on a Tyrrhenian amphora of c. 560 BCE from Tarquinia, Artemis and Apollo shoot arrows at the fleeing Niobids (Hamburg, Museum für Kunst und Gewerbe, 1960; *CVA* Hamburg, Museum für Kunst und Gewerbe 1, 23–24, Fig. 4, pls. 1978–80, 12.1–2, 13.1–2, 14.1–4).

34. Paris, Louvre G341, *ARV*² 601.22, 1601, *CVA* Paris, Louvre 2, III.Id.3, pls. 95–98: 1.1–4, 2.1–4, 3.1–5, 4.1.

35. According to Paus. 5.11.1–9. On the chryselephantine statue of Zeus at Olympia, see Lapatin 2001: 79–85, and on its throne, Fink 1967.

36. Ridgway 1981: 56–58; some stylistic discrepancies have been noted among the three sculptures. Collapsing female Niobid shot in the back with an arrow, the only one securely association with the Gardens of Sallust: Rome, Terme 72274; Hartswick 2004: 93–104; Geominy 1992: 918, no. 21a; Paribeni 1979, 176–79. Fleeing female Niobid: Copenhagen, Ny Carlsberg Glyptothek 520; Geominy 1992: 918, no. 21b; Poulsen 1951: 267–69). Supine, wounded, male Niobid: Copenhagen, Ny Carlsberg Glyptothek 472; Geominy 1992: 918, no. 21c; Poulsen 1951: 269–71. On the Roman findspot of these sculptures, see Hartswick (2004: 93–104) and Moltesen (1998).

37. Rome, Museo Nazionale 72274.

38. Ridgway 1981: 56.

39. On the myth: Huskinson 1996: 30–31; Motte 1996: 190–97; Beaumont 1995: 341–44; Siebert 1990: 286, 309–11, nos. 315–21; Baratte 1989; Price 1978: 70–72; Loeb 1979: 28–56; Zanker 1965: 45–55; Griefenhagen 1931: 27–43; Heydemann 1885.

40. Most divinities whose lives as children were explored in ancient sources and depicted in art have a close relationship with the mortal youths they protect. Their own progress through childhood represented important and sometimes challenging or dangerous stages in the lives of mortals. Thus Artemis, Apollo, Dionysus, Heracles, Hermes, and even Zeus, all linked with human young, appear as babies and children in Greek literature and art.

41. Boston, Museum of Fine Arts 95.39, *ARV*² 533.58.

42. Frazer 1921: 319–20; Apollodoros reports that Hermes convinced the Theban royal couple to raise Dionysus as a girl, perhaps emphasizing the god's broad jurisdiction over both sexes.

43. Athens, Kyrou Collection 71.

44. Vatican Museum 16586, *ARV*² 1017.54, 1678.

45. Rome, Mus. Naz. Etrusco di Villa Giulia, 49002, *ARV*² 1067.8. This expression of intimate relationships between adults and babies appears on Classical Attic grave reliefs as well.

46. On the Anthesteria festival, and specifically on the day called Chous, see Hamilton (1992: 5–33) and Guazzelli (1992: 30–31).

47. Raftopoulou 2000.
48. Agora I 7154, discovered reused in a Late Roman house on the north slope of the Areopagus, is discussed by Camp 1990: 201. See also Ridgway 1997: 198, 199.
49. Wycherley 1957: 67–74. Most sources date from the first to third centuries CE.
50. But Syracuse in Sicily was said to have been the first city to establish an altar for *Eleos* (Diodorus Siculus 13.22.6–8); Konstan 2001: 89–90; Wycherley 1957: 69, no. 169.
51. Wycherley 1957: 74, no. 190 = EM 8423. The inscribed stele, preserving a fragmentary relief, was found in the Odeion of Herodes Atticus.
52. Freyburger 1988; Gould 1973. For example, the Chicago Painter's pelike, c. 450 BCE, Palermo, Mus. Arch. Regionale, 2186, *ARV²* 630.24.

A Crying Shame: Pitying the Sick in the Hippocratic Corpus and Greek Tragedy

Jennifer Clarke Kosak

◎▣◎

IF FREQUENCY OF MENTION IS ANY MEASURE, PITY WAS NOT A contentious subject among writers of medical treatises in fifth- and fourth-century Greece. The most common words for pity, *eleos* and *oiktos*, do not appear in any form in the Hippocratic Corpus except for three occurrences in the *Letters*, works dating to the Roman period. Despite the absence of direct discussions of pity in the treatises, I wish to ask whether the Hippocratic doctor was expected to pity or did in fact pity his patients, and if not, why not. This line of inquiry leads to the larger question of whether anyone was supposed to feel pity for the sick, and if so, who and under what circumstances. My analysis traces several aspects of the complex relationship between pity and power in the private realm of sickness and healing. Pity can be felt by almost anyone but does not necessarily translate into the power to help. The sick may seek pity for their condition, but arguably they seek relief even more. And although healers certainly present themselves as capable of curing disease and providing a release from pain, they do not, apparently, do so out of pity.

Perhaps the reader will immediately object: why should we expect to find any mention of pity in the Hippocratic Corpus? Should we expect pity to motivate or affect those who, after all, are only doing their job? Do we regularly expect pity from modern doctors? In fact, there is a debate within modern Western medical ethics not only over whether doctors should be emotionally affected by the plight of their patients but also over exactly what kind of emotions they ought to register. At the end of the nineteenth century, the influential doctor William Osler urged his medical students to maintain "equanimity" in their dealings with patients.[1] Indeed, the process of medical education in the West arguably encouraged medical students to develop a sense of emotional detachment.[2] Yet the importance of emotional commitment on the part of the doctor has played a significant role in recent discussions of the doctor-patient relationship: these have come increasingly to focus on a model of mutual decision making and patients' rights.[3] Doctors now are often urged to cultivate their emotions – above all, to experience and reveal empathy. In defining empathy, Howard Spiro writes: "Empathy is the feeling that 'I might be you' or 'I am you,' but it is more than just an intellectual identification; empathy must be accompanied by feeling" (1993: 2). Others suggest that empathy can comfortably coexist with "detached concern" because it enables insight into what the patient is going through mentally and emotionally as well as physically. Thus empathy allows the doctor to get a complete clinical picture of the patient's situation (Halpern 1993).

Even those who consider the emphasis on empathy misplaced often find room for sympathy and compassion.[4] Sympathy, it is argued, is surely the human emotion that motivates people to become doctors: they see and understand the suffering of others and desire to alleviate it. On the contrary, say the empathy advocates, sympathy is based too much on a sense of identification with the patient: complete identification is not desirable since the overly sympathetic doctor will feel powerless to help the patient. The term "pity" rarely enters this debate over the nature and degree of emotional identification appropriate in the doctor-patient relationship;[5] and when it does, pity may be dismissed as a feeling less virtuous (Lascombe 1993: 59–60) or more primitive (Wilmer 1987: 404–6) than either sympathy or empathy. Pity "may involve little understanding of another" (Halpern 1993: 164) and "may be a defense against identification" (Wilmer 1987: 405). Thus, while it is true that members of modern Western societies do not normally see pity as a characteristic emotion or attitude of doctors, this fact poses the same question: why not? Are not sick people deserving of pity? What is it about pity that makes it an emotion less appropriate for doctors than, for example, sympathy? Why does pity play such a small role in modern – and classical Greek – discussions of the place of emotion in the practice of medicine?[6] Indeed, one might argue that the ancients pay even less attention to prescribing the appropriate emotions for doctors than the moderns, given that, at least in the fifth century BCE, *oiktos* can connote what English means by both pity and compassion or sympathy – and yet both this word and its more restricted companion *eleos* make so poor a showing in the Corpus.[7]

Although I cannot investigate here the role of pity in modern Western medicine,[8] let me suggest four possible reasons why pity is not mentioned in the classical treatises of the Hippocratic Corpus. First, it might be that pity is simply assumed – but, given the various nuances involved in discussions of pity in both ancient and modern sources, we would still need to explain why. Second, if pity is indeed an emotion felt by those who are in a superior position (in the sense of being currently trouble free or "outside" the situation themselves) to the pitied,[9] the term might be inappropriate in medical contexts. Issues of superiority in Greek healing are complex. Although some doctors enjoyed high social status, many were regarded as practitioners of a banausic occupation. Since they worked with their hands for compensation, to act as a healer was not to act from some distant position, lofty or otherwise.[10] Furthermore, ancient medical writers generally saw themselves as one corner of a triangle comprised of the disease, the patient, and the healer,[11] and subordinate to the art of medicine itself; hence, they may not have considered themselves in a position of relative advantage vis-à-vis their patients and so did not feel it necessary to pity them. A third possible reason for the absence of pity in medical texts is that pity, as I suggested earlier, does not require action – it is an emotion that allows for some distance between the pitier and the pitied and does not impel the pitier to intervene – whereas the work of the doctor is all about action. Fourth and last, the medical writers may have felt that pity and personal emotions had no place in the world of the rationalist medicine they were trying to establish, although they often note the emotions of grief or distress suffered by the patients themselves; thus, they thought their task was to bring the patients out of pain, and in order to do so they suppressed feelings of pity and asserted expressions of control. I consider all of these reasons at various points in this discussion, and argue that at least two of them contribute to the lack of Hippocratic discussions of pity.

ATTITUDES OF HEALERS

I would like to begin by examining a variety of passages in the Hippocratic Corpus that deal with the attitudes of healers toward their patients. Thereafter, since pity per se receives little explicit treatment in the Hippocratic Corpus, I will draw upon other textual evidence in my attempt to shed light on the role of pity in the treatment of the sick. Let us return to the Hippocratic letters already mentioned. Although written in the Roman period, these were clearly meant to represent Hippocratic ideas and doctrines; many include extensive quotations from works that were present in the Corpus at a much earlier date.[12] The two letters that mention pity retell the story about how Hippocrates was called to Abdera to treat the philosopher Demokritos, who had apparently gone mad. Hippocrates refused money in recompense for this service; as he says in letter 11, addressed to the Abderites, money is a ruinous force, and because of it, "Man's life is a pitiful thing (*oiktros*)" (11). As evidence of Demokritos' madness, Hippocrates recounts in letter 17 that he rebuked Demokritos for laughing at things one should pity (17.4):

> *Don't you think you are strange at any rate to laugh at the death of a human or illness or delusion, or madness, or melancholy, or butchery, or something still worse, or again at marriages or festivals or births or initiations or offices and honors or anything else completely good? For things that demand pity you laugh at* (ha deon oikteirein gelêis*), and you mock those things in which one should take pleasure, such that in your case there is no distinguishing between good and bad.*

Demokritos defends himself by arguing that he can only laugh because all he sees are constant instances of human folly. Nonetheless, humans are pitiable in that they bring evil upon themselves (17.9):

> *Man as a whole is from birth a disease* (nousos*): while being raised, without resource, a suppliant for assistance; while growing up, he is incorrigible, foolish under the guidance of a teacher; reckless when grown up, past his prime, pitiable* (oiktros*), having sowed his own personal sufferings with irrationality* (alogistiêi*).*

According to the letters, Hippocrates recognizes the validity of Demokritos' position and reports to the Abderites that Demokritos is of sound mind.

These two occurrences of pity in letter 17 reflect rather different ideas concerning pity: the first use (*oiktirein*) suggests that we should pity people who are suffering from bad things – and that they do not deserve their suffering. The second (*oiktros*) suggests that people are pitiable or pitiful because they irrationally bring their suffering upon themselves. It is this second use, representing Demokritos' opinion, that is ultimately vindicated: Demokritos is declared sane. But even though Hippocrates is convinced that Demokritos' view of human nature is correct, he does not subsequently decide to give up medical practice on the grounds that people do not deserve treatment.[13] If, as I have suggested, pity is an emotion most tenable for those not called upon to act, then the philosopher may appropriately pity (or not), but the doctor must intervene, or, if he refrains, should ideally do so out of concern that he will harm the patient more than help him (I say ideally because we shall see that this motivation does not always account for non-intervention).

According to the physician Galen, who practiced in the Roman era, the motivations of doctors to give treatment to patients were various (*On the Doctrines of Hippocrates and Plato* 9.5.4):

> For some for the sake of compensation work at the medical art, others because of the relief from taxation given them by law, others on account of philanthrôpia, *just as others on account of the reputation that comes with the art or on account of honor.*[14]

In Galen's system of medical ethics, *philanthrôpia* (concern for one's fellow human beings) is the appropriate motivation for serving as a physician. Because he believes that Hippocratic medical ethics are generally consistent with his own, Galen places Hippocrates himself among those doctors who act out of *philanthrôpia*.[15] And even though pity is not named in Hippocratic treatises, the medical authors represented in the Corpus *do* discuss attitudes that doctors should have toward their patients. In a number of places they indicate that one needs to treat patients with respect, with kindness, and without disapprobation. Let me start with some evidence from the later treatises and work backward. The little treatise *Physician* (*Peri iatrou*) dates most probably to the late fourth century (Potter 1995: 298–99) and in its opening sections describes the qualities that the good doctor must possess: as with any number of texts, the treatise is concerned to show how the doctor can acquire a good reputation. In section 1, the author urges the reader, presumably a prospective doctor, to have a character that is *kalos kai agathos*, thus aspiring to the behavior and status of the upper classes. Moreover, as part of being *kalos kai agathos*, he will be *semnos* (serious, grave) and *philanthrôpos* (humane) toward all. A little later, the writer urges the prospective doctor to avoid harsh expressions because these indicate that the doctor is *authadês* (self-involved, arrogant) and *misanthrôpos* (hateful, unkind).[16] It is unclear whether such an attitude is to be avoided because it will affect the health of the patient or merely the standing of the doctor – that is, the harsh-mannered doctor will not attract customers. Nonetheless, earlier in the chapter, the writer had urged the doctor to be clean and sweet-smelling, as these things are pleasant for the patient. Hence, the author pays attention to the means by which the doctor may succeed and at the same time expresses interest in the well-being of the patient.

The language of the treatise is unusual: the word *philanthrôpos* occurs only here in the Corpus; the related word *philanthrôpia* occurs once, in the treatise *Precepts* (probably of late Hellenistic date[17]), in which we find the rather well-known aphorism, "where there is *philanthrôpiê*, there also is *philotekhniê* (wholehearted commitment to one's craft)" (6). The context of this sentiment concerns money: the writer urges the medical practitioner to provide treatment regardless of the patient's ability to pay. By the time we come to Galen, as I noted earlier, *philanthrôpia* has been established as one of the guiding principles of appropriate medical ethics – but, like terms for pity, we do not see it in the early works of the Corpus.[18] It may seem odd that this term that was to become so central in later medical literature is largely missing from the Corpus itself. But the word *philanthrôpia* and its cognates are not common in the literature of the fifth century generally, and even one of the earliest uses shows the potential challenges faced by those who aspire to this quality: in the *Prometheus Bound*, Kratos and Hephaistos wonder at Prometheus' *philanthrôpos tropos* (his "human-loving way," 11, 28) because he engages in activities that help humankind despite great personal cost and suffering. One of the benefactions Prometheus provides humankind is instruction in medicine (478–83).[19] The behavior of Prometheus finds a parallel in the first chapter of the Hippocratic treatise *Breaths* (discussed later), where the author describes how the doctor helps others even though he suffers in the attempt.

Despite the absence of exhortations to *philanthrôpia*, the overall well-being of the patient is clearly of concern in earlier treatises. In the treatise *Epidemics VI*,[20] the author urges "kindnesses (*kharites*) towards the sick," which include keeping the patients' food and drink clean and keeping what he or she touches soft; moreover, it includes bending the rules of the *tekhnê* slightly in order to give the patient comfort (6.4.7).[21] But the concern for the doctor's reputation and its effect on treatment, even to the detriment of the patient, occurs as well. So, for example, the author of *Fractures* reveals a conflict between good standards of medical practice and the need to bow to the pressures of public expectation. In his opening chapter he severely criticizes those who attempt to put theory ahead of sense in their approach to healing: they apparently believe that "outlandishness" (*to xenoprepês*) is to be preferred to the "obvious" (*to eudêlon*). Although this behavior is rejected, possible motives for such treatment become increasingly apparent as the treatise progresses. For the author himself indicates the need to be sensitive to the expectations of the public and to the aesthetic values of the patients. Thus, in his discussion of the use of hollow splints, he confesses his *aporia* over what to advise: the splints are useful to some degree, but are not really conducive to health. Yet, as he says, the public expects them to be used and, he states, "the practitioner will be more free from blame" if he uses a hollow splint, even if it is "rather lacking in *tekhnê*" (*atekhnesteron ge*, 16). Later in the treatise, he speaks of how the doctor should be careful in the case of a broken femur to try to ensure that the leg when healed will not be shorter than before, since this would result in both *aiskhunê* (shame, disgrace) and *blabê* (harm) for the patient (19). This attentiveness to the feelings of the patient (the doctor wishes to preserve the patient's dignity and avoid giving him a sense of shame), as opposed to the physical problems presented by disease and injury, is fairly widespread in the Corpus. But doctors also maintain a healthy regard for their own reputations: there are a number of places where we hear of doctors not intervening in order to remain "free from blame" if something goes wrong.[22]

How in fact did doctors decide whom to treat? Did pity play a role in this decision? As we have seen, one expectation mentioned openly in the later treatises is that doctors should treat any patient, regardless of his or her ability to pay. We know from other fifth-century sources that doctors often did charge a fee, and it is unclear how often they offered free treatment. However, as Jacques Jouanna (1999: 114) notes, the more than 450 patients mentioned in the *Epidemics* came from a variety of social and economic backgrounds: men, women, rich, poor, slave, free.[23] Furthermore, the writers do make rather subtle moral judgments about the lifestyles of patients, but these do not and apparently should not stand in the way of treatment. Here are but two of many examples from the *Epidemics*. The first is *Epidemics III*, case 11, where a woman easily troubled (*gunê dusanios*) falls sick "from justifiable grief " (*ek lupês meta prophasios*): the symptoms of her disease – sleeplessness and loss of appetite – sound remarkably like a case of serious depression. Although the woman is apparently predisposed to be gloomy and therefore could perhaps be accused of overreacting to a problem, the writer specifically removes her from blame: she had a good reason for doing what she did. The same cannot be said for a young man in Meliboea, who took to his bed "having been heated for a long time by drinking and lots of sex" (*Epid. III*, case 16). Clearly, he has brought his illness on himself. Nonetheless, the writer does not chastise him but merely records his observations of the patient over the course of twenty-four days. Now it is true that the woman in case 11 recovers whereas the young man in case 16 dies. But the writer records their symptoms in both cases; and, despite the hints as to who is responsible for his own suffering and who is not, both are apparently worthy of treatment.

Furthermore, medical writers sometimes take a stand against long-held superstitions in order to remove personal responsibility from patients. I think particularly of the treatise *On the Sacred Disease*, in which the author castigates those who explain epilepsy as an attack by divine forces. Admittedly, the writer focuses mostly on removing the blame from the *gods*, arguing that the gods, pure as they are, are unlikely to pollute human beings – indeed, they are more likely to purify them (1.44).[24] But he suggests that sufferers feel shame because of the attacks: they try to remove themselves from company and cover up their heads due to embarrassment ("this happens because of shame at their malady, and not because of fear, as the many hold, of the divine" 12.2). Small children, he explains, who are as yet unaware of the effects of the disease and haven't learned how to anticipate it, will often fall down right where they are, apparently in full view: as he says, they feel fear and fright, but "they do not yet know the feeling of shame" (12.4). The older patients feel shame presumably because of their loss of self-control and perhaps also because others will think that they are subject to divine punishment of some kind. But the author of *On the Sacred Disease* seems determined to remove blame and shame from the sufferers by providing a naturalistic explanation for the disease. It seems possible that in this treatise we see not only an assertion of the author's superior knowledge in understanding the nature of disease, but also an intimation of pity: the author, seeing persons suffering shame undeservedly, feels pity for them, and is moved to the action of writing the treatise and arguing against the traditional understanding of the sacred disease.

One treatise that I have not yet mentioned is rather exceptional, and that is *Breaths*. Here we see not only intimations of the doctor's pity for his patients, but also, I would argue, an invitation to the reader to pity or commiserate with the doctor. In the opening chapter, the author

argues for the existence of some *tekhnai* that cause pain (and the word
for "causing pain," *epiponos*, as used in the Hippocratic Corpus usually
has very physical connotations of pain)[25] to the practitioners, but are
helpful – a common good – to their beneficiaries (*Breaths* 1.1–3):

> *There are certain* tekhnai *which cause pain for those who practice*
> *them, but are beneficial for those who use them, and while they are a*
> *common good (*xunon agathon*) for the public, they are painful for those*
> *who actually do the handiwork (*tois metakheirizomenoisi*).*
> *Belonging to such a group of* tekhnai *is what the Greeks call medical*
> tekhnê: *for while the healer sees terrible things (*ta deina*) and touches*
> *unpleasant ones (*thinganei . . . aêdeôn*) and reaps his own pains in the*
> *sufferings of others, the sick are relieved by means of the* tekhnê *from*
> *the greatest evils, diseases, grief, toils, death. Opposed to all these things*
> *is medical* tekhnê.

Medicine is a painful art, explains the author. The doctor, like a tragic
spectator, sees *ta deina*,[26] but he does not do so from a distance, for he
is in physical contact with his patients, as the passage stresses through
the use of the word *metakheirizomenoisi* to describe the practitioners of
the medical art, as well as in the phrase "touches unpleasant things."
Moreover, while providing for the common good, he himself reaps a
harvest of personal suffering. Apparently, he is willing to bring pain
onto himself in order to bring good to others.[27] Indeed, he makes great
claims for his art, which frees others from the greatest evils, diseases,
suffering, pains – and even death. Is it pity that motivates the doctor
here? Or is it a mixture of motives: the humanitarian desire to help
those who are suffering combined with the quest for *timê* (honor, privilege), to be acquired by contributing to the *xunon agathon*? Are we as
readers supposed to admire the doctor or commiserate with him or pity
him or all of these? Note also the distinction here between *tekhnê* and
practitioner. It is the *tekhnê* that frees people from all these evils; it is

the *tekhnê* that opposes all these things, as he stresses at the end of the passage. The doctor is, it seems, merely the instrument through which this very powerful and admirable *tekhnê* operates, so is he to receive credit, too?

The status issues concerning doctors seem relevant here. As I mentioned earlier, doctors saw themselves in a subservient position not only to the *tekhnê*, as we see in this passage, but also to the disease itself, as we learn in the famous passage from *Epidemics I*, 11:

> Practice two things regarding diseases: to be helpful or to do no harm. The tekhnê *consists of three things, the disease, the patient and the doctor: the doctor is the servant of the* tekhnê; *the patient is to oppose the disease together with the doctor.*

In this passage, doctor and patient are a team, working together to fight the disease. With two against one, they may defeat this apparently superior foe. But if the doctor and the patient are on the same level, then it is difficult for the doctor to pity the patient, since pity may require, as has been argued by David Konstan,[28] a position of superiority to, or at least a level of detachment from, the person being pitied. In other words, pity cannot operate in situations where equality among the participants is established or immediate reciprocity is expected.[29] The passage from *Breaths*, although it invites us to observe the suffering of the doctor himself, does not indicate that the doctor feels pity for his patients, even though they, too, are suffering. Despite the fact that they are not family members or intimates, the doctor and patient form a bond that allows the doctor to feel with rather than for his patients.

PHYSICAL CONTACT

The issue of physical contact and its role in situations arousing pity requires further consideration. The physical contact may in fact further the bond developed between doctor and patient, since, as I have argued elsewhere (Kosak 1999), physical contact between the sick and the healthy requires that either a bond of kinship exist or one of fictive kinship be established.[30] But the physical contact also diminishes the level of pity per se and introduces a more reciprocal type of emotion. Here, material from other genres or institutions may help frame the argument. Let us first consider supplication: in situations of supplication, the suppliant often demands pity from the powerful.[31] At the same time, the act of supplication is intimately connected to the particular circumstances of the supplicated and the suppliant and requires more than the mere appeal for pity in order to succeed: suppliants will often call upon family connections and past experiences familiar to the supplicated as part of their efforts to persuade.[32] But the suppliant also attempts to supplement such verbal demands with physical contact that creates a bond with the supplicated person and establishes the mutual mortality and humanity of each participant. Indeed, it has been suggested by John Gould in his seminal article on *hiketeia* that supplication is incomplete without the physical contact, although it sometimes succeeds even without it (1973: 77–78). Kevin Crotty argues that "the suppliant's gestures of self-abasement" serve to remind the supplicated of the vital importance of life itself, in contrast to the premium placed on reputation when one's life is not at stake (1994: 90–91). It seems to me that physical contact transforms the position of the supplicated person from one who can merely pity to one who is called upon to act, to make a choice – one who must now *reciprocate* rather than one who can be passively affected by emotion only.[33] Of course, the people being supplicated may respond as though they are still acting out of pity, and out of their own free choice, since it is in their interest to appear in control of the situation. Likewise, the suppliant does not want to threaten the self-control of the supplicated too much, provoking anger rather than pity, and so usually remains in a kneeling position, visually marking the distinction in status between suppliant and supplicated.

The supplication scene in Sophocles' play *Philoctetes* provides a useful comparison. In this scene, the older Philoctetes, suffering from a hideous wound, supplicates the younger (and healthier) Neoptolemus, begging him to take him home, but does not succeed in touching him.[34] Neoptolemus does not in fact respond to Philoctetes' supplication immediately; it is the chorus who respond and urge that Neoptolemus accede to Philoctetes' request. They give two reasons: Philoctetes is worthy of pity (506–509) *and* such an action would serve to punish the Greek leaders (510–515), with whom Neoptolemus is at odds in the fictive story that he has constructed for the purposes of deceiving Philoctetes. Hence, the chorus provide a reason that does not involve pity and that therefore allows Neoptolemus to act only in his own self-interest.[35] The absence of physical contact is important in the play for a number of reasons,[36] but I wish to stress how it enables Neoptolemus to retain more self-control in a delicate situation where the balance of power is not in fact clear: Philoctetes, although sick, is older. He is also indispensable to the success of the Greek mission – so he has some power, though he is not aware of it.

Scenes from Tragedy

The passage in *Breaths*, then, suggests two things: first, that the doctor wants to be seen as suffering along with his patient, creating a bond that allows him to move out of the role of distant observer and into the role of intimate; second, that the doctor-patient relationship must be defined as intimate because of the physical contact that is almost invariably involved in the doctor-patient relationship.[37] Because the material from the Hippocratic Corpus on the subject of pitying the sick is limited, however, it is important to consider other genres that may provide additional evidence for Greek attitudes on the appropriate relationship between patient and caregiver. Greek tragedy offers us a number of scenes depicting interactions between a sick person and a caregiver that may help us understand more fully the importance of both status and physical contact in the construction of proper emotional responses. For, although it presents these issues in a stylized or even ironic way, tragedy, unlike medical literature, allows us to see caregivers and their patients in action. Furthermore, the relationship between pity and action for which I have argued may also be rendered more clearly in Athenian tragedy, where the external audience is frequently invited to pity, but never to act, but the internal audience faces a more complex set of demands. Thus, I shall now examine some sickness scenes from tragic plays in order to discover whether these scenes reinforce what we see (or do not see) in the Hippocratic Corpus. The corpus represents a medical tradition that is non-Athenian in origin (though it is very clear that the Athenians, or at least some Athenians, were well aware of Hippocrates and Hippocratic medical ideas).[38] Nonetheless, the comparisons with tragedy may also show whether the emotions attributed to healers and sufferers in the medical literature were typical in Athenian culture, too.

In Euripides' *Hippolytus*, the Nurse caring for the sick Phaedra speaks words that provide a tragic parallel to the passage from *Breaths* discussed earlier.[39] She enters to inform the audience of Phaedra's condition and also to complain about her difficulty in tending her (186–88):

> *It is better to be sick than to tend the sick,*
> *Sickness is a single issue, but involved in tending the sick are*
> *Pain of the mind* (lupê . . . phrenôn) *and toil with the hands*
> (khersin . . . ponos).

It is striking how the issue of touch reappears as the Nurse speaks of working with her hands. The Nurse takes an even stronger position than the author of *Breaths*, however, as she indicates that the healer actually suffers *more* than the patient. This seems in keeping with the

Nurse's character: she is, after all, someone inclined to thrust herself into the limelight whenever possible. The Nurse seems to be determined to rescue Phaedra no matter what Phaedra herself desires; as she says at 496–97, "now there is a great *agôn* (struggle, contest) to save your life, and this is no trifling matter." Here then is clearly one healer intent on freeing her patient from death. Phaedra, by contrast, is interested in whether any life will do or whether only a life that rests on morally sound foundations (cf. esp. 377–409). Finally, while the Nurse is obviously of a lower social class than Phaedra, she seems determined, when she is not complaining about the difficulty of caring for the sick, to equate her suffering to that of Phaedra – so, for example, when she finally learns the truth about Phaedra's secret love for Hippolytus (and she herself says the words, as Phaedra points out), she begins to carry on in true tragic fashion (353–57):

> *Alas, what will you say, child? How you have utterly destroyed me.*
> *Women, it is not bearable, I will not endure*
> *Living: I see a hateful day, a hateful light.*
> *I shall throw, hurl my body, I shall be relieved of*
> *Life by dying: farewell, I no longer exist.*

It is as if she were the tragic heroine, not Phaedra; although she later changes her mind about dying, both for her own and for Phaedra's sake, she clearly feels that she is suffering, if not more than Phaedra, then at least at an equal level.[40] If the Nurse pities anyone in this play, it is herself. But more important to my argument is the playwright's emphasis on the physical contact between caregiver and patient and the Nurse's insistence that she suffers with or even more than Phaedra. At the same time, Euripides, drawing on ideas about the behaviors and attitudes of healers that are also found in the Hippocratic Corpus, has taken them to an extreme in order to produce what is surely a dislikeable – and even dangerous – character.

We find plaintive language about caring for the sick in Euripides' *Orestes* also – from Electra, although she calls it "sweet slavery" (221; and cf. 229–30). Indeed, complaints about playing the role of caregiver or healer come from female characters and low-status males, such as the Old Man in *Trachiniae*, not elite males – and to this issue I shall turn briefly now. Elite males may not complain about caregiving,[41] but they do take the issue of touching one another very seriously. Four scenes in extant tragedy represent one elite male caring on stage for another elite male who is sick. Heracles is tended by the Old Man and then by his son Hyllos in *Trachiniae*; he is also tended by Theseus in *Heracles*. Philoctetes is cared for by Neoptolemus in *Philoctetes* and Orestes is cared for by Pylades in *Orestes*. Touch plays a role in each of these scenes, as the caregiver either embraces the sick character, or in the case of *Philoctetes*, suggests an embrace. In each case, a bond of kinship or of fictive kinship is clearly indicated or established. Thus, Hyllos' status as Heracles' son is stressed in *Trachiniae*. Likewise, in the final scene of *Heracles*, Theseus initially offers his help as "a friendly subordinate" (*huperetês philos*), but as the embrace between the two men occurs, Heracles calls Theseus his son ("bereft of children I nevertheless have you as my child," 1401). The subordination of Theseus does not last long: once he is convinced that Heracles, now on his feet, will live and come to Athens, he asserts his own authority. Hence, in the final image of the play, Heracles himself becomes the child as he is supported off stage like *epholkides* (1424), using the same expression he applied to his own children earlier in the play as he led them to apparent safety (631–32). In *Philoctetes*, Philoctetes actually rejects the proffered embrace of Neoptolemus in the sickness scene (761–62), and thus Neoptolemus is pointedly not established as a caregiver. Hence it is not surprising that words of pity remain in effect throughout the play; only when a strong bond of friendship and equality between the two has been established at the end of the play does anything close to the embrace take place (1403).[42] In *Orestes*, Pylades is represented as both an outsider and a relative; his status is constantly shifting.[43] He is determined, like the Nurse in *Hippolytus*, to show that his suffering is equivalent to that of Orestes. Pylades not only insists that he had a role in the murder of Clytemnestra, but also keeps bringing up his own problems. As he says at 763, "now ask me what I am suffering: for I myself am a goner (*oikhomai*) too." Pylades eagerly cares for his sick friend/relative; his insistence on equating their suffering seems to obviate the need for expressions of pity.[44] In a play where the manliness of the protagonist is subject to frequent debate, it is perhaps not surprising to see an elite male unconcerned to justify his behavior in touching another elite male. But Pylades' behavior is, I think, deliberately meant to contribute to the ambiguity over the moral status of Orestes that pervades this play.[45]

CONCLUSION

Of the four possible explanations I offered earlier as to why pity does not appear in the Hippocratic Corpus, two at least seem likely. Because male healers place themselves into a position of relative equality with their patients, subordinate to both the treatment and the disease, they are not in a position to pity; furthermore, because they must and do act by touching their patients, pity is not a word or a feeling that appropriately describes their disposition toward these sufferers. The patients are usually not related to the healers, but this does not prevent the healers from feeling compassion or empathy rather than pity. We see these issues reflected in Athenian tragedy, too, with a much stronger emphasis on status negotiation: for females and slaves, the relationship of caregiver and sick is de facto intimate since they operate or should operate only within their own *oikos*, but for men, a bond of kinship or fictive kinship enables the caregiver to act not with pity but with sympathy or even empathy toward the patient. Handling the sick is unpleasant, says the author of *Breaths*, so it is not something lightly done. Not wishing to bring shame on themselves or cause shame for their patients, the healers in both tragedy and the Hippocratic Corpus establish themselves as intimates, fictive kin, who then do not pity but instead suffer along with those who are sick. Pitying the sick may be humane, but it will not bring results. To heal, one must get closer – even if such proximity is in some way uncomfortable – and get to work.

▣◎▣

ENDNOTES

I would like to thank Rachel Hall Sternberg for her many helpful comments on earlier versions of this paper.

1. Osler's influential address "Aequanimitas" was first published in Philadelphia in 1889; it thereafter was put together with other papers and republished in a book entitled *Aequanimitas, With Other Address to Medical Students, Nurses and Practitioners of Medicine* (Philadelphia 1904).

2. Hafferty 1991.

3. See, for example, Budd and Sharma 1994, *passim*.

4. So Landau: "[Effective physicians] will be sensitive, sympathetic, imperturbable, understanding, and occasionally empathic, but by far the least employed of these traits will be empathy" (1993: 109).

5. Targeted readings in the literature of modern medical ethics and keyword searches for "pity" in databases of medical journals and library catalogs failed to turn up many discussions of pity, whereas compassion, sympathy, and empathy are everywhere to be found.

6. Given the limited role of pity in both the modern and ancient sources, it might be reasonable to ask: has pity *ever* been deemed an important emotion or motivating factor in the practice of western medicine? Pity does appear to play a role in the early Christian and medieval periods, especially with the development of charitable medicine (consider especially the history of hospitals). Even here, however, the concept of *agapê* (humane love) is more dominant than pity. For a general overview, see Amundsen and Ferngren 1986 and Temkin 1991.

7. On the range of meanings for these words, see Stanford (1983: 23–26), who suggests a translation of "compassionate grief" for the uses of *oiktos* in tragedy. Konstan (2001: 53–54) points out that Aristotle uses the word *eleos* in his discussion of the pity in the *Rhetoric* and also notes that *eleos* is the standard word used in oratory.

8. It is perhaps natural to think of experiences of disease as universal, cutting across cultural boundaries, but as the work of anthropologists and sociologists has demonstrated (e.g., Kleinman 1980; Douglas 1994), such experiences are in fact culturally determined. The biological processes of disease may be universal, but reactions to disease, expectations for treatment, and definitions of sickness and health all vary from culture to culture and even within cultures. Hence the experience of modern Western medicine may help us locate questions but will not necessarily supply answers.

9. See Konstan's discussions of modern definitions, which, as he points out, avoid using the term "pity" (2001: 12–15), and ancient ones (2001: 60–66).

10. The status of medical practitioners is neither static nor standardized in ancient Greece; different times and locations offer different windows on the status question. Thus Burford (1972: 220–21 n. 6) explains that she has omitted doctors from her discussion of ancient craftspeople: the norms that apply to such people do not regularly apply to doctors because their craft is less predictably successful than other crafts. Nonetheless, many doctors were seen as craftspeople, worked with their hands, and charged a fee for their services, none of which were activities or characteristics of the elite. For discussions of the social status of healers, "banausic" and otherwise, see, for example, Cohn-Haft 1956; Horstmanshoff 1990; Jouanna 1999: 75–111; Nutton 1992; Pleket 1995.

11. So, for example, *Epidemics I*, 11, quoted and discussed in the text later.

12. At least some of the letters had been written by the first century CE, since portions are attested in the oldest papyrus containing part of the Corpus. None of the letters, however, are listed by Erotian, the first century CE grammarian who compiled a Hippocratic lexicon. For discussions of date and overview of Hippocratic content, see Smith (1990: 29), who argues that the Democritean letters were written sometime between 200 BCE and the early first century CE.

13. On the significance of the encounter as a "triumph for Cynicism and a defeat for Hippocrates," see Temkin 1991: 61–71.

14. All translations, unless otherwise noted, are my own.

15. On Galen and his attribution of motives of *philanthrôpia* to Hippocrates, see, for example, Temkin 1991: 48–50.

16. "Then he must be clean in person, well dressed, and anointed with sweet-smelling unguents that are beyond suspicion. For all these things are pleasing to people who are ill, and he must pay attention to this. In matters of the mind, let him be prudent, not only with regard to silence, but also in having a great regularity of life, since this is very important in respect of reputation; he must be a gentleman in character and grave and kind to all. For an over-forward obtrusiveness is despised, even though it may be very useful. . . . In appearance, let him be of serious but not harsh countenance; for harshness is taken to mean arrogance and unkindness" (*Physician* 1, trans. Potter).

17. Jouanna 1999: 405–6.

18. As Konstan (2001: 88) points out, *philanthrôpia* in our ancient sources is generally considered a virtue rather than an emotion. There is often, however, a connection with pity; thus, as Konstan also argues, Aristotle's use of the phrase *to philanthrôpon* (*Poet.* 13,

1453a2) involves a recognition that pitiful situations "may excite a kind of commiser-ation or fellow-feeling independently of the merits of the sufferer" (2001: 47). In his analysis of the medical ethics and attitudes expressed in *Decorum, Precepts, Physician* and *Epidemics VI*, Temkin (1991) argues that the emphasis on *philanthrôpia* in *Precepts* probably has some connection to the concept of *philanthrôpia* in Stoic philosophy. He cites Seneca's discussion of Stoic *philanthrôpia* (*On Mercy* 2.5.1–3), in which he argues – against the view that Stoics reject pity as an emotion appropriate to the wise person – that love of one's fellow man and concern for the common good do motivate the Stoic; pity alone is inappropriate since it is an emotion stemming from easy impression-ability. Temkin goes on to link Stoic ethics with exhortations to pity (*misericordia*) in the Roman medical writers Scribonius Largus and Celsus – exhortations tempered by reminders not to become so emotionally involved as to undermine one's capacity for good judgment. Although Temkin maintains that the author of *Precepts* felt both "pity and compassion for the sick," he argues that a reserved form of pity is meant. Yet it is sig-nificant, in my view, that the word *misericordia* appears in the Roman materials while the equivalent does not in the Greek, even in the second-century CE author Soranus. Temkin cites the latter's *Gynecology* 1.2.4 as evidence for "compassion" – the Greek is a form of *sumpaskhô* – as an appropriate medical virtue. Nonetheless, Temkin argues that the emphasis on *misericordia* and *philanthrôpia* in the sources from the Roman era is not a new phenomenon in medicine but probably has a long history obscured by the paucity of our sources from the third to first centuries BCE. See Temkin 1991: 23–35.

19. Plato also uses the word in association with healing imagery at *Symposium* 189d1–3, where Aristophanes describes Eros: "He is the most human loving (*philanthrôpotatos*) of gods, being both a helper of humankind and a healer of those things the cure of which is the greatest blessing for the human race." Attic writers in the fourth century make frequent use of the word, where it is used in a complimentary sense to describe behavior that is "kind" or "humane": it connotes generosity of spirit (see, for example, Arist. *Eth. Nic.* 1155a20 and Dem. 21.48–49) and has no specific medical resonance. But it seems possible that the fifth-century uses in tragedy and philosophy point to an association with medicine in this period, even if there is no direct evidence in the medical literature.

20. This treatise probably dates to the late fifth century BCE; for brief discussion, see Smith (1994: 10) and Jouanna (1999: 389–90). The treatises under discussion in the rest of this chapter (*Fractures, Epidemics I, Epidemics II, On the Sacred Disease, Breaths*) are also dated to the late fifth or early fourth century; for summaries of scholarly discussions on dates, see Appendix 3 in Jouanna (1999: 373–416).

21. "Gentleness" seems to have been a point of pride for healers of ancient Greece as well. As early as Homer, we hear of *êpia pharmaka*, soft, soothing, or gentle remedies (cf. *Il.* 4.218, 11.515, 11.830); the point is made explicitly in the story of Demokedes, who healed Darius, the King of Persia, with gentle remedies, in contrast to the violent ones that had already been attempted by Egyptian healers (Hdt. 3.130).

22. See numerous examples and discussion in von Staden 1990.
23. Epigraphy supplies good evidence for doctors who apparently went the extra mile for their communities: a number of inscriptions have been found in which the grateful public thanks the enthusiastic and equitable treatment received from a particular doctor; for examples, see Hands 1968: 202–5 (documents 62–68). Such evidence is post-fifth century. Nevertheless, there is also Thucydides' famous description (2.47.4) of the unstinting efforts of doctors during the plague at Athens, which began in 430. Thucydides does not suggest that the doctors acted out of pity or even compassion, but he implies admiration for their sense of duty – they continued to treat victims even though their remedies were ineffective (they treated with *agnoia*, ignorance, at least at first), and they were particularly likely to catch the disease because they kept visiting the sick.
24. The enumeration of chapters here is from Grensemann 1968.
25. So, for example, *Diseases* 3.16 describes a "bloody" form of pleurisy as strong, painful (*epiponos*), and deadly.
26. For the tragic element in this description, see also Jouanna 1987: 109.
27. As Temkin and others have pointed out, this passage received much attention in the development of Christian medical ethics, in which suffering for the sake of others was valued (cf. Temkin 1991: 141–45, and esp. 141 n. 78, for references to the substantial body of scholarship on the *Nachleben* of this passage).
28. See Konstan 2001 (esp. 59–62, 65) with references to scholarship on pity in other situations.
29. Tom Falkner's contribution to this volume underscores the fellow-feeling that tragic characters reveal in their expressions of pity for others and points out the similarities between Deianeira and Neoptolemus as they recognize and feel pity for the suffering of Iole and the captive women, and Philoctetes, respectively. The difference between the two pitiers is also important, I believe: Neoptolemus is able to act, to make a successful transition from spectator to helper and friend, whereas Deianeira (in keeping with her vulnerable, feminine position) can do nothing to appease the suffering of herself or of Iole. She tries to, of course, but with disastrous consequences.
30. On theories of fictive kinship, see Pitt-Rivers 1997, and for applications in ancient Greece, see Herman 1987.
31. Konstan, however, argues that pity is not central to the act of supplication, but that the act and institution of supplication deserves honor in and of itself (2001: 79). While I agree with his argument, it remains true that appeals to pity often form part of the strategy used by the suppliant. On supplication and pity, see also the essays of Konstan, Angeliki Tzanetou, and James Johnson and Douglas Clapp in this volume.
32. See Crotty 1994, esp. 20–24.
33. Gould (1973: 97) discusses two "not necessarily mutually exclusive" explanations for the importance of the physical contact: first, that it actually represents the "vital power" of the suppliant flowing into the supplicated, helping the latter to perform the request; and second, that it is a "symbolically aggressive, yet unhurtful" act on

the part of the suppliant, in that he or she touches "the most vital, most vulnerable and most closely guarded parts" of the supplicated's body. Such an act is "a threat to the integrity of the person supplicated" (100). To restore or maintain his position as powerful, the supplicated must (it is hoped) respond. Significantly, Gould suggests that, in the absence of physical contact, the supplicated may more successfully avoid the demands of the suppliant (77).

34. So I believe: cf. Kosak 1999: 115–17.

35. Konstan (1997: 278) discusses this passage in the course of a convincing argument that pity (over and above friendship) is a central theme of *Philoctetes*, but he does not note that the chorus suggest self-interest as one reason for Neoptolemus to grant Philoctetes' request. The chorus' need to provide a reason beyond pity may indicate that it is not plausible (both for the characters in the fictive situation set up in the play and for the Athenian audience watching the whole) for Neoptolemus to act out of pity at this stage of the play. It is in the course of Philoctetes' attack of illness that his pitying response seems real and unguarded (cf. esp. 759–61 and 805), and this of course occurs after he has had the opportunity to examine closely the bow of Heracles (662–670). Seeing the bow of Heracles and hearing Philoctetes promise to let him touch it as a favor to a benefactor has established that Philoctetes can in fact reciprocate to some degree.

36. See further Kosak 1999.

37. It is true that doctors did not always touch their patients directly: there is evidence of assistants who are doing the touching (including female assistants in the case of female patients; on this issue, cf. Lloyd 1983: 70–76). But it remains unlikely that a doctor would never personally touch a patient; furthermore, it remains *notionally* part of their job at all times.

38. The identities and origins of these writers are a knotty problem. The Corpus is written in Ionic dialect, but various places of origin have been postulated for different treatises. For a discussion of the many issues involving Hippocrates' own career, the Hippocratic tradition, and the origins of the Hippocratic Corpus, see Jouanna 1999: 3–71.

39. Noted by Ulrich von Wilamowitz-Moellendorff (1891: 197).

40. This would accord well with the argument of Johnson and Clapp in this volume, that the *Hippolytus* puts negative situations before us in order to instruct the audience in the positive value of compassion.

41. And, it should be noted, Greeks did not believe that nursing the sick was inherently a female activity; indeed, for the Greeks, as Helen King puts it, "A woman in a nursing role with a male patient is presented not as some natural order, but as deeply unnatural" (1998: 171). See also Sternberg (2000) for an analysis of a nursing situation reported in Isocrates' *Aegineticus* involving male caregiver and male patient: the caregiver insists that he did all he could and suffered much in the process.

42. Neoptolemus is most likely to express pity when he is unsure how to act; when he is decisive, he justifies his actions on the basis of honor and shame. Thus, when he finally decides to give the bow back (1221–1309), he does not mention pity as a

motivation. Indeed, he goes on to suggest that Philoctetes does not deserve pity if he insists on bringing his suffering on himself (1318–20). This suggests that men cannot simultaneously feel pity and act on it: to be a man is to get beyond pity and into performance. On the significance of gender in pity, see Falkner in this volume.

43. Pylades describes their relationship as one of *sungeneia* (kinship) at 732, a relationship underscored by the two uses of words based on the stem *kêdeu-* at 791 and 795, which here refer to caregiving but are words that can stress kinship bonds in other contexts (see Willink 1986 *ad* 795 and *LSJ* under κηδεύω and κῆδος). However, at 805–6, Orestes places him in the category of *thuraioi* (outsiders), when he contrasts his helpful behavior to that of the useless behavior of Menelaos, his *homaimos* (same-blooded).

44. Konstan (2001: 54–59) calls attention to the absence of appeals to pity in *Orestes*, and explains it in part through Aristotle's contention that pity is not an emotion felt or expected between those who are intimate friends or kin (cf. *Rhetoric* 2.8, 1386a18–23). Thus, Orestes uses other strategies in his attempt to win Menelaos' support, such as reminding him of what he owes to Agamemnon.

45. For a much more detailed analysis of these scenes, see Kosak 1999.

PITY IN PLUTARCH

CHRISTOPHER PELLING

◎▣◎

THE THEME OF THIS COLLECTION IS "PITY AND POWER," AND BY Plutarch's time power – the power of the Romans – had changed everything. Explicit use of pity words is something like three times more frequent in the Roman *Lives* than in the Greek. It was the Athenians who prided themselves on pity as a national virtue;[1] but it was the Romans who most frequently raised questions of pity in action. Their power was much greater than that of Athens had ever been, and often, perhaps surprisingly often, they show pity too.

It is interesting to see which of these questions of pity Plutarch found most morally engaging. Sometimes he avoids an issue that we might have expected to absorb him. Julius Caesar, for instance, used *misericordia*, as close as Latin gets to "pity," to describe his pardoning of his enemies,[2] and this famously cut both ways. It was enough of a virtue for Caesar himself (no political numbskull, after all) to think it worth parading;[3] yet it could be debated practically whether he was wise to raise up the men who would contrive his fall.[4] It also seems likely that it was debated morally too: the *hauteur* that it implied, with the great man granting mercy to men within his power, could also be felt as deeply humiliating, inappropriate for one fellow-citizen or fellow-senator to express to another.[5] Plutarch is most interested in tracing the reasons for Caesar's overthrow, in *Caesar* from the dictator's perspective – the mistakes that he made, perhaps that he was forced to make by the pressures of rule – and in *Brutus* from the conspirators'. Yet he makes no mention of mercy as an issue. When a temple to *Clementia*[6] is founded, Plutarch presents it simply as a gesture of genuine appreciation from the Romans, something to suggest how unfair and malicious were the gibes of his enemies (*Caes.* 57.4): the word he uses for *Clementia* is *Epieikeia*, "Reasonableness." Earlier, when Caesar was ostentatiously sparing so many of his enemies in the first months of the civil war, Plutarch again portrays it as straightforwardly a *good* action, and one with good results: it is most effective in winning over the goodwill of his adversaries (*Caes.* 34.7–9).[7] The word this time is *philanthrôpia*, "humane feeling to fellow-humans." True, Plutarch was not the first to translate *clementia* by *epieikeia*,[8] and true, ideas of pity and *philanthrôpia* had been linked for centuries.[9] *Philanthrôpia* had also become an especially appropriate word for generosity to enemies within one's power.[10] But both *philanthrôpia* and *epieikeia* are much more unequivocally good things than pity, and are classed as virtues rather than emotions. Such language left less room for debate whether the actions were good or bad,[11] and so there is no suggestion of their double-edged effect. Yet that theme (we might think) would have fitted *Caesar* in particular very well, for that *Life* is most interested in the way that Caesar in power is trapped by his own past actions, actions that in their day were skillful and well-judged.

Plutarch knew this period so well that he must have known about the theme. He does indeed make something of it elsewhere, when he has the younger Cato repudiate any chance of safety at Caesar's hands. "If I had wanted to be saved thanks to Caesar," he said, "it would have been my role to go to him alone. But I do not wish to owe gratitude to the tyrant for his lawlessness: for lawlessness is what this is – to save people as if he was their master, when it was wrong for him to be lord over them at all" (*Cat. Min.* 66.2). But even in *Cato* this does not become a focused *issue*: there are other times in that *Life* and pair where Plutarch encourages an interest in whether Cato is being too stiff and unbending (cf. esp. *Phoc.* 3, *Cat. Min.* 30.9–10, 44.1), but not here. It suggests the strength of his principles; and that is underlined by a contrast with the pity Cato himself shows for others, as we shall see. But the moral and practical questionability of Caesar's clemency was *not* the sort of theme that interested Plutarch about pity at Rome: not in *Caesar*, not really in *Cato* either. Perhaps he was reluctant to provide a paradigm for the powerful men of his own day of clemency's dangers:[12] more likely, the issue was simply too parochial in time and space, too limited to associations which one people at one time gave to pity. Plutarch's tastes are usually for the more timeless themes, and the same is true here.

Other themes interested him more. Often the interest is pity for Rome's subjects or victims: the pity that a general like Flamininus would feel for the Greeks (*Flam.* 13.7, 15.6); the pity, it seems ill-judged, that leads the Romans to allow Philip to retain Macedonia (*Arat.* 54.5); the pity, we shall see later in this chapter, that Aemilius and the people of Rome might feel for the captured Perseus; the pity that Lucullus tries to show for the captured Amisos but that cannot save the city (*Luc.* 19.4), or that Marcellus felt as he gazed at the doomed Syracuse (*Marc.* 19). Sometimes this sort of pity develops into a more elaborate theme, with pity overseas in some sort of counterpoint with pity – or pitilessness – for fellow Romans. Thus there is the pity that the younger Cato showed for his fellows in accepting command (*Cat. Min.* 56.4), and then also showed for the threatened Utica (58.1–2, 63.5–6, 64.4, 65.2);[13] the pity he showed for "the weakness" of those under his command who admitted that they did not have it in them to be Catos themselves (64.5), and then for those who sail away as he dies (70.6, cf. 67.4) – and the mercy that he refused to take from Caesar, as we saw. There is the pity too that Sulla is begged to show to Athens (*Sull.* 13.4), the pity of which the Athenians despair (13.6) and yet which they strangely receive (14.9), so that in the epilogue Plutarch can contrast Sulla's treatment of the city with Lysander's pitilessness (43[5].5); the pity indeed to which Sulla had been prone as a young man "so that he often burst into tears" – but he changed so much in his later years that "he brought upon great power the reproach that it does not allow character to remain the same in power, but turns it to be crazed and conceited and inhuman" (*Sull.* 30.6).

So far we have been investigating the themes that Plutarch found *most* interesting, themes he thought he could do something with: we will return to that approach later in the chapter, and look at some ways in which he develops themes of pity in particular narratives. There is another way in which we can explore literary texts to illuminate the moral concepts of their milieu, and that is to dwell on what Plutarch took for granted, what he found *least* problematic. Such cases illuminate moral assumptions that come so naturally that neither he nor his audience would think they needed explanation or invited questioning. In the next section I will often be following that approach – though on one or two occasions we may find more thoughtful discussion or insights, in both *Lives* and *Moralia*, which may illuminate in a different way the unconscious assumptions which will be our main focus. In particular, Plutarch – so immersed both in the literature of the classical past and in the cultural swirl of second-century CE Greece – may be a particularly interesting filter for exploring how and whether pity changed.

Pity Transformed?

Pity's Closeness

The pair *Nicias–Crassus* deals with terrible disasters. Few pairs have more of a tragic tinge.[14] The closing chapters of *Nicias* are particularly interesting here, as we can trace in detail Plutarch's retelling of Thucydides' original narrative (*Nic.* 25.5, 26.4–6):

> *Before their eyes were the sick and wounded that they were leaving behind. Their plight seemed* more pitiful *even than that of the dead they left unburied; yet those who were departing thought themselves more burdened still, for they would suffer more and anyway reach the same end.*

... There were many terrible sights in the camp but the most pitiful was Nicias himself. *Ravaged by sickness, he was reduced against all dignity to the most meagre of food and the slightest of bodily provisions, at a time when he needed so much more because of his disease. Yet despite his weakness he carried on performing and enduring more than many of the healthy. It was clear to all that it was not for himself that he bore the toil, nor because he was clinging to life; it was for the sake of his men that he refused to give up hope. Others were forced by their terror and suffering into tears and lamentation, but if Nicias himself was ever driven to this it was clearly because he was measuring the disgrace and dishonor of the expedition's outcome against the greatness and glory of what he had hoped to achieve. Nor was it only the sight of the man that was so moving. They also recalled his words and advice when he had warned against the expedition, and that made it even clearer how undeserved were his sufferings. They were dispirited too when they thought of the hopes they might place in Heaven, reflecting how this pious man, who had performed so many religious duties with such great splendor, was faring no better than the lowest and humblest of his army.*

Most of this, it is clear, is Plutarch's own imaginative rewriting,[15] and it is interesting to see how much of it concentrates on pity. There are the explicit uses of pity words at the beginning; there are also many of the other features that we so frequently find in pity narratives, the way people are "moved," the emphasis on sight and on sound (the sound of lamentation), the contrast with past glory and hopes, the emphasis on undeserved suffering. In Thucydides' original we find some of the same features, in particular a highly visual register; that is a highly emotional narrative too, and one that surely evokes pity in the reader. But pity was not the word used for the emotions of the characters in Thucydides' text. Things were there "dreadful" (*deinon*), people saw things that were "painful to the sight and to think about," they suffered "pain together with fear," "the whole army was filled with tears," then things were "too great to cry at." A chapter later Plutarch gives Nicias direct speech for a plea to the victorious Spartan general Gylippus: "let pity come over you, Gylippus, in your victory – not pity for me, who used to have such a name and reputation for such good fortune, but pity for the other Athenians. Remember how the fortunes of war are alike for everyone, and the Athenians themselves used those fortunes moderately and gently when they were the ones who fared well" (*Nic.* 27.5). Pity again, and this is another elaboration of Thucydides' original (that had no direct speech); and the appeal to past services and to the shared human condition represents further aspects that we shall see as typical of Plutarchan pity.

One possible explanation of the increased stress on pity would be simply in terms of narrative technique. Plutarch – it is often clear elsewhere – likes to reconstruct the responses of onlookers and use them to guide his own readers' response;[16] is this a case where he is "guiding" in a particularly straightforward way, using the participants' response to instill similar responses in the reader or hearer's mind? Is the participants' pity infectious, so that we feel pity too? In contrast Thucydides, especially in Book Seven, had been particularly skilled at creating an audience response that had no direct analogue in the response of characters in the text – indeed his guidance may be in terms of opposites, with pitilessness in the text generating readerly pity. Nicias had claimed that the Athenians were now more deserving of divine pity than envy (7.77.4), but the reader of Thucydides knows how little can really be expected of that; nor do enemies give any pity either. But that can generate more compensating pity in readers, just as the reader may feel more pity for the victims at Mykalessos because of the pitilessness of their attackers (7.29), just indeed as the audience of Sophocles' *Antigone* may feel more pity for the girl because she is emotionally isolated within the text itself. So Thucydides had managed to construct a "pitiful" response to the sufferings of the Athenians (so this explanation may run) in one way; Plutarch does the same thing more crudely.

There is something in that "explanation"; but explanation is what it is not. For Plutarch too was skilled at guiding audience responses in less crudely direct a way: the magnificence, and perhaps the pitifulness too (though this is an issue to which we will return, p. 303), of Cleopatra's death is accentuated by the insensitivity of her Roman attackers, so that a Roman can ask, "Is this well done, Charmian?" without even realizing that he is setting up for one of the most beautifully crushing rejoinders of world literature. "It is well done, and fitting for a princess descended of so many royal kings" – Shakespeare's words, but Plutarch's phrase (*Ant.* 85.6–7, Shakespeare *Antony & Cleopatra* V.2.325–26). Nor does *Crassus* use pity words for the carnage of the Carrhae campaign,[17] nor *Antony* for the hardships of Antony's Parthian retreat:[18] the awfulness of the Roman predicament is brought out in other ways. We can still ask why it was natural for Plutarch to create more immediate an empathy between audience and characters in *Nicias* than he does elsewhere; why it was natural for Thucydides to avoid pity language here and for Plutarch to use it.

In terms of the Aristotelian theory of pity, there is a clear explanation why Thucydides avoids pity terms, and David Konstan's book puts us in a good position to identify it.[19] Pity, claims Aristotle (*Rh.* 2.8, 1386a17–24), requires an emotional distance. If one is in the same position of fearfulness or suffering as the victim, one does not pity, one simply shares the emotion. If a ship is hit by a storm at sea, those aboard do not pity one another, they each feel the same fear.[20] Konstan cites the passage where Isocrates looks back on Sparta's domination: "because of the mass of our own evils we stopped pitying one another, for they left no one enough time to share another person's pain."[21] This would seem to be a similar case: Thucydides' Athenians do not pity Nicias, for their suffering leaves them no room for that; his suffering and theirs are as one.

This may be right for Thucydides, which makes it all the more interesting that it is clearly not right for Plutarch. That may be partly because, for him, Nicias' suffering and that of his men are not as one, not quite. Nicias is made into a particularly intense version of that suffering, and it is testimony to the soldiers' admiration that they can recognize that his case is even worse, even more moving, than theirs. But that is only part of the explanation; still, the proximity of suffering and emotion is too close for pity to have been a natural word to use within Aristotelian conceptions.

The more fundamental explanation is that this "emotional distance" requirement does not seem to function for Plutarch, or at least not in the same way. For instance, Aristotle seems to have thought that one would not feel pity for very close kin: parents would not feel pity for a dead child, for instance, they would feel grief (*Rh.* 2.8, 1386a20–2).[22] Nor, it seems, would one feel pity for a loved one who was very recently dead;[23] again, the pain would be too raw, too close, and only time would give the sort of distance that would render pity the appropriate response. Neither postulate seems to work for Plutarch. When he writes, most movingly, to his wife Timoxena to console her on the recent death of their daughter, pity, precisely, is what he assumes his wife may be feeling (611c). The ps.-Plutarchan *Consolation to Apollonius* describes such behavior as normal: we should congratulate those who have just died "rather than pity and lament them, as most people do through their ignorance" (107c).[24] Others who are recently dead, too, evoke pity, and that tends to come as the emotional pitch of mourning heightens rather than reduces: take the crowd's pity for Julius Caesar at his funeral (*Caes.* 67.7, *Cic.* 42.4) – not close kin, admittedly, but still one who is intensely mourned.[25] Elsewhere too people feel pity for kin – for brothers in mortal danger

(*Greek Questions* 300f), or Coriolanus for his mother and wife,[26] or for lovers, as Cleopatra for the dying Antony (*Ant.* 77.5); or sometimes they do not feel pity when pity is expected or appropriate.[27] Nor is this the only sort of pity that comes specially close to home. When Athens is faced by mass slaughter, many killed themselves "in pity and love for their country, thinking it was on the point of destruction" (*Sull.* 14.7), a "destruction" in which they are of course closely implicated themselves. Less fraught, but still telling, is Apollonius' "pity for the Greek nation" when he hears the young Cicero speaking, "for the one honour which remained *to us* is now passing to the Romans, culture and rhetoric" (*Cic.* 4.7, cf. *On the Pythian Oracles* 401c); or for that matter Plutarch's own "pity for the weakness of human nature" (*Ag.–Cl.* 37.8), a passage to which we will return later (p. 291).

Ag.–Cl. 17 is a specially interesting case. Chilonis is supplicating her father Leonidas on behalf of her husband Cleombrotus. In the past she had shared her father's exile; now she takes her husband's side. "My father, the way I appear and the way I look do not come from pity for Cleombrotus; no, grief has remained as my sibling and housemate [literally 'fellow-nurtured and fellow-dweller,' σύντροφον καὶ σύνοικον] from *your* suffering and your exile. . . . Both as wife and as daughter it has been my lot to share the misfortunes and the dishonour (συνατυχεῖν καὶ συνατιμάζεσθαι] of my family . . . then I was counted with you . . . [συνεξεταστθεῖσα], now you think it right to kill sons-in-law and disregard your children." She calls for pity from her father (17.8); her tears (17.7) evoke tears from bystanders too, who again, explicitly, are "pitying" (17.4). The recurrent *sun-* (with-) language is expressive. She has shared her father's fate and dishonor and grief; her appearance is now one of pity, even if it is not quite the pity for husband that it seems; and her appearance of pity and calls for pity are infectious, so that others come to pity her. Evidently, pity language is not at all inappropriate for close relatives, and here it starts with close kin. But it spreads. And it does not look as if the pity changes its nature as it moves away to those more emotionally distant.[28]

The extreme example of pity "close to home" would be self-pity, and, as Konstan brings out, this is problematic for Aristotelian conceptualization. Where classical self-pity occurs, Konstan argues that it is usually felt as a self-conscious paradox, with a fragmentation of self into observer and observed that is more extreme and expressive than in any modern counterpart.[29] Yet for Plutarch, at least, the concept does not seem problematic.[30] When Eumenes comes upon the dying Craterus, "he grasped his hand, and poured much abuse on Neoptolemus; he vented too his pity for Craterus because of his fortune, and for himself because of the necessity which had forced him to fight an intimate friend, and kill or be killed" (*Eum.* 7.13).[31] (And notice again the pity for a man who is very recently dead, indeed one who is not quite dead yet, just as with Cleopatra and the dying Antony.) As Pompey and Caesar settle to fight at Pharsalus, observers muse on how dreadful it all is. These men "have not even taken pity on their own fame and reputation, for until that time they were both hailed as undefeated" (*Pomp.* 70.6): that would not have been "self-pity" in our sense, but certainly pity for a part of oneself that is fundamental to the identity of men like these. It does look as if Plutarch is not operating with any Aristotle-like notion of a spectrum of closeness, where we need to feel close (bonded by a shared humanity and fragility) but not too close, where some relationships are too thick for pity and some too thin. Such picking and choosing among pitiable fellow humans is not for him.

Pity's Reflections

For Plutarch pity is an emotion, as it is for Aristotle and for other classical authors, but – again as for classical authors, and indeed for us – it has a heavy cognitive aspect. It is usually connected with sight and eyes: hence tears are the natural response, and sometimes the pitier's tears are triggered by the tears of the pitiable, expressing how close their emotions come to being the same, just as we saw Chilonis' tears evoking the tears of others.[32] There is often an aural as well as a visual element too, as pity is evoked by cries and laments; this may help to explain why in Plutarch, as in classical historians, the words *oiktos*, *oiktirein* and their cognates are used rather more frequently than *eleos* or *eleêmôn*. The words are clearly very close in meaning, and often cluster together in the same context;[33] but the etymological link, or at least affinity, of *oiktos* with the cries of *oi* or *oimoi* may still be felt.[34]

There is more to "cognition" than simply perception, and in Plutarch – as once again in classical precedents – pity tends both to trigger and to be affected by rational reflection. This is where questions of merit come in, and Plutarch is certainly aware of the dangers of pity being aroused for the undeserving. He is alert to the abuse of pitiful display here,[35] and also to the dangers of rhetoric;[36] but *logos* in a different sense, that of rationality, is essential as one reflects on any case for pity. In all this he is again close to his classical models, but there is a difference in what form such a "case for pity" could take. In classical authors – especially, and unsurprisingly, in oratory – the case typically rests on the merits or otherwise of the pitiable. One does not pity suffering which is deserved, so Aristotle thought (*Rh.* 2.8, 1385b14, 2.9 1386b8–15, 25–33 etc).[37] Plutarch's pitiers too reflect on merit and desert, but the musings tend to be more general. Plutarch more regularly makes his pitiers concede that in *this* case the actions of the pitied man were wrong, but in a wider sense so fine a man, with so many *other* deserts and services to the state, did not deserve to fall into such misfortune. Thus with the trial of Manlius: his guilt is clear, but the "sight" that moves the Romans to pity is the sight of the Capitol where he had fought the Gauls, and the memory of his past services is a strong counter to his present culpability (*Cam.* 36.6). So also with Marius three hundred years later: when a band of men is about to kill Marius, they suddenly take pity and are ashamed of the thought of killing "the saviour of Italy," despite his current murderous course (*Mar.* 39.5).[38] Even after so great an outrage as that of L. Flamininus – the execution of a criminal to satisfy the whim of a girlfriend – the people took pity on him after his expulsion from the senate, and Plutarch's language suggests that he rather approved: "the people were doing what they could to correct what had happened and make things better" (*Cat. Mai.* 17.6). The broader view comes quickly and readily – and always to increase pity, never to reduce it (never for instance to say that he may not have been guilty in this case, but so dreadful a villain was anyway undeserving of pity).

It is interesting too how swiftly the reflections often move to more general musings on the human condition. When the people of Messene saw the aged Philopoemen "dragged along as a prisoner, it seemed so unworthy of his glory and his achievements and triumphs of old, and most were moved to pity him and share his pain: they wept as they reflected on the emptiness, fragility, and worthlessness of human capacity" (*Phil.* 19.1).[39] In that case the reflections go with the "broader view" of the man himself and his "glory and his achievements and triumphs of old," and such a mood can extend to whole cities and their past. When Marcellus supervises the fall of Syracuse he is as moderate as he can be, "but still thought the city was suffering piteously, and even in the midst of such great joy his soul showed how he shared their grief and pain, seeing the destruction of such great and brilliant prosperity in so short a time" (*Marc.* 19.6, cf. § 2). Sometimes the register is suggested more subtly. At *Marius* 40.6 Marius is expecting pity as he lands in Africa, but he gets none. His reply is "go and tell the governor that you have seen Marius sitting among the ruins of Carthage": as Plutarch says, that elegantly compares his own ruin to that of the city whose fall was so paradigmatic of human vulnerability. At *Lysander* 15 there is a debate whether to destroy Athens and "leave it as pasture for flocks," but opinions turn when a Phocian sings the song from Euripides' *Electra* where the chorus greet "Agamemnon's child." "Everyone was broken,[40] and it seemed a dreadful thing to destroy and annihilate so glorious a city and one which had borne such great men." Euripides was one of those great men, and that is part of the point here; but there is also the further suggestion that Athens has herself come to play Electra's role, so humbled and unfitting to her ancestors, past glory, and proper status. Just as with Marcellus at Syracuse, we have the broader view of a city's past as well as its present, and also the broader (and more "tragic") theme still, the humbling mutability that could be anyone's lot.

This *sub specie aeternitatis* register is not alien to classical pity either. Aristotle is clear that pity depends on a perception that "it," or something like "it," could happen to me or someone close to me (*Rh.* 2.8, 1385b11–16), and that this perception depends upon an awareness of humanity's shared fragility or vulnerability. It remains true that in classical authors the generalizing reflection may be *assumed* by pity, but is rarely expressed (though it is sometimes: cf. pp. 291–92 later). In Plutarch it more regularly comes to the surface.

Pitying Flawed Humanity

What it is that could happen to me, or someone close to me, can also be different. Consider the following passage, from *Marius*. A new war with Mithridates is brewing, and Marius is eager for the command despite his years (*Marius* 34.5–7):

> *Marius was like a young man full of ambition as he tried to shake off his old age and weakness. He would go down to the Campus Martius every day and train with the young men, and he showed that he was still nimble in weapon-work and had a good seat on a horse, even though he had grown bulky and awkward with age and had become very fat and heavy. Some approved of this activity and would go down as spectators*

> to view his keenness in competition [literally "his ambition and his
> contests"], but the best people found themselves pitying his greed and his
> lust for glory. He had started poor and become very rich; he had started
> small and become very great; but he recognised no bounds to his
> prosperity, he was not content to enjoy in peace and quiet what he had
> already, but as if he had nothing he was planning to go careering off to
> Cappadocia and the Black Sea. After all those triumphs and all that
> glory he was now, at his age, to fight it out with Archelaus and
> Neoptolemus the satraps of Mithridates. As for the justifications Marius
> gave himself, they seemed totally ridiculous: for he said he wanted to
> train his son by being present himself on campaign.

So the "best people" found themselves "pitying" this crazy glory-
hunting and greed. It is hard to think that pity would have been an
appropriate response within Aristotelian conceptualization. It is clear
that Marius is stigmatized for his untimely war-lust; and yet his culpability is not militating against pity, it seems essential to it. We might
compare the Romans' response to Antony when Octavia bears her bad
treatment so nobly: "the Romans pitied not her but Antony" (*Ant.* 57.5) –
and again, clearly, pitied him *the more* because he behaved so badly and
she behaved so well.

   In part that is a further instance of observers taking a "broader view"
on Marius or on Antony. So great a man has merits that are greater than
his current defects. But that is not the basic point. It is not so much
that other piteous considerations can outweigh this nonpitiable flaw:
instead the emotional defect is itself an *object* of pity, something that
promotes and adds to pity rather than counting in the other side of
the balance. In Marius' case these "best people" share a perspective that
Plutarch himself develops elsewhere in the pair, the notion that the
quest of a Pyrrhus or a Marius for more and more is senseless. That is
the theme of the great exchange of Pyrrhus and Cineas at *Pyrrh.* 14. At

the end of it all Pyrrhus might hope to relax peaceably and enjoy good cheer with his friends – and yet that option is already available. Why not take it now?

Those reflections suggest that this crazed quest is not just a quirk of Pyrrhus or Marius, but something one finds and regrets more widely: it is this that explains why "pity" is still an appropriate reaction. In *Agis–Cleomenes* Plutarch records how Aratus' animosity against Cleomenes led him to bring Antigonus into Greece. "We include this," he says, "not in any desire to accuse Aratus, for in many cases this man was the epitome of Greek spirit and greatness; no, it is in pity for the weakness of human nature, if even in characters that are so remarkable and so exceptionally virtuous it cannot produce what is fine without anything which deserves indignation and retribution" (*Ag.–Cl.* 37.8).[41] Plutarch too, like those observers of Marius, finds it natural to pity such flawed conduct: human nature after all generates it, even in characters as great as these.

So by now the "it" that could happen to anyone is an "it" that is more capaciously interpreted. The "it" that could happen classically is externally driven calamity: the gods can bring anyone down, everyone can be reduced to slavery, everyone can be subject to death or bereavement or terrible agony. In Marius' or Aratus' case the "it" is internally generated, an emotion that is culpable and drives one to culpable action. If that is generalizable, it suggests that we all have the capacity for bad actions, not simply the capacity to suffer bad things. And once *that* is conceded, the link of pity with merit becomes a good deal more complex. It no longer becomes so easy to deny pity to one who has brought about his own downfall through culpable actions, for that too or something like that could happen to me or someone close to me. Two of Aristotle's basic postulates have come to be in conflict with one another.

Plutarch's phrase "in pity at human nature" requires thought too: this is an extreme form of the *sub specie aeternitatis* register that Plutarch's pitiers so regularly adopt. In one way this too seems alien to Aristotle's theorizing, this time to his expectation of emotional distance: for are we too not implicated in this human nature that we are supposed to be pitying? This would come to be a form, though a highly generalized form that is both diluted and deep, of the self-pity that we saw to be problematic. Yet there is a sense in which this "pity at human nature" is not so alien to classical conceptions after all. Take that *locus classicus* of tragic pity, Odysseus' pity for Ajax in Sophocles' play (*Ajax* 121–26):

> *I pity him, wretched as he is, even though he is my enemy, for he is yoked together with terrible, destructive madness* (atê). *And in this I am not considering his lot any more than my own: for I see that we all are nothing more than phantoms or an empty shadow, all of us who are alive.*

"Human nature" is within Odysseus' perspective too: we are all vulnerable, this could happen to any of us. For Odysseus the shared vulnerability, the feeling of bond with any other human, is an underlying presumption or precondition for pity, but what is pitied is still the individual, Ajax, not human nature as a whole. In closely similar cases in other authors Cyrus pities (or at least spares) Croesus and Odysseus fails to pity Hecuba, not in either case all humanity.[42] What in classical authors is conceptual underpinning has become for Plutarch the object of pity itself. Another difference, again, is that Odysseus is pitying Ajax for a stroke from outside: *atê* combines the ideas of madness and destruction, but in either case is typically viewed as a blow from a god. Yet both these differences bring out also how fine the distinction is between those classical concepts and Plutarch's development. Any human might come to be pitiable, even if all humanity is not quite pitiable because of it; and Ajax's internally driven emotions and actions are central to the play, even if the precise form his catastrophe takes is shaped externally by Athena. Plutarch's thought marks a development, but it is not an unnatural one.

Not unnatural, but not insignificant either. The extension of "it could happen to me" thinking to flaws as well as calamities shows a more capacious, more forgiving approach to one's fellow humans. We see this in his moral essays too, for instance where he urges us to feel "pity, rather than disgust, for greed," or finds it "pitiful" for someone to follow the worse course when recognizing the better (*How to Listen to the Poets* 27d, 33f).[43] As for greedy injustice and indiscriminate licentiousness, one should "pity them and criticise them at the same time" (*On Superstition* 165b). When old men want to rush off on public jobs that are undignified and humiliating, "it seems to me pitiful, my friend, while others may think it hateful and vulgar" (*Should an Old Man Take Part in Public Life?* 794a). And this sympathetic capaciousness is certainly a hallmark of Plutarch's approach to his own characters. Even his more negative examples – Coriolanus, Alcibiades, Demetrius, Antony – are treated with understanding and "sympathy," and in each case we are left to comprehend how a great nature could achieve so much and yet go astray.[44] Whether this response is quite "pity" is another question, and we will return to it at the end of the chapter.

THEMES OF PITY
Pity and Blame

One danger with Plutarch's moral capaciousness, allowing that human flaws as well as suffering might happen to anyone, is that it may paralyze censure. Is it not simply bad luck that a human propensity should have manifested itself in one person's case rather than another's, and how can we blame that person for what might so easily have happened to anybody? So, if we pity, if indeed we try to understand how a flawed character could come about, can we also blame? That was a familiar train of thought to Gorgias, Euripides, Antiphon, Thucydides, and Aristotle;[45] it may still be a problem (though not a debilitating one) for modern philosophy; it has become much more of a problem for modern legal practice, with its rhetoric of "one-downmanship"[46] – those claims that the person in the dock is the real victim. But it is not one that Plutarch himself found difficult. He can blame very well. He blames Coriolanus, even in a *Life*, which is unusually concerned to understand how the man's character could come out the way it did, and to criticize the weaknesses of a harsh, one-sided military upbringing. British prime minister Tony Blair once declared that his party would be tough on crime, tough on the causes of crime. Plutarch is tough on Coriolanus, and tough on the causes of Coriolanuses.[47]

He blames Marius too, as the passage we have already quoted makes clear. The *Life* goes on to blame him even more, and is exceptional in that its closing cadences are phrased in an unusually unsympathetic and censorious register.[48] Pity in that *Life* soon needs to be redirected; yet the precise form that redirection takes comes as a surprise. When Marius returns to Rome (*Marius* 41.6):

> *he wanted to appear pitiful, but with the piteousness was mixed the aspect which was more typical of the sight of the man, the terror which he inspired. A display of shame could not conceal the way his spirit was not humbled but made more ferocious by his change of fortune.*

(Yet again, that emphasis on "sight" and "display.") Marius has benefited from others' pity in his distress, especially the pity of the men who "could not kill Gaius Marius" and remembered his past services (39.5: earlier, p. 288); then he had turned himself into a paradigm of shifting destiny at Carthage (40.7). But now it looks as if he is himself less sensitive to his own mutability than he expected others to be: "his spirit was not humbled but made more ferocious by the change of fortune."

So will pity be more appropriate for Marius' victims than for the old man himself? We might have thought so – but in fact the terror turns out too great even for that: "as headless bodies were thrown out and trampled underfoot on the streets, there was no pity, but a shuddering and trembling of everyone at what they saw" (44.9). With Aristotelian conceptions we might infer that this was simply too close to home for pity to be appropriate: just as one may not feel pity for the others in the same danger (earlier, p. 283), so one does not feel pity when one is under so immediate a threat. Yet we saw reason to doubt whether that Aristotelian conceptualization works for Plutarch, and probably this is not the right explanation here. Pity, we shall see, can jostle with anger or with admiration too, and even when pity might be an appropriate or possible response another emotion can be more powerful still. However we explain it, the rhythm of the *Life* is interesting: it seems to be preparing first for a conclusion pitying Marius, then for one switching that pity to others, then that final adjustment gives the even more suggestive nuance when pity is no longer felt at all.[49]

Pity in Conflict

Pity becomes a leading theme in some other *Lives* as well: this is the point where we turn more firmly to those cases where Plutarch is not simply taking points about pity for granted, but developing them thoughtfully and artistically. In particular, this is where we can examine where pity is problematic, where observers' pity comes into conflict with – something else. But what is this "something else"? In Marius' case, as we saw, it was eventually fear. In modern sensibility pity more often clashes with justice: that is the conflict that most typically preoccupies legal theorists and juries (and preoccupied Tony Blair), in those cases when a criminal may seem to deserve punishment for the crime but also pity for the personal circumstances that generated such desperation. As Konstan observes, this is not a clash that fits neatly on to classical conceptions, where pity itself has a closer link with merits and deserts. Even with Plutarch, with that greater capacity for moral indulgence, this is not the most usual form for a pity conflict to take, and when it does it is felt as an abuse of language. Thus at the siege of Clusium Brennus calls on the Romans "to stop feeling pity for the people of Clusium lest you teach the Gauls too to be fine people and lovers of pity at the expense of those who are wronged (*adikoumenois*) by Rome" (*Cam.* 17.5). The suggestion in Brennus' irony is clearly that the Romans are presently pitying those "wronged" by the Gauls. Yet all the people of Clusium have done is to occupy soil that the Gauls wanted. To phrase that as a "wrong" or "injustice" is the way barbarians speak.[50]

Often it is anger that pity has to struggle with. As Plutarch comments in *On Restraining Anger* (463b), anger usually wins. In that essay, this is evidently most regrettable, one of the worst things about rage; yet in the *Lives* it can be more morally complex, and sometimes (though rarely) it seems even to be right for anger to carry the day.[51] Take, once again, *Camillus*. At *Cam.* 11.3 it is clearly regrettable that anger wins, when the Roman people are too angry to pity Camillus for his private bereavement. Yet at *Cam.* 36.7 Camillus seems to be acting rightly in removing Manlius from the sight of the Capitol (earlier, p. 287), so that the jurors can properly show their anger for his crimes; then two chapters later (38.5) he seems equally right in pitying some conspirators and offering them the chance to deflect the senate's anger. Those last two are cases where we might naturally have phrased it in terms of a conflict between pity and justice; for Plutarch it is more natural, and more interesting, to put it in terms of a conflict with anger.

Pity and Contempt; Pity and Admiration

Yet it is still true that pity is made more problematic by the sufferer's bad behavior; but now the bad behavior more typically is in the present or future tense, what a man (and it usually is a man rather than a woman) is doing *now*, at the time when he might be pitied, or is likely to go on to do later.

Take, for instance, the closing chapters of *Dion*, where Dion's philosophical idealism comes into conflict with the needs of the real world, and pity (or at least mercy) becomes a difficult issue. At ch. 47 Dion's scurrilous opponent Heracleides has fallen into his power. His friends and allies press him to remove this "disease" (νόσημα, 47.3) from the state. The demagogues on the other side shrewdly urge Dion to show his superiority over anger and spare his adversary: that is exactly the thing to say to the philosophically correct Dion, and he duly *is* merciful, explicitly relating his decision to his training in the Academy (47.4–9). But is he right? It is a difficult question, as difficult as the parallel question in the *Brutus* whether it was right to spare Antony on the Ides of March (18.3, 20.2). It certainly *seems* not to be right; within a chapter Heracleides is up to his old tricks, and Dion's friends can reasonably criticize him for being too high-minded to take their advice (48.9). A few chapters later, and things have worsened further; and this time Dion gives in to his friends, and orders the killing of Heracleides – and, interestingly, gets quite a good press from Plutarch for it (53.6), just as Brutus will get a bad press for sparing Antony (*Brut.* 20.2). The Syracusans "came to realize" that this town was not big enough for both Heracleides and Dion to practice politics. This is, indeed, a very hard-nosed and not specially idealistic picture, one where indeed "the end may justify the means,"[52] and one where the dangers for the future can make mercy or pity inadvisable.

Elsewhere it is present rather than past or future bad behavior that affects the case. In *Aemilius Paullus*, the fate of the Macedonian king Perseus ought to be pitiable, yet he fails to win that pity because of his undignified way of bearing it. When he is captured by the Romans (*Aem.* 26.7–12),

> he showed that he had a flaw that was worse than his love for money, and that was his love for life [philopsukhia, *a more negative quality in Greek than in any English translation*[53]]. It was because of this that he robbed himself of pity (eleos), the one thing that fortune does not take away from those who are brought low. For when he was brought before

> *Aemilius in chains, Aemilius treated him as a great man who had*
> *suffered retribution and bad fortune, and rose and went to meet him in*
> *tears with his friends; but Perseus hurled himself headlong before him*
> *(a most terrible sight), grabbed his knees, and uttered ignoble words and*
> *pleas. Aemilius did not allow him to continue, but gave him a grieving*
> *and pained look and said: "Why, you wretch, do you take away from*
> *Fortune what would be the greatest of charges against her? For by*
> *acting like this you will give the impression that your suffering is*
> *deserved, and that you were unworthy of your past fate rather than your*
> *present one. Why do you diminish my victory? Why do you make my*
> *success seem trivial, showing yourself an ignoble and unworthy rival of*
> *Rome? When men fall into bad fortune, virtue plays no small part in*
> *winning the respect even of enemies, but even in good fortune cowardice*
> *is the most disgraceful thing of all for Romans."*

This crucial scene seems to be largely Plutarch's invention,[54] and it shows Aemilius behaving with the magnanimity which the Romans liked to claim as their own. There are the usual accompaniments of pity – a "sight," tears, reflections in the *sub specie aeternitatis* register. It is Plutarchan rather than Aristotelian pity too, for there is little hint that Perseus did not deserve his fall; this is "retribution," apparently from the gods.[55] The universality of such vulnerability still makes pity an appropriate response in a sensitive man of power. But Perseus himself does not get his lines right, and it is the contemptible in his behavior that drives out the pitiful.[56] The past is not forgotten, but it is this present behavior that makes it seem that his past good fortune was undeserved, and that this humiliation now is right.

Similar points recur when Perseus reaches Rome, and the issue is his triumph. There is a hint that Rome as a whole, not just Aemilius, might naturally and properly have felt pity toward the defeated enemy:

if the triumph was to be withheld, "it should have been because of pity towards the foe, not envy towards the general" (M. Servilius at 31.6, with that contrast of pity and envy that is so familiar from the classical world).[57] The triumph is held, and pity is indeed the response, in particular pity and tears for Perseus' infant children (33.9). Perseus himself walks as though dumbstruck: his friends and attendants walk as a "chorus" – the tragic suggestions are interesting – as they lament Perseus' fate, and show that they are so overwhelmed by his sufferings that they think little of their own (34.1). Pity and piteousness are certainly in the air; yet still Aemilius has been unrelenting in his demand for the triumph, and the reason is again that *philopsukhia* of Perseus, that clinging to life that is so undignified and unworthy of a great man (34.3). Pity, though, Aemilius still feels (37.2), and he wants to help Perseus; but he can find no way of showing it other than to arrange a move from the prison to a better "and more *philanthrôpos*" location. There finally Perseus dies: perhaps he starved himself, but one version was that his guards tormented him to death by depriving him of sleep. Even at the end, then, amid all that piteousness and pity, Perseus cannot manage or be allowed true dignity.

In that *Life* Perseus' fate is skilfully interwoven with Aemilius' own. Perseus' sons survive; Aemilius loses his. The pity of the observers at Perseus' triumph is mirrored by the emotion of the Roman people as they feel Aemilius' loss and shudder at the harshness of fortune (35, 36.2). And Aemilius, natural philosopher as he is, does get his lines right in response: he addresses the people with "noble and great words" (37.1), dwelling on the way that they have "no less clear an example of human weakness in the fate of the triumphator than in that of the man he led in triumph" (36.9). He had always known that Fortune gave no man "anything that is great which was unmixed and without balancing retribution" (36.6) – retribution again, the same word and concept as the "retribution" that he saw in Perseus' fate.[58] Aemilius, however, knew how to expect and now knows how to bear such "retribution," when Perseus did not. One notices the familiar *sub specie aeternitatis* register too: Aemilius' fate might be something that could happen to any human.

Is Aemilius then the one who deserves pity? Is that where the *Life* is heading? One might think so; the theme is there, and so are many of the ingredients; but once again there is a final tweak. For it is noticeable that pity words are not used for Aemilius' fate, despite all the sensitive emotion and fellow-feeling of everyone around. Perhaps the observers' grief is simply so intense that, as with Marius' terror, it forces out pity, but more likely this very dignity of Aemilius renders pity an inappropriate word. People's admiration for the man is simply too great. In that case we have a paradox indeed: the abasement of Perseus makes pity natural, yet he behaves too badly to deserve it; Aemilius' own suffering comes close to evoking pity too, but Aemilius behaves too well to make pity appropriate.

If so, this is not the only case where pity may be denied or deniable because a person behaves well. Take the story that forms the climax of *Amatorius* (770d–771c): that position is important, for this is a tale that inspires wonder and thought. A Gaul named Sabinus was involved in the great revolt of Civilis in 69–70 CE. Once the revolt was over, Vespasian's men began hunting him down. He fled, and spent months hiding in a cave. At first he sent a message to his wife to say he had died, hoping that her grief would add plausibility to the tale; but her grief was then so great that he began to fear for her life, and he sent to tell her the truth. She kept visiting him in the cave, and "it was almost as if she was living with him in Hades for seven months." She smuggled him to Rome when there seemed a hope of safety; nothing came of it, so they returned and resumed subterranean life. She even bore his twins, managing a difficult birth on her own. Eventually she was caught, and Vespasian executed her. Yet "*observers' pity was driven out* by her confidence and magnificence of speech, something that particularly inflamed Vespasian: when she gave up hope of being spared, she said that she had been happier living as she had in the dark than he was now, living the way he did as king" (771c).[59]

CONCLUSION: READERLY PITY?

Pity had long been linked with something that was more clearly a virtue, τὸ φιλάνθρωπον, that fellow-feeling for all humanity that was the mark of a humane and civilized mortal.[60] So it is for Plutarch too: Aemilius' pity at least allows him to find Perseus a more *philanthrôpos* imprisonment (*Aem.* 37.2, earlier pp. 299–300); it is *philanthrôpia* that Caesar shows toward those he spares (*Caes.* 34.7–9, earlier p. 278).[61] When Sulla loses his capacity for pity he is accordingly *apanthrôpos*, "inhuman," losing his human sensibility altogether (*Sull.* 30.6: earlier, p. 279). But Plutarch theorizes the link more sharply than his predecessors: for him pity is still not equivalent to τὸ φιλάνθρωπον, but is an indispensable element in it (*On Moral Virtue* 451d–e):

> The emotions produce elements which are very useful to rationality and pull in the same direction as virtues: with bravery goes spirit (when it is moderate); with justice, hatred for evil and also indignation against those who are undeservedly fortunate ... And who would take affection away from friendship, or pity from philanthrôpia, or the sharing of joy and pain from genuine goodwill? Even if one wanted to, one could not separate them nor melt one away from the other.

So pity would seem, at least in that sort of theorizing, to be an almost unequivocally good thing.[62]

That suggests a further question. Plutarch's own writing, very clearly, is crafted to inspire and promote virtue, both in his listeners and in himself. As it happens, the proem to one of our prime examples, the *Aemilius*, is a place where he articulates this aspiration explicitly. As the virtue of *philanthrôpia* implies pity, is pity too something which his own heroes are meant to inspire? We have seen how Plutarch himself operates with a very capacious interpretation of pity: he, or the authorial *persona* he projects, is not one to deny pity to someone because he or she is too close or too distant, nor because they have brought such suffering on themselves. If he, and we, spread pity so widely and so readily, should we not extend it also to those great and engaging human beings of whom he writes?

The answer is I think "no," or at least less than we would expect. It is striking how Plutarch's comparative epilogues raise many moral issues about the narratives and suggest many possible responses, but only very rarely use pity terms. There may be moments, certainly, where pity has been appropriate, particularly when a great man meets a pathetic end; that is so with Cicero, for instance (*Cic.* 54[5].1). Pity may be evoked in particular sections of the narrative too, as it was in the *Nicias*, and that can be so even when pity terms are not used: the end of Cato may be one case, and in a different way the end of Demetrius would be another. (What is pitiable in Cato's case is mainly the circumstances, in Demetrius' case mainly the style of his decadent final years: so the "it" that could happen to anyone is more external in one case, more internal in another.) But pity for a life *as a whole* seems inappropriate; nor is pity for a particular aspect of that life normally the note on which Plutarch chooses to leave.

One reason for this may be suggested by the cases of Aemilius Paullus or of Vespasian's victim: many of Plutarch's heroes meet their end or cope with extreme adversity admirably, and they behave well enough to make pity inappropriate. But even when they do not – and Plutarch does not spare his heroes from blame in such cases, when Demosthenes for instance or Cicero copes badly with exile – pity is inappropriate for such great men. Consider Antony: his death may seem piteous – "eye-witnesses say that no sight was more pitiful" (*Ant.* 77.3) – and in the epilogue it seems that it was blameworthy too (93[6].4, Antony took himself off "in a cowardly, pitiful, and dishonourable way"). But the narrative itself encourages a different response. As he dies, Cleopatra is lost in pity for him (77.6), but he tells her "not to mourn for him because of these last shifts of fortune, but to congratulate him on the good things of his life. He had been the most famous and most powerful man alive, and now it was not ignoble for him, a Roman, to be defeated by a Roman" (77.7). Pity this "Roman, by a Roman valiantly vanquished"?[63] Hardly! Nor indeed does pity seem appropriate for Cleopatra at her own end, as she wins that final, magnificent victory in death (earlier, p. 283). And Nicias, we remember, called on Gylippus for pity, but "not for me, who used to have such a name and reputation for such good fortune" (*Nic.* 27.5: earlier). Elsewhere, too, heroes are given credit for dwelling on the positive aspects of their life. The end of *Marius* may be harsh on the hero, but it also points (and in unusually lyrical language) to a better way to end one's days. "Plato, they say, when he came to die praised his destiny and his fortune, first for being born a human rather than an irrational beast, secondly for being a Greek rather than a barbarian, and lastly for being born into the time of Socrates" (*Mar.* 46.1). It is the memory of the good things that should dominate at the end.

So it may be that a truly "philanthropic" response to the hero is here, paradoxically, one that makes pity inappropriate. We extend to the hero the generosity of spirit we might offer (at least provisionally) to any fellow human, and that means that we should concentrate on what is admirable. The opposite of this is the "malice," literally *kakoêtheia* or "badness of character," which Plutarch so oddly found in Herodotus: using severe words when mild ones would suffice, bringing in irrelevant bad acts or omitting the good, preferring less creditable versions and motives, and so on (*Malice of Herodotus*, esp. 855b–856d). Such generosity should not be applied so unthinkingly as to avoid treating a hero's reverses completely: as Plutarch comments in the proem to *Nicias* (1.5), it is so often the reverse that shows a person's true qualities.[64] Still less should one try to conceal a person's flaws, for those can aid our understanding of the human condition and the range of personalities that greatness can admit. One should simply avoid accentuating the bad things too much (*Cimon* 2.3–5):

> *It is just as with artists when they are painting things of beauty and elegance: when there is some little blemish, we think they should not omit it completely but they should not concentrate on it either, for the one makes the picture ugly and the other makes it untrue. In the same way it is difficult, perhaps indeed impossible, to put on display any man's life which is irreproachable and pure. So we should dwell on the good parts and fill out the truth as a way of providing a likeness. When we see the mistakes and flaws which spring from emotion or from political necessity and adhere to a person's actions, we should think of these as deficiencies in virtue rather than manifestations of vice. We should not be too eager and emphatic in indicating them in our narrative, but write as if ashamed of human nature, if it produces no character which is purely noble nor indisputably virtuous.*

"As if ashamed of human nature": the similarity to the *Agis–Cleomenes* passage is clear, where Plutarch expressed his "pity for human nature" (*Ag.–Cl.* 37.8, earlier, p. 285). Both flaws and reverses need to be noticed, and it needs to be understood that this is the coin in which human experience deals. As we see them, pity may be one response. But to allow pity to dominate at the end of a great life would show an insensitivity to what is good and admirable; and that is not Plutarch's way, nor the way he encourages in his readers.

Much of what we have seen in Plutarch suggests a more engaging and forgiving sensibility than Aristotle's conceptualization would allow. Some of it sounds very "modern," especially the way in which moral problems so often come when issues of pity combine with issues of power, or the way it is felt to be condescending to offer pity to the highly virtuous. Yet the biggest question remains, and it can only be sketched here, not answered: how much *has* pity changed from "classical conceptions"? Or is Plutarch's distance from Aristotle rather a pointer to ways in which Aristotle failed to do justice even to those classical conceptions? The answer is doubtless a little of both. The sympathetic capaciousness of Plutarch, the willingness to feel pity even for moral failings, the broader approach to merit – all of that builds on classical ideas but takes them much further. Yet we have also seen one or two cases where classical texts as well as Plutarch suggest reservations about Aristotle's schemata.

Of course, the debate on the adequacy of Aristotle's analysis has to extend over a good deal more material than this, and other chapters in this collection contribute to that discussion more squarely than this one has been able to do. Yet Plutarch may at least remind us that Aristotle's was not the only, nor necessarily the most thought-provoking, conception of pity in the ancient Greek world.[65]

ENDNOTES

1. As Plutarch knew, *Advice on Public Life* 799c.
2. Along with *misericordia* Caesar used *liberalitas* and *lenitas* rather than *clementia*: cf. esp. Cic. *Att.* 9.7c (174c).1, Caes. *BC* 1.72.3, 1.74.7, 3.98.2 with Wickert (1937: 243), Treu (1948: 200), Syme (1958: 703). *Clementia* is more Cicero's word for Caesar's practice: Weinstock (1971: 236–37). But presumably that word too was not *objectionable* to Caesar: see next note.
3. In 44 BCE a coin depicts the temple of Clemency with the legend CLEMENTIAE CAESARIS on the obverse (Crawford, *RRC* 480/21). Clemency was enough of a virtue too for Augustus, sensitive as he was to avoiding the propaganda errors of the last generation, still to parade it, most notably on the golden shield in the *Curia Iulia* (*RG* 34.2): cf.

for example, Syme (1939: 159–60, 259). Tiberius paraded it too: Levick 1975 and 1976: 87–88, 91; add now the *senatus consultum de Cn. Pisone patre* 11. 91–2.

4. Compare esp. Cic. *Att.* 14.22 (376). 1, Vell. Pat. 2.57.1, Plin. *NH* 7.93; Griffin 2003: 165.

5. For the development of this theme in Lucan (e.g., 2.519–21), see the discussion of Leigh (1997: 54–67) and the earlier contributions to the debate that he cites. It is reasonably clear that talk of "pardon" or "mercy" could be double-edged by the time of the early principate. Konstan (2001: 99) doubts whether it was so regarded in Caesar's own time, but Cic. *Phil.* 2.5 is particularly suggestive: Cicero is there dismissing Antony's claim that he deserves particular gratitude for sparing Cicero's life at Brundisium in 48. "Is this not the consummate example of a bandit's kindness, members of the senate – to be able to claim that they have given life to people when they did not take it away? If this *were* a kindness, those who killed the man who had saved them – men whom you yourself are accustomed to call 'most distinguished' – would never have gained so much glory." That passage shows how such "kindness" could be regarded and represented as reprehensible; the link to the case of Caesar's assassins suggests that this is picking up on an even stronger form of the debate in their case. Compare also Jal (1963: 464–68) and especially now Griffin (2003).

6. More properly *Clementia Caesaris*, as the coin suggests (n. 3), or (less likely) *Clementia et Caesar*, as Appian and Dio (n. 8) have it: cf. Weinstock (1971: 241), Griffin (2003: 159–63). I am most grateful to Miriam Griffin for help on the difficult issues of Caesarian clemency.

7. De Romilly (1979: 282–83) notes that Caesar's *philanthrôpia* elsewhere has a hint of demagogy about it: *Cat. Min.* 22–3, *Caes.* 4.8–9; cf. also Martin (1961: 170–1) for this as a possible association of the word. But it is surely hard to extract that nuance here. Later, too, Caesar's generosity to captured opponents is noted without a hint of any double edge: *Caes.* 46.4, 48.3–4. Notice also *Cic.* 39.6–7, where Plutarch treats Caesar's magnanimity toward Cicero in the Ligarius case with no suggestion that such generosity of spirit had dangers as well as merits.

8. The translation is not at all exact, but no Greek word precisely captures *clementia*: cf. Weinstock (1971: 235), Dahlmann (1917: 26), Griffin (1976: 149), and (2003: 165). In the present context both App. *BC* 2.106.443 and Dio 44.6.4 use *epieikeia* as well, and so does the Greek version of *RG* 34.2 (n. 3, this chapter). On the suggestions of the word cf. de Romilly (1979: 53–63): it is linked with pity as early as Homer, *Il.* 23.534 and 537.

9. Compare later below, and n. 60.

10. Compare *Sulla* 14.8, *Ant.* 32.1, 41.1, *Alex.* 44.5, *On Alexander's Fortune or Virtue* 338e, and other cases listed by Martin (1961: 171); see also de Romilly (1979: 49–50) and Konstan (2001: 89–90). This usage gives special point to *Cor.* 31.5, where the Romans try to save face and promise to treat the Volscians with *philanthrôpia* if they withdraw: but Rome is no longer in control, and the language is expressively inappropriate.

11. Notice that Dio 43.10.3, when explaining how Cato was offended by Caesar's offer of pardon (earlier), uses pity, *eleos*, rather than *epieikeia*: Konstan 2001: 101.

12. Or possibly clemency was no longer felt an appropriate paradigm for a ruler, who should now be "mild" rather than "clement" or "merciful": on this see the suggestive remarks of Schettino (1998).

13. Admittedly, pity *words* occur in the Utica sequence only in the plea of the "senators" "to pity them" at 64.5, though Cato's actions and motives throughout seem very close to pity. Cato's rhetoric to the Uticans employs neither *hauteur* nor condescension (esp. 59, 64.7–9), and that may make pity an inappropriate word for the way he treats them: cf. n. 18.

14. For the tragic aspects of *Nicias* cf. Pelling (1992), esp. 27–28 = (2002), ch. 5, esp. 130–1; of *Crassus*, cf. Braund (1993) and Zadorojniy (1997). The question of "tragic influence" on Plutarch is difficult and delicate: at Pelling 2002: 27, n.111, I try to outline the debate.

15. For fuller analysis of the rewriting, and for arguments against the alternative view that Plutarch is combining Thucydides with another source: cf. Pelling 1992: 14–16 = 2002: 120–1; 2000: 48–49.

16. Pelling 1988, index s.v. "characterisation by reaction," and for examples Russell 1963: 23, 25 (= Scardigli 1995: 362, 365); Moles 1988: 38; Duff 1999a: 180 and 185, n. 45.

17. *Crass.* 24.5, 25.5–11, 26.3, 26.5, 27.4–8, 28.1–2, 30.3–5, and 31.8 are places where, for example, *oiktros* language might have been used, but we find it only at 26.7 when Crassus calls on his soldiers' sense of "pity" for him at the death of his son. Even there the reflections of "wise observers" a chapter later – that he had brought it on himself through senseless ambition, 27.6 – suggest that pity was not the only or most appropriate response at the time.

18. At *Ant.* 40.8–9 and 44.4 soldiers respond warmly to Antony's distress, and pity might have been the way it was put; but it is not, perhaps because the suggestions of condescension would be inappropriate (cf. n. 13) for a man they so respected (43.3–6). The sufferings are intense, but not explicitly pitiful, at, for example, 45.7–12, 47.4–8, and 48.3–5. The enemies' response is eventually admiration for the troops' *aretê* (*Ant.* 49.2–3), another reason why pity might be an inappropriate ingredient in the scenes (later).

19. Compare Konstan 2001, esp. 49–74, 132: "pity begins where love leaves off," p. 59.

20. Konstan 2001: 50.

21. Isoc. 4.112, cited by Konstan (2001: 50). It is not clear, however, that Konstan's explanation of the Isocrates passage is the right one: Isocrates' point is that the sufferings did not allow "time" or "leisure," σχολή, to feel a shared grief. On Aristotelian principles the point should rather be that the same grief *was* felt, and it was this that excluded pity. It may be that the Isocrates passage is closer to the point of Plut. *Ant.* 77.5, where Cleopatra "almost forgot her own troubles in pity for Antony's": one emotion can drive out, or almost drive out, another without either being in itself inappropriate. The same issues arise with Plut. *Mar.* 44.9 (later). But, however we explain it, the Isocrates passage still gives a close analogy to the situation in Thucydides.

22. This is treated elaborately by Konstan 2001: 50–51, 54–58.

23. Konstan 2001: 63.

24. Compare fragment 177.1 (p. 106 Sandbach) from the *On the Soul*, where it is normal to call the recently dead "the poor and pitiful one" (τὸν ἄθλιον καὶ τὸν οἰκτρόν).

25. So also with Demetrius' funeral barge at *Demetr.* 53.6: the bystanders' pity for the recently dead Demetrius is there evoked by the sight of the tearful Antigonus, Demetrius' son, and this would naturally be taken as another example of "spreading pity" like that of Chilonis (later).

26. In the comparative epilogue, Plutarch is explicit that it was pity (*oiktos*) and pleading that swayed Coriolanus, *Alc.* 43[4].5. The narrative itself was less explicit, but left the same impression. The gods have pitied the women at *Cor.* 33.4 (a very rare instance of divine pity in the *Lives*), which raises the question whether Coriolanus will pity them too; "the sight and the piteousness" of the suppliants made "the enemies *too*" react with shame and silence. Coriolanus is then "broken," ἐπικλασθέντα (36.7), a word often used of being overcome by pity (later).

27. Thus at *Demetr.* 47.3, Demetrius calls successfully on Seleucus "to take pity on a kinsman"; at *Sulla* 9.13 it is particularly remarkable that Sulla shows no pity toward "friends and kinsmen and family" (cf. *Popl.* 6.4). At *Rom.* 19.5–6, the Sabine women comment scathingly on the pity (*eleos*) that their fathers are finally showing by coming to fight: this attack is more pitiable (*oiktroteran*) than their earlier neglect. (If this case were isolated it might be claimed that this period of neglect had rendered them more distant than normal "kin"; Konstan (2001: 66–67) explains Eur. *Hipp.* 1089 in a similar way. But in Plutarch's case the other parallels render this unnecessary.)

28. Nor indeed when it moves in the opposite direction, from one more distant to one who is closer. When Thespesius sees terrible punishments in the underworld, they are "pitiful" and the victims hold out their hands to him and plead for pity: the climax comes when he sees his own father there (*God's Slowness to Punish* 566e) pleading similarly. It is not said that pity is his response to his father; but, in the light of the other passages collected here, that seems a reasonable inference. Note too, incidentally, that pity is here thought appropriate even for those who are punished for dreadfully evil lives: 554b, 564f, 566e, 567d. That is relevant for the link of pity and desert that I discuss later in the chapter.

29. Konstan 2001: 64–71; cf. Konstan 1999. He may overstate the case: cf. Sternberg in this volume.

30. Compare too the related notion of "compassion for oneself." As Coriolanus goes into exile he is so carried away with rage that "he alone was without the compassion for himself (ἀσυμπαθὴς ἑαυτῷ) that all around felt" (*Cor.* 21.1); as Alexander sees the wife and daughters of the defeated Darius, "he felt compassion (συμπαθής) for their own fate rather than his own" (*Alex.* 21.2). True, it may well be that those phrases are both emphatically paradoxical and influenced by the juxtaposition with the "compassion" of or for others: see next note. But such notions are also made easier by the ease with which ancient psychology divided the human soul or personality into "parts" that may or may not work in harmony: just as a city can be at one with itself "sharing its

emotions and being united with itself" (συμπαθὲς καὶ οἰκεῖον αὑτῷ, *God's Slowness to Punish* 559a), just as indeed there can be a universal *sympatheia* of the whole *kosmos* (*On the Face in the Moon* 924c, *On Fate* 574e), so the different parts of a human organism can be more or less in "sympathetic" harmony with one another (e.g., *Table Talk* 626c, 721e, 736a, *Epicurus Makes a Pleasant Life Impossible* 1096e, *Generation of the Soul in Timaeus* 1024a–b, cf. *Consolation to Apollonius* 112e); so indeed can nonhuman plants or organisms (*Table Talk* 696a).

31. Not that this passage is wholly without classical parallels: it is helped by the juxtaposition with "pity for Craterus" (Konstan 2001: 70–71 here has some good points), and also ᾠκτίσατο, "vented pity," is not quite the same as ᾠκτίρει, "pitied" (Burkert 1955: 31–2, noting that this nuance is especially frequent when middle rather than active forms are used, Konstan 2001: 71 and 143, n. 26). Elsewhere too one can write piteously about one's own fate and try to arouse the pity of others (*Demetr.* 47.3) without it quite being "self-pity."

32. *Ag.–Cl.* 17.4 and 7 (earlier). For tears evoking tears cf. *Aem.* 33.6–8; at *Demetr.* 53.6 the sight of tears evokes crying and laments, thus moving from the visual to the aural; at *Alex.* 71.7–8 it is the other way round. Tears that do not evoke pity but might have been expected to: *Them.* 10.9. Tears that are evoked but the person who evokes them stays surprisingly tearless: *Socrates' Sign* 595d.

33. *Rom.* 19.5 (cf. n. 27), *Them.* 10.8–9, *Aem.* 33.8, *Mar.* 41.6. For similar clustering in Thucydides and Xenophon cf. Burkert 1955: 51–52.

34. This is suggested by various word plays linking *oiktos* language with words for cries or groans: οἶκτον . . . οἰμωγάς at *Them.* 10.8; οἰκτρότερον στεναγμόν at *Aem.* 26.4; οἶκτον καὶ ὀλοφύρμον at *Demetr.* 53.6; ὀλοφύρσεις . . . οἰκτρῶν, *Progress in Virtue* 83d; οἰκτρὰ καὶ ὀδυρτά, *Is Vice Enough to Make One Unhappy?* 499f. For similar plays in classical authors, cf. Burkert 1955: 30–31.

35. Pitiful display: *Gracch.* 10.9, where the rich make a display of going around "humbled and piteous": the texture of that narrative is not such as to encourage much sympathy for their uncompromising selfishness. In two of his three treatments of the frenzy aroused at Caesar's funeral, Plutarch does not even mention Antony's funeral speech, concentrating instead on the effect of the display of the bloodstained robes (*Cic.* 42.4, *Brut.* 20.4). The speech is mentioned at *Ant.* 14.7, but even there more space is given to the display.

36. Dangers of rhetoric: cf. esp. *On Harmful Feelings of Shame* 536a, where a danger of flattery is that people will be led to give up their animosities with evil people "so that they may be called pitying (*eleêmones*) and kind to their fellow-humans (*philanthrôpoi*) and compassionate." At *Dem.* 22.7 the choice of language is interesting. Aeschines has there attacked Demosthenes for celebrating a public success only a week after his daughter's death, and Plutarch is indignant: Aeschines' unfair rhetoric "breaks" people (ἐπικλῶντα, cf. n. 40) and "makes them effeminate" as it drives them toward pity. Pity is not usually feminized in Plutarch, and it is indeed notable how few of his memorable women are marked by pity; pity may be especially aroused *by* the sight of suffering

women, but it is not an especially female thing to feel. It remains interesting that it *can* be stigmatized in this way. Classical authors are again not too different: cf. Soph. *Ajax* 580, 651–3 with Pelling 2000: 297, n. 37.

37. This postulate of Aristotle is explored interestingly by Konstan 2001, esp. 34–48.

38. Not that this pity is necessarily commended: see later.

39. Compare *Tim.*14.2, where the word used of one response to the exiled Dionysius is "sympathy" or "compassion" – συμπαθοῦντες – but the musings are in a similar register: some of the Greeks "reflected on the power of unforeseen and divine causes amid what was weak and visible in human life."

40. The word is ἐπικλασθῆναι, often used of the response of pity: cf. *Marc.* 23.9, *Demetr.* 47.4, *Ant.* 18.4, and *Cor.* 36.7 with n. 26.

41. "Deserves indignation and retribution" is ἀνεμέσητον: this suggests the sort of balancing or punishment, whether divine or human or both, which is likely to come. Compare n. 55, this chapter, for some cases where such retribution is traced. Here it prepares for the following narrative of Cleomenes' successes (esp. *Ag.–Cl.* 38–9) and Aratus' humiliation (esp. 40). With the sentiment cf. *Cimon* 2.5, quoted at the end of the chapter.

42. Hdt. 1.86.6, Eur. *Hec.* 282–85, 321–26 (the second is discussed by Konstan 1999: 125). Compare also Philoctetes' appeal to Neoptolemus to pity him, remembering the human condition, at Soph. *Phil.*501–6, and Heracles' pitying of Meleager at Bacch. 5.158 – though there Heracles' reflections on suffering humanity (160–62) are swiftly overtaken by more immediate concerns (165–69). Closer to Plutarch is Hdt. 7.46.2, discussed by Sternberg in her chapter in this volume: Xerxes there is brought to "feel pity as I reflect how short is human life, when so many people are here and none of them will be alive in a hundred years." The pity is probably for the people arrayed before him rather than for everyone, but the elegant imprecision of the language points out how easily one thought can blur into the other.

43. This makes it less surprising that earlier in the same essay he interprets – deeply implausibly – the Homeric phrase "wretched mortals" (δειλοῖσι βροτοῖσι) as meaning not all mortals, but only those who are "pitiful because of their bad character" (διὰ μοχθηρίαν), *How to Listen to the Poets* 22c. The notion "pitiful *because of* bad character" does not fit Aristotelian notions, nor such denials of pity to the morally bad as Deinarchus in *Dem.* 10.3.

44. For Plutarch's treatment of such characters cf. esp. Duff 1999a, index s.v. "great natures," and Duff 1999b.

45. That is, in Gorgias' *Helen*, in the debate of Helen and Hecuba in Euripides' *Trojan Women*, in Antiphon's *Tetralogies*, in Thucydides' Plataean debate, and in Aristotle *Eth. Nic.* 3.1110b9ff, 1111a21ff and elsewhere. I explore this more in Pelling 2000: 71–72, 94–95, and 100–1.

46. For the phrase cf. Minow 1996: 31–32.

47. I have developed this point, and tried to elucidate some of the principles involved in such characterization, at Pelling 2002: 321–29.

48. I have developed this point too elsewhere, this time in Pelling 1997a, esp. 245 = 2002, ch. 17, esp. 377–78.

49. Or, to be more precise, no longer felt by characters in the text. Whether the audience – "we" – feel pity is a separate and more difficult question, and we return to it later.

50. It is true that Brennus is allowed some thought-provoking points at Rome's expense too, observing that the Romans too have gone in for the sort of expansion that they are now criticizing in the Gauls. That does not make his rhetoric any less disquieting; it just means that we might feel disquieted about Rome's behavior too.

51. Pity wins, to Marcellus' credit, at *Marc.* 23.9; anger wins, to the consul Acilius' discredit, at *Flam.* 15.6. It is more morally complex at *Popl.* 6.4–5, where Brutus does not allow pity to force his anger to relent, an action that "defeats both those who wish to blame and those who wish to praise: neither can do so adequately."

52. On this cf. Nikolaidis (1995), bringing out that "[m]oralist and idealist as he may be, Plutarch is also an alert pragmatist, a man of real life, . . . and his moral outlook feeds constantly on his experience and common sense." He therefore several times justifies or condones questionable means in the service of laudable ends: Nikolaidis' examples include some other cases where pity or mercy seems not to be commended, for instance Plutarch's approval for the rape of the Sabine women (*Rom.* 35[6].2) and Timoleon's fratricide tyrannicide (*Tim.* 5.1, 41[2].11). In such cases Plutarch tends to regard the service of the state as the higher good: cf. Frazier 1995: 166–71. I discuss the *Dion* case more fully in Pelling (2004).

53. It is the same word as at *Nic.* 26.4, where Nicias wins more pity from onlookers because they know that it is not through 'clinging to life' that he is continuing to endure (quoted earlier).

54. Swain (1989: 325), observing that the equivalent speech in Livy 45.8.1–6 has Aemilius offering "Rome's familiar clemency" (*cognita populi Romani clementia*). Livy is more likely than Plutarch to be following Polybius' original.

55. The word is νεμεσητόν: for this use cf. *Ages.* 22.2 and esp. *Per.* 37.5 with Stadter (1989) *ad loc.*, where the Athenians are broken by the sight of Pericles' personal bereavement and think that "he had suffered retribution and now needed human comfort" (νεμεσητά τε παθεῖν ἀνθρωπίνων τε δεῖσθαι). That is again interesting in terms of justice and merit. Here as there, the supernatural "retribution" implies that there had been some good reason for the gods to intervene, but that gives a reason why human sympathy should be extended, not why it should be denied.

56. That is already hinted even before his capture: "Perseus suffered pitiably (*oiktra*)... but he let out an even more pitiful groan" (*Aem.* 26.4). Paradoxically, a pitiful groan that is out of proportion to the pitiful suffering may raise, or at least hint at, the question whether pity is the appropriate response.

57. Compare esp. Arist. *Rh.* 2.9, 1386b16–29. One classical instance is Thuc. 7.77.4 (earlier). For the pity/envy contrast in Plutarch cf. also *Demetr.* 50.5 and *On Envy and Hatred* 538b.

58. For fortune as a major theme of *Aemilius–Timoleon* cf. Swain 1989, esp. 323–27.

59. Compare *Virtues of Women* 258a, where a woman is praised for bearing her sufferings "not pitifully nor humbly, but with the sort of spirit that has rationality too"; *On Self-praise* 541b, where those who have fallen on bad times are admired when they struggle up from the low and pitiable to seem jubilant and lofty, and in such cases they seem "great and irrepressible." Such cases help us to understand *Alc.* 27.1, when Alcibiades does not want to come home "through the pity and generosity of the people," but to achieve something so that he can come home in glory: he wants to align with those who seem not pitiful or humble, but great, irrepressible, and admirable.

60. Compare de Romilly 1979: 43–52, 274–307 and on Plutarch's usage also Martin 1961. *Philanthrôpia* was often grouped with pity (e.g., Dem. 25.76, 25.81; Diod. 17.38.3, 27.18.1; Luc. *Timon* 8; App. *BC* 3.9.64, 5.4.38, though ctr. Arist. *Poet.* 1453a3); pardon (Dem. 21.148, 25.81); or gentleness (Isoc. 5.116, 7.12; Dem. 24.51; Hyp. 5 Frag. 6); and at Dem. 21.185 we see praise for the man who is "moderate, *philanthrôpos*, and pitying many." I am grateful to Rachel Sternberg here.

61. Compare also *On the Fortune of the Romans* 320c, where a servant is *eleêmon* and *philanthrôpos*; *On the Cleverness of Animals* 960a, where *philanthrôpia* is linked with a "love of pity"; *Dtr.* 50.5, where the *philanthrôpia* of the king generates pity (*eleos*) but it turns to envy cf. n.57; *On Harmful Feelings of Shame* 536a (earlier, n. 36); *Alex.* 71.8.

62. "Almost" unequivocally because pity is here phrased as a typical stimulus to *philanthrôpia* rather than a sufficient (or perhaps even a necessary) condition for it. The formulation leaves it open for other considerations to outweigh pity, so that in a particular case the truly *philanthrôpos* person should suppress or qualify the pity he or she might feel. That leaves Plutarch able to admire without contradiction Aemilius' insistence on the triumph or to share the observers' response to Vespasian's victim. If the argument of the rest of this chapter is on the right lines, that qualification is important. Compare de Romilly (1979: 278–79, 301–2) for other ways in which Plutarch links *douceur* words with virtues.

63. Shakespeare, *A&C* IV.15.57–58.

64. On the textual problem here (we need to read ἀποκαλυπτομένην or ἀνακαλυπτομένην rather than καλυπτομένην) cf. Duff 1999a: 25.

65. Many thanks to Rachel Sternberg, Judith Mossman, Miriam Griffin, and the referees for their help.

WORKS CITED

Adam, Sheila. 1966. *The Technique of Greek Sculpture in the Archaic and Classical Periods.* London: Thames and Hudson.

Adkins, Arthur. 1960. *Merit and Responsibility: A Study in Greek Values.* Oxford: Oxford University Press.

Allan, W. 2001. *Euripides: The Children of Heracles.* Warminster: Aris & Phillips.

Allen, Danielle S. 2000. *The World of Prometheus: The Politics of Punishing in Democratic Athens.* Princeton: Princeton University Press.

Amundsen, Darrel W., and Gary B. Ferngren. 1986. "The Early Christian Tradition." In *Caring and Curing: Health and Medicine in the Western Religious Traditions*, ed. R. L. Numbers and D. W. Amundsen, 40–60. New York: Macmillan.

Annas, Julia. 1993. *The Morality of Happiness.* New York: Oxford University Press.

Ashmole, Bernard, and Nicholas Yalouris. 1967. *Olympia: The Sculptures of the Temple of Zeus at Olympia.* London: Phaedon.

Baratte, François. 1989. "La naissance de Dionysos sur un couvercle de sarcophage de Musée d'Amiens." *Revue Archéologique*, 143–48.

Barnes, Jonathan. 1995. "Rhetoric and Poetics." In *The Cambridge Companion to Aristotle*, ed. Jonathan Barnes, 259–85. Cambridge: Cambridge University Press.

Barrett, William S. 1964. *Euripides: Hippolytos.* Oxford: Oxford University Press.

Barton, Carlin A. 1993. *The Sorrows of the Ancient Romans: The Gladiator and the Monster.* Princeton: Princeton University Press.

Baslez, Marie-Françoise. 1984. *L'étranger dans la Grèce antique.* Paris: Belles Lettres.

Beare, John I. 1984. *Greek Theories of Elementary Cognition from Alcmaeon to Aristotle.* Oxford: Clarendon Press. First published 1906.

Beaumont, Lesley. 1995. "Mythological Childhood: A Male Preserve?" *Annual of the British School at Athens* 90: 339–61.

Belfiore, Elizabeth. 1983. "Plato's Greatest Accusation against Poetry." *Canadian Journal of Philosophy*, supplementary vol. 9: 39–62.

————. 1992. *Tragic Pleasures: Aristotle on Plot and Emotion.* Princeton: Princeton University Press.

————. 1998. "Harming Friends: Problematic Reciprocity in Greek Tragedy." In *Reciprocity in Ancient Greece*, ed. Christopher Gill, Norman Postlethwaite, and Richard Seaford, 139–58. Oxford: Oxford University Press.

Bisel, Sarah C., and J. L. Angel. 1985. "Health and Nutrition in Mycenaean Greece." In *Contributions to Aegean Archaeology: Studies in Honor of W.A. McDonald*, ed. N. C. Wilkie and W. D. E. Coulson, 197–209. Dubuque, IA: Kendall/Hunt.

Blundell, Mary Whitlock. 1989. *Helping Friends and Harming Enemies: A Study in Sophocles and Greek Ethics.* Cambridge: Cambridge University Press.

————. ed. 1990. *Sophocles' Oedipus at Colonus.* Newburyport, MA: Focus Classical Library.

————. 1993. "The Ideal of Athens in *Oedipus at Colonus*." In *Tragedy, Comedy, and the Polis*, ed. A. H. Sommerstein et al., 287–306. Bari: Levante Editori.

Boardman, John. 1985. *Greek Sculpture: The Classical Period.* London: Thames and Hudson.

Boedeker, D. 1998. "Presenting the Past in Fifth-Century Athens." In *Democracy, Empire and the Arts*, ed. D. Boedeker and K. A. Raaflaub, 185–202. Cambridge, MA: Harvard University Press.

Boedeker, D., and K. A. Raaflaub. 1998. *Democracy, Empire and the Arts in Fifth-Century Athens*. Cambridge, MA: Harvard University Press.

Boegehold, Alan L. 1995. *The Lawcourts at Athens*. The Athenian Agora, vol. 28. Princeton: American School of Classical Studies at Athens.

———. 1999. *When a Gesture Was Expected*. Princeton: Princeton University Press.

Bond, G. 1988. *Euripides: Herakles*. Oxford: Clarendon Press.

Borg, Barbara E. 2002. *Der Logos des Mythos: Allegorien und Personifikation in der frühen griechischen Kunst*. Munich: Fink.

Braund, David C. 1993. "Dionysiac Tragedy in Plutarch, *Crassus*." *Classical Quarterly* 43: 468–74.

Bremer, Robert H. 1988. *American Philanthropy*. 2nd ed. Chicago: University of Chicago Press.

Brouskari, Maria S. 1974. *The Acropolis Museum: A Descriptive Catalogue*. Translated by Judith Binder. Athens: Commercial Bank of Greece.

———. 1996. *Ta Mnêmeia tês Akropolês*. Athens: Tameio Archaiologikôn Porôn kai Apallotriôseôn.

Brown, J. C. 1996. *Rings: Five Passions in World Art*. New York: Harry N. Abrams.

Budd, Susan, and Ursula Sharma, eds. 1994. *The Healing Bond: The Patient-Practitioner Relationship and Therapeutic Responsibility*. London: Routledge.

Buitron, Diana. 1972. *Attic Vase Painting in New England Collections*. Cambridge, MA: Fogg Art Museum.

Buitron-Oliver, Diana. 1995. *Douris*. Mainz: Philipp von Zabern.

Burford, Alison. 1972. *Craftsmen in Greek and Roman Society*. Ithaca, NY: Cornell University Press.

Burian, Peter. 1974. "Suppliant and Saviour: Oedipus at Colonus." *Phoenix* 28: 408–29.

———. 1985. "*Logos* and *Pathos*: The Politics of the *Suppliant Women*." In *Directions in Euripidean Criticism*, ed. P. Burian, 129–55. Durham, NC: Duke University Press.

Burkert, Walter. 1955. "Zum altgriechischen Mitleidsbegriff." Ph.D. diss., Friedrich-Alexander University.

Burn, Lucilla. 1987. *The Meidias Painter*. Oxford: Oxford University Press.

Burnett, Anne Pippin. 1998. *Revenge in Attic and Later Tragedy*. Berkeley: University of California Press.

Cairns, Douglas L. 1993. Aidôs: *The Psychology and Ethics of Honour and Shame in Ancient Greek Literature*. Oxford: Clarendon Press.

———. 1996. "Veiling, αἰδώς, and a Red-Figure Amphora by Phintias." *Journal of Hellenic Studies* 116: 152–58.

_____. 1999. "Representations of Remorse and Reparation in Classical Greece." In *Remorse and Reparation*, ed. M. Cox, 171–78. London: Jessica Kingsley.

_____. 2001. "Anger and the Veil in Ancient Greek Culture." *Greece & Rome* 48: 18–32.

_____. 2002. "The Meaning of the Veil in Ancient Greek Culture." In *Women's Dress in the Ancient Greek World*, ed. L. Llewellyn-Jones, 73–93. London: Duckworth and the Classical Press of Wales.

Camp, John M. 1990. *The Athenian Agora: A Short Guide*. Athens: American School of Classical Studies at Athens.

Campbell, A.Y., ed. 1950. *Euripides: Helena*. Liverpool: University Press of Liverpool.

Cartledge, Paul. 1997. "'Deep Plays': Theatre as Process in Greek Civic Life." In *Cambridge Companion to Greek Tragedy*, ed. P. E. Easterling, 3–35. Cambridge: Cambridge University Press.

Christ, Matthew. 1994. "Herodotean Kings and Historical Inquiry." *Classical Antiquity* 13(2): 167–202.

Clark, Candace. 1997. *Misery and Company: Sympathy in Everyday Life*. Chicago: University of Chicago Press.

Clay, Jenny Strauss. 1983. *The Wrath of Athena*. Princeton: Princeton University Press.

Clifford, Orwin. 1984. "The Just and the Advantageous in Thucydides: The Case of the Mytilenaian Debate." *American Political Science Review* 78: 485–94.

Cohen, B. 2001. "Ethnic Identity in Democratic Athens." In *Ancient Perceptions of Greek Ethnicity*, ed. Irad Malkin, 235–74. Washington, DC: Center for Hellenic Studies.

Cohn-Haft, Louis. 1956. *The Public Physicians of Ancient Greece*. Northampton, MA: Smith College.

Conacher, Desmond J. 1967. *Euripidean Drama*. Toronto: University of Toronto Press.

Connor, W. Robert. 1984. *Thucydides*. Princeton: Princeton University Press.

Cook, Robert M. 1964. *Niobe and Her Children*. Cambridge: Cambridge University Press.

Cooper, John M. 1999. *Reason and Emotion: Essays on Ancient Moral Psychology and Ethical Theory*. Princeton: Princeton University Press.

Crane, Gregory R., ed. 2002. *The Perseus Project*.

Crawford, Neta C. 2000. "The Passion of World Politics: Propositions on Emotion and Emotional Relationships." *International Security* 24: 116–56.

Crotty, Kevin. 1994. *The Poetics of Supplication: Homer's* Iliad *and* Odyssey. Ithaca, NY: Cornell University Press.

Dahlmann, Hellfried. 1934. "*Clementia Caesaris.*" *Neue Jahrbücher für Wissenschaft* 10: 17–26.

Damasio, Antonio R. 1994. *Descartes' Error: Emotion, Reason, and the Human Brain*. New York: G. P. Putnam's Sons.

David, Ephraim. 1989. "Laughter in Spartan Society." In *Classical Sparta*, ed. A. Powell, 1–25. Norman: University of Oklahoma Press.

Davies, Malcolm. 2000. "The Man Who Surpassed All Men in Virtue: Euripides' *Hippolytus* and the Balance of Sympathies." *Wiener Studien* 113: 53–69.

Dawe, R. D. 1996. *Sophoclis Oedipus Rex*. Stuttgart: Teubner.

Debnar, Paula. 2001. *Speaking the Same Language*. Ann Arbor: University of Michigan Press.

de Lauretis, Teresa. 1984. *Alice Doesn't*. Bloomington: Indiana University Press.

———. 1987. *Technologies of Gender*. Bloomington: Indiana University Press.

Den Boer, Willem. 1979. *Private Morality in Greece and Rome*. Leiden: Brill.

Denyer, Nicholas, ed. 2001. *Plato: Alcibiades*. Cambridge: Cambridge University Press.

de Romilly, Jacqueline. 1961. *L'évolution du pathétique d'Eschyle à Euripide*. Paris: Presses Universitaires de France.

———. 1974. "Fairness and Kindness in Thucydides." *Phoenix* 28: 95–111.

———. 1975. *Magic and Rhetoric in Ancient Greece*. Cambridge, MA: Harvard University Press.

———. 1979. *La douceur dans la pensée grecque*. Paris: Belles Lettres.

———. 1988. "Le conquérant et la belle captive." *Bulletin de l'Association Guillaume Budé*, 3–15.

Detienne, Marcel, and Jean-Paul Vernant. 1989. *The Cuisine of Sacrifice Among the Greeks*. Chicago: University of Chicago Press.

Devereux, George. 1985. *The Character of the Euripidean Hippolytus: An Ethno-Psychoanalytical Study*. Chico, CA: Scholars Press.

Diels, Herman. 1954. *Fragmente der Vorsokratiker*. 2 volumes. Berlin: Weidmannsche Verlagsbuchhandlung.

Dimock, George E. Jr. 1977. "Euripides' *Hippolytus*, or Virtue Rewarded." *Yale Classical Studies* 25: 239–58.

Dobrov, Gregory W. 2001. *Figures of Play: Greek Drama and Metafictional Poetics*. Oxford: Oxford University Press.

Dodds, Eric R. 1951. *The Greeks and the Irrational*. Berkeley: University of California Press.

———. 1960. *Euripides: Bacchae*. 2nd ed. Oxford: Clarendon Press.

Dougherty, C. 1996. "Democratic Contradictions and the Synoptic Illusion of Euripides' *Ion*." In *Dēmokratia: A Conversation on Democracies, Ancient and Modern*, ed. J. Ober and C. Hedrick, 228–49. Princeton: Princeton University Press.

Douglas, Mary. 1994. "The Construction of the Physician." In *Healing Bond*, ed. Susan Budd and Ursula Sharma, 23–41. London: Routledge.

Dover, Kenneth J. 1974. *Greek Popular Morality in the Time of Plato and Aristotle*. Berkeley: University of California Press.

Duff, Timothy. 1999a. *Plutarch's Lives*. Oxford: Oxford University Press.

———. 1999b. "Plutarch, Plato, and 'Great Natures.'" In *Plutarco, Platòn Aristoteles*. Actas del V Congreso Internacional de la I.P.S., ed. A. Pérez Jiménez, J. García López, and Rosa M. Aguilar, 313–32. Madrid: Ediciones Clásicas.

Dunn, Francis M. 1996. *Tragedy's End: Closure and Innovation in Euripidean Drama.* Oxford: Oxford University Press.

Durrant, Michael. 1993. *Aristotle's* De Anima *in Focus.* New York: Routledge.

Eagleton, Terry. 1991. *Ideology: An Introduction.* London: Verso.

Easterling, P. E., ed. 1982. *Sophocles: Trachiniae.* Cambridge: Cambridge University Press.

————. 1997. "A Show for Dionysus." In *Cambridge Companion to Greek Tragedy,* ed. P. E. Easterling, 36–53. Cambridge: Cambridge University Press.

Easterling, P. E., ed. 1997. *The Cambridge Companion to Greek Tragedy.* Cambridge: Cambridge University Press.

Edmunds, L. 1996. *Theatrical Space and Historical Place in Sophocles'* Oedipus at Colonus. Lanham, MD: Rowman & Littlefield.

Ehrenberg, V. 1947. "*Polypragmosyne.*" *Journal of Hellenic Studies* 67: 46–67.

Eisenberg, Janet, Sandra Losoya, and Tracy Spinrad. 2003. "Affect and Prosocial Responding." In *Handbook of Affective Sciences,* ed. Richard J. Davidson et al., 787–803. Oxford: Oxford University Press.

Elkins, James. 2001. *Pictures & Tears: A History of People Who Have Cried in Front of Paintings.* New York: Routledge.

Else, Gerald F. 1967. *Aristotle's* Poetics*: The Argument.* Cambridge, MA: Harvard University Press.

Falkner, Thomas. 1989. " Ἐπὶ γήραος οὐδῷ: Homeric Heroism, Old Age, and the End of the *Odyssey.*" In *Old Age in Greek and Latin Literature,* ed. Thomas Falkner and Judith de Luce, 21–67. Albany: State University of New York Press.

————. 1993. "Making a Spectacle of Oneself: The Metatheatrical Design of Sophocles' *Ajax.*" In *Text and Presentation: Journal of the Comparative Drama Conference* 14, ed. K. Hartigan and B. Richardson, 35–40. Lanham, MD: University Press of America.

————. 1998. "Containing Tragedy: Rhetoric and Self-Representation in Sophocles' *Philoctetes.*" *Classical Antiquity* 17(1): 25–58. Berkeley: University of California Press.

————. 1999. "Madness Visible: Tragic Ideology and Poetic Authority in Sophocles' *Ajax.*" In *Contextualizing Classics,* ed. Thomas Falkner, Nancy Felson, and David Konstan, 173–201. Lanham, MD: Rowman & Littlefield.

Falkner, Thomas, Nancy Felson, and David Konstan, eds. 1999. *Contextualizing Classics: Ideology, Performance, Dialogue.* Lanham, MD: Rowman & Littlefield.

Fallaci, Oriana. 2002. *The Rage and the Pride.* New York: Rizzoli International Publications.

Ferguson, N. 2003. *Empire: The Rise and Demise of the British World Order and the Lessons for Global Power.* New York: Basic Books.

Ferguson, W. S. 1927. "The Athenian Expedition to Sicily." *The Cambridge Ancient History* 5: 282–311.

Ferrari, Gloria. 1990. "Figures of Speech: The Picture of Aidos." *Metis* 5: 185–200.

————. 1997. "Figures in the Text: Metaphors and Riddles in the *Agamemnon.*" *Classical Philology* 92: 1–49.

————. 2002. *Figures of Speech: Men and Maidens in Ancient Greece*. Chicago: University of Chicago Press.

Fink, Josef. 1967. *Der Thron des Zeus in Olympia*. Munich: Heimeran.

Fitzpatrick, David. 2001. "Sophocles' *Tereus*." *Classical Philology* 51: 90–101.

Forbes Irving, Paul M. C. 1992. *Metamorphosis in Greek Myths*. Oxford: Oxford University Press.

Fornara, Charles. 1983. *The Nature of History in Ancient Greece and Rome*. Berkeley: University of California Press.

Forsdyke, S. 2001. "Athenian Ideology and Herodotus' *Histories*." *American Journal of Philology* 122: 329–58.

Fortenbaugh, William W. 2002. *Artistotle on Emotion*. 2nd ed. London: Duckworth.

Frank, Robert H. 1988. *Passions within Reason: The Strategic Role of the Emotions*. New York: Norton.

Frazer, James G., trans. 1921. *Apollodorus: The Library*. Vol. 1. Loeb Classical Library. London: Heinemann.

Frazier, Françoise. 1995. "Principes et décisions dans le domaine politique d'après les *Vies* de Plutarque." In *Teoria e prassi politica*, ed. Italo Gallo and Barbara Scardigli, 147–71. Naples: M. D'Auria.

Frede, Dorothea. 1996. "Mixed Feelings in Aristotle's *Rhetoric*." In *Essays on Aristotle's* Rhetoric, ed. Amélie Oksenberg Rorty, 258–85. Berkeley: University of California Press.

Freedberg, David. 1989. *The Power of Images: Studies in the History and Theory of Response*. Chicago: University of Chicago Press.

French, Peter A. 2001. *The Virtues of Vengeance*. Lawrence: University Press of Kansas.

Freyburger, Gérard. 1988. "Supplication grecque et supplication romaine." *Latomus* 47: 501–25.

Frijda, Nico H. 1986. *The Emotions*. Cambridge: Cambridge University Press.

Frijda, Nico H., Antony S. R. Manstead, and Sacha Bem, eds. 2000. *Emotions and Beliefs: How Feelings Influence Thoughts*. Paris: Cambridge University Press.

Gadbery, Laura. 1992. "The Sanctuary of the Twelve Gods in the Agora: A Revised View." *Hesperia* 61: 447–89.

Gallo, Italo, and Barbara Scardigli, eds. 1995. *Teoria e prassi politica nelle opere di Plutarco: Atti del V Convegno plutarcheo (Certosa di Pontignano, 7–9 giugno 1993)*. Naples: M. D'Auria.

Garvie, Alexander F. 1998. *Sophocles: Ajax*. Warminster, England: Aris & Phillips.

Gauthier, P. 1988. "Métèques, périèques et paroikoi: bilan et points d'interrogation." In *L'étranger dans le monde grec*, ed. R. Lonis, 23–46. Nancy: University Press of Nancy.

Geominy, Wilfred. 1992. In *Lexicon Iconographicum Mythologiae Classicae* vol. 6, 914–29. Zurich, s.v. "Niobidae."

Gera, Deborah Levine. 1993. *Xenophon's* Cyropaedia: *Style, Genre, and Literary Technique.* Oxford: Clarendon Press.

Gilby, Dena M. 1996. "Weeping Rocks: The Stone Transformation of Niobe and her Children." PhD diss., University of Washington.

Gill, Christopher. 1998. "Altruism or Reciprocity in Greek Ethical Philosophy?" In *Reciprocity in Ancient Greece*, ed. Christopher Gill, Norman Postlethwaite, and Richard Seaford, 303–28. Oxford: Oxford University Press.

Gill, Christopher, Norman Postlethwaite, and Richard Seaford, eds. 1998. *Reciprocity in Ancient Greece.* Oxford: Oxford University Press.

Giordano, Manuela. 1999. *La supplica: rituale, istituzione sociale e tema epico in Omero.* Naples: Istituto Universitario Orientale.

Goemann, Elke. 1991. *Euphronios der Maler.* Milan: Fabbri.

Goff, Barbara. 1990. *The Noose of Words: Readings of Desire, Violence and Language in Euripides'* Hippolytus. Cambridge: Cambridge University Press.

Golden, Mark. 1981. "Demography and the Exposure of Girls at Athens." *Phoenix* 35: 316–31.

———. 1990. *Children and Childhood in Classical Athens.* Baltimore: Johns Hopkins University Press.

Golder, Herbert. 1990. "Sophocles' *Ajax*: Beyond the Shadow of Time." *Arion*, 3rd ser., 1: 9–34.

Goldhill, Simon. 1986. *Reading Greek Tragedy.* Cambridge: Cambridge University Press.

———. 1990. "The Great Dionysia and Civic Ideology." In *Nothing to Do with Dionysos?*, ed. John Winkler and Froma Zeitlin, 97–129. Princeton: Princeton University Press. First published in *Journal of Hellenic Studies* 107(1988): 58–76.

———. 1997. "The Audience of Athenian Tragedy." In *Cambridge Companion to Greek Tragedy*, ed. P. E. Easterling, 54–68. Cambridge: Cambridge University Press.

———. 1999. "Programme Notes." In *Performance Culture and Athenian Democracy*, ed. Simon Goldhill and Robin Osborne, 1–28. Cambridge: Cambridge University Press.

Gomme, A., K. Dover, and A. Andrewes. 1956–1981. *A Historical Commentary on Thucydides.* 5 vols. Oxford: Oxford University Press.

Gould, John P. 1973. "*Hiketeia.*" *Journal of Hellenic Studies* 93: 74–103.

Gould, Thomas. 1990. *The Ancient Quarrel between Poetry and Philosophy.* Princeton: Princeton University Press.

Greifenhagen, A. 1931. "Kindesheitmythos des Dionysos." *Rheinisches Museum* 46: 27–43.

Grensemann, Hermann, ed. and trans. 1968. *Die hippokratische Schrift "Über die heilige Krankheit."* Berlin: De Gruyter.

Grethlein, J. 2003. *Asyl und Athen: die Konstruktion kollektiver Identitäten in der griechischen Tragödie.* Beiträge zum antiken Drama und seiner Rezeption 21. Stuttgart: Metzler.

Griffin, Jasper. 1998. "The Social Function of Attic Tragedy." *Classical Quarterly* 48: 39–61.

Griffin, Miriam T. 1976. *Seneca: A Philosopher in Politics.* Oxford: Clarendon Press.

————. 2003. "*Clementia* after Caesar." In *Caesar against Liberty? Perspectives on his Autocracy*, ed. Elaine Fantham and Francis Cairns, 157–82. Cambridge: Francis Cairns.

Griffiths, Alan. 1999. "Euenius the Negligent Nightwatchman (Herodotus 9. 92–6)." In *From Myth to Reason?* ed. R. Buxton, 169–82. Oxford: Oxford University Press.

Griffiths, Paul E. 1997. *What Emotions Really Are: The Problem of Psychological Categories.* Chicago: University of Chicago Press.

Guazzelli, Teresa. 1992. *Le Antesterie.* Florence: Firenze libri.

Hafferty, Frederic. 1991. *Into the Valley: Death and the Socialization of Medical Students.* New Haven, CT: Yale University Press.

Hall, Edith. 1989. *Inventing the Barbarian.* Oxford: Clarendon Press.

————. 1997. "The Sociology of Athenian Tragedy." In *Cambridge Companion to Greek Tragedy*, ed. P. E. Easterling, 93–126. Cambridge: Cambridge University Press.

Halleran, Michael R. 1995. *Euripides: Hippolytus.* Warminster, UK: Aris & Phillips.

Halliwell, Stephen. 1996. "Plato's Repudiation of the Tragic." In *Tragedy and The Tragic*, ed. Michael S. Silk, 332–49. Oxford: Clarendon Press.

————. 2002. *The Aesthetics of Mimesis.* Princeton: Princeton University Press.

Halperin, David, John Winkler, and Froma Zeitlin, eds. 1990. *Before Sexuality. The Construction of Erotic Experience in the Ancient Greek World.* Princeton: Princeton University Press.

Halpern, Jodi. 1993. "Empathy: Using Resonance Emotions in the Service of Curiosity." In *Empathy and the Practice of Medicine*, ed. Howard M. Spiro et al., 160–73. New Haven: Yale University Press.

Hamilton, Richard. 1992. *Choes and Anthesteria: Athenian Iconography and Ritual.* Ann Arbor: University of Michigan Press.

Hammer, Dean. 2002. "The *Iliad* as Ethical Thinking: Politics, Pity, and the Operation of Esteem." *Arethusa* 35: 203–35.

Hancock, Graham. 1989. *Lords of Poverty: The Power, Prestige, and Corruption of the International Aid Business.* New York: Atlantic Monthly Press.

Hands, Arthur R. 1968. *Charities and Social Aid in Greece and Rome.* Ithaca, NY: Cornell University Press.

Harris, William V. 2001. *Restraining Rage: The Ideology of Anger Control in Classical Antiquity.* Cambridge, MA: Harvard University Press.

Harrison, Evelyn B. 1979. "The Iconography of the Eponymous Heroes on the Parthenon and in the Agora." In *Greek Numismatics and Archaeology: Essays in Honor of Margaret Thompson*, ed. Otto Mørkholm and Nancy M. Waggoner, 71–85. Wetteren: NR.

————. 1996. "The Web of History: A Conservative Reading of the Parthenon Frieze." In *Worshipping Athena*, ed. Jenifer Neils, 198–218. Madison: University of Wisconsin Press.

Hartog, François. 1988. *The Mirror of Herodotus: The Representation of the Other in the Writing of History*. Translated by Janet Lloyd. Berkeley: University of California Press.

Hartswick, Kim J. 2004. *The Gardens of Sallust*. Austin: University of Texas Press.

Heath, Malcolm. 1987. *The Poetics of Greek Tragedy*. Stanford: Stanford University Press.

Heiden, Bruce. 1989. *Tragic Rhetoric: An Interpretation of Sophocles' Trachiniae*. New York: Peter Lang.

Herman, Gabriel. 1987. *Ritualised Friendship and the Greek City*. Cambridge: Cambridge University Press.

Heydemann, Heinrich. 1885. "Dionysos Gebürt und Kindheit." *Hallisches Winckelmannsprogramm* 10: 3–58.

Hogan, James C. 1972. "Thucydides 3.52–68 and Euripides' *Hecuba*." *Phoenix* 26: 241–57.

Hornblower, Simon. 1991. *A Commentary on Thucydides*. Vol. 1. Oxford: Clarendon Press.

Horstmanshoff, Herman F. J. 1990. "The Ancient Physician: Craftsman or Scientist?" *Journal of the History of Medicine and Allied Sciences* 45: 176–97.

Hume, David. 1998. *An Enquiry Concerning the Principles of Morals: A Critical Edition*. Edited by Tom L. Beauchamp. Oxford: Clarendon Press. First published 1751.

Humphrey, Sally C. 1980. "Family Tombs and Tomb Cult in Ancient Athens." *Journal of Hellenic Studies* 100: 96–126.

Hunter, Virginia. 1994. *Policing Athens*. Princeton: Princeton University Press.

Hurwit, Jeffrey M. 1982. "Palm Trees and the Pathetic Fallacy in Archaic Greek Poetry and Art." *Classical Journal* 77: 192–99.

————. 1987. "Narrative Resonance in the East Pediment of the Temple of Zeus at Olympia." *Art Bulletin* 69: 6–15.

————. 1999. *The Athenian Acropolis: History, Mythology, and Archaeology from the Neolithic Era to the Present*. Cambridge: Cambridge University Press.

Huskinson, Janet. 1996. *Roman Children's Sarcophagi: Their Decoration and its Social Significance*. Oxford: Clarendon Press.

Irwin, Terence. 1977. *Plato's Moral Theory: The Early and Middle Dialogues*. Oxford: Oxford University Press.

Jal, Paul. 1963. *La Guerre Civile à Rome: Étude littéraire et morale*. Paris: Presses Universitaires de France.

Janko, Richard, trans. and ed. 1987. *Aristotle: Poetics*. Indianapolis, IN: Hackett.

Jebb, Sir Richard, ed. 1883. *Sophocles: Oedipus Tyrannus*. Cambridge: University Press.

———. ed. 1889, reprinted 1930. *Sophocles: Oedipus Coloneus.* Cambridge: University Press.

———. ed. 1907. *Sophocles: Ajax.* Cambridge: University Press.

Jenkins, Ian. 1994. *The Parthenon Frieze.* Austin: University of Texas Press.

Johnson, James Franklin. 1980. "Compassion in Sophocles' *Philoctetes*: A Comparative Study." PhD diss., University of Texas at Austin.

———. 2002. "Compassion and Friendship in Euripides' *Herakles*." *Classical Bulletin* 78(2): 123–37.

Jones, Christopher. 1999. *Kinship Diplomacy in the Ancient World.* Cambridge, MA: Harvard University Press.

Jones, William H. S. 1918. *Pausanias: Description of Greece.* Vol. 1. Loeb Classical Library. London: Heinemann.

Jouanna, Jacques. 1987. "Médecine hippocratique et tragedie grecque." *Cahiers du GITA* 3: 109–31.

———. 1999. *Hippocrates.* Baltimore: Johns Hopkins University Press.

Kakridis, Johannes. 1949. *Homeric Researches.* Lund: Gleerup.

Kamerbeek, Jan C. 1984. *The Plays of Sophocles: Commentaries.* Part 7, *Oedipus Coloneus.* Leiden: Brill.

Kant, Immanuel. 1960. *Observations on the Feeling of the Beautiful and Sublime.* Translated by John T. Goldthwait. Berkeley: University of California Press. First published 1764.

Kappeler, Susanne. 1986. *The Pornography of Representation.* Minneapolis: University of Minnesota Press.

Kaufhold, S. D. 1997. "Ovid's Tereus, Fire, Birds, and the Reification of Figurative Language." *Classical Philology* 92: 66–71.

Kavvadias, G. G. 2000. *O Zographos tou Sabouroff.* Athens: Tameio Archaiologikon Poron kai Apallotrioseon Dieuthunsi Demosieumaton.

Kearns, Emily. 1989. *The Heroes of Attica.* London: University of London, Institute of Classical Studies.

Kennedy, George A. 1959. "The Earliest Rhetorical Handbook." *American Journal of Philology* 80: 169–78.

———. 1963. *The Art of Persuasion in Greece.* Princeton: Princeton University Press.

———, trans. and ed. 1991. *Aristotle on Rhetoric: A Theory of Civic Discourse.* New York: Oxford University Press.

———. 1994. *A New History of Classical Rhetoric.* Princeton: Princeton University Press.

Kierdorf, W. 1966. *Erlebnis und Darstellung der Perserkriege.* Hypomnemata 16. Göttingen: Vandenhoeck & Ruprecht.

Kim, Jinyo. 2000. *The Pity of Achilles: Oral Style and the Unity of the* Iliad. Oxford: Rowman & Littlefield.

King, Helen. 1998. *Hippocrates' Woman: Reading the Female Body in Ancient Greece.* London: Routledge.

Kitto, Humphrey D. F. 1939. *Greek Tragedy: A Literary Study.* London: Methuen.

————. 1956. *Form and Meaning in Drama*. London: Methuen.

Kleinman, Arthur. 1980. *Patients and Healers in the Context of Culture*. Berkeley: University of California Press.

Knell, Heiner. 1978. "Die Gruppe von Prokne und Itys." *Antike Plastik* 17: 9–19.

Knox, Bernard M. W. 1952. "The *Hippolytus* of Euripides." *Yale Classical Studies* 13 = *Word and Action: Essays on the Ancient Theater*, ed. Bernard Knox, 205–30. Baltimore: Johns Hopkins University Press, 1979.

————. 1961. "The *Ajax* of Sophocles." *Harvard Studies in Classical Philology* 65 = *Word and Action: Essays on the Ancient Theater*, ed. Bernard Knox, 125–60. Baltimore: Johns Hopkins University Press, 1979.

————. 1964. *The Heroic Temper*. Sather Classical Lectures 35. Berkeley: University of California Press.

Konstan, David. 1997. "Philoctetes' Pity: Commentary on Moravcsik." *Proceedings of the Boston Area Colloquium in Ancient Philosophy* 13: 276–82. Leiden: Brill.

————. 1999. "Pity and Self-Pity." In *Electronic Antiquity* 5.2. http://scholar.lib.vt.edu/ejournals/ElAnt/V5N2/konstan.html.

————. 2000a. "Altruism." *Transactions of the American Philological Association* 130: 1–17.

————. 2000b. "Pity and the Law in Greek Theory and Practice." *Dike* 3: 125–45.

————. 2001. *Pity Transformed*. London: Duckworth.

Kopperschmidt, Josef. 1971. "Hikesie als dramatische Form." In *Die Bauformen der griechischen Tragödie*, ed. Walter Jens, 321–46. Munich: Wilhelm Fink.

Kosak, Jennifer. 1999. "Therapeutic Touch and Sophocles' *Philoktetes*." *Harvard Studies in Classical Philology* 99: 93–134.

Kovacs, David. 1980. "Euripides *Hippolytus* 100 and the Meaning of the Prologue." *Classical Philology* 75: 130–37.

————. 1995. *Euripides*. Vol. 2. Loeb Classical Library. Cambridge, MA: Harvard University Press.

Kövecses, Zoltán. 2000. *Metaphor and Emotion: Language, Culture, and Body in Human Feeling*. Cambridge: Cambridge University Press.

Kreikenbom, Detlev. 2003. "Raumkonzeptionen in der nachparthenonischen Plastik." In *Zum Verhältnis von Raum und Zeit in der griechischen Kunst*, ed. Peter C. Bol, 183–208. Möhnesee: Bibliopolis.

Kron, Uta. 1976. *Die zehn attischen Phylenheroen*. Berlin: Mann.

Kunisch, Norbert. 1997. *Makron*. Mainz: Philipp von Zabern.

Kurtz, Donna C., and J. Boardman. 1971. *Greek Burial Customs*. Ithaca, NY: Cornell University Press.

Kyrieleis, Helmut. 1997. "Zeus and Pelops in the East Pediment of the Temple of Zeus at Olympia." In *The Interpretation of Architectural Sculptural in Greece and Rome*, ed. D. Buitron-Oliver, 13–37. Washington, DC: National Gallery of Art.

Lada, Ismene. 1993. "'Empathic Understanding': Emotion and Cognition in Classical Dramatic Audience-Response." *Proceedings of the Cambridge Philological Society* 39: 94–140.

————. 1996. "Emotion and Meaning in Tragic Performance." In *Tragedy and The Tragic*, ed. Michael S. Silk, 397–413. Oxford: Clarendon Press.

Landau, Richard L. 1993. "And the Least of These is Empathy." In *Empathy and the Practice of Medicine*, ed. Howard M. Spiro et al., 103–9. New Haven: Yale University Press.

Lapatin, Kenneth D. S. 2001. *Chryselephantine Statuary in the Ancient Mediterranean World*. Oxford: Oxford University Press.

La Rocca, Eugenio. 1986. "Prokne ed Itys sull' Acropoli: una motivazione per la didica." *Mitteilungen des Deutschen Archäologischen Instituts* 101: 153–66.

Lascombe, Michael A. 1993. "Letters of Intent." In *Empathy and the Practice of Medicine*, ed. Howard M. Spiro et al., 54–66. New Haven: Yale University Press.

Lateiner, Donald. 1977a. "Heralds and Corpses in Thucydides." *Classical World* 71: 97–106.

————. 1977b. "Pathos in Thucydides." *Antichthon* 11: 42–51.

————. 1985. "Nicias' Inadequate Encouragement." *Classical Philology* 80(3): 201–13.

————. 1989. *The Historical Method of Herodotus*. Toronto: University of Toronto Press.

Leigh, Matthew. 1997. *Lucan: Spectacle and Engagement*. Oxford: Oxford University Press.

Levene, Daniel S. 1997. "Pity, Fear and the Historical Audience: Tacitus on the Fall of Vitellius." In *The Passions in Roman Thought and Literature*, ed. S. Braund and D. Gill, 128–49. Cambridge: Cambridge University Press.

Levick, Barbara M. 1975. "Mercy and Moderation on the Coinage of Tiberius." In *The Ancient Historian and his Materials: Essays presented to C. E. Stevens on his Seventieth Birthday*, ed. Barbara Levick, 123–37. Farnborough: Gregg.

————. 1976. *Tiberius the Politician*. London: Thames and Hudson.

Lewis, David M. 1955. "Notes on Attic Inscriptions (II)." *Papers of the British School at Athens* 50: 1–36.

Lewis, Michael, and Jeannette M. Haviland-Jones, eds. 2000. *Handbook of Emotions*. 2nd ed. New York: Guilford Press.

Lloyd, Geoffrey E. R. 1983. *Science, Folklore and Ideology*. Cambridge: Cambridge University Press.

Lloyd-Jones, Hugh, ed. 1971. *Aeschylus*. Vol. 2. Cambridge, MA: Harvard University Press.

————. ed. 1994. *Sophocles*. Vols. 1–3. Loeb Classical Library. Cambridge, MA: Harvard University Press.

Lloyd-Jones, Hugh, and N. G. Wilson. 1990. *Sophoclis Fabulae*. Oxford: Oxford University Press.

Loeb, Ehud Herbert. 1979. *Die Geburt der Götter in der griechischen Kunst der klassischen Zeit*. Jerusalem: Shikmona.

Lonis, R. 1988. *L'étranger dans le monde grec*. Nancy: University Press of Nancy.

Loraux, Nicole. 1977. "'La belle mort' spartiate." *Ktema* 2: 105–20.

———. 1986. *The Invention of Athens: The Funeral Oration in the Classical City.* Translated by A. Sheridan. Cambridge: Harvard University Press.

———. 1987. *Tragic Ways of Killing a Woman.* Translated by A. Forster. Cambridge, MA: Harvard University Press.

———. 1990. "Herakles: The Super-Male and the Feminine." In *Before Sexuality*, ed. David Halperin, John Winkler, and Froma Zeitlin, 21–52. Princeton: Princeton University Press.

———. 2002. *Mourning Voices: An Essay on Greek Tragedy.* Translated by E. T. Rawlings. Ithaca, NY: Cornell University Press.

Lutz, Catherine A. 1988. *Unnatural Emotions: Everyday Sentiments on a Micronesian Atoll and their Challenge to Western Theory.* Chicago: University of Chicago Press.

Lyons, Deborah. 1997. *Gender and Immortality: Heroines in Ancient Greek Myth and Cult.* Princeton: Princeton University Press.

Macleod, Colin. 1977. "Thucydides' Plataean Debate." *Greek, Roman and Byzantine Studies* 18: 227–46. Reprinted in Macleod 1983b, 130–22.

———. 1978. "Reason and Necessity: Thucydides 3.9–14, 37–48." *Journal of Hellenic Studies* 98: 64–78. Reprinted in Macleod 1983b, 88–102.

———. 1982. *Homer: Iliad Book XXIV.* Cambridge: Cambridge University Press.

———. 1983a. "Homer on Poetry and the Poetry of Homer." In *Collected Essays*, ed. Colin Macleod, 1–15. Oxford: Oxford University Press.

———. ed. 1983b. *Collected Essays.* Oxford: Oxford University Press.

MacMullen, Ramsay. 2003. *Feelings in History, Ancient and Modern.* Claremont, CA: Regina Books.

Macurdy, Grace. 1940. *The Quality of Mercy: The Gentler Virtues in Greek Literature.* New Haven: Yale University Press.

Mahaffy, John P. 1883. *Social Life in Greece from Homer to Menander.* 5th ed. London: Macmillan. First published 1874.

Mahoney, Anne. 2001. Review of *Figures of Play: Greek Drama and Metafictional Poetics* by G. W. Dobrov. *Bryn Mawr Classical Review* (June 19, 2001).

March, Jenny. 2000. "Vases and Tragic Drama: Euripides' *Medea* and Sophocles' Lost *Tereus*." In *Word and Image*, ed. N. Keith Rutter and Brian A. Sparkes, 119–39. Edinburgh: Edinburgh University Press.

Martin, Hubert M. 1961. "The Concept of *Philanthropia* in Plutarch's *Lives*." *American Journal of Philology* 82: 164–75.

Mattusch, Carol. 1994. "The Eponymous Heroes: The Idea of Sculptured Groups." In *The Archaeology of Athens and Attica under the Democracy*, ed. W. D. E. Coulson, O. Palagia, T. L. Shear, H. A. Shapiro, and F. J. Frost, 73–81. Oxford: Oxbow Books.

Meiggs, R. 1972. *The Athenian Empire.* Oxford: Oxford University Press.

Mendelsohn, D. 2002. *Gender and the City in Euripides' Political Plays.* Princeton: Princeton University Press.

Menlowe, Michael A., and Alexander McCall Smith, eds. 1993. *The Duty to Rescue: The Jurisprudence of Aid.* Hants, UK: Dartmouth Publishing.

Messerschmidt, Wolfgang. 2003. *Prosopopoiia Personifikationen politischen Charakters in spätklassischer und hellenistischer Kunst.* Cologne: Böhlau.

Mills, Sophie. 1997. *Theseus, Tragedy, and the Athenian Empire.* Oxford: Clarendon Press.

Minow, Martha. 1996. "Stories in Law." In *Law's Stories: Narrative and Rhetoric in the Law*, ed. P. Brooks and P. Gewirtz, 24–36. New Haven: Yale University Press.

Moles, John L., ed. and trans. 1988. *The Life of Cicero / Plutarch.* Warminster, UK: Aris & Phillips.

Moltesen, Mette. 1998. "The Sculptures from the *Horti Sallustiani* in the Ny Carlsburg Glyptothek." In *Horti Romani*, ed. M. Cima and E. LaRocca, 175–88. Rome: L'Erma di Bretschneider.

Monroe, Kristen. 1996. *The Heart of Altruism.* Princeton: Princeton University Press.

Moore, John. 1977. "The Dissembling-Speech of Ajax." *Yale Classical Studies* 25: 47–66.

Moreau, Alain. 1995. "La Niobe d'Eschyle: quelques jalons." *Revue des Études Grecques* 108: 288–307.

Most, Glen W. 2003. "Anger and Pity in Homer's *Iliad.*" In *Ancient Anger: Perspectives from Homer to Galen*, ed. S. Braund and G. W. Most, 50–75. Cambridge: Cambridge University Press.

Motte, André. 1996. "Le thème des enfances divines dans le mythe grec." *Les Études Classiques* 64: 109–25.

Mulvey, Laura. 1975. "Visual Pleasure and Narrative Cinema." *Screen* 16(3): 6–18.

Murdoch, Iris. 1977. *The Fire and the Sun: Why Plato Banished the Artists.* Oxford: Oxford University Press.

Naiden, F. S. 2000. "Greek Supplication Prior to 300 BCE." Ph.D. diss., Harvard University.

Neils, Jenifer, ed. 1996. *Worshipping Athena: Panathenaia and Parthenon.* Madison: University of Wisconsin Press.

————. 1999. "Reconfiguring the Gods on the Parthenon Frieze." *Art Bulletin* 81: 7–20.

————. 2001. *The Parthenon Frieze.* Cambridge: Cambridge University Press.

Neils, Jenifer, and John H. Oakley. 2003. *Coming of Age in Ancient Greece: Images of Childhood from the Classical Past.* New Haven: Yale University Press.

Nercessian, Andy. 1994. In *Lexicon Iconographicum Mythologiae Classicae.* Vol. 7, 162–63, s.v. "Pandion." Zurich: Artemis.

Nietzsche, Friedrich. 1964. *Thus Spake Zarathustra.* Translated by Thomas Common. New York: Russell & Russell. First published 1883–1891.

Nikolaidis, Anastasios G. 1995. "Plutarch's Heroes in Action: Does the End Justify the Means?" In *Teoria e prassi politica*, ed. Italo Gallo and Barbara Scardigli, 301–12. Naples: M. D'Auria.

Norwood, Gilbert. 1954. *Essays on Euripidean Drama.* Berkeley: University of California Press.

Nussbaum, Martha. 1986. *The Fragility of Goodness*. Cambridge: Cambridge University Press.

———. 1994. *The Therapy of Desire*. Princeton: Princeton University Press.

———. 2001. *Upheavals of Thought: The Intelligence of Emotions*. Cambridge: Cambridge University Press.

Nutton, Vivian. 1992. "Healers in the Medical Market-Place: Towards a Social History of Graeco-Roman Medicine." In *Medicine in Society*, ed. A. Wear, 15–58. Cambridge: Cambridge University Press.

Oakley, John H. 1990. *The Phiale Painter*. Mainz: Philipp von Zabern.

———. 1997. *The Achilles Painter*. Mainz: Philipp von Zabern.

———. 2004. *Picturing Death in Classical Athens: The Evidence of the White Lekythoi*. Cambridge: Cambridge University Press.

———. Forthcoming. "Bail-Oinochoai." In *Periklean Athens and Its Legacy*, ed. J. M. Barringer and J. M. Hurwit. Austin: University of Texas Press.

Oatley, Keith, and Jennifer M. Jenkins. 1996. *Understanding Emotions*. Oxford: Blackwell.

Ober, J., and B. Strauss. 1990. "Drama, Political Rhetoric and the Discourse of Athenian Democracy." In *Nothing to do with Dionysos?*, ed. John Winkler and Froma Zeitlin, 237–70. Princeton: Princeton University Press.

Olasky, Marvin. 1992. *The Tragedy of American Compassion*. Lanham, MD: Regnery Publishing.

Oliver, Graham J. 2000. "Athenian Funerary Monuments: Style, Grandeur, and Cost." In *The Epigraphy of Death*, ed. G. J. Oliver, 59–80. Liverpool: Liverpool University Press.

Ormand, Kirk. 1999. *Exchange and the Maiden: Marriage in Sophoclean Tragedy*. Austin: University of Texas Press.

Orwin, Clifford. 1984. "The Just and the Advantageous in Thucydides: The Case of the Mytilenaian Debate." *American Political Science Review* 78: 485–94.

———. 1994. *The Humanity of Thucydides*. Princeton: Princeton University Press.

Osborne, M. J. 1983. *Naturalization in Athens*. Verhandelingen van de Koninklijke Academie voor Wetenschappen, Letteren en Schone Kunsten van België. Klasse der Letteren 98 III–IV Brussels.

Osborne, Robin. 2000. "Archaic and Classical Greek Temple Sculpture and the Viewer." In *Word and Image*, ed. N. Keith Rutter and Brian A. Sparkes, 228–46. Edinburgh: Edinburgh University Press.

Ostwald, Martin. 1979. "Diodotus Son of Eucrates." *Greek, Roman and Byzantine Studies* 20: 5–13.

———. 1986. *From Popular Sovereignty to the Sovereignty of Law: Law, Society, and Politics in Fifth-Century Athens*. Berkeley: University of California Press.

Padel, Ruth. 1990. "Making Space Speak." In *Nothing to Do with Dionysos?*, ed. John Winkler and Froma Zeitlin, 336–65. Princeton: Princeton University Press.

———. 1992. *In and Out of the Mind. Greek Images of the Tragic Self*. Princeton: Princeton University Press.

Palagia, Olga. 1993. *The Pediments of the Parthenon.* Leiden: Brill.

Paribeni, Enrico. 1979. *Museo Nazionale Romano.* Vol. 1. Rome: De Luca.

Parker, Laetitia P. E. 2001. "Where is Phaedra?" *Greece & Rome* 48: 45–52.

Pearson, Lionel. 1962. *Popular Ethics in Ancient Greece.* Stanford: Stanford University Press.

Pedrick, Victoria. 1982. "Supplication in the *Iliad* and the *Odyssey.*" *Transactions of the American Philological Association* 112: 125–40.

Pelliccia, Hayden. 1995. *Mind, Body, and Speech in Homer and Pindar.* Göttingen: Vandenhoeck and Ruprecht.

Pelling, Christopher B. R. 1992. "Plutarch and Thucydides." In *Plutarch and the Historical Tradition,* ed. P. A. Stadter, 10–40. London: Routledge. Reprinted with revisions in Pelling 2002, 117–42.

———. 1997a. "Is Death the End? Closure in Plutarch's *Lives.*" In *Classical Closure: Endings in Ancient Literature,* ed. D. H. Roberts, F. M. Dunn, and D. Fowler, 228–50. Princeton: Princeton University Press. Reprinted with revisions in Pelling 2002, 365–86.

———. 2000. *Literary Texts and the Greek Historian.* London: Routledge.

———. 2002. *Plutarch and History.* London: Classical Press of Wales and Duckworth.

———. 2004. "Do Plutarch's Politicians Never Learn?" In *The Statesman in Plutarch's Works,* ed. L. de Blois, J. Bons, T. Kessels, and D. M. Schenkeveid, vol. 1, 87–103. Leiden: Brill.

Pelling, Christopher B. R., ed. 1997b. *Greek Tragedy and the Historian.* Oxford: Oxford University Press.

Pickard-Cambridge, A. 1988. *The Dramatic Festivals of Athens.* 2nd ed. Revised by J. Gould and D. M. Lewis. Oxford: Clarendon Press and NY: University Press.

Pitt-Rivers, Julian. 1997. *The Fate of Shechem or the Politics of Sex: Essays in the Anthropology of the Mediterranean.* Cambridge: Cambridge University Press.

Pleket, Henry W. 1995. "The Social Status of Physicians in the Graeco-Roman World." In *Ancient Medicine in its Socio-Cultural Context,* ed. P. J. van der Eijk, H. F. J. Horstmanshoff, and P. H. Schrijvers, 27–34. Amsterdam: Rodopi.

Pomeroy, Sarah B. 1997. *Families in Classical and Hellenistic Greece.* Oxford: Oxford University Press.

Potter, Paul. 1995. *Hippocrates.* Vol. 8. Loeb Classical Library. Cambridge, MA: Harvard University Press.

Poulsen, Frederik. 1951. *Catalogue of Ancient Sculpture in the Ny Carlsberg Glyptotek.* Copenhagen: Nielsen & Lydiche.

Prag, A. J. N. W. 1985. *The* Oresteia: *Iconographic and Narrative Tradition.* Warminster: Aris & Phillips.

Price, Theodora Hadzisteliou. 1978. *Kourotrophos: Cults and Representations of the Greek Nursing Deities.* Leiden: Brill.

Raaflaub, K. 2004. *The Discovery of Freedom in Ancient Greece.* Translated by R. Franciscono. Chicago: University of Chicago Press.

Rabinowitz, Nancy S. 1992. "Tragedy and the Politics of Containment." In *Pornography and Representation in Greece and Rome*, ed. Amy Richlin, 36–52. Oxford: Oxford University Press.

Radt, S. L., ed. 1999. *Tragicorum Graecorum Fragmenta*. 4 vols. Göttingen: Vandenhoeck & Ruprecht.

Raftopoulou, Eliana G. 2000. *Figures enfantines du Musée national d'Athènes, Département des sculptures*. Munich: Hirmer.

Reddy, William M. 2001. *The Navigation of Feeling: A Framework for the History of Emotions*. Cambridge: Cambridge University Press.

Reeder, Ellen D. 1995. *Pandora. Women in Classical Greece*. Princeton: Princeton University Press.

Reinhardt, Karl. 1979. *Sophocles*. Translated by H. and D. Harvey. Oxford: Blackwell. First published 1947.

Richlin, Amy, ed. 1992. *Pornography and Representation in Greece and Rome*. Oxford: Oxford University Press.

Richter, Gisela, and L. F. Hall. 1936. *Red-figured Athenian Vases in the Metropolitan Museum of Art*. New Haven: Yale University Press.

Ridgway, Brunilda S. 1970. *The Severe Style in Greek Sculpture*. Princeton: Princeton University Press.

———. 1981. *Fifth Century Styles in Greek Sculpture*. Princeton: Princeton University Press.

———. 1984. *Roman Copies of Greek Sculpture: The Problem of the Originals*. Ann Arbor: University of Michigan Press.

———. 1997. *Fourth-Century Styles in Greek Sculpture*. Madison: University of Wisconsin Press.

———. 1999. *Prayers in Stone: Greek Architectural Sculpture ca. 600–100 B.C.E.* Berkeley: University of California Press.

———. 2002. *Hellenistic Sculpture* III. Madison: University of Wisconsin Press.

Ringer, Mark. 1998. *Electra and the Empty Urn*. Chapel Hill: University of North Carolina Press.

Robertson, Noel. 1996. "Athena's Shrines and Festivals." In *Worshipping Athena*, ed. Jenifer Neils, 27–77. Madison: University of Wisconsin Press.

Roccos, Linda J. 1986. "The Shoulder-Pinned Back Mantle in Greek and Roman Sculpture." Ph.D. diss., New York University.

Roisman, Joseph. 1988. "On Phrynichos' *Sack of Miletos* and *Phoinissai*." *Eranos* 86: 15–23.

Rolley, Claude. 1994–1999. *La Sculpture Grecque*. 2 vols. Paris: Picard.

Rosivach, Vincent J. 1976. "Sophocles' *Ajax*." *Classical Journal* 72: 47–61.

———. 1991. "Some Athenian Presuppositions about 'The Poor.'" *Greece and Rome* 38: 189–98.

Rousseau, Jean-Jacques. 1972. *Émile*. Translated by B. Foxley. London: Everyman Library. First published 1762.

Rubidge, Bradley. 1993. "Tragedy and the Emotions of Warriors: The Moral Psychology Underlying Plato's Attack on Poetry." *Arethusa* 26: 247–76.

Russell, Donald A. 1963. "Plutarch's *Life of Coriolanus.*" *Journal of Roman Studies* 53: 21–28. Reprinted in Scardigli 1995, 357–72.

Rutter, N. Keith, and Brian A. Sparkes. 2000. *Word and Image in Ancient Greece.* Edinburgh: Edinburgh University Press.

Salkever, Stephen. 1986. "Tragedy and the Education of the *Dêmos*: Aristotle's Response to Plato." In *Greek Tragedy and Political Theory*, ed. J. P. Euben, 274–303. Berkeley: University of California Press.

Scardigli, Barbara, ed. 1995. *Essays on Plutarch's Lives.* Oxford: Oxford University Press.

Schachter, Albert. 1996. In *Der Neue Pauly*, Vol. 1, 142, s.v. "Aëdon." Stuttgart: Metzler.

Scheff, Thomas. 1994. *Bloody Revenge.* Boulder, CO: Westview Press.

Schefold, Karl, and F. Jung. 1989. *Die Sagen von den Argonauten, von Theben und Troia in der klassischen und hellenistischen Kunst.* Munich: Hirmer.

Schenker, David J. 1995. "The Victims of Aphrodite: *Hippolytus* 1403–1405." *Mnemosyne* 48: 1–10.

Scheper-Hughes, Nancy. 1992. *Death without Weeping: The Violence of Everyday Life in Brazil.* Berkeley: University of California Press.

Schettino, M. T. 1998. "Perdono e 'clementia principis' nello stoicismo del II secolo," *CISA* 24: 209–38.

Schmidt, M. 1992. In *Lexicon iconographicum mythologiae classicae.* Vol. 6, 908–9, s.v. "Niobe." Zurich: Artemis.

Schopenhauer, Arthur. 1995. *On the Basis of Morality.* Translated by E. F. J. Payne. Indianapolis, IN: Hackett. First published 1840.

Schröder, O. 1914. "De laudibus Athenarum." Ph.D. diss., Göttingen.

Schuchhardt, Walter-Herwig. 1977. *Alkamenes.* Berlin: de Gruyter.

Scott, Mary. 1979. "Pity and Pathos in Homer." *Acta Classica* 22: 1–14.

Scullion, Scott. 2002. "Tragic Dates." *Classical Quarterly* 52: 81–101.

Scully, Stephen. 1995. "Introduction." In *Euripides: Suppliant Women.* Translated by Rosanna Warren and Stephen Scully, 3–19. Oxford: Oxford University Press.

Seaford, Richard. 1998. "Introduction." In *Reciprocity in Ancient Greece*, ed. Christopher Gill, Norman Postlethwaite, and Richard Seaford, 1–11. Oxford: Oxford University Press.

Segal, Charles. 1981. *Tragedy and Civilization.* Norman: University of Oklahoma Press.

———. 1993. *Euripides and the Poetics of Sorrow: Art, Gender and Commemoration in* Alcestis, Hippolytus *and* Hecuba. Durham, NC: Duke University Press.

Sen, Amartya K. 1990. "Rational Fools: A Critique of the Behavioral Foundations of Economic Theory." In *Beyond Self-Interest*, ed. Jane J. Mansbridge, 25–43. Chicago: University of Chicago Press.

Shapiro, Harvey A. 1981. *Art, Myth, and Culture: Greek Vases from Southern Collections.* New Orleans: New Orleans Museum of Art and Tulane University.

———. 1993. *Personifications in Greek Art.* Kilchberg/Zurich: Akanthus.

———. 1994. *Myth into Art: Poet and Painter in Classical Greece.* London: Routledge.

———. 1996. "Democracy and Imperialism: The Panathenaia in the Age of Perikles." In *Worshipping Athena,* ed. Jenifer Neils, 215–25. Madison: University of Wisconsin Press.

Shapiro, Harvey A., C. A. Picón, and G. D. Scott III. 1995. *Greek Vases in the San Antonio Museum of Art.* San Antonio: San Antonio Museum of Art.

Shaw, Michael H. 1982. "The ἦθος of Theseus in *The Suppliant Women.*" *Hermes* 110: 3–19.

Shay, Jonathan. 1994. *Achilles in Vietnam.* New York: Maxwell Macmillan.

Shear, T. Leslie. 1973. "The Athenian Agora: Excavations of 1971." *Hesperia* 42: 121–79.

Sheets, George. 1994. "Conceptualizing International Law in Thucydides." *American Journal of Philology* 115: 51–73.

Sheppard, John T. 1920. *The* Oedipus Tyrannus *of Sophocles.* Cambridge: Cambridge University Press.

Sicherl, Martin. 1977. "The Tragic Issue in Sophocles' *Ajax.*" *Yale Classical Studies* 25: 67–98.

Siebert, G. 1990. In *Lexicon Iconographicum Mythologiae Classicae.* Vol. 5, 283–387, s.v. "Hermes." Zurich: Artemis.

Silk, Michael S. 1985. "Heracles and Greek Tragedy." *Greece and Rome* 32: 1–22.

———, ed. 1996. *Tragedy and the Tragic: Greek Theatre and Beyond.* Oxford: Clarendon Press.

Simon, Erika. 1969. "Zu den Giebeln des Zeustempels vom Olympia." *Athenische Mitteilungen* 83: 147–66.

Simon, Erika, and M. Hirmer. 1976. *Die griechischen Vasen.* Munich: Hirmer.

Smith, Amy Claire. 1997. "Political Personifications in Athenian Art." Ph.D. diss., Yale University.

Smith, Wesley, ed. and trans. 1990. *Hippocrates: Pseudepigraphic Writings.* Leiden: Brill.

———. 1994. *Hippocrates.* Vol. 8. Loeb Classical Library. Cambridge, MA: Harvard University Press.

Smyth, Herbert W., ed. 1926. *Aeschylus.* Vol. 2. Loeb Classical Library. London: Heinemann.

Sober, Elliott, and David Sloan Wilson. 1998. *Unto Others: The Evolution and Psychology of Unselfish Behavior.* Cambridge, MA: Harvard University Press.

Solmsen, Friedrich. 1938. "Aristotle and Cicero on the Orator's Playing upon the Feelings." *Classical Philology* 33: 390–404.

———. 1975. *Intellectual Experiments of the Greek Enlightenment.* Princeton: Princeton University Press.

Sontag, Susan. 2003. *Regarding the Pain of Others*. New York: Farrar, Straus and Giroux.

Sorabji, Richard. 2000. *Emotion and Peace of Mind: From Stoic Agitation to Christian Temptation*. Oxford: Oxford University Press.

Sparkes, Brian A. 1985. "Aspects of Onesimos." In *Greek Art: Archaic into Classical*, ed. C. G. Boulter, 18–39. Leiden: Brill.

Spiro, Howard M., Mary G. McCrea Curnen, Enid Peschel, and Deborah St. James, eds. 1993. *Empathy and the Practice of Medicine: Beyond Pills and the Scalpel*. New Haven: Yale University Press.

Spiro, Howard M. "Empathy: An Introduction," in *Empathy and the Practice of Medicine*, ed. Howard M. Spiro, Mary G. M. Curnen, Enid Peschel, and Deborah St. James, 1–6. New Haven: Yale University Press.

Sprague, Rosamond Kent, ed., and Hermann Diels. 1972. *The Older Sophists*. Columbia: University of South Carolina Press.

Stadter, Philip A. 1989. *A Commentary on Plutarch's* Pericles. Chapel Hill: University of North Carolina Press.

Stafford, Emma. 2000. *Worshipping Virtues: Personification and the Divine in Ancient Greece*. London: Duckworth.

Stahl, Hans-Peter 1966. *Thukydides. Die Stellung des Menschen im geschichtlichen Prozess*. Zetemata 40. Munich: Beck.

———. 1975. "Learning Through Suffering?" *Yale Classical Studies* 24: 1–36.

———. 1977. "On 'Extra-Dramatic' Communication of Characters in Euripides." *Yale Classical Studies* 25: 159–76.

Stanford, William B., ed. 1963. *Sophocles: Ajax*. London: Macmillan.

———. 1983. *Greek Tragedy and the Emotions*. London: Routledge & Kegan Paul.

Sternberg, Rachel Hall. 1998. "Pity and Pragmatism: A Study of Athenian Attitudes Toward Compassion in Fifth- and Fourth-Century Historiography and Oratory." Ph.D. diss., Bryn Mawr College.

———. 2000. "The Nurturing Male: Bravery and Bedside Manners in Isocrates' *Aegineticus* (19.24–9)." *Greece & Rome* 47(2): 172–85.

Stevens, Edward B. 1944. "Some Attic Commonplaces of Pity." *American Journal of Philology* 65: 1–25.

Stevens, Gorham P. 1946. "The Northeast Corner of the Parthenon." *Hesperia* 15: 1–26.

Stevens, Philip T. 1986. "Ajax in the *Trugrede*." *Classical Quarterly* 36: 327–36.

Stewart, Andrew. 1990. *Greek Sculpture: An Exploration*. 2 vols. New Haven: Yale University Press.

Strassburger, H. 1958. "Thykydides und die politische Selbstdarstellung der Athener." *Hermes* 86: 17–40.

Swain, Simon. 1989. "Plutarch's *Aemilius* and *Timoleon*." *Historia* 38: 314–34.

Sykes, Charles J. 1992. *A Nation of Victims: The Decay of the American Character*. New York: St. Martin's Press.

Syme, Ronald. 1939. *The Roman Revolution*. Oxford: Oxford University Press.
———. 1958. *Tacitus*. Oxford: Clarendon.
Szlezák, Thomas A. 1982. "Zweitlige Dramenstruktur bei Sophokles und Euripides." *Poetica* 14: 1–23.
Taplin, Oliver. 1986. "Fifth-Century Tragedy and Comedy: A *Synkrisis*." *Journal of Hellenic Studies* 106: 163–74.
Tatum, James. 1989. *Xenophon's Imperial Fiction*. Princeton: Princeton University Press.
Temkin, Oswei. 1991. *Hippocrates in a World of Pagans and Christians*. Baltimore: Johns Hopkins University Press.
Tersini, Nancy D. 1987. "Unifying Themes in the Sculptures of the Temple of Zeus at Olympia." *Classical Antiquity* 6: 139–59.
Thesaurus Linguae Graecae (TLG). 1999. Irvine: University of California at Irvine.
Thompson, Homer A. 1952. "The Altar of Pity in the Athenian Agora." *Hesperia* 21: 47–82.
———. 1977. "Dionysos Among the Nymphs in Athens and in Rome." *Journal of the Walters Art Gallery* 36: 73–84.
Thompson, Homer A., and R. E. Wycherley. 1972. *The Agora of Athens*, Agora XIV. Princeton: American School of Classical Studies.
Touloupa, Eve. 1994. In *Lexicon Iconographicum Mythologiae Classicae*. Vol. 7, 527–29, s.v. "Procne et Philomela." Zurich: Artemis.
Traulos, John. 1971. *Pictorial Dictionary of Ancient Athens*. London: Thames and Hudson.
Treu, Max. 1948. "Zur clementia Caesaris." *Museum Helveticum* 5: 197–217.
Triandi, Ismene. 1998. *To Mouseio Akropoleos*. Athens: National Bank of Greece.
Tsiafakis, Despoina. 2000. "The Allure and Repulsion of Thracians in the Art of Classical Athens." In *Not the Classical Ideal: Athens and the Construction of the Other in Greek Art*, ed. Beth Cohen, 364–89. Leiden: Brill.
Tsitsiridis, S. 1998. *Platons* Menexenos: *Einleitung, Text und Kommentar*. Beiträge zur Altertumskunde 107. Stuttgart und Leipzig: Teubner.
Turner, Chad. 2001. "Perverted Supplication and Other Inversions in Aeschylus' Danaid Trilogy." *Classical Journal* 97: 27–50.
Tyler, James. 1974. "Sophocles' *Ajax* and Sophoclean Plot Construction." *American Journal of Philology* 95: 24–42.
Tyrrell, William B. 1985. "The Unity of Sophocles' *Ajax*." *Arethusa* 18: 155–85.
Vanderpool, Eugene. 1974. "The 'Agora' of Pausanias I, 17, 1–2." *Hesperia* 43: 308–10.
van Wees, Hans. 1992. *Status Warriors*. Amsterdam: Gieben.
———. 1998. "A Brief History of Tears: Gender Differentiation in Archaic Greece." In *When Men Were Men: Masculinity, Power and Identity in Classical Antiquity*, ed. L. Foxhall and J. Salmon, 10–53. London: Routledge.
Vellacott, Philip. 1975. *Ironic Drama: A Study of Euripides' Method and Meaning*. London: Cambridge University Press.

Vernant, Jean-Pierre, and Pierre Vidal-Naquet. 1990. *Myth and Tragedy in Ancient Greece*. Rev. ed. Translated by Janet Lloyd. New York: Zone Books.

Veyne, Paul, ed. 1987. *A History of Private Life from Pagan Rome to Byzantium*. Translated by Arthur Goldhammer. Philippe Ariès and George Duby, general editors. Vol. 1. Cambridge, MA: Belknap Press of Harvard University Press.

Vickers, Brian. 1973. *Towards Greek Tragedy*. London: Longman.

Vidal-Naquet, Pierre. 1990. "Oedipus between Two Cities." In *Myth and Tragedy*, ed. Jean-Pierre Vernant and Pierre Vidal-Naquet, 329–359. New York: Zone Books.

———. 1997. "The Place and Status of Foreigners in Tragedy." In *Greek Tragedy and the Historian*, ed. Christopher B. R. Pelling, 109–119. Oxford: Oxford University Press.

Visser, M. 1982. "Worship Your Enemy: Aspects of the Cult of Heroes in Ancient Greece." *Harvard Theological Review* 75: 403–28.

von Staden, Heinrich. 1990. "Incurability and Hopelessness in the Hippocratic Corpus." In *La maladie et les maladies dans la Collection hippocratique*, ed. Paul Potter, Gilles Maloney, and Jacques Desautels, 75–112. Quebec: Éditions du Sphinx.

Wagner, David. 2000. *What's Love Got to Do with It? A Critical Look at American Charity*. New York: New Press.

Walbank, Frank W. 1955. "Tragic History: A Reconsideration." *Bulletin of the Institute of Classical Studies of the University of London* 2: 4–14.

———. 1960. "History and Tragedy." *Historia* 9: 216–34.

Walker, Andrew D. 1993. "*Enargeia* in Greek Historiography." *Transactions of the American Philological Association* 123: 353–77.

Walker, Henry J. 1995. *Theseus and Athens*. Oxford: Oxford University Press.

Wardy, Robert. 1996. *The Birth of Rhetoric: Gorgias, Plato and their Successors*. London: Routledge.

Weinstock, Stefan. 1971. *Divus Julius*. Oxford: Clarendon Press.

Whitehead, David. 1993. "Cardinal Virtues: The Language of Public Approbation in Democratic Athens." *Classica et Mediaevalia* 44: 37–75.

Wickert, Lothar. 1937. "Zu Caesars Reichspolitik." *Klio* 30: 232–53.

Wiemann, Elsbeth. 1986. *Der Mythos von Niobe und ihren Kindern*. Worms: Wernersche Verlagsgesellschaft.

Wierzbicka, Anna. 1992. *Semantics, Culture, and Cognition: Universal Human Concepts in Culture-Specific Configurations*. New York: Oxford University Press.

———. 1999. *Emotions across Languages and Cultures*. Cambridge: Cambridge University Press.

Wilamowitz-Moellendorff, Ulrich von, ed. 1891. *Euripides: Hippolytos*. Berlin: Weidmann.

Wiles, D. 1997. *Tragedy in Athens: Performance Space and Theatrical Meaning*. Cambridge: Cambridge University Press.

Wilkins, John, ed. 1993. *Euripides: Heraclidae*. Oxford: Clarendon Press.

Willink, C. W., intr. and comm. 1986. *Euripides: Orestes*. Oxford: Clarendon Press.

Willis, Ellen. 1996. "Down with Compassion: Morality Isn't All It's Cracked up to Be." *The New Yorker*, 30 September 1996.

Wilmer, Harry A. 1987. "The Doctor-Patient Relationship and the Issues of Pity, Sympathy and Empathy." In *Encounters between Patients and Doctors*, ed. John Stoeckle, 403–11. Cambridge, MA: Harvard University Press.

Wilson, Donna. 2002. *Ransom, Revenge and Heroic Identity in the* Iliad. Cambridge: Cambridge University Press.

Winkler, John, and Froma Zeitlin, eds. 1990. *Nothing to Do with Dionysos? Athenian Drama in its Social Context*. Princeton: Princeton University Press.

Winnington-Ingram, Reginald P. 1980. *Sophocles: An Interpretation*. Cambridge: Cambridge University Press.

Wiseman, T. Peter. 1979. *Clio's Cosmetics*. Leicester, UK: Leicester University Press.

Wohl, Victoria. 1998. *Intimate Commerce: Exchange, Gender, and Subjectivity in Greek Tragedy*. Austin: University of Texas Press.

Woodford, Susan. 2003. *Images of Myth in Classical Antiquity*. Cambridge: Cambridge University Press.

Wuthnow, Robert. 1991. *Acts of Compassion: Caring for Others and Helping Ourselves*. Princeton: Princeton University Press.

Wycherley, Richard E. 1954. "The Altar of *Eleos*." *Classical Quarterly* 4: 143–50.

————. 1957. *Literary and Epigraphical Testimonia*. The Athenian Agora, vol. 3. Princeton: Princeton University Press.

Zacharia, Katerina. 2001. "'The Rock of the Nightingale': Kinship Diplomacy and Sophocles' *Tereus*." In *Homer, Tragedy and Beyond: Essays in Honour of P. E. Easterling*, ed. Felix Budelmann and Pantelis Michelakis, 91–112. London: Society for the Promotion of Hellenic Studies.

Zadorojniy, Alexei V. 1997. "Tragedy and Epic in Plutarch's *Crassus*." *Hermes* 125: 169–82.

Zanker, Graham. 1994. *The Heart of Achilles. Characterization and Personal Ethics in the* Iliad. Ann Arbor: University of Michigan Press.

Zanker, Paul. 1965. *Wandel der Hermesgestalt in der attischen Vasenmalerei*. Bonn: Habelt.

Zeitlin, Froma. 1990a. "Playing the Other: Theater, Theatricality, and the Feminine in Greek Drama." In *Nothing to Do with Dionysos?*, ed. John Winkler and Froma Zeitlin, 63–96. Princeton: Princeton University Press.

————. 1990b. "Thebes: Theater of Self and Society in Athenian Drama." In *Nothing to Do with Dionysos?*, ed. John Winkler and Froma Zeitlin, 130–67. Princeton: Princeton University Press.

Zgusta, Ladislav. 1971. *Manual of Lexicography*. Prague: Academia Publishing House of the Czechoslovak Academy of Sciences.

Zielinski, T. 1896. "Excurse zu den Trachinierinnen des Sophokles." *Philologus* 9: 491–540 and 577–633.

Zimmermann, Bernhard. 1991. *Greek Tragedy: An Introduction.* Translated by T. Marier. Baltimore: Johns Hopkins University Press.

Zuntz, Günther. 1953. "The Altar of Mercy." *Classica et Mediaevalia* 14: 71–85.

————. 1955. *The Political Plays of Euripides.* Manchester: Manchester University Press.

Zwicky, Arnold M., and Jerrold M. Sadock. 1975. "Ambiguity Tests and How to Fail Them." In *Syntax and Semantics*, Vol. 4, ed. John P. Kimball, 1–36. New York: Academic Press.

INDEX OF ANCIENT PASSAGES

SUBJECT INDEX

Achilles, 69–70, 73, 139–40
  public grief of, 143, 144, 145
  vase paintings of, 205–6, 212–14
Achilles Painter, 198–200, 202
Acropolis, civic art on, 229, 234–37
Adrastus, 54–59, 100–4, 136
Adrestos, 19, 22, 29, 74, 78, 80
advantage, decisions based upon, 48, 54–60,
  98
Aedon, 226–27
Aegeus, 141
Aemilius Paullus, 279, 298, 301, 302
Aeneas, 107
Aeschines, 32, 39
Agamemnon, 69, 127, 140, 187, 189
aged. *See* old age
aidôs, 7, 112, 134, 140
Aithra, 54, 58–60, 65, 136, 219
Ajax
  as model of masculinity, 187
  public grief of, 147
  suicide of, vase painting of, 207–8, 224
Ajax (Sophocles), modes of compassion in,
  125–30
Alcibiades, 28, 31, 65, 293
Alkamenes, 229–30
Alkimachos Painter, 207–8, 242–43
Alkmaeon of Kroton, 38
Alkmene, 115–16
Altar of Pity, 13, 196, 246
Altar of the Twelve Gods, 196, 246
Amasis, 22, 86
Anaximines, 51
Anchises, 106–7
anger, 8, 53, 83, 94, 97
  emotional response of, 150
  struggle of pity with, 19–20, 37, 296,
  297
Antigone, 112, 238
Antinoös, 70
Antony, 285, 286, 290, 293, 297, 302
Aphrodite, 126, 172
  in civic art, 236

Apollo
  in civic art, 238–39
  vase paintings of, 214–15
Apollodoros, 30, 32
appeals for pity. *See also* suppliants
  function of reciprocity and self-interest in,
  125, 135–37, 139, 265–66
  as weakness, 87, 139
Aratus, 291
Archaic pity, *versus* classical pity, 71
Archidamos, 35
aretê, 3, 100, 135–36
Argives, 98, 100–4, 136–37
Aristotle
  definition of pity, 18, 21, 51, 60, 68, 179, 219
  on emotional distance, 283–84, 295
  on emotions, 65, 153
  and knowledge of human frailty, 289
  on location of emotion, 39
  on pitilessness, 73
  on pity, 5, 12, 26, 42, 50–54, 75, 79, 92, 102,
  223
  versus Plutarch, 291, 304
  on poetics of pity, 71
  sight and pity in, 36
  on tragedy and pity, 71, 123–24, 133, 153,
  165
Artabanos, 15, 20, 77
Artemis, 132, 236, 238–39
Aryandes, 19, 80
asylum, 62
Athena, 70, 137, 293
  in civic art, 235–36
Athens
  civic ideology of
    lessons in, 111–18
    and tragedy, 123, 137–40, 166, 169–70
  as generous city, 98–118
  as leader of Delian League, 104–8
  as liberator of Greece, 105
  nature of pity in, 3
  public grief in, 74
  self-image of, 1, 12, 98, 104, 117–18, 124, 277